Novell ZENworks™ for Desktops 4

ADMINISTRATOR'S HANDBOOK

Brad Dayley,
Lisa DaNae Dayley, and
Ron Tanner

Novell
PRESS™

Novell®

201 West 103rd Street, Indianapolis, Indiana 46290 USA

Novell ZENworks™ for Desktops 4 Administrator's Handbook

International Standard Book Number: 0-7897-2985-7

Library of Congress Catalog Card Number: 2003100656

Printed in the United States of America

First Printing: April 2003

06 05 04 03   4 3 2

Trademarks

All terms mentioned in this book that are known to be trademarks or service marks have been appropriately capitalized. The Publisher cannot attest to the accuracy of this information. Use of a term in this book should not be regarded as affecting the validity of any trademark or service mark. Novell, NetWare, the Novell Press logo, GroupWise, ManageWise, Novell Directory Services, and NDPS are registered trademarks; Novell Press, NDS, Novell BorderManager, ZENworks, and Novell Distributed Print Services are trademarks; CNE is a registered service mark; and CNI and CNA are service marks of Novell, Inc. in the United States and other countries. All brand names and product names used in this book are trade names, service marks, trademarks, or registered trademarks of their respective owners.

Warning and Disclaimer

Every effort has been made to make this book as complete and as accurate as possible, but no warranty or fitness is implied. The information provided is on an "as is" basis. The authors and the publisher shall have neither liability nor responsibility to any person or entity with respect to any loss or damages arising from the information contained in this book or from the use of the CD or programs accompanying it.

Acquisitions Editor
Jenny Watson

Development Editor
Emmett Dulaney

Managing Editor
Charlotte Clapp

Project Editor
George E. Nedeff

Copy Editor
Kezia Endsley

Indexer
Chris Barrick

Proofreader
Juli Cook

Technical Editors
Jay Raines
Ron Tanner

Team Coordinator
Vanessa Evans

Interior Designer
Gary Adair

Contents At a Glance

IV

Table of Contents

Preface

The computer industry has made incredible progress with information sharing since the introduction of local area networks (LANs) in the 1980s. These advancements have produced services and tools that increase user productivity while decreasing their workload. Companies have come to rely on networks for virtually all aspects of business, such as accounting, payroll, mail, communications, advertising, and banking—the list goes on and on. All this comes at a price, however. In return for having a high-speed network to increase employee and company productivity, each business must also incur an often enormous support cost. Novell recognizes this and provides a solution—Zero Effort Networks, or ZENworks, for Desktops.

ZENworks is the first directory services-based desktop management tool that reduces the cost of owning networked PCs and makes using networks easier. ZENworks for Desktops builds on this initial release and leverages the functionality of NDS to make Windows-based desktops easier to use and manage without sacrificing power or flexibility. It allows the network administrators to leverage NDS to ensure that users can focus on their business, not their PC. With automated application delivery and repair, desktops customized for user's needs, and with easy problem resolution, ZENworks for Desktops gives users all the power of the PC without as high an administrative cost for making it work.

This book is your guide to leveraging ZENworks for Desktops to distribute applications, manage users, and maintain desktop PCs. This book provides steps to set up and use the advanced features of ZENworks for Desktops to cut your administrative efforts and costs, while making the network environment much more friendly to users.

About the Authors

Brad Dayley is a software engineer on Novell's Critical Problem Resolution team. He has nine years of experience installing, troubleshooting, and coding Novell's products. He co-developed an advanced debugging course used to train Novell's support engineers and customers and is the co-author of *Novell's Guide to Resolving Critical Server Issues*.

Lisa DaNae Dayley has a bachelor's degree in advertising copywriting from Brigham Young University and has owned and operated her own digital media services business for eight years. She provides a wide range of services from copywriting and graphic layout to digital video editing and publishing. DaNae's current biggest project is keeping track of her husband and three sons wherever their Jeep will take them.

Ron Tanner is a networking computer professional who has been with Novell since 1993; he is currently a ZENworks Product Manager, defining future ZENworks products. Prior to being with Novell, Ron worked at AT&T Bell Laboratories developing advanced networking systems. Ron has been involved with the ZENworks project since its inception.

Dedication

For D, A & F!
—*Brad Dayley*

I did this one all for Brad.
—*DaNae Dayley*

For my Peach Queen, who gives me a reason. And to my engineering buddies that are fun to work with and make great stuff.
—*Ron Tanner*

Who Should Read This Book?

This book is for anyone responsible for setting up or maintaining a Novell network. If you are a network administrator, technical support staff, CNE, or consultant, this book will give you the edge you need to streamline application distribution and manage users and desktops much more efficiently. You will save valuable time by using the advanced features of ZENworks for Desktops to automate time-consuming tasks such as application distribution and workstation management.

How This Book Is Organized

This book is organized into the following chapters to guide you through installing ZENworks, setting up ZENworks in NDS, and then leveraging the advanced features of ZENworks to reduce your network-management costs.

Chapter 1: The ZENworks Family

Chapter 1 provides a high-level overview of the ZENworks for Desktops system and its components. Additionally, it discusses the different types of packaging of ZENworks for Desktops that are available and what is new in this latest release.

Chapter 2: Installing ZENworks for Desktops 4

Chapter 2 discusses the prerequisites and design considerations of installing ZENworks for Desktops. It also takes you through the installation of the server and client pieces of ZENworks for Desktops, thus helping you avoid any pitfalls that could result in later problems.

Chapter 3: Setting Up ZENworks for Desktops 4 in Your Tree

Chapter 3 identifies the steps that must be taken following the install to get your ZENworks for Desktops system up and functioning. In order to get the full effects of ZENworks for Desktops, you must deliver the proper agents to the workstations in your system and import workstations into your tree, allowing you to manage all of your desktops centrally from your NDS tree.

Chapter 4: Novell Clientless Operation

Chapter 4 discusses the ZENworks for Desktops 4 components that allow for Web-based delivery of ZENworks services through a Web browser. It discusses the client and server agents that you will use to enable the ZENworks for Desktops management features to distribute applications, maintain hardware and software inventory, create images, and remotely manage workstations that do not have a Novell client installed, whether they reside inside or outside of your corporate firewall.

Chapter 5: Creating Application Packages Using snAppShot

Chapter 5 discusses the snAppShot utility and how to use it to create an application object template for later distribution. It discusses why and when you should use snAppShot and describes how snAppShot creates the application object template. It also discusses how to use snAppShot's advanced features, including preferences, special macros, and partial installation detection.

Chapter 6: Creating and Using Application Objects

Once you have an understanding of application object templates from Chapter 5, Chapter 6 covers using the template to create application objects and setting them up for distribution. This chapter also familiarizes you with how to set up properties to customize your application objects and how the new application system incorporates Microsoft MSI.

Chapter 7: Setting Up Application Distribution

Once you have set up the application object into your eDirectory, as described in Chapter 6, you need to set up the application distribution environment. This chapter covers using ConsoleOne to set up application users to receive applications, use application foldering, and automate application object distribution.

Chapter 8: Setting Up User Policies

ZENworks for Desktops provides several policies that describe how the system should deal with users. Chapter 8 discusses the various policies that are associated with users of the tree, how to set them up, and the value that they can provide to your system.

Chapter 9: Setting Up a Workstation Policy Package

Chapter 9 identifies the various workstation policies that are available in the ZENworks for Desktops system. These policies affect the behavior, security, and desktop of all the workstations in your network. This chapter tells you how to set up these policies and make them effective in your network.

Chapter 10: Creating a Container Policy Package

Additional policies are available for ZENworks for Desktops that help in describing how the ZENworks for Desktops system can be most effective in your tree and network. Chapter 10 discusses these policies and how they affect the behavior of the agents that are doing the work of getting your settings to your desktops.

Chapter 11: Creating a Service Location Policy Package

ZENworks for Desktops agents must locate several resources in the network in order to perform their jobs. These resources can be SMTP servers or databases. Chapter 11 discusses how you can use the Service Location Policy Package to identify where these resources are found by the agents.

Chapter 12: Creating a Server Policy Package

ZENworks for Desktops has now introduced agents that are located on your NetWare or NT servers and are used to facilitate such activities as imaging and inventory. This chapter discusses how the policies in the Server Policy Package can affect the behavior of these server agents.

Chapter 13: Using ZENworks Workstation Inventory

The inventory system in ZENworks for Desktops allows you to capture the hardware and software components on every workstation in the tree.

This chapter discusses the inventory system of ZENworks for Desktops and how to best deploy the inventory system throughout the network and tree to get all of your information about your workstations in the right place.

Chapter 14: Imaging a Workstation

ZENworks for Desktops allows you to take images of your workstations and apply them to any and all other workstations in the network. Imagine being able to fix a workstation by simply requesting that it re-image itself from your administration workstation. Can you believe that you can even include application objects into these images? This chapter defines how the imaging system works and how you can get those images to contain exactly what you want and the most efficient way to get them onto those workstations.

Chapter 15: Maintaining a Workstation

Chapter 15 identifies the other programs and systems that accompany the ZENworks for Desktops product that will help in identifying problems with desktops in the network and getting those problems fixed. These tools include Remote Control and Remote Diagnostics.

Chapter 16: Using Software Metering with ZENworks for Desktops

Chapter 16 discusses how to use the ZENworks for Desktops software metering features to give your organization the capability to manage software licenses and track software usage by using ZENworks for Desktops application management and Novell's Licensing Services (NLS). This chapter discusses how to create a license meter certificate and how to assign users to licenses.

Chapter 17: Integrating ZENworks for Desktops with ZENworks for Servers

Novell has introduced additional ZENworks type products. One of these is ZENworks for Servers, which allows you to perform tasks on the server much like you do for the workstation. ZENworks for Servers includes a function called Tiered-Electronic Distribution, which will move files efficiently through the network and place them on servers. ZENworks for

Desktops can interact with ZENworks for Servers, making it easy for you to move your application objects and files throughout the network to your various application servers, and keeping all of them up-to-date with the latest software. This chapter discusses this interaction between these two ZENworks products.

Chapter 18: Deploying Novell ZENworks for Desktops 4 in a Pure Microsoft Windows Environment

Using Novell's eDirectory and DirXML products allows you to install ZENworks for Desktops 4 into a pure Windows network with minimal requirements on the network side. This chapter covers how to set up and configure your network to install and use ZENworks for Desktops 4 in your pure Windows environment.

Chapter 19: Troubleshooting ZENworks

ZENworks for Desktops is an extremely powerful tool that will save network administrators much needed time. However, because of the complexity of network environments, problems can occur that prevent ZENworks for Desktops from doing its job. Chapter 19 covers how to troubleshoot and diagnose those problems in the following areas: desktop management, distributed applications, policy packages, NDS, and NetWare errors.

Appendix A: Understanding eDirectory Changes

Appendix A identifies all of the objects and attribute changes that ZENworks for Desktops performs on your Novell eDirectory tree.

Appendix B: Using snAppShot to Create an Application Object Package

Appendix B first explains a detailed example of using the snAppShot utility to create an application object package for distribution to other workstations. Second, Appendix B gives a detailed review of the application object template created. The purpose of Appendix B is to give you practical experience and knowledge of application object templates.

Appendix C: Other ZENworks for Desktops Resources

This appendix lists other places you can go to get more help with your ZENworks for Desktops implementation.

Appendix D: ZENworks Inventory Database Schema

This appendix discusses the inventory schema that is used in the database to record the inventory of the workstation. This appendix describes each of the tables in the database and gives SQL examples to extract your own information from the database.

Acknowledgments

Our sincere gratitude goes out to the following persons, without whom this book could not have come in to being:

To the ZENworks team that, although leaner, has put a great number of significant features in this update. Thanks for making a great product that can benefit all those who have a network and users to support. We're looking forward to many new versions to make the product even better.

To everyone at Novell who allowed us to pick their brains, including but not limited to (with apologies to any whose names we have forgotten) Matthew Lewis, Krishnan R., Kelly Norman, Alan Jex, Frank Morse, David Rivers, Drake Backman, Kevin Wilkins, and Nile Thayne.

We Want to Hear from You!

As the reader of this book, *you* are our most important critic and commentator. We value your opinion and want to know what we're doing right, what we could do better, what areas you'd like to see us publish in, and any other words of wisdom you're willing to pass our way.

You can email or write me directly to let me know what you did or didn't like about this book—as well as what we can do to make our books stronger.

Please note that I cannot help you with technical problems related to the topic of this book, and that due to the high volume of mail I receive, I might not be able to reply to every message.

When you write, please be sure to include this book's title and author as well as your name and phone or email address. I will carefully review your comments and share them with the author and editors who worked on the book.

Email: feedback@novellpress.com

Mail: Mark Taber
Associate Publisher
Que Publishing/Novell Press
201 West 103rd Street
Indianapolis, IN 46290 USA

Reader Services

For more information about this book or others from Novell Press or Que Publishing, visit our Web site at www.quepublishing.com. Type the ISBN (excluding hyphens) or the title of the book in the Search box to find the book you're looking for.

CHAPTER 1

The ZENworks Family

Although this book is about ZENworks for Desktops, several other ZENworks products are now available from Novell, Inc. Currently Novell offers the following products in the ZENworks family:

- *ZENworks for Desktops*—A desktop management system that manages many workstation aspects.
- *ZENworks for Servers*—A system that enables you to manage servers and to distribute files across the network.
- *ZENworks for Handhelds*—A system that enables you to manage policies, applications, and inventory on PDA devices.

All ZENworks products rely significantly on the directory, specifically Novell Directory Services, to provide a greater manageability level, and greater ease, for each component in the network.

All of the ZENworks products are cross-platform compatible; they can run not only in NetWare environments, but also in Windows, Linux, and Solaris environments (without the need for NetWare). Novell is bundling these products into a suite—expected in 2003—that will continue the trend toward integration of all of the ZENworks management components.

What Is ZENworks for Desktops?

ZENworks for Desktops is a desktop management system that has been developed by Novell, Inc. The ZENworks in ZENworks for Desktops stands for Zero Effort Networks and is named to reflect the lack of effort required for users and the minimum effort necessary for the administrator to manage the desktops in their systems.

The goal of ZENworks for Desktops is to reduce the total cost of ownership (TCO) for dealing with all the workstations in the network. This is achieved by special attempts to reduce the effort necessary to manage the desktops.

ZENworks for Desktops is segmented into three desktop management and maintenance areas, which are discussed in the following sections. These include Application, Workstation, and Remote Management.

Application Management

The ZENworks Application Management area for Desktops is designed to easily deploy applications from the network to individual desktops. These applications can be automatically installed on the workstation, cached for later installation, or just have an icon applied to a desktop that references a software executable or installation bundle on a server in the network. All the applications that are deployed to the desktop enable the administrator to control when they are deployed, how they are applied, and who or which desktops get certain applications.

ZENworks for Desktops also enables you to customize the settings for each user by referencing values in Novell Directory Services (NDS) or eDirectory and embedding them in the Registry keys and files for the particular applications. Then, when that application is deployed to the desktop, these values are customized for the particular user. In addition to customization, the ZENworks for Desktops Application Management portion includes the capability to help you equalize the usage on the network through its load-balancing features. ZENworks attempts to make the application always available with its fault-tolerance features.

With the integration of NDS, ZENworks for Desktops Application Management ensures that the applications follow the users to whichever desktop they use in the network, keeping their connection to the network always functioning in a familiar way.

ZENworks for Desktops Application Management has features that enable you to distribute and assign applications to users, thus making the management of application for desktops and your users on the desktop simple and consistent.

ZENworks for Desktops Application Management features are currently provided for the following platforms: Windows 95, Windows 98, Windows NT, Windows 2000, and Windows XP.

Workstation Management

Workstation Management refers to the capability of the administrator to affect direct changes on the desktop and manage the Registry, Novell clients, desktop images, printers, and even ZAW and ZAK policies (that is, Windows Group Policies) of the Windows operating systems. With the Novell Directory Services advantages, you can make changes to a Configuration object that affects the client, for example, and then apply those changes to all or a portion of the workstations in your entire organization. Due to the inheritance rules of NDS, and the introduction of Workstation objects into the tree, these Configuration objects can be applied to many users and workstations in the tree by associations with objects, groups, or containers.

Microsoft introduced to their Windows environments the products ZAW (Zero-Administration Workstation) and ZAK (Zero-Administration Kit) as a first step in enabling administrators to manage the workstation. These products resulted in Registry settings that could be stored in a .POL file and then accessed by each workstation as it attaches to the server. These Registry settings would then be applied to the workstation, resulting in the interface the administrator wanted for the users.

ZENworks for Desktops has taken the ZAW and ZAK features of Windows to the next level by providing these Registry manipulations (resulting in desktop changes) and placing them into the NDS tree. Rather than having to create a .POL file and deploy it across the network servers, an administrator can administer the same features in NDS. Once the ZAW and ZAK features have been administered into the NDS system, that "policy" can then be applied to any workstation in the system or follow any users as they move from desktop to desktop, regardless of which server they are working on in the tree. Novell, through ZENworks for Desktops, has truly introduced fault-tolerance and manageability to these policies introduced by Microsoft.

ZENworks for Desktops also enables the administrator to create a Configuration object for the Novell client. Then all workstations that are associated with this Configuration object use the configurations specified to manage the client. There was one customer that was told by Novell that in order to fix the problem they needed to change only one line in the NET.CFG file of the client. The customer was not too happy because they had over 10,000 clients of that type and determined that it would take them years with their current staff to make that change. Now, with ZENworks for Desktops, the administrator can make the change in one Client configuration policy object and the change is then forwarded to clients of all associated workstations. The change becomes effective the next time the users log into the system. This one change is made in minutes instead of years.

In addition, the ZENworks for Desktops Workstation Management feature includes a desktop hardware inventory. An inventory *sweet spot* is stored in the Workstation object. It is associated with the physical workstation device. This inventory can be useful to administrators in understanding the workstation capabilities as they manage and maintain the desktop.

Additionally, ZENworks for Desktops provides a complete hardware and software scanning capability that is stored in a separate database. A link exists between the Workstation objects and the database, allowing you easy access to the scanned information. Reports are also included with ZENworks for Desktops that provide you useful, tabular information of what is stored in the scanned database.

Included with the ZENworks for Desktops Workstation Management features are enhanced versions of the original Workstation Manager 1.0 (WSM) features that include dynamic Windows NT/2000 account management. Enhanced versions of the account management give even greater control to the NT administrator. When these users log into NDS, they have a local account automatically created and customized for the particular user. When they log out, this account can remain or can be removed from the local Windows NT/2000 system.

Through the ZENworks for Desktops Workstation Management features, Novell provides the capability to manage all desktop aspects including access to basic Windows features and to the automatic printer deployment. Like many ZENworks for Desktops features, these capabilities follow users as they move across the organization from one workstation to another, including the printer drivers and printers.

ZENworks for Desktops Workstation Management features are currently provided for the following platforms: Windows 95, Windows 98, Windows NT, Windows 2000, and Windows XP.

Remote Management

The ZENworks for Desktops Remote Management feature includes the capability to discover information about the workstation and to perform some remote diagnostics and repairs on that workstation. As mentioned earlier, ZENworks for Desktops introduces into the tree a new object representing the workstation. This Workstation object is associated with the physical desktop and is a repository for information about the specific desktop. The administrator can then use this information in determining how to most effectively maintain and repair that desktop.

In addition to the introduction of the Workstation object, the Remote Management feature of ZENworks for Desktops provides the administrator with the capability of eDirectory Authenticated Remote Control. The eDirectory Authenticated Remote Control feature keeps anyone who does not have rights to control a *particular* workstation from being able to control the system remotely. This way administrators and users are assured that only authorized personnel can remote control their desktops.

To help in workstation diagnostics and repair, Remote Management of ZENworks includes remote diagnostics, and file transfer capabilities. These also require proper rights in the eDirectory tree in order to perform the tasks.

ZENworks for Desktops Remote Management features are currently provided for the following platforms: Windows 95, Windows 98, Windows NT, Windows 2000, and Windows XP.

What's New in ZENworks for Desktops 4?

ZENworks for Desktops continues to mature with new developments in desktop platforms, such as Windows XP, and with collaborating software. ZENworks for Desktops 4 is more user friendly for administrators and users alike.

ZENworks for Desktops 4 has been updated to fully support the Windows XP environment and still supports Windows 98, Windows NT, and Windows 2000.

NOTE You can no longer create new policies for Windows 95 workstations or users. Continued support for Windows 95 workstations can be provided by running both ZENworks for Desktop 3.2 and ZENworks for Desktops 4 in the same tree.

ZENworks for Desktops 4 works on a NetWare only, Windows only, or NetWare and Windows mixed server environment. If you need ZENworks for Desktops 4 to work in a pure Windows environment, you need to run NDS for Windows Servers or eDirectory for Windows Servers in order for the NDS directory to be available.

ZENworks Clientless Workstation Management

ZENworks for Desktops 4 uses standard Internet protocols and commonly open ports to communicate between desktops and the ZENworks server. This creates exciting new possibilities by allowing you to manage workstations outside your firewall.

It is no longer necessary to have the Novell Client installed on the workstation in order to utilize the Application Management features of ZENworks. ZENworks services—including software distribution and update, shortcuts, HTTP links, and thin client sessions—are now available through Web-based service delivery. All ZENworks for Desktops features are fully available without the client and through this HTTP connection to a Web server.

Policies and Workstation Management

Novell iPrint Policy

This policy replaces the traditional printer policies, creating a universal print policy that is highly effective. The new Novell iPrint policy allows you to install the Novell iPrint client to user workstations, giving users the capability to use their Web browsers to install printers on their workstation. Once these printers have been installed, they can be used just as any other printer regardless of the physical location of that printer. For instance, a user in Colorado could print a needed document on a printer located in the California extension of the company.

ZENworks for Desktops Policy

The ZENworks for Desktops policy takes advantage of the new clientless management features and allows you to configure two agents within the policy. The ZENworks Management Agent allows clients to access the

Middle Tier server (Web server with ZENworks servlets) using an IP address from outside the firewall.

Policies No Longer Supported by ZENworks for Desktops 4

The Client Configuration, RAS Configuration, and Restrict Login policies have been replaced by the ZENworks for Desktops Policy. The traditional printer policies have been replaced by the Novell iPrint policy.

Application Management

The Application Launcher/Explorer is no longer dependent on the Novell Client. This makes for several changes in this area:

▶ Access to eDirectory can be provided to the user through the ZENworks Management Agent and ZENworks Middle Tier software. It is also possible to use the Application Browser (a Web browser view) instead of or in addition to Application Launcher or Application Explorer to view distributed applications.

▶ Application Dependencies enables you to establish a list of applications that must be installed before an application can be distributed, thus allowing you to install dependent applications in the order that they are required.

▶ Application Launcher/Explorer can generate event reports including install, uninstall, launch, and cache in XML format and send the reports via HTTP to a specified target URL.

▶ Application Launcher/Explorer supports script engines other than the Novell Client script engine, which means that you can specify your own engine when running a distribution script or launch script.

▶ The Application object for an MSI (Microsoft System Installer) application now enables you to define patches you want applied during the distribution process. You can also specify actions (such as reinstall all files, reinstall old file, and so on) that will occur when a user verifies an MSI application. You can also affect the individual configuration settings within an MSI file through the Application object.

▶ The Random Refresh feature instructs Application Launcher/Explorer to retrieve its application information from the user's cache directory during startup and then refreshes that information from eDirectory at a later time. This allows you to reduce network traffic during peak times.

▶ Rogue Processes Management enables you to find and stop application processes not launched by Application Launcher/Explorer. You can administer these processes to not only be tracked, but also terminated.

▶ In order to accommodate different connections, Application Launcher/Explorer now supports three modes. The local mode is used when Application Launcher/Explorer is connected to eDirectory through a fast connection; for example, a LAN connection. The Remote mode is used when the connection is slow, as in a modem connection. The Disconnect setting is used when the user is not connected to the network and Application Launcher/Explorer access to eDirectory is not possible. All directory information is retrieved from a local cache.

The following features have been added to enhance Application Launcher/Explorer's new remote capabilities:

▶ Terminal server applications and Web applications that work across slower connections better than standard applications do.

▶ Checkpoint Restart provides users with a timeframe for how long it will take to download a standard application during distribution and, when remotely connected, enables users to postpone an in-progress download.

▶ Remote Alternate Application enables you to specify an alternative application to use when a user is in remote mode rather than local mode. For example, when the user is accessing the application while in remote mode, you might want it run through a terminal server.

Workstation Imaging

ZENworks for Desktops 4 introduces the following enhancements to workstation imaging:

▶ Performance enhancements that enable you to restore images on IDE hard disks much faster.

▶ Support for USB keyboards, thus enabling you to use USB keyboards in the imaging engine on the workstation.

▶ The capability to start a multicast session from the imaging server console.

▶ The capability to store DNS information for a workstation in the policies/image-safe data.

▶ PXE support, which was previously delivered through another ZENworks product. Using PXE, you can deliver images and applications to your workstations at boot time.

Workstation Remote Management

ZENworks for Desktops 4 introduces the following new features for remote workstation management:

▶ Remote management independent of the Novell client—even across a firewall—through a middle-tier server.

▶ Support for initiation remote management operations from the user object as well as the Workstation object. This enables you to administrate users from whatever workstation they are logged into.

▶ Remote management of workstations across a firewall, through a middle-tier server.

▶ An optional password security feature for remote control. This feature allows you to remote control a workstation with an IP address and a password that is set by the remote user. You no longer are required to have a Workstation object in order to perform remote control.

Workstation Inventory

ZENworks for Desktops 4 introduces the following new features for workstation inventory:

▶ Support for using a NetWare 6 server as an inventory server.

▶ Support for using MS SQL Server 2000 as the inventory database engine.

▶ Support for roll-up of inventory across multiple Novell eDirectory trees.

▶ Support for roll-up of inventory data across a firewall.

▶ Additional scanning support allowing you to use user-defined attributes to collect inventory data that is not collected from the workstation by default.

▶ Additional scanning support that collects the product identification number of any application, including Microsoft applications from workstations.

▶ Additional scanning support that allows you to scan the full path of applications on workstations.

▶ Additional status data allowing you to view the scan status of a workstation in the inventory database from a specified time.

▶ Additional support for ZENworks for Servers 3.

▶ Support allowing workstation inventory to access the eDirectory through LDAP.

Additional Novell Products

ZENworks for Desktops 4 includes the following Novell products to simplify the use of ZENworks in non-NetWare, non-eDirectory environments: (wow!

▶ *eDirectory*—A license for eDirectory for Windows 2000 is included in the product, allowing you to fully run ZENworks in a Windows only environment.

▶ *DirXML*—A license is also included with ZENworks for Desktops 4. This technology allows you to synchronization users between Active Directory/NT Domains and eDirectory. This allows you to continue to manage your Windows systems in AD or NT and still receive the benefits of ZENworks for Desktops.

▶ *Password Synchronization*—This add-on driver to DirXML is also available as part of the ZENworks for Desktop product. It provides you the capability to synchronize passwords between Active Directory/NT Domains and eDirectory. You can now provide single-sign on for your users between their domains and eDirectory.

Benefits to Using ZENworks for Desktops

Significant benefits exist in using the ZENworks for Desktops product in your NetWare and NT/2000 environments. The greatest benefit comes from effectively leveraging existing information that is currently in your directory, and combining this with the new components and tree extensions provided in ZENworks for Desktops. By building these relationships in the directory between users and their desktops, enormous management potential surfaces and is easily available to the administrator. Using the eDirectory tree and its hierarchical nature enables you to manage all the desktops in your tree from one place, or delegate to local administrators and containers in sub-trees.

ZENworks for Desktops also is an easy extension of the current administration system. All the administration requirements for ZENworks for Desktops can be administered via snap-ins that are provided and plugged directly into the ConsoleOne Administration utility. Additionally, ZENworks for Desktops uses the familiar rights associated with your tree to govern how accessible the features are to each user in your system.

The cost of managing the desktops that you have in your network is the single largest cost of having your network at all. Some analysts estimate the desktop maintenance cost to be 78% of all network costs. ZENworks for Desktops helps reduce this cost and specifically makes the administrator's life easier by enabling the administrator to manage most user's desktop needs from the office.

From the office, you can deploy applications to any user in the tree, deliver printers and printer drivers, create Windows NT/2000 workstation accounts, and configure Novell clients on any set, or all desktops across the network. While in the office, you can cite specific policies to be applied to each user's desktop, or desktop groups, that can lock down a system or just customize a background screen. Without leaving the office, you can receive help requests from the user, look at the desktop hardware and operating system information, remotely control and repair the problems, and even re-image the workstation if necessary. Among the greatest costs in maintaining a workstation is that which is involved in traveling from one desktop to the next. With ZENworks for Desktops, that effort is largely minimized.

## CHAPTER 2

Installing ZENworks for Desktops 4

Among the biggest keys to using software tools effectively is properly installing them. Properly installing a software product enables you to get started faster and avoid problems later. This chapter focuses on helping you prepare to install ZENworks for Desktops and its components.

This chapter breaks the installation of ZENworks for Desktops into the following main sections. This breakdown helps you prepare and install the product fast and correctly:

- ▶ Prerequisites for installing ZENworks for Desktops
- ▶ Installing ZENworks for Desktops Server Components
- ▶ Installing ZENworks for Desktops Middle Tier Server Components
- ▶ Installing ZENworks for Desktops Management Agent on Workstations

Prerequisites for Installing ZENworks for Desktops

The first step you should take to install ZENworks for Desktops is to make certain your network hardware and software meet the requirements. The following sections discuss the hardware and software requirements needed to install ZENworks for Desktops as well as pre-install checklists that you should perform to make certain you are ready to begin the install.

Hardware and Software Requirements

The following tables list both the hardware and software requirements that must be met on your NetWare and Windows servers before you can install ZENworks for Desktops. Taking the time to review the hardware and software requirements will help you resolve any deficiencies in your network and help eliminate problems during and after installation.

Table 2.1 contains the hardware and software requirements that must be met on NetWare 5.1, NetWare 6, and Windows NT/2000 servers to install the ZENworks for Desktops server software.

TABLE 2.1 ZENworks for Desktops Server Requirements

REQUIREMENT	NETWARE 5.1	NETWARE 6	WINDOWS NT	WINDOWS 2000
Minimum Free Disk Space	128MB	220MB	220MB	220MB
Processor	Pentium III (minimum)	Pentium III (minimum)	Pentium III (minimum)	Pentium III (minimum)
RAM	256MB or 1GB if scaled to 200 concurrent users	256MB or 1GB if scaled to 200 concurrent users	256MB or 1GB if scaled to 200 concurrent users	256MB or 1GB if scaled to 200 concurrent users
JVM	JVM 1.3.1 (included on companion CD)	JVM 1.3.1 (included on companion CD)	N/A	N/A
eDirectory	Novell eDirectory 8.5	(shipping)	NDS Corporate Edition of NDS eDirectory	Novell eDirectory 8.5
Software Updates	NW51SP34EXE (or later) patch applied	N/A	N/A	N/A

Table 2.2 contains the hardware and software requirements that must be met on NetWare 5.1, NetWare 6, and Windows 2000 servers to install the ZENworks for Desktops Middle Tier server software.

TABLE 2.2   ZENworks for Desktops Middle Tier Server Requirements

REQUIREMENT	NETWARE 5.1	NETWARE 6	WINDOWS 2000
Minimum Free Disk Space	160MB	160MB	160MB
Processor	Pentium III (minimum)	Pentium III (minimum)	Pentium III (minimum)
RAM	256MB or 1GB if scaled to 200 concurrent users	256MB or 1GB if scaled to 200 concurrent users	256MB or 1GB if scaled to 200 concurrent users
Web Server	Apache HTTP Server, version 1.3.22	Apache HTTP Server (shipping)	Microsoft IIS Web Server
Installed Software	Novell Certificate Server version 2.20	Novell NetStorage	N/A
Software Updates	NW51SP4.EXE (or later) patch applied	N/A	Windows 2000 Server Service Pack 2

Table 2.3 contains the hardware and software requirements that must be met on NetWare 5.1 and NetWare 6 servers to install the ZENworks for Desktops Inventory server software.

TABLE 2.3   NetWare Inventory Server Requirements

REQUIREMENT	NETWARE 5.1	NETWARE 6
Novell eDirectory	8 with Certificate Server v2.03 and LDAP	8 with Certificate Server v2.03 and LDAP
Support Pack	3	N/A
JVM	1.3.1 (or later)	1.3.1 (or later)
JVM Disk Space	105MB	N/A
Memory	256MB	512MB
CPU Speed	Pentium II	Pentium II

TABLE 2.3   Continued

REQUIREMENT	NETWARE 5.1	NETWARE 6
Inventory Disk Space	35MB without database 50MB with database	35MB without database 50MB with database
ConsoleOne Disk Space	70MB	70MB
Miscellaneous	Valid IP address Long name support	Valid IP address Long name support

Table 2.4 contains the hardware and software requirements that must be met on NetWare 5.1 and NetWare 6 and Windows NT/2000 servers to install the ZENworks for Desktops Inventory server database.

TABLE 2.4   Inventory Server Database Requirements

REQUIREMENT	NETWARE 5.1 AND NETWARE 6	WINDOWS NT/2000
Database	Sybase ASA 7.0.1.1583 Oracle 8i can be used as an alternative	Sybase ASA 7.0.1.1540 Oracle 8.1.5, 8.1.6, 8.1.7 MS SQL Server on Windows 2000 servers
Memory	256MB minimum 512MB recommended	256MB minimum 512MB recommended
CPU Speed	Pentium III	Pentium III
Disk Space	1.5GB leaf level 20GB root level (varies from 1-25GB)	1.5GB leaf level 20GB root level (varies from 1-25GB)

Installation Prerequisite Checklist

The following sections contain checklists that you should review prior to beginning the installation of ZENworks for Desktops server and Middle Tier software. These checklists help you ascertain whether your network is ready for the install.

ZENworks for Desktops Server Pre-Install Checklist

► Make and archive a reliable backup!

► Make sure that all of the hardware and software requirements are met. In particular, make sure that the recommended version of ConsoleOne is installed on the server where you will install the ZENworks for Desktops server software.

► Make sure you have Admin rights to all NetWare servers where you will install ZENworks for Desktops server software.

► Make sure you have Admin rights to extend the directory schema.

► Make sure that the workstation from where you will run the installation program is authenticated to the server or servers where you are installing the software.

► If you are installing on a NetWare server, you need to unload JAVA.NLM by executing the `java -exit` command.

► Exit any program that uses files in the `SYS:PUBLIC` directory on any server where you will be installing ZENworks for Desktops server software.

► Exit any Windows programs on the network workstation from which you will be running the installation program.

► Set your screen display for 1024×768.

► Novell Client must be installed on the workstation or server where you will be running ConsoleOne for administering the ZENworks for Desktops server.

► A Windows 2000 workstation or server is recommended for running the ZENworks for Desktops server installation.

► Uninstall any third-party remote control agent or remote control application running on the managed workstation.

► Associate the Remote Management policy settings for the managed workstation.

► Ensure that you have installed Novell Certificate Server and LDAP on the NetWare server that will be your Inventory server.

► Stop Sybase Adaptive Server Anywhere by typing **Q** at the Sybase console prompt.

► Use top-down deployment for Inventory installation.

ZENworks for Desktops Middle Tier Server Pre-Install Checklist

▶ Verify that the hardware and software requirements in Table 2.2 are met on the servers you are planning to install the Middle Tier server components on.

▶ On NetWare 5.1 and NetWare 6 servers, edit the *ThreadsPerChild* \APACHE\CONF\ADMINSERVER.CONF file. You should change the value from the default of 50 to 512.

Installing ZENworks for Desktops Server Components

Once you have reviewed the hardware and software requirement and completed the pre-install checklist for the servers you plan to install ZENworks for Desktops on, you can begin the installation procedure to install the ZENworks for Desktops server components as outlined in this section. The following sections detail the steps to install the ZENworks for Desktops server components.

Login to Tree As Admin

The first step to installing the ZENworks for Desktops server components is to log in to the eDirectory tree as Admin or as a user with supervisor rights to the NetWare servers and eDirectory containers where you want to install ZENworks for Desktops.

Launch Install from CD

Once you are logged in as Admin or an Admin equivalent, you are ready to launch the ZENworks for Desktops install. The ZENworks for Desktops installation CD-ROM is supplied with an auto-run feature, which is automatically launched when you insert the CD-ROM into your client. You can also start the install by executing the WINSETUP.EXE file on the root of the CD-ROM.

Start ZENworks Install

To install the ZENworks for Desktops components on servers in your tree, select New Install, Install ZENworks for Desktops Server from the main install screen. This will launch the install for the ZENworks for Desktops server components.

The first screen you will see in the ZENworks for Desktops Server install is the welcome screen. Read the contents and click Next to continue.

The second screen you will see is the license agreement screen. Read the license agreement and select the Accept button if you agree to the terms. Click Next to continue.

The next screen you will see is the verification screen reminding you of the requirements that must be met to install ZENworks for Desktops server components. Review the requirements one last time and click Next to continue.

The next screen in the install is the tree selection screen, shown in Figure 2.1. This screen enables you to specify which tree you want to install ZENworks into. The ZENworks for Desktops install can install ZENworks to only one tree at time. Therefore, if you are authenticated to multiple trees, you must select one tree to update with ZENworks schema extensions, programs, and files.

To select a tree, click the Browse button and find the tree you want to use. You can log in to the tree, if you are not already authenticated, by clicking the login button and entering the login information.

If you have not already extended the schema on this tree, check the Extend schema option to have the install do it prior to installing the software and creating eDirectory objects. Once you are finished selecting the tree, click Next to continue.

Select ZENworks for Desktops Components to Be Installed

The next screen in the install is the ZENworks for Desktops server component selection screen, shown in Figure 2.2. This screen enables you to specify which ZENworks for Desktops components you want to install on your network.

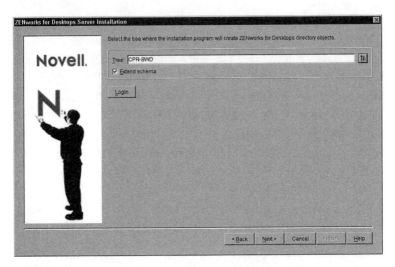

FIGURE 2.1
Tree selection screen for the ZENworks for Desktops install.

Select which of the following components you want to install and then click the Next button:

- ▶ *Application Management*—Installs the desktop software distribution components and creates Application objects on the eDirectory.

- ▶ *Automatic Workstation Import*—Installs the programs and files necessary to complete the automatic workstation import to the servers.

- ▶ *Workstation Imaging*—Installs the programs and files necessary to perform workstation management functions.

- ▶ *Remote Management Tools*—Installs the programs and files necessary to manage workstations remotely.

- ▶ *Workstation Inventory*—Installs the programs and files necessary to inventory workstations.

- ▶ *Workstation Management*—Installs the workstation manager on the selected servers. This option allows you to have DLU and workstation policies and applications.

- ▶ *Sybase Database*—Installs Sybase to the selected servers and sets up the database for workstation inventory management.

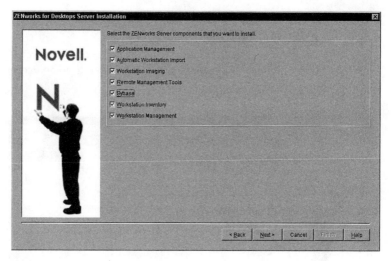

FIGURE 2.2
Component selection screen for the ZENworks for Desktops install.

Select Servers for Installation

The next screen in the install is the ZENworks for Desktops server selection screen, shown in Figure 2.3. You can select which servers to install ZENworks for Desktops to by clicking the Add Servers button and selecting NetWare and Windows servers.

You do not need to install ZENworks to every server in your tree, just the ones that ZENworks for Desktops server components will be used on.

Once you have selected which servers you want to install ZENworks for Desktops on, you need to define which of the following components should be installed and then click Next to continue:

▶ *ConsoleOne Snapins*—Installs the ZENworks for Desktops snap-ins to the `SYS:\PUBLIC\MGMT\CONSOLEONE\1.2\SNAPINS` directory.

▶ *Import*—This server automatically imports workstations, but does not remove them. There must be at least one import server.

▶ *Removal*—This server removes workstations, but does not import them. This server type is optional. However, you should have at least one removal server if your workstation count changes very much.

▶ *ZEN Preboot*—Installs components for ZENworks for Desktops Preboot Services.

▶ *XML Proxy Service*—Installs the XML proxy service on the server if you are planning on configuring a proxy server to roll up and scan data that is across a firewall.

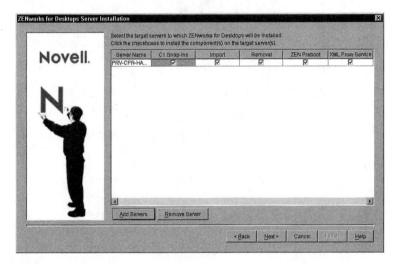

FIGURE 2.3
Server selection screen for the ZENworks for Desktops install.

NOTE Make certain that you have verified the server hardware and software prerequisites for installing ZENworks for Desktops on all of the servers you check in this menu before proceeding.

Select Path for Inventory Database Installation

The next screen in the install, if you selected the workstation inventory component, is the Inventory installation screen, shown in Figure 2.4. This screen enables you to set the volume and path to install the workstation inventory files and database to.

To set the path, select the server in server list and then click the Browse button or simply specify a path that exists on that server. Once you have set the path for all servers, click the Next button to continue.

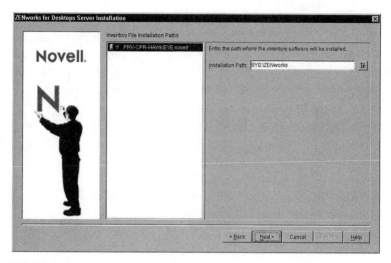

FIGURE 2.4
Inventory installation screen for the ZENworks for Desktops install.

NOTE Be sure to consider growth. As you add more workstations to the inventory, the database grows. Make certain that you have enough disk space on the volume you select to accommodate the addition of new workstations.

Configure XML Proxy

The next screen in the install, if you selected the XML Proxy service component, is the XML Proxy service configuration screen, shown in Figure 2.5. This screen enables you to set the volume and path as well as the port that the XML Proxy service will use.

To set the path and port, select the server in the server list, set the port number and then click the Browse button or simply specify a path that exists on that server. Once you have set the path for all servers, click the Next button to continue.

NOTE The firewall must allow XLM RPC requests to the XML Proxy service on the port you specify for them to pass through.

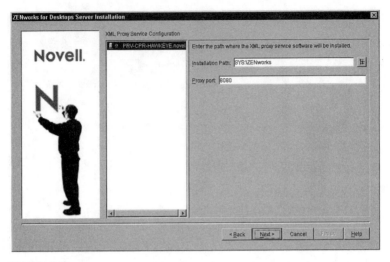

FIGURE 2.5
XML Proxy service configuration screen for the ZENworks for Desktops install.

Configure Remote Management

The next screen in the install, if you selected the remote management component, is the remote management installation screen. This screen enables you to set the volume and path to install the workstation remote management components to.

To set the path, select the server in the server list and then click the Browse button or simply specify a path that exists on that server. Once you have set the path for all servers, click the Next button to continue.

Complete the Install

Once you have completed the setup options, you see the summary screen as shown in Figure 2.6. This screen shows you the product components you selected and the servers that they will be installed on. If you need to make any changes you can click the Back button; otherwise, click Finish and the ZENworks for Desktops install performs the tasks listed in the following sections.

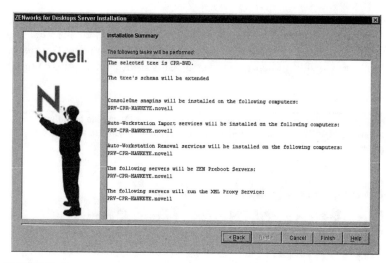

FIGURE 2.6
Installation summary screen for the ZENworks for Desktops install.

Check File System

The ZENworks for Desktops install checks for available disk space on the servers you requested to install to. If there is insufficient disk space, you can proceed. The ZENworks for Desktops install installs some files that already exist on the server. The older files are overwritten. Therefore, there may be enough disk space to install ZENworks for Desktops even if the available showing is less than needed.

Check Schema

The ZENworks for Desktops install also checks the DS schema for problems prior to updating it. If no problems are found, the schema is extended to include new objects and attributes necessary for the components you selected to install.

Copy Files

Once the file system, schema, and DS objects are checked and any problems are resolved, the ZENworks for Desktops install copies the files to each server selected in the previous menu in sequential order. A status screen lets you know which server is being installed and a percentage of progress to completion. Once the file copy is done you can click the Finish button. The ZENworks for Desktops server component install is complete.

Log Problems

All problems with the file system, schema, or DS objects are reported in a log file that can be displayed once the installation is complete. You can review the log file and correct any errors and re-install necessary components.

NOTE It's highly recommended that you carefully review the log file for all errors and review the README file (available from the same screen). If there are any errors, they are much easier to correct at this point than they will be later.

Installing ZENworks for Desktops Middle Tier Server Components

Once you have verified the hardware and software prerequisites for the servers you plan to install the ZENworks for Desktops Middle Tier Server components to, you can begin the installation procedure to install the Middle Tier server components as outlined in this section. The following sections detail the steps to install the ZENworks for Desktops server components.

Start ZENworks Middle Tier Install

To install the ZENworks for Desktops Middle Tier server components on servers in your tree, you need to authenticate to the tree and start the install as described the ZENworks for Desktops Server install section. Once you have started the install, select New Install, Install ZENworks Middle Tier Server from the main install screen. This will launch the install for the ZENworks for Desktops Middle Tier server components.

The first screen you will see in the ZENworks for Desktops Middle Tier server install is the welcome screen. Read the contents and click Next to continue.

The second screen you will see is the license agreement screen. Read the license agreement and select the Accept button if you agree to the terms. Click Next to continue.

The next screen you will see is the verification screen reminding you of the requirements that must be met to install ZENworks for Desktops Middle Tier server components. Review the requirements one last time and click Next to continue.

Select Server(s) for Installation

The next screen in the install is the server selection screen, shown in Figure 2.7. This screen enables you to specify which servers you want to install the ZENworks for Desktops Middle Tier components to. You can select which servers to install ZENworks for Desktops Middle Tier components to by clicking the Add Servers button and selecting NetWare and Windows servers.

Once you have selected which servers you want, you need to define the following primary eDirectory tree information for each server:

▶ *DNS Name or IP Address of eDirectory Server and Context*—Specify the DNS name or the IP address and the eDirectory context of a NetWare or Windows server that has the ZENworks for Desktops Server components installed on it. Use the following format:

```
<dns_name_or_ip_address>:<context> i.e. ZfD_Server.
novell.com:xAccess.novell
```

▶ *Full DN and Password of Admin User*—Specify the full username and password of a user who has admin rights to the server.

Once you have configured the primary eDirectory tree information for each server, click Next to continue.

Complete the Install

Once you have completed the setup options, you see the summary screen as shown in Figure 2.8. This screen shows you servers you selected and the primary eDirectory tree info you specified for each. If you need to make any changes, you can click the Back button; otherwise click Finish. The ZENworks for Desktops Middle Tier server install will install the components to the servers you specified.

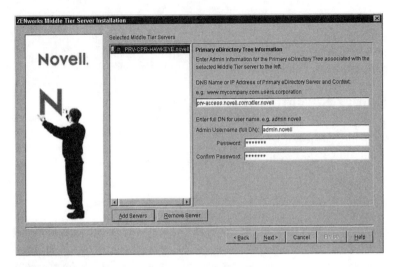

FIGURE 2.7
Server selection screen for the ZENworks for Desktops Middle Tier server
install.

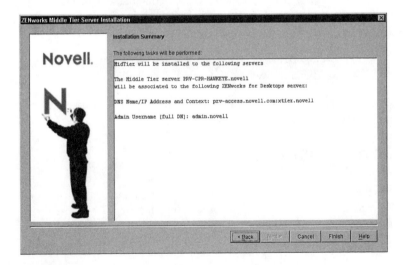

FIGURE 2.8
Summary screen for the ZENworks for Desktops Middle Tier server install.

Post Install Checks

Once the ZENworks for Desktops Middle Tier server install is complete, you should perform the following checks on the network:

▶ *Allow Clear Text Passwords*—Make certain that the servers you specified in the primary eDirectory tree info section of the install have the Allows Clear Text Passwords option enabled.

▶ *IP Address*—If you are running the Apache Web server on a secondary IP address on your NetWare 6 server, make certain that the `add secondary IP address` lines are placed towards the top of the `SYS:\SYSTEM\AUTOEXEC.NCF` file instead of at the bottom.

▶ *Reboot Middle Tier Server*—You must reboot the NetWare or Windows servers that you installed the Middle Tier software on.

▶ *Check Middle Tier Server*—Check that the Middle Tier Server is running by entering the following address in your Web browser:

`http://<dns_name_or_IP_address_of_Middle_Tier_Server>/oneNet/zen`

Installing ZENworks for Desktops Management Agents

The ZENworks for Desktops management agents must be installed on each workstation that you want to distribute applications to, remotely manage, or maintain inventory for. The following sections discuss running the install for the management agent for the first time. This agent creates an install record that you can use to distribute the management agents to your workstation through NAL or as a silent install from a central network location.

Start Management Agents Install

You can start the management agent install by running SETUP.EXE from the `\AGENTINSTALL` directory on the CD-ROM, or from the `\\SYS\public\zenworks` directory on the ZENworks for Desktops server. Use the `/r` parameter to instruct the install to record the settings in the SETUP.ISS file located in the `\Windows` or `\WINNT` directory of the workstation. You can also use the /f1 parameter to specify your own path and filename for the .ISS file. For example:

```
setup /r /f1"c:\temp\standard.iss"
```

The first screen you will see in the ZENworks for Desktops management agent install is the welcome screen. Read the contents and click Next to continue.

The second screen you will see is the license agreement screen. Read the license agreement and select the Accept button if you agree to the terms. Click Next to continue.

The next screen you will see is the destination screen, which enables you to specify where to install the agents. Keep in mind that if you specify a drive other than C:, workstations with only a C: drive will be unable to use the .ISS file. Browse to the path you want workstations to use and click Next to continue.

Select Management Agent Features

The next screen is the ZENworks for Desktops workstation component selection screen, shown in Figure 2.9. This screen enables you to specify which ZENworks for Desktops components you want to install on your workstations.

Select the following components you want to install and then click the Next button:

▶ *Application Management*—Installs the Application Launcher agent and software to the workstation, thus allowing it to receive application distributions.

▶ *Workstation Manager*—Installs the agent and files to allow administrators to import, configure, and manage the workstation using eDirectory.

▶ *Workstation Imaging*—Installs the agent and drivers necessary for ZENworks to create and maintain an image of the workstation.

▶ *Remote Management Tools*—Installs the agents and files necessary to manage the workstation from a remote console.

▶ *Workstation Inventory*—Installs the agent and scan utilities necessary to scan the workstation for hardware and software inventory data.

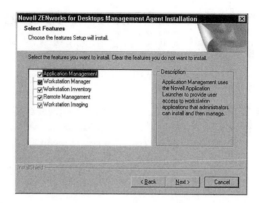

FIGURE 2.9
Component selection screen for the ZENworks for Desktops Management
agent install.

Set the ZENworks for Desktop Middle Tier Server

The next screen in the install is the Middle Tier server selection screen,
shown in Figure 2.10. This screen enables you to specify which Middle
Tier server the ZENworks for Desktops agent will use to connect to the
network. Set the DNS name or the IP address of the Middle Tier server
and click Next to continue.

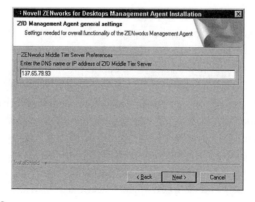

FIGURE 2.10
Middle Tier server selection screen for the ZENworks for Desktops
Management agent install.

Configure Workstation Manager Settings

The next screen in the install, if you are installing on a workstation without the Novell Client, is the Workstation Manager settings screen. This screen enables you to specify how the workstation manager behaves on the workstation through the following settings:

▶ *Display ZENworks Middle Tier authentication dialog box*—Enabling this option displays the Middle Tier authentication dialog box whenever a user logs in or tries to access a resource that requires authentication. This dialog box will replace the standard Microsoft login dialog box. If you leave this check box blank, ZENworks will log in in the background and the standard Microsoft login dialog box will pop up on the workstation.

▶ *Let users change the ZENworks Middle Tier Server address on authentication dialog box*—Enabling this option allows the users to specify the IP address or DNS name of the Middle Tier server they want to authenticate to. If you are restricting access through specific Middle Tier servers, disable this option. However, if you need to give users dynamic access to resources that lie beyond different Middle Tier Servers, enable this option.

Once you have set the options correctly, click Next to continue.

Configure the NAL Windows Startup Options

The next screen in the install is the Novell Application Launcher/Windows Startup options screen, shown in Figure 2.11. This screen enables you to specify how you want Novell Application Launcher (NAL) to behave on startup:

▶ *Launch Application Explorer*—Enabling this option starts the Novell Application Launcher when the workstation is booted. Use this option if you have updates that you want to periodically install on user workstations as soon as they are booted, for example, when updating anti-virus software. Any pending applications that are associated with the workstation or user will be executed.

▶ *Launch Application Window*—Enabling this option launches the application window when a user logs in. This gives the users easy access to their applications as soon as they log in.

▶ *None*—If you do not select either of the two options, the workstation will boot normally and the users must access the Application Explorer and Application window through the Program menu. Use this option if you are trying to impact users minimally.

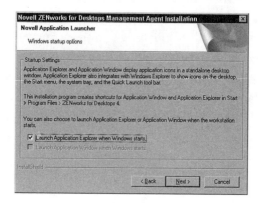

FIGURE 2.11
Novell Application Launcher/Windows Startup options selection screen for the ZENworks for Desktops Management agent install.

Once you have set the options correctly, click Next to continue.

Complete the Install

Once you have completed the setup options, you see the summary screen. This screen shows you the settings that you have selected for the management agent install. If you need to make any changes, you can click the Back button; otherwise click Next. The ZENworks for Desktops management agent will be installed on the workstation. Once the agent has been installed on the workstation, you will be prompted to either reboot the workstation immediately or to wait. The workstation must be restarted in order to activate the agents.

Further Install Options

After you run the initial install and create an .ISS file, you can automate future installs by using the .ISS file to create an application object, or enable users to run a silent install from the network or other source. The following sections discuss how to use the ISS file to automate the Management agent install.

Application Object

The easiest and fastest way to install the ZENworks for Desktops management agent on workstations is to create an Application object and distribute it. This works only when the workstations already have the Novell Client and Application Launcher running on them.

Use the following steps to create an Application object for the management agent and to distribute it to users who are currently running Application Launcher:

1. Create a network directory for the management agent source files.

2. Copy `\AgentInstall\SETUP.EXE` and the .ISS file you created into the source file directory.

3. Create a simple Application object (no .AOT/.AXT/.MSI file).

4. Modify the command line of the application object to include the `/s` option. This option tells the install to use an .ISS file and to not display dialog boxes. For example:

   `setup.exe /s /f1"E:\WAGENT\SETUP.ISS"`

5. Define the system requirements for the workstation to receive the distribution.

6. Add the Source directory you created in step 1 to the application object.

7. Associate the Application object with the users and workstations that you want to receive the Management agent install.

8. Set the Run Application Once option and schedule the distribution.

9. Save the Application object settings by clicking Finish.

NOTE The install will run in silent mode using the `/s` option. Instead of displaying errors to the screen, errors will be saved to a SETUP.LOG file in the same directory as the .ISS file. You can specify a different log file by using the following option on the setup command line: `/f2"<path_and_filename>"`.

Silent Install

If you need to install the ZENworks for Desktops management agent on workstations that do not have Application Launcher running on them, you need to make the SETUP.EXE application and the .ISS file you created available to the user from a different source. There are many ways to do this:

▶ You can create a directory on the network that those workstations have access to and copy the SETUP.EXE and .ISS files to it. The workstations can then copy the files.

▶ You can Zip the files up and e-mail them to users and they can extract them to their local workstations.

▶ You can also create an install CD containing the files and distribute the CD to users so they can copy the files to their local workstations.

▶ You can also deliver SETUP.EXE through a Web browser. For example, you can copy SETUP.EXE to the root of your Web server. You then edit the MYAPPS.HTML file that is created automatically by the Middle Tier installation so it replaces the ZFDWEBSW.EXE with SETUP.EXE.

Once the files are installed on the local workstation, the users will need to run the setup using the /s option and use the .ISS file settings. For example:

```
setup.exe /s /f1"c:\Zclient\setup.iss"
```

## CHAPTER 3

Setting Up ZENworks for Desktops 4 in Your Tree

This chapter provides a quick overview of the ZENworks for Desktops system and a high-level view of the changes that occur within your tree. Try to follow and understand this system and how it impacts your current Novell Directory Services installations. Other chapters delve into the details of installation and feature execution.

General ZENworks for Desktops Architecture

Novell ZENworks for Desktops requires some changes to your tree structure in addition to installation and extensions to the new ConsoleOne administration tool. Additionally, you need to place new agents on the workstation. This section details the changes that need to occur to implement ZENworks for Desktops into your tree.

Objects in eDirectory and Their Impact on the Tree

When you install ZENworks for Desktops into your tree, it not only copies the executable files necessary to run the software, but it also extends the schema in your tree. The schema extension in your tree introduces several new objects and attributes to your system. Following is a high-level list of the changes to your schema. For a more detailed view of the schema changes, refer to Appendix A.

▶ *Container package object*—This object collects for your administration all of the policies that can be associated with a container. You create one of these objects when you want to affect a container policy. One such policy is search, which affects the order of searching for all policies in and below the container.

▶ *Server package object*—This object collects all of the policies that are available for servers. The policies for servers in the ZENworks for Desktops product include policies for automatic workstation import. Other server policies that are compatible with this object are included in the ZENworks for Servers product.

▶ *Server group object*—This object enables the creation of a group of servers. This is useful when you want to apply a Server Policy Package to a group of servers.

▶ *Service location package object*—This package collects the policies in the system that are related to locating services in the network.

▶ *User package object*—This object holds all of the policies that are associated with users. This includes such policies as the Dynamic Local User, Remote Control, and Novell iPrint policies.

▶ *Workstation package object*—This package contains all of the registered policies for a workstation. These policies can be such items as workstation imaging and inventory policies.

▶ *Workstation image object*—This object represents an image taken from a workstation. This image can then be applied to any workstation in the network from some commands in Novell's eDirectory or through a boot process with a floppy.

▶ *Workstation group object*—This object enables you to collect a set of workstations into a group. This is useful when you want to apply policies to a set of workstations that are not all in the same container.

▶ *Application object*—This object is associated with an application that you want to distribute or make available to any desktop in the network.

▶ *Application folder object*—This object enables you to create a menuing/foldering system for the presentation of your applications on the user's Start menu or windowed desktop.

▶ *Database object*—This object represents the database in the network where you are storing such information as logs of ZENworks activity and events, as well as hardware and software inventory information.

▶ *Inventory service object*—This object represents the inventory service that is configured and running on the network, collecting your hardware and software configurations of your workstations.

▶ *Several policy objects*—This is a set of Policy objects that represents policies contained in the User, Server, or Workstation policy packages. These can be such policies as the Help Desk policy, Remote Control policy, or Restrict Login policy, just to name a few. Currently ZENworks for Desktops creates and uses over 36 policies.

Introducing most of these objects to the tree has minimal impact. The only objects that you need to consider because of their size are the Application and the Workstation objects:

The Application object can grow depending on the amount of Registry settings that a particular application contains. You need to be careful where you place these objects because they can be large, especially for some applications such as Microsoft Office.

The Workstation object only introduces approximately 4KB of information. However, the culmination of all Workstation objects in your environment needs to be managed carefully. Be sure to use good design techniques when placing your partitions to make your tree most efficient.

Novell ZENworks Management Agents

ZENworks Management agents are a collection of services and executables that are required to be on the workstation. These agents communicate with eDirectory either through the Novell Client (optionally installed) or through the Middle Tier Web server. These agents include Workstation Management Agent, Application Management Agent, Inventory Agent, and Remote Control Agent. A supplied executable or downloadable MSI (Microsoft System Installer) version is available for delivery to your workstations. This delivery can be through a push, remote install, or through a Web browser.

Additionally, ZENworks also provides a small agent, called Application View Agent, that only provides delivery of applications to the workstations through a browser. This agent is considerably smaller and can easily be delivered via e-mail or via a browser to help you kick-start your rollout of ZENworks.

Policy Packages and Policies

To help in the administration of the features and policies of ZENworks for Desktops, the various policies are conveniently grouped into policy packages. These policy packages are logical groupings of policies.

Policy packages can be associated with the various appropriate objects. For example, User Policy Packages can be associated with a single user, a group of users, or a container. Workstation Policy Packages can be associated with a single workstation, a group of workstations, or a container. A single policy package can also be associated with several users, groups, and containers.

Because the system looks for policies by searching up the tree from the User or Workstation object (depending on the application), it is desirable to keep this search from proceeding too far up the tree. Therefore, ZENworks for Desktops includes a search policy found in the Container Policy Package. This policy limits the number of levels and the search order that all ZENworks for Desktops systems use to discover and apply policies.

Various services are used by the ZENworks for Desktop system, and these services are located by the Services Location Policy Package. This package is typically associated with a container and identifies where SNMP traps and the database is located. The applications in the system then use the database specified in the location policy.

ZENworks for Desktops Policy Package Wizard

In order to assist you in constructing policies, ZENworks for Desktop includes a wizard that is activated with the creation of a policy package object. The Policy Package Wizard is launched when you go to a container and request that a new policy package object be created. Previous

versions of ZENworks had a wizard that could be executed from the
Tools menu of NWAdmin32; this is no longer supported in ConsoleOne.

Policy Package Wizard

The Policy Package Wizard is activated when you create a policy package
from the Create menu choice or from the Policy Package Wizard icon on
the ConsoleOne toolbar. The first screen, shown in Figure 3.1, presents
you with the list of all available policy packages and the list of policies
that are contained in each policy.

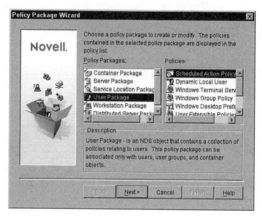

FIGURE 3.1
Initial screen of the Policy Package Wizard.

Once you select a policy package, the right side of the wizard fills in with
the various policies that are available. You need to press Next in order to
proceed in the creation of the policy package you have selected. You are
then asked to enter the name of the policy package and the container
where the package should reside. This screen is shown in Figure 3.2.

After selecting the name and container, you are presented with a page
that lets you go back to create another package or select the option to
define additional properties for the package you are about to create.
When you select the additional properties option and press Next, the
wizard creates the object and then opens the object properties, just as if
you had browsed to the object and selected properties. Now you can
modify and activate specific policies in the package.

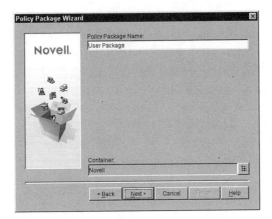

FIGURE 3.2
Prompt for package name screen from the Policy Package Wizard.

Setting Up User Packages in the Tree

Once you have user objects in your tree and have the ZENworks management agents installed on your users' workstations, you can begin to manage your users in the tree.

The following sections describe at a high level some of the things that you can manage with the User Policy Package.

Creating User Policy Packages

You can quickly create a User Policy Package by using the following described steps. You'll learn about the details of each policy in later chapters.

1. Launch ConsoleOne.

2. Browse in ConsoleOne to the container where you want to create the policy package. Remember that you can set the package to reside in any container and still associate it with any other container in the tree; but be careful not to replicate large partitions all over your tree just to get to the policy packages.

3. Select the Container object and then click the right mouse button and select the policy package object. This opens the Policy Package Create Wizard to walk you through the creation.

4. Select User Package and follow the wizard to identify the container and the name of the object. Pick Define Additional Properties in the last wizard page so you can activate some policies. If you didn't do this, browse in ConsoleOne to the container that has your User Policy Package and select that object. You can double-click or right-click and choose properties from the menu.

5. You are presented with the property page for the user package you have defined. The screen should look like the one in Figure 3.3.

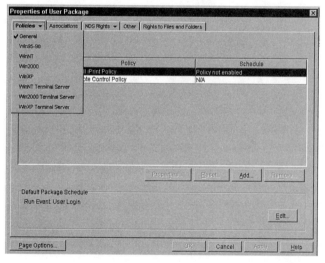

FIGURE 3.3
Properties of User Policy Package.

6. Under the general category, you can activate both the Remote Control and the Novell iPrint policies. Clicking the small triangle next to the Policies tab and then selecting the desired workstation type from the drop-down menu can access the workstation specific policies. Once you select the workstation type, the policies tab for that specific workstation is displayed.

7. Mark the Remote Control policy check box.

8. Go into Remote Control policy properties by either double-clicking to get to the properties or by selecting the details button.

9. Once in the properties of the Remote Control policy, you can select various configuration options on the pages displayed to enable the user to see and run the Remote Control application. The Remote Control policy is described in detail in later chapters.

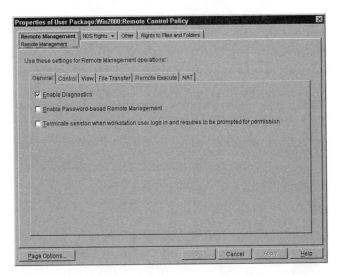

FIGURE 3.4
Properties of the Remote Control policy in the User Policy Package.

10. Press OK to complete the changes. If you have not associated this policy package with a container, group, or user object, a notification is displayed (see Figure 3.5).

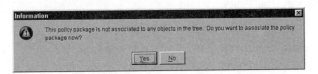

FIGURE 3.5
Notification of unassociated User Policy Package.

11. Click Yes to associate this User Policy Package with a container in the tree. This once again brings up the property pages of the User Policy Package and displays the Associations page (see Figure 3.6). You need to then press the Add button and browse to the container, group, or user you want to receive this policy package. Remember, every user below the identified container, within the specified group or the associated user, receives this policy package and all policies activated in this package.

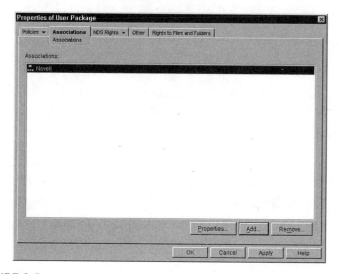

FIGURE 3.6
Associations page of the User Policy Package.

12. Press OK to complete the change.

You have now created a simple User Policy Package and turned on the Remote Control policy for all of the users associated with this policy package. Now when the remote control agent reads this policy, it will enforce the configurations specified.

Setting Up Workstations in the Tree

Before you can start really managing the workstation, you must create Workstation objects and associate them with physical workstations. This step is not necessary if you do not want to manage the physical device, but instead want only to manage the desktop. For example, if you only want to deliver applications to the workstation and apply Microsoft policies to the desktop when a user is logged into the workstation, it's best to associate a user policy to the particular user. However, if you want to manage the physical inventory in *addition* to managing the workstation accounts, you must first have the Workstation object.

The following sections describe the automatic workstation methods of importing a workstation into the tree.

To get the system up and running, you must first have an Import Policy active in your tree and the agents running on the server and workstations. You must do the following to get a functioning Import Policy in your tree:

1. Activate workstation agents.

2. Activate server agent (only for automated workstation import).

3. Create a policy package (User package for manual, Server package for automated).

4. Turn on the Import Policy in the policy package.

5. Associate the policy package.

6. Set the Registry keys or DNS host file on the workstation through an application package to notify the workstation which eDirectory tree or Middle Tier to use as its primary tree.

7. Enable login cycles to register the workstation to the tree and have the server agent automatically create the Workstation object and associate it to the device.

8. Associate other policies to the Workstation objects to affect management.

Activate Server Agents

If you want to have automated workstation import in your network, you should have installed the automatic workstation agents onto the server as part of the installation process.

These agents on the workstation get into contact with the agents on the server through DNS services. You must either have a DNS server in your network with the DNS name of the automatic workstation import server registered (you gave the name at installation time) or each workstation must have the DNS name and address in the host file. The hostname must be `zenwsimport`, because the agents will be doing a hostname lookup with that name to find the IP address of the server with the service. This can also be done through a Registry key on the workstation (`HKEY_LOCAL_MACHINE\Software\Novell\ZENworks\zenwsreg` with the string value of `ImportServer=DNS` or IP address of the import server).

The agents must be running on the server. You accomplish this by executing the ZENWSIMP.NCF file for NetWare or by having the install process install the automatic workstation import service on the NT/2000 servers.

NOTE A `NoSuchMethodError` event can occur when workstations attempt to register the agent if you do not have the latest JNCP.NLM and NJCL.JAR files loaded on the server before running the automatic workstation import agent. You can also look in the WSREG32.LOG file in the root drive of the workstation for additional clues. The correct versions can be found on the ZENworks for Desktops 4 CD under the companionCD/NJCL directory or from www.novell.com.

Creating a Policy Package

To begin the automatic workstation process, you must have a workstation import policy activated and associated with the server that is running the import agents. This is done by creating a Server Policy Package, activating the import policy, and then associating the Server Policy Package with the server via a container, server group, or direct association. Follow these steps:

1. Start ConsoleOne.

2. Select a container to hold the Server Policy Package object.

3. Create the Server Policy Package in the container.

4. Go through the Policy Package Wizard and select a Server Policy Package for the type of package and name the object. Follow the wizard and associate the policy package with the container that has the Server object with the import agent running. Remember that these policies are effective in sub-containers as well, so you can associate the policy package high enough in the tree to affect as many servers as desired.

Creating a Workstation Import Policy

Now that you have created the Server Policy Package and associated it with a container that holds the server, you need to activate the Workstation Import Policy in the package. To activate the Workstation Import Policy, do the following:

1. Start ConsoleOne.

2. Browse to the container that has the Server Policy Package you want to administer.

3. Select the Server Policy Package and bring up the properties on the object.

4. Select the Workstation Import Policy from the list of policies available. When you select and activate the import policy, the check box will be checked.

5. Perform details of the Workstation Import Policy if desired.

6. Select OK and close out the dialog boxes.

Once you have created a Workstation Import policy, the workstations that have not been registered with the tree will attempt to contact the workstation import agent on the server when rebooted. If a connection is made, the agent receives information from the workstation (to help in the naming), and then creates the Workstation object in the tree and returns that object name back to the workstation. The workstation then stores that information in a secure portion of the Registry and it is associated with that object in the tree.

In the preceding Step 5, you had the option of modifying the details of the Import Policy. Let's discuss briefly some of these options. If you decide to take the default Import policy, when you create workstations, they will be located in the same container as the Server object and will be named by the concatenation of the computer name and the MAC address of the network card. You can change the Import Policy to identify under which container you want the Workstation object to reside (can be absolute or relative to server or policy container) and to name the Workstation object.

Associations of Policy Packages

The ZENworks for Desktops system always starts with the relevant User, Server, or Workstation object, depending on the feature being executed. Once the User, Server (for agents), or Workstation object is located, the system will walk the tree until it locates the first policy package it can find. Generally once a package is found the configuration set in that policy is applied to the system, and the ZENworks for Desktops feature is activated.

Some features, such as the Microsoft Windows desktop policies, are an accumulation of several ZAW/ZAK policies to which the user can be associated. These policies require that the search proceed until the root of the tree.

Walking to the root of the tree for policy packages can be time-consuming, especially when the tree spans across a WAN link. Therefore, ZENworks for Desktops introduced the search policy that is contained in the Container Policy Package. This search policy limits the levels of containers that all processes search to find their policies.

Novell Workstation Registration and Object Creation

If the import policy has been created and associated with the Server object and the workstation import agents are running on the server, when a user logs into the system, it activates a workstation registration process. Based on the policy, it might take several logins before the registration occurs.

The registration process includes an agent running on the workstation attempting to resolve the DNS name of `zenwsimport`. It uses that address to contact the automated workstation import process running on the server. Alternatively, the agent will use the Registry key (`HKEY_LOCAL_MACHINE\Software\Novell\ZENworks\zenwsreg`) with the string value of `ImportServer=DNS` or the IP address of the import server. The server process receives information about the workstation and the user and then, based on the naming description administered in the import policy associated with the server, it creates a Workstation object for the workstation. Once the object is created, it returns the distinguished name of the Workstation object back to the registration process on the workstation. The workstation then stores the workstation DN information in a secure portion of the Registry and it becomes associated with the given Workstation object.

You can un-register a workstation by running `zwsreg -unreg` from the workstation (it was installed when the agents were placed on the workstation) that you want to disassociate with an object. The initial rules of Workstation object creation go into effect and a new object is created at the proper time and given to the workstation.

NOTE Once you have your users associated with their appropriate policy packages, you can create other policies in that package and have them affect the user's environment. This is also true with Workstation objects and their associated policy packages.

Remote Management Rights

A majority of the remote management features are available to users and administrators via rights in the eDirectory tree on the objects that represent the target device. For example, in order to remote control a target workstation, you can configure ZENworks such that one must have rights in the target Workstation object in order to perform the remote control function.

You must grant individual rights in the tree in order to enable users to perform remote management functions on workstations and user desktops. The following objects in the tree can be granted remote management rights: User, Group, Organizational Role, Organization, Organization Unit, Country, Locality, [Root], and [Public]. Two methods exist that you can use to set up these rights. The following subsections discuss these methods.

Remote Operators Page

A Remote Operators Page is associated with each Workstation object. Figure 3.7 displays this page.

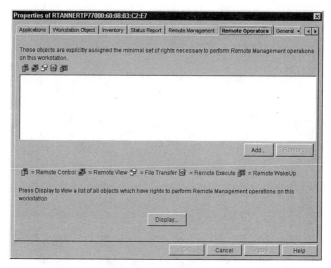

FIGURE 3.7
Remote Operators page in a Workstation object.

From within this page, you can add users or groups to the list of operators. With each addition, you can check which of the remote management utilities this addition has rights to perform. The choices available
are Remote Control, Remote View, File Transfer, Remote Execute, Remote
Wakeup, and Diagnostics. Check the box to grant the user or group the
rights to perform these functions on this particular workstation.

You can also discover who in the tree has rights to perform some remote
management on a specific workstation. You can do this by selecting a
workstation in ConsoleOne and running Remote Management Rights
from the Tools menu, or by pressing the Display button on the remote
operators page of the Workstation object. When this program is activated, it displays a report detailing who has rights to which portions of
rights management. A sample output report is shown in Figure 3.8.

With ZENworks for Desktops 4, you can also set a remote control policy
that allows you to remote control without a workstation object and without the need to have rights on the object to perform remote control. This
option is called Password-based Remote Management and it allows you
to remote control a workstation by selecting Tools, Remote Management,
Windows from the ConsoleOne tools menu. When prompted, you must
enter the IP address of the workstation along with a user password.

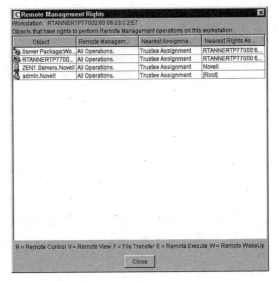

FIGURE 3.8
Report of rights management on a specified workstation.

Inventory, Event, and Logging Databases

In order to keep track of the logging events generated by the workstation agents, other ZENworks server agents, SNMP events, and hardware and software inventories for your workstations, you need to install at least one database into your tree. This database holds all of the events, inventory, and reporting information. You can then generate reports against that database to display information about your workstations in the tree.

You can have a server collect inventory information and then forward it to a local database on that server, or another in the area. You can also have that information rolled up into another enterprise-level database. This allows you the capability to have a local site database that just contains local information and then have that information also included in an enterprise-level database that might contain information from many site databases.

When you installed the database on the server at installation time, a ZfD Database object was created in the same container where the server is located. This Database object represents the database that resides on that server. The object enables you to administer the server where the database is located and the passwords that are used by the agents to gain entry into the database. This object is also used in the Service Location Policy Package that tells the workstation and server agents what database to use for storing their event and logging information.

To get the databases up and functioning for events and logging, you need to do the following:

1. Install the Sybase database onto a server. This places a blank database on the server and puts in the MGMTDBS.NCF file on NetWare to get it started.

2. Create a Service Location Policy Package and activate the database policy. You need to create the package and turn on the database policy that also needs to have a reference to the Database object in the database page.

3. Associate the Service Location Policy Package with a container. This enables agents of users or desktops in that container to locate the database.

4. Application objects that you want to track have a page where you can specify which events you want logged in the database. See additional information in Chapter 5, "Creating Application Packages Using snAppShot."

Additional administration needs to be accomplished in order to get workstation inventory data into the database. See Chapter 13, "Using ZENworks Workstation Inventory," for additional information.

Reporting

Once you have set up an inventory database and identified what you want to store in the database (such as inventory, application launching or failures, and so on), you can run reports against that database.

ZENworks for Desktops 4 uses a JDBC interface to connect and query from the database. You can get to the reports by selecting the Tools,

Inventory Reports from the ConsoleOne menu. You are asked to configure the database first, so the system knows which database to communicate with. When you configure the database by selecting Tools, Configure
DB, you are prompted for the IP address of the server containing the
database. Under the advance options, you can tell the system whether the
database is a Sybase or an Oracle server.

In ZENworks for Desktops 4, you can launch semi-custom reports that
present you with a screen that lists the available reports and the items in
the report that you can customize. When you select a report, you are
allowed to select a set of values that must match for the data to be
included in the report. This enables you to create reports that are much
more informative without the reams of data that were printed out in
prior versions. Figure 3.9 displays a sample screen from the Novell
Application Launcher report selection.

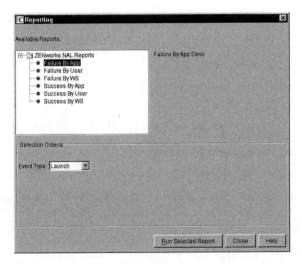

FIGURE 3.9
Application Launcher semi-report screen.

Once you have selected a report, the system connects with the configured
database and then queries the information with a JDBC connection. The
results are then placed in a canned styled report and presented in the
viewer that pops up to display the information. From the viewer you can
save or print the report.

Reports for ZENworks for Desktops are built upon a runtime Crystal Reports engine. Using your own Crystal Reports designer, you can create any number of custom reports for your particular business needs.

Setting Up TED Distributions

ZENworks for Desktops 4 ships with some agents that plug into the Tiered Electronic Distribution system that is included with the ZENworks for Servers product.

These agents allow you to distribute Application objects and the installation files associated with them throughout the servers in your network. They also keep the files and objects up-to-date with the identified "golden" versions.

For more information about how to use the integrated ZENworks for Desktops 4 agents to distribute application objects as TED distributions, check out *Novell ZENworks for Servers 3 Administrator's Handbook* (ISBN 0-7897-2986-5).

## CHAPTER 4

Novell Clientless Operation

Since the philosophy of Novell's ZENworks line of product is to reduce the cost while increasing the productivity of managing servers, workstations, and networks, it was only a matter of time before a clientless solution was introduced. ZENworks for Desktops 4 introduces new architecture that enables you to manage workstations that do not have the Novell client installed on them.

This allows you to use the ZENworks for Desktops management features to distribute applications, maintain hardware and software inventory, create images and remotely manage workstations that do not have a Novell client installed, whether they reside inside or outside of your corporate firewall.

ZENworks for Desktops Clientless Workstation Management Components

ZENworks for Desktops 4 includes new components that allow for Web-based delivery of ZENworks services through a Web browser. This section discusses the components that allow the ZENworks workstation management tools to work without an installation of the Novell client on the workstation.

ZENworks for Desktops Management Agent

The ZENworks for Desktops Management agent is a small set of workstation applications that enable the workstation to be managed from a ZENworks for Desktops server. You can install the Management agent on a workstation that does not have the Novell client or on workstations that do have the Novell client. The agent provides full functionality regardless of whether the client is present. If the client is present, however, the Management agent may use some client features to provide additional access points (for example, no Middle Tier server specified). Additionally, if the client is present and for some reason cannot make connections to the services needed, the ZENworks for Desktop Management agent will automatically divert its requests through any specified Middle Tier Web server.

You can install the following Management agent components on a workstation:

▶ *Application Management*—Provides users with access to distributed desktop applications through the Novell Application Launcher (NAL).

▶ *Workstation Manager*—Allows administrators to configure and manage workstations through Novell eDirectory.

▶ *Workstation Inventory*—Collects hardware and software inventory information from scanned workstations, thus allowing administrators to track and manage what hardware and software is currently installed on managed workstations.

▶ *Remote Management*—Allows administrators to remotely manage workstations through a remote console.

▶ *Workstation Imaging*—Allows administrators to create an image of a workstation's hard drive and put it on other workstations over the network.

Corporate Firewall

Corporate firewalls are simply combinations of hardware and software that restrict access to the internal corporate network from the rest of the Internet. This feat is accomplished by restricting access to certain addresses and ports.

ZENworks for Desktops Middle Tier Server

The ZENworks for Desktops Middle Tier server is a NetWare or
Windows 2000 server that has ZENworks agents installed in the
`SYS:\XTIER\` directory on NetWare servers and `<Windows Source`
`Drive>:\oneNet` directory on Windows 2000 servers. These agents
provide the NCP communication necessary to provide clientless authentication to the network as well as facilitate ZENworks for Desktop workstation management traffic to and from a clientless workstation. Clientless
workstations attach through the DNS name or IP address of the Middle
Tier server.

NOTE If you are running ZENworks for Desktops in a Windows only environment,
the ZENworks for Desktops Middle Tier server must be a member of the same domain as
your ZENworks for Desktops servers. The Middle Tier server can be the same server
as your ZENworks for Desktops server.

Web Server

The ZENworks for Desktops Middle Tier server must have one of the following Web server engines running on it to provide the HTTP communication between the workstations' browser and the Middle Tier agents:

▶ *NetWare 6*—Apache HTTP Server (Shipping)

▶ *NetWare 5.1*—Apache HTTP Server (version 1.3.22)

▶ *Windows 2000*—Microsoft IIS Web Server (Shipping)

ZENworks for Desktops Server

The ZENworks for Desktops server provides the final piece of the clientless workstation management model by providing NCP access between
the administrator using the ZENworks for Desktops management tools
and the Middle Tier server that is providing the HTTP communication to
the clientless workstation. The ZENworks for Desktops server can treat
the clientless workstation as any normal managed workstation and can
distribute files to it, gather inventory data, and provide remote control
sessions.

How ZENworks for Desktop Clientless Workstation Management Works

The ZENworks for Desktops management agent allows a clientless workstation to authenticate to the network by establishing an HTTP connection, at port 80 and port 443, to a ZENworks for Desktops Middle Tier server. The workstation can be inside or outside the corporate firewall.

When a workstation authenticates to a ZENworks for Desktops Middle Tier server, the Middle Tier server establishes an NCP connection to a ZENworks for Desktops server. The ZENworks for Desktops 4 server can be in the same eDirectory tree or a different tree; however, user licenses are only consumed in the eDirectory tree that the ZENworks for Desktops 4 server is installed in. The capability to connect through a Middle Tier server that does not belong to the same tree enables ZENworks to provide a much more secure and dynamic clientless access environment. It does this by separating the access point from corporate data and services.

Once a clientless workstation has authenticated to the network through a ZENworks for Desktops Middle Tier server, the ZENworks for Desktops policies and application distributions can use the HTTP to NCP series of connections to manage the workstation. In other words, NAL Application objects can be applied on the workstation, the workstation can be remotely managed, and inventory data can be collected from it.

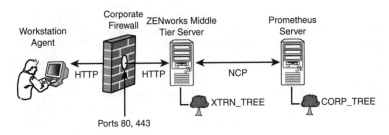

FIGURE 4.1
ZENworks for Desktops 4 clientless workstation management diagram.

This can be an extremely powerful tool for managing user workstations that must access the network through the corporate firewall.

For example, administrators can use the ZENworks for Desktops Management agent to manage corporate PCs that employees have at home because they work from a home office, or occasionally work from home. Corporate applications can be distributed to the home office workstation, the workstation can be remotely managed, and inventory can be tracked.

Another example of when this feature can be useful is with remote sales offices that reside outside the corporate firewall.

Using the ZENworks for Desktops Middle Tier Server

The ZENworks for Desktops Middle Tier server works mostly in the background to allow you to manage clientless workstations the same as you do workstations that have the Novell Client installed. Once it is installed and configured, there is not much maintenance involved. However, there are times when you'll need to interact with the Middle Tier server. The following sections discuss tasks such as logging into, viewing the status of, starting and stopping, and modifying settings for the Middle Tier server.

Logging Using the Middle Tier Login Page

When you have installed the ZENworks for Desktops Management agent on a workstation that does not have a Novell Client installed, you can configure the Windows NT/2000/XP workstation to display the ZENworks Middle Tier Authentication dialog box on startup or when user authentication is requested. You can also specify whether users can change the ZENworks for Desktops Middle Tier server address.

If you have only one Middle Tier server or if you have restricted access through the ZENworks for Desktops Middle Tier server, you should not allow users to change the Middle Tier server address. This allows you to control which users access the network through a specific server.

However, if you have several Middle Tier servers and are less restrictive about which server your users can authenticate through, allowing users to change the address of the ZENworks for Desktops Middle Tier server will make accessing the network easier. Consider this option if users might need to access different Middle Tier servers to gain access to different resources on the Internet.

Logging into the network using the Middle Tier login page works the same as the Novell Client login page. The users must enter their network user IDs and passwords. Once users click OK, they will be authenticated to the network.

You can also use a pass-through method to authenticate to the network by disabling the login page when you install the ZENworks for Desktops agent. This allows you to use only the workstation login page to authenticate to the network as long as the user ID and passwords are synchronized between the local workstation and the network. If the passwords are not synchronized, a second login prompt will appear after the user enters their ID and password to log in to the local machine.

Viewing the Statistics of the Middle Tier Server

Once you have installed and configured the ZENworks for Desktops Middle Tier server, you can view the current request statistics at any time. This allows you to determine whether the Middle Tier server is currently up, view the number of current requests and sessions, see the bytes read and written, and view any failures that have occurred while clientless workstations tried to authenticate.

If the ZENworks for Desktops Middle Tier server is running, you can access the statistics page, shown in Figure 4.2, by accessing following Web page:

```
http://Server_DNS_or_IP/oneNet/xtier-stats
```

Viewing the Sessions on the Middle Tier Server

In addition to viewing the statistics for the ZENworks for Desktops Middle Tier server, you might also want to look at the currently active sessions through the xtier-session page. This page allows you to see the DN, session ID, number of requests, session timeout setting, login time, and last request time of all sessions that are currently active on the Middle Tier server. You can use the xtier-session page to monitor access as well as troubleshoot session problems on the Middle Tier server.

Running xtier-session will show only your session, whereas an administrator can see all sessions with the xtier-sessions command.

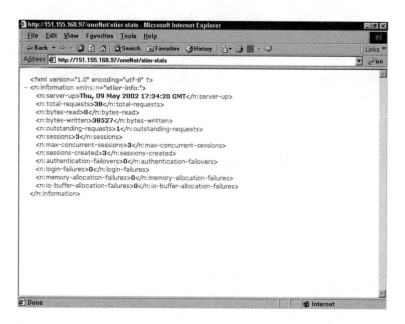

FIGURE 4.2
xtier-stats XML page for a ZENworks for Desktops Middle Tier server in Internet Explorer.

If the ZENworks for Desktops Middle Tier server is running, you can access the xtier-session page, shown in Figure 4.3, by accessing following Web page:

```
http://Server_DNS_or_IP/oneNet/xtier-sessions
```

Viewing the NCPL Stats on the Middle Tier Server

Another page that you might find useful when managing the ZENworks for Desktops Middle Tier server is the xtier-ncplstats page. This page allows you to see statistical information about modules that are currently active on the Middle Tier server. This information can be useful when you are troubleshooting issues across the Middle Tier server. For example, if you are troubleshooting the process of importing workstations across the Middle Tier server, you can look at the module information about the `ZEN-XWSIMPORT` module to see whether threads are running and events are being seen (to determine whether the Middle Tier server is receiving import data from the clientless workstation).

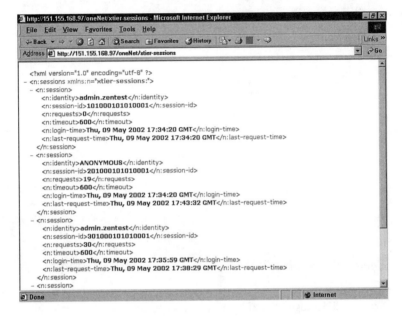

FIGURE 4.3
xtier-session XML page for a ZENworks for Desktops Middle Tier server in Internet Explorer.

If the ZENworks for Desktops Middle Tier server is running, you can access the xtier-ncplstats page, shown in the Figure 4.4, by accessing following Web page:

```
http://Server_DNS_or_IP/oneNet/xtier-sessions
```

Starting and Stopping the Middle Tier Server

You might need to stop the Middle Tier server at times to inhibit users from authenticating though it or to perform maintenance on the server. When the Middle Tier server is stopped, users cannot authenticate to the network through it and you cannot manage workstations through it.

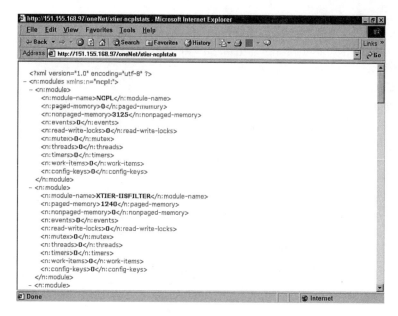

FIGURE 4.4
xtier-ncplstats XML page for a ZENworks for Desktops Middle Tier server in
Internet Explorer.

You can execute the following commands at the NetWare console of the
server where you installed the ZENworks for Desktops Middle Tier server:

▶ nvxadmdn—Executes the NVXADMDN.NCF script that halts the
ZENworks for Desktops Middle Tier server.

▶ nvxadmup—Executes the NVXADMUP.NCF script that restarts the
ZENworks for Desktops Middle Tier server after it has been halted.

On Windows 2000, go to the Internet Services Manager and click on the
properties of your Web site. Then, from the ISAPI Filter tab, you can disable and enable the oneNet filter.

Increasing the Session Timeout

User sessions that have been established through the ZENworks for
Desktops Middle Tier server will time out after 10 minutes of inactivity
by default. Once that threshold has been reach and the session has timed
out, users are required to re-authenticate when they attempt to access the
session.

You can increase the session timeout threshold if you have users that access the network through a Middle Tier server. You can use the NSADMIN utility located at the following Web address to increase or decrease the default timeout:

```
http://middle_tier_server_IP_address_or_DNS_name/oneNet/
nsadmin
```

When you enter this address in your Web browser, you are asked to authenticate to the utility using your network user ID and password. Once you have authenticated to the NSADMIN utility, you will see the General settings page by default. You can also access the General settings page by selecting Manage Xtier, General.

To increase the session timeout, you need to increase the value of the Session Timeout field on the General settings page, shown in Figure 4.5. The Session Timeout specifies the session length in seconds using hexadecimal notation. The default value is **0x258** (decimal 600, which is 10 minutes). You can increase this value to allow users a greater amount of inactivity time before the session is timed out.

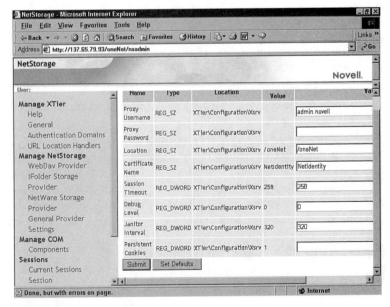

FIGURE 4.5

General xtier settings page for the ZENworks for Desktops Middle Tier server in Internet Explorer.

## CHAPTER 5

Creating Application Packages Using snAppShot

One of the most useful tools provided in ZENworks for Desktops is the snAppShot utility. As an administrator installing and updating applications on client workstations, you'll save a lot of time using the snAppShot utility. It enables you to create a template during a single install that can be used to easily distribute applications and upgrades to several workstations on your network.

This chapter familiarizes you with the snAppShot utility and describes how to use it to create application packages. The following topics are discussed:

- ▶ What snAppShot is
- ▶ When you should use snAppShot
- ▶ How snAppShot works
- ▶ Advanced features of snAppShot
- ▶ Limitations of snAppShot
- ▶ Using snAppShot
- ▶ snAppShot application packages versus .MSI files

What Is snAppShot?

The first step in using the snAppShot utility is to understand what it is. The snAppShot utility is an application used to create before and after images of a model workstation when installing or upgrading an application. So in effect, snAppShot takes a picture of the workstation before an application is installed or upgraded to it, and another picture after the application has been fully installed or upgraded.

Once snAppShot has the two pictures, it can then discern the differences between the two pictures. It saves the differences and can use them later to upgrade or install applications to other workstations on the network.

When Should You Use snAppShot?

Now that you understand what snAppShot is, you need to know when to use it. By default, snAppShot is generally used to package an application to distribute to several other users based on the eDirectory and the application properties.

However, because snAppShot captures changes made to a workstation during install, many situations exist in which you can use it to save time. The following sections describe how snAppShot is useful in three situations.

Complex Installations or Upgrades

Using snAppShot to aid in complex installations or upgrades can save you a considerable amount of time otherwise spent repeating the same steps over and over. By using snAppShot, you simply need to perform the complex installation or upgrade once, record the differences, and then apply those differences to the other workstations.

An example of when snAppShot is useful in a complex upgrade is when installing and configuring a printer driver on a Windows XP client. To do so, use the following steps:

1. Enter the network path to the printer or browse the network to find the appropriate queue.

2. Use the Windows XP CD-ROM or the path to the CAB files that have the necessary files to install the printer driver.

3. Configure the printer drivers for the desktop.

4. Make the appropriate configuration changes for the printer.

The preceding steps are tolerable if it is for one or two workstations, but if 100 or more workstations need the printer set up, the task becomes monumental.

Using snAppShot on one Windows XP machine to "package" a printer installation enables you to create an Application object template that you can use to create an Application object.

Once the Application object is created for the printer installation, other Windows XP clients can install the printer, with drivers, without having to use CAB files, the Windows XP CD-ROM, or make configuration changes!

Numerous Installations or Upgrades

Using snAppShot to aid in installations that must be done on numerous workstations can also save you a lot of time. Often, application upgrades or installations are very simple to perform and only take a short time on one workstation. However, that time is multiplied by the number of clients you have on your network. Many companies have thousands of clients, and, although installing an application takes only a few minutes on one client, the installation takes days to complete on all network clients.

snAppShot enables you to configure the upgrade or install to be automatically performed throughout the network. Instead of running the install or upgrade on workstation after workstation, you simply perform it once on the model workstation and use snAppShot to record the differences. Once recorded, the changes can be made to several other workstations easily and efficiently.

Using snAppShot to record the changes during the update and packaging into an Application object enables you to have the upgrade performed automatically as the users log in to the network. This saves a lot of time and effort when upgrading a large number of users. It also guarantees that every client has been upgraded.

Verifying Changes Made During an Install or Upgrade

Another situation where snAppShot is very useful is to verify or view the changes made by an application install or upgrade. Although snAppShot was not designed for this purpose, it works well because it captures the changes made during the install.

Application installations can create difficulties for other applications. snAppShot enables you to detect what the application install did to your client and enables you to correct it without un-installing or re-installing an application.

A good example of where snAppShot can help with reviewing an application install is installing a new application that updates shared DLLs in the **SYSTEM** directory for Windows 98. The application replaces a working DLL with a newer DLL that has bugs.

Once the new DLL is installed, the new application works fine, but a previously installed application fails to load properly. Normally you would have two options: to re-install the application that is failing to unload, or to un-install the new application and hope that its un-install mechanism backed up the old DLLs before copying over them.

Using snAppShot, however, enables you to see which DLLs were replaced by the new application install, so that you can simply replace them from a backup, CD-ROM, or other source.

How snAppShot Works

Now that you know what snAppShot is and what it is for, you need to understand how it works. This section discusses how snAppShot can analyze and store the changes made by an installation or upgrade.

Files Created by snAppShot

When snAppShot is used to determine the changes made by an installation or upgrade, many files are created to store information. These files are used later when the installation or upgrade needs to be performed again. They contain all the information needed to update other clients without having to run the installation program or upgrade again.

The following sections describe the file types created by snAppShot when recording the changes during an installation or upgrade.

.AXT Files

AXT stands for Application Object Text Template, meaning that the .AXT file is written in human-readable, text format. Therefore, you can open it in a text editor and edit the contents.

NOTE The .AXT file takes longer to import into an Application object than an .AOT file, and it is prone to inaccuracies if certain .AXT file format standards are not followed.

An .AXT file contains information about what happened on a workstation when an application was installed to it. You can also think of it as a "change log" that contains the differences between the pre- and post-application installation states of a workstation. snAppShot discovers these differences and records them in the .AXT file, as shown in Figure 5.1.

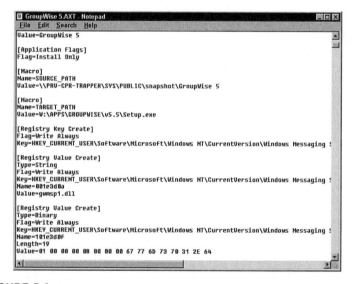

FIGURE 5.1
Sample excerpt from a snAppShot .AXT file.

You use the .AXT file when creating and setting up Application objects using Application Launcher for large-scale distribution. The .AXT file delivers the information about the application to the new Application object.

.AOT Files

AOT stands for Application Object Template. The .AOT file is written in binary format and cannot be edited in a text editor.

NOTE .AOT files import faster into an application object and can be more accurate than their text-based counterpart, the .AXT file.

An .AOT file contains information about what happened on a workstation when an application was installed to it. You can also think of it as a "change log" that contains the differences between the pre- and post-application installation states of a workstation. snAppShot discovers these differences and records them in the .AOT file.

You use the .AOT file when creating and setting up Application objects using Application Launcher for large-scale distribution. The .AOT file delivers the information about the application to the new Application object.

.FIL Files

One .FIL file represents one application file that was installed to a workstation. Because there can be hundreds of files installed to a workstation during an application's installation or upgrade, there can also be hundreds of .FIL files representing that application.

Think of .FIL files as the Application object's copy of the originally installed application files.

NOTE For convenience, it's recommended that you store .FIL files in the same place as the .AOT file. If you place these files in a network location, it is easier to access them as you build and distribute the Application object.

A list of the .FIL files that need to be copied to run an application appears in the .AOT file. This list can be viewed from the Application Files property page in the Application object in ConsoleOne.

FILEDEF.TXT

The FILEDEF.TXT file is a "legend" that compares originally named installed files with the newly named .FIL files. snAppShot copies the FILEDEF.TXT file to the same directory where the .FIL files are created. You then use it to compare .FIL files to the originally installed files. A sampling from the FILEDEF.TXT file is shown in Figure 5.2.

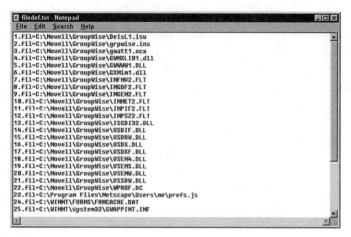

FIGURE 5.2
Sample excerpt from a snAppShot FILEDEF.TXT file.

Information Saved by snAppShot

snAppShot can determine what changes have been made during an installation or upgrade by saving information before and after, and then determining the differences. Installations and upgrades can change many files and settings on a workstation; therefore, snAppShot saves many different types of information about the configuration of the workstation.

The following sections describe the information that snAppShot stores before and after an installation or upgrade.

Files and Folders

First and foremost, snAppShot saves a list of all files that were added or modified during the installation or upgrade. It also saves a copy of the file as a .FIL file to be used in later installations or upgrades.

.INI Files

snAppShot saves any changes to application or system .INI files, so that those files can be modified when the Application object is used later. The following are some of the files snAppShot monitors for changes:

▶ *WIN.INI*—This file contains information about the Windows workstation setup, such as desktop settings, file types, and so on.

▶ *SYSTEM.INI*—This file contains information about device and driver settings for the Windows workstation.

▶ *PROTOCOL.INI*—This file contains information about the network settings for the Windows network protocols.

System Configuration Text Files

snAppShot records any changes to system configuration text files. That way any changes to drivers being loaded, paths being set, or environment variables being added or changed are recorded. You can then apply such changes to other systems when you use the Application object to install or upgrade the workstation.

The following are the two files snAppShot monitors for system configuration changes:

▶ AUTOEXEC.BAT

▶ CONFIG.SYS

Windows Shortcuts

Any changes to Windows shortcuts are also recorded by snAppShot. Therefore, if an application installation or upgrade adds a new shortcut to the desktop or Start menu, or modifies the path in an existing shortcut, those changes are applied to other systems as well along with the Application object.

Registry

snAppShot can record any changes made to a Windows workstation's Registry by an installation or upgrade. This is extremely important later, because even if you copy all files installed by an installation or upgrade and make the appropriate changes to configuration files, the application often fails to run, because Registry settings have not been made.

Using snAppShot to save the Registry settings fixes that problem by saving the changes to the Registry and then applying them when the Application object is used to install or upgrade the application on a new workstation.

Advanced Features of snAppShot

Although snAppShot is a relatively easy program to run, some advanced features make it an extremely powerful tool. This section discusses the following advanced features included in the snAppShot utility.

Using snAppShot Preferences

If you think of snAppShot as a camera, and the .AOT file as the out-putted "picture," you can think of snAppShot preferences as the adjustments you make to the camera (aperture settings, film speed, and focus) before you take the picture.

snAppShot preferences let you control what snAppShot "sees" as it discovers the changes made to a workstation as a result of installing an application. In other words, you can specify/control information recorded about the certain items (described in the following sections) during an installation or upgrade.

Files/Folders

Using snAppShot preferences, you can include or exclude the recording of certain changes to particular folders and files. This enables you to protect certain directories that you do not want to alter on other workstations when the Application object is used on them to install or upgrade an application.

Windows Shortcuts

Using snAppShot preferences, you can exclude particular Windows shortcut files from being recorded. This allows you to protect certain application shortcuts from being created or altered on other workstations during the installing or upgrading of an application.

.INI Files

Using snAppShot preferences, you can exclude particular application .INI files from being recorded. This enables you to protect certain application .INI files from being created or altered on other workstations when the Application object is used on them to install or upgrade an application.

System Configuration Files

Using snAppShot preferences, you can define which system configuration file changes are recorded. This enables you to set which system configuration changes should be recorded and created or altered on other workstations when the Application object is used on them to install or upgrade an application.

Registry Entries

Using snAppShot preferences, you can also include or exclude changes from particular portions of the Windows Registry from being recorded. This enables you to protect certain areas of the Windows Registry that you do not want to be altered on other workstations when the Application object is used on them to install or upgrade an application.

Special Macros

Special macros are built-in machine- and user-specific values that the snAppShot utility is able to use to control how Application object templates are created. These special macros read from the Registry, enabling for the customization of Application objects in snAppShot. This customization enables you to distribute the same application to several machines that might have Windows installed or configured differently.

The following is a list of some common macros:

▶ *WinDir*—Directory containing the Windows OS, typically `C:\Windows` or `C:\WINNT`.

▶ *WinSysDir*—Directory containing the Windows system files (DLLs).

▶ *TempDir*—Windows temporary directory, typically `C:\Windows\temp`.

▶ *Favorites*—File system directory that serves as a common repository for the user's favorite items.

▶ *Fonts*—Virtual folder containing system fonts.

▶ *Personal*—File system directory that serves as a common repository for personal documents.

TIP The online help that appears when you click the Help button on the Application Object Macros property page in ConsoleOne provides a detailed list of the macros available to snAppShot.

When snAppShot starts, it asks the client library for a list of the special macros. This list combined with the user macros (created in the custom mode) make up the complete list of macros, which are then placed in order from the longest value to the shortest.

While snAppShot runs, it records the differences between the pre-installation scan and the second scan. It then creates an entry in the .AOT file, during which snAppShot calls the routine that searches and replaces data with the macro's name. Later, when the Application Launcher is used to distribute the object, it gets the macro values from the .AOT file.

The Application Launcher receives the values and names for these special macros by looking in the Registry under the key:

```
HKEY_CURRENT_USER
+Software
+Microsoft
+Windows
+CurrentVersion
+Explorer
+Shell Folders
```

The Application Launcher client creates a special macro using the name and value.

NOTE If the value does not exist, the special macro is returned and the data value is set to blank.

Let's say that a special macro is defined for a directory containing temporary files. The entry in the Windows Registry would appear as:

```
HKEY_CURRENT_USER
+Software
+Microsoft
+Windows
+CurrentVersion
+Explorer
+Shell Folders
TempDir=C:\DATA\TEMP
```

This Registry entry would correspond to the special macro:

```
%*TempDir%
```

Therefore, when snAppShot adds the creation information for the Registry entry in the .AOT or .AXT file, it writes an entry similar to the following:

```
[Registry Value Create]
Type=String
Flag=Write Always
Key=HKEY_CURRENT_USER\Software\Microsoft\Windows\
➥CurrentVersion\Explorer\SHell
Folders
Name=TempDir
Value=%*TempDir%
```

When the Application Launcher tries to distribute the settings, it sees the special macro value and then, in an attempt to set this Registry key, tries to read the value from this exact Registry key.

If the Registry value was set before the application is distributed, this process works beautifully; however, if it is not set until after the application is distributed, the Application Launcher tries to use data from the same Registry entry that it is trying to create.

This problem can be remedied in two ways:

1. The first way to resolve this problem is to set the Registry value before the user clicks on the icon (perhaps using ZENworks for Desktops workstation policies discussed later in this book). Then when the Application Launcher client reads the data for these special macros, it reads the correct value and knows how to replace the special macro correctly.

2. The second and better/more difficult solution is to manually edit the .AXT file created for the Application object template. Instead of using the macro you are trying to create, add an entry with a different macro name but the same value.

Partial Install Detection

If your application needs to reboot the workstation to finish the installation, snAppShot recognizes this and picks up where it left off before the reboot. All snAppShot data is stored in a hidden directory on the C: drive. Furthermore, snAppShot is automatically run after the machine is restarted. When snAppShot restarts, it detects a partial installation, and a window pops up and allows you to continue with the previous installation.

Limitations of snAppShot

Now that you know how snAppShot works and understand some of its advanced features, you need to understand its limitations. snAppShot is a very powerful tool; however, it cannot be used for the tasks described in the following sections.

Capturing Install Logic

snAppShot is unable to capture the "logic" of an installation involving choices based on existing hardware, software, or other settings. For example, if the application's setup program installs a particular video driver or modem setting file to a workstation, these settings might not be valid when transferred to another workstation.

The following sections describe some of the things you should be aware of when using snAppShot to create application packages.

Hardware Specific Drivers

Some applications query the computer system to determine what hardware is installed and only install necessary drivers for the hardware that actually exists. This often results in problems if you distribute the application to clients that do not have the same hardware as the computer in which the application package was created. You can use the hardware inventory feature of ZENworks for Desktops, discussed later in this book, to quickly determine what specific hardware is installed on clients.

Available Disk Drives

Occasionally, an application install prompts the user to input additional paths of locations to store files. When you use snAppShot to create an application package, make certain that any additional paths you specify, both local and network, exist on all clients you want to distribute the application to. For example, if you specify a path on the D: drive, all clients must have a D: drive on their computer. If necessary, you can use macros and user prompts when distributing the application to handle this; however, that must be defined in the Application object.

Prerequisite Drivers and Applications

Another thing you should watch for when creating application packages using snAppShot is prerequisites for application installs. For example, if the application needs to determine which version of DirectX is installed on the computer, it might determine that the current version is correct and then not install needed DirectX drivers. This results in the drivers not being included in the Application object. If a client that is receiving the application from ZENworks for Desktops does not have the correct version of DirectX drivers, the application might not function properly.

Guaranteeing Impact on All Workstations

Although, you can use snAppShot to install or upgrade applications on all workstations, it cannot guarantee the impact the application install or upgrade will have on all workstations. The following sections describe some rare occasions when an application distributed to a client might result in problems.

Conflicting Local Applications

It is possible that an application distributed with ZENworks for Desktops could conflict with a local application that was installed by the user of that workstation. For example, you distribute a corporate virus scanner to all workstations. An existing application then cannot open files correctly because the virus scanner believes it is a virus that is trying to modify the files.

Most companies have some sort of standard for applications that can be installed on clients. This standard usually ensures that applications being distributed with ZENworks for Desktops do not conflict with any other applications on the users' systems.

Specialized Shared DLLs

When an Application object is delivered to a workstation, it can be configured to copy files only if they are newer. This usually protects shared DLLs because the older functionality is usually available in newer versions.

However, some applications have DLLs that have functionality written specifically for them. This functionality does not exist in newer versions, and, if they are overwritten with a newer file, the application they supported might no longer function.

Hardware Requirements

Many applications are written for computer systems that have a high level of CPU speed, RAM, video memory, disk speed, and so on. If this type of application is distributed down to a client workstation that does not have the hardware capability to support them, they will not function properly.

This potential problem can be controlled somewhat by configuring the Application object to check for hardware levels before installing (discussed in the next chapter). You can use the hardware inventory feature of ZENworks for Desktops, discussed later in this book, to quickly determine what hardware is installed on clients.

Imaging an Entire Workstation

snAppShot is designed to record changes made by a single application install, and therefore, it cannot image an entire workstation for disaster recovery purposes. When snAppShot discovers a workstation, it only saves some information about the files, such as the date, time, and size of the files. It does not save a copy of all the files on the workstation.

If you have a need to image an entire workstation, refer to Chapter 14, "Imaging a Workstation."

Using snAppShot

Once you are familiar with when and why to use the snAppShot utility and understand some of its advanced features, you are ready to begin using it to create Application objects. When you start snAppShot, you see a screen similar to the one in Figure 5.3.

This startup screen for snAppShot allows you to select from standard, custom, express, or super express (command-line) modes (explained in detail in the following sections) depending on your needs, and on whether you already have a preference file ready.

Using Standard Mode

You should use the standard mode in snAppShot to discover the application installation changes on a workstation using default settings. If you have never run snAppShot before, and are unfamiliar with the available settings, this is the best option. It requires little intervention.

To use the standard mode, simply select it and perform the operations outlined in the following sections to create the needed files.

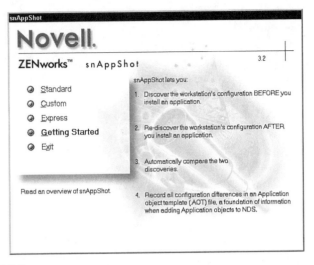

FIGURE 5.3
The Main menu in the snAppShot utility, which allows users to select which discovery mode they want to use.

Name the Application Object Icon Title

Once you select the standard mode installation from the main screen in snAppShot, a window similar to the one shown in Figure 5.4 is displayed. From this screen, you need to input the name that the Application object has in the eDirectory tree and include a title for the icon that represents the Application object.

NOTE It is recommended that you choose object and icon names that are descriptive enough to distinguish among applications, and often, among versions. This saves confusion and time later.

Specify the Network Location of the Application Source (.FIL) Files

Next, a screen similar to the one in Figure 5.5 enables you to set the network location to store the application source files (.FIL).

When setting this location, remember the following two issues:

▶ Make sure you select a location that all users who will need the Application object have access to.

▶ Make sure there is enough disk space in the network location to store the entire application.

FIGURE 5.4
snAppShot window for naming the Application object and the application's icon.

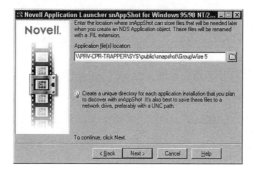

FIGURE 5.5
This snAppShot window allows users to specify the location to store the application source files.

Specify the Network Location of the Application Template (.AOT and .AXT) Files

Once you have specified a network location for the .FIL files, snAppShot enables you to set a network location for the application template (the .AOT and .AXT files). Set the network location by either entering it into the text window or by clicking on the folder button and navigating to the appropriate directory.

Specify the Drives That Will Be Discovered

Once you have selected the network location to store the Application object support files, you need to select which disk drive to scan on the workstation to determine changes, as shown in Figure 5.6.

You can add drives to the list by clicking on the Add button and selecting the drives you want to scan. Conversely, you can remove drives from the list by selecting the drive and then clicking on the remove button. You can select network drives as well, but only if they are mapped. This allows you to install applications to a larger network drive if needed and still discover the changes.

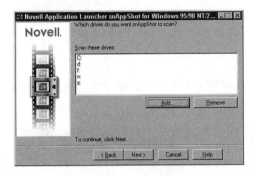

FIGURE 5.6
snAppShot window for specifying which disk drives, network and local, are scanned during discovery.

TIP Make sure you select all drives that the application install or upgrade affects. If you do not select a drive and the application install or upgrade adds, removes, or modifies files on that drive, the changes will not be discovered.

Read the Pre-Discovery Summary to Check Settings

Once you have all the drives you want to select added to the list of drives to be scanned, click Next and a summary of the preferences is displayed in the next window, as shown in Figure 5.7. The information displayed includes:

- ▶ Application object name
- ▶ Application icon title
- ▶ Template filename
- ▶ Application files directory
- ▶ snAppShot's working drive
- ▶ Scan options
- ▶ Disks to scan

▶ Directories to exclude

▶ Files to exclude

▶ System text files to scan

FIGURE 5.7
This snAppShot window allows you to review the current preference settings before starting the first discovery.

TIP Click Save Preferences to save the snAppShot preferences you have defined thus far to a file. Later, during a similar snAppShot session, you can choose the preferences you save now to accelerate the process.

Run the First snAppShot Discovery

The first snAppShot discovery runs when you click Next from the Preference Summary window. A screen shows the status of the discovery and a count of the following items that have been discovered:

▶ Folders and files

▶ Windows shortcuts

▶ .INI files

▶ System configuration files

▶ Registry entries

Run Application's Installation or Upgrade

Once the first snAppShot discovery is complete, a Run Application Install button is available. When you select the Run Application Install button, a pop-up menu appears. You can navigate to the application install executable and execute it.

Once the application install is complete, you can continue with the discovery process of the snAppShot application.

TIP Write down where the installation program installs the application's executable file. This information will be useful later when creating and distributing the Application object.

Enter the Path to the Application's Executable

Once you have completed the application install, snAppShot gives you the option to specify a path to the application's executable on this workstation. You can enter the location of the installed application files on this workstation in the text field.

Of course, if you do not want snAppShot to set a target distribution location, leave this field blank and continue.

Run the Second snAppShot Discovery

Once you are finished setting the path to the application's executable and you click the Next button, snAppShot runs the second discovery. Once again, you can monitor the status of the discovery by noting the count of the following items:

- ▶ Folders and files
- ▶ Windows shortcuts
- ▶ .INI files
- ▶ System configuration files
- ▶ Registry entries

Once the discovery is finished, snAppShot begins generating an object template. This is where the differences between the two discoveries are discerned and the template files are created.

NOTE Depending on the number of folders, files, and Registry entries on your workstation, the second discovery process can take a considerable amount of time. However, both the discovery and the template generation screens have status counters to let you know how far along they are.

Read the Completion Summary

Once the second snAppShot discovery is complete and the template files are generated, a completion summary of what took place is displayed in the window shown in Figure 5.8. The completion summary contains information about the application template creation, including:

- ▶ The location of the new Application object template (.AOT)
- ▶ The location of the new .FIL files
- ▶ The location of the textual version of the Application object template (.AXT)
- ▶ Listing of the steps to take to create the Application object
- ▶ Statistical totals from the second discovery
- ▶ Statistical totals from entries added to the Application object template (.AOT)

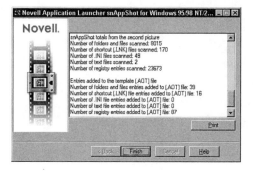

FIGURE 5.8
This snAppShot window allows users to review the summary of the Application object template generation.

TIP You have the option from this window to print the summary. It is recommended that you do so and keep the printout as a record to aid in troubleshooting future problems if they happen to occur.

Using Custom Mode

You should use the custom mode in snAppShot to set specific options when discovering the application installation or upgrade changes on a workstation. Custom mode is much like standard mode except that it gives you the added opportunity to specify the drives, files, folders, Registry hives, and shortcuts that you want to include or exclude in the discovery process. You can save these settings in a preference file for later use if you need to run snAppShot for a similarly configured application.

Only in custom mode can you see and use all of snAppShot's features. To use the custom mode, simply select it and perform the following operations to create the needed files:

1. Choose the snAppShot preferences file.

2. Name the Application object and icon title.

3. Specify the network location of the application source (.FIL) files.

4. Specify the network location of the application template (.AOT and .AXT) files.

5. Specify which parts of the workstation to include or exclude.

6. Specify the drives that will be discovered.

7. Read the pre-discovery summary.

8. Run the first snAppShot discovery.

9. Run the application's installation or upgrade.

10. Specify how to handle the creation of files, folders, .INI file entries, and Registry settings.

11. Enter the path to the application's executable file.

12. Define macros for distribution automation.

13. Run the second snAppShot discovery.

14. Read the completion summary.

Choose the snAppShot Preferences File

The first window that comes up after you select the custom mode in snAppShot is the Choose snAppShot Preferences window. From this window, you have the option of either using a previously saved preference file, or using the snAppShot default settings.

If you have previously created and saved a preferences file in a previous custom mode, you can navigate to that file or enter the path to it into the text field as shown in Figure 5.9.

Name the Application Object and Icon Title

Once you select the preference file option in custom mode in snAppShot, a window is displayed. From this screen, you need to input the name that the application object will have in the eDirectory tree and a title for the icon that represents the application object.

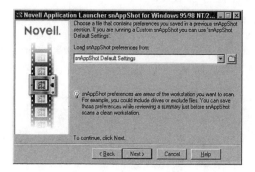

FIGURE 5.9
The snAppShot window for specifying a pre-created preference file or for using the default settings.

Specify the Network Location of the Application Source (.FIL) Files

Once you have set the name for the application object and title for its icon in the custom mode install, a screen enables you to set the network location to store the application source files (.FIL).

When setting this location, you should remember the following two points:

▶ Make sure you select a location that all users who will use the application object have access to.

▶ Make sure there is enough disk space in the network location that you set to store the entire application.

Specify the Network Location of the Application Template (.AOT and .AOT) Files

Once you have specified a network location for the .FIL files, snAppShot enables you to set a network location for the application template (.AOT and .AXT files). Set the network location by either entering it into the text window, or by clicking on the folder button and navigating to the appropriate directory.

NOTE If files already exist with the same object name, you have the option of overwriting the older ones.

Specify Which Parts of the Workstation to Include or Exclude

Once you have selected the network location to store the Application object support files, you can select which of the following parts of the workstation you want to include or exclude, as shown in Figure 5.10:

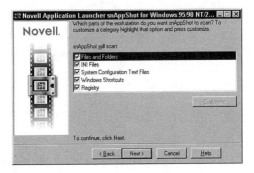

FIGURE 5.10
The snAppShot window for specifying which parts of the workstation to include or exclude.

> ▶ *Files and folders*—From the Workstation Scan Customization menu in snAppShot, you can modify which files and folders you want to include or exclude. Simply select the files and folders option and click the Customize button. A window similar to the one in Figure 5.11 pops up, and you must select which files and folders to ignore.

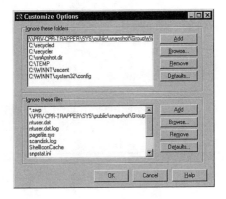

FIGURE 5.11
The snAppShot window for specifying how and which files and folders are created in the Application object template.

TIP Wildcards are valid here. For example, if you want to exclude all .DAT files, you could specify *.DAT in the list of files to ignore.

▶ *.INI files*—From the Workstation Scan Customization menu in snAppShot, you can modify which .INI files to exclude. Simply select the .INI files option and click the Customize button. A window pops up from which you select which .INI files to ignore.

▶ *System configuration text files*—From the Workstation Scan Customization menu in snAppShot, you can modify which system configuration text files you want to include in the scan. Simply select the system configuration text files option and click the Customize button. A window similar to the one in Figure 5.12 pops up, from which you select which system configuration text files you want to include.

FIGURE 5.12
This snAppShot window allows you to specify which system configuration files are created in the Application object template.

▶ *Windows shortcuts*—From the Workstation Scan Customization menu in snAppShot, you can modify which Windows shortcuts to exclude. Simply select the Windows shortcuts option and click the Customize button. A window pops up, and you select which Windows shortcuts to ignore.

▶ *Registry*—From the Workstation Scan Customization menu in snAppShot, you can modify which Registry hives you want to include or exclude. Simply select the Registry option and click on the Customize button. A window similar to the one in Figure 5.13 pops up, and you select and deselect from a list of hives to include.

FIGURE 5.13
This snAppShot window indicates which Windows Registry hives are created in the Application object template.

Specify the Drives That Will Be Discovered

Once you have specified which parts of the workstation to include or exclude, you must select which disk drive to scan on the workstation to determine changes.

You can add drives to the list by clicking on the Add button and selecting the drives you want to scan. Conversely, you can remove drives from the list by selecting the drive, and then clicking on the Remove button.

NOTE You can select network drives as well, however, only if they are mapped. This enables you to install applications to a larger network drive if needed and still discover the changes.

Read the Pre-Discovery Summary

Once you have all the drives you want to select added to the list of drives to be scanned, click Next and a summary of the preferences are displayed. The information displayed includes:

- ▶ Application object name
- ▶ Application icon title
- ▶ Template filename
- ▶ Application files directory
- ▶ snAppShot's working drive
- ▶ Scan options
- ▶ Disks to scan
- ▶ Directories to exclude
- ▶ Files to exclude
- ▶ System text files to scan

TIP Click Save Settings to save the snAppShot preferences you have defined thus far to a file. Later, during a similar snAppShot session, you can choose the preferences you save now to accelerate the process.

Run the First snAppShot Discovery

The first snAppShot discovery runs when you click Next from the preference summary window. A screen shows the status of the discovery, and a count of the following items that have been discovered:

▶ Folders and files

▶ Windows shortcuts

▶ .INI files

▶ System configuration files

▶ Registry entries

Run the Application's Installation or Upgrade

Once the first snAppShot discovery is completed, a Run Application Install button is available. When you select the Run Application Install button, a file pop-up menu appears, from which you navigate to the application install executable and execute it.

Once the application install is complete, you can continue with the discovery process of the snAppShot application.

NOTE Record where the installation program installs the application's executable file. This information is useful later when creating and distributing the Application object.

Set Options for Creating Files, Folders, .INI File Entries, and Registry Settings

Once the application's installation or upgrade is complete, snAppShot enables you to specify how to handle the creation of entries for the Application object. From the screen shown in Figure 5.14, you can set the additional criteria for the entries described in the following sections.

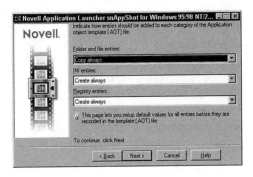

FIGURE 5.14
The snAppShot window for specifying how snAppShot handles the creation of file, folder, .INI file, and Registry entries in the Application object template.

▶ *Folder and file entries*—From the Application Object Entry Addition window in snAppShot, you can choose whether files and folders are added to the Application object. Click the down arrow under the folders and files option and select one of the following additional criteria, as shown in Figure 5.15:

- ▶ Copy always
- ▶ Copy if exists
- ▶ Copy if does not exist
- ▶ Copy if newer
- ▶ Copy if newer and exists
- ▶ Request confirmation
- ▶ Copy if newer version
- ▶ Copy if different

▶ *.INI files*—From the Application Object Entry Addition window in snAppShot, you can configure whether .INI files are added to the Application object by clicking the down arrow under the .INI files option and selecting one of the following additional criteria, as shown in Figure 5.16:

- ▶ Create always
- ▶ Create if does not exist

- ▶ Create if exists
- ▶ Create or add to existing section

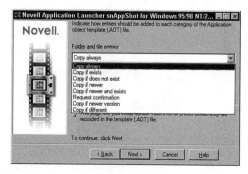

FIGURE 5.15
The snAppShot window that allows the users to specify how snAppShot handles the creation of file and folder entries in the Application object template.

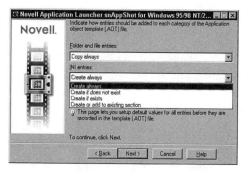

FIGURE 5.16
The snAppShot window for indicating how snAppShot handles the creation of .INI file entries in the Application object template.

- ▶ *Registry entries*—From the Application Object Entry Addition window in snAppShot, you can configure whether Registry entries are added to the Application object. Click the down arrow under the

Registry entries option and select one of the following additional criteria, as shown in Figure 5.17:

- ► Create always
- ► Create if does not exist
- ► Create if exists

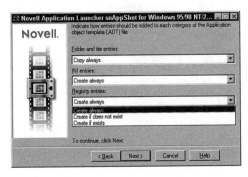

FIGURE 5.17
The snAppShot window that allows the users to specify how snAppShot handles the creation of Registry entries in the Application object template.

Enter the Path to the Application's Executable File

Once you have defined the additional criteria for entries into the Application object, snAppShot gives you the option to specify a path to the application's executable on this workstation. You can enter the location of the installed application files on this workstation in the text field.

Of course, if you do not want snAppShot to set a target distribution location, leave this field blank and continue.

Define Macros for Distribution Automation

Once you are finished setting the path to the application's executable and have clicked the Next button, you can define macros to control the distribution of Application objects. A screen similar to the one shown in Figure 5.18 enables you to add, edit, or remove macros to control automation of application distribution.

When you click the Add button in the Macro Definition window, you can specify a variable name and a string that is replaced within the template data, as shown in Figure 5.19.

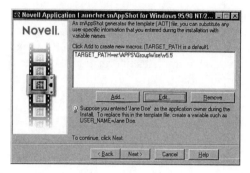

FIGURE 5.18
This snAppShot window allows the users to add, edit, or remove macros to be used in the Application object template.

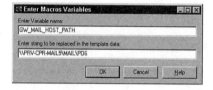

FIGURE 5.19
The snAppShot window for specifying a variable name and string in macros.

Run the Second snAppShot Discovery

Once you are finished with defining macros to automate Application object distribution, click Next, and snAppShot runs the second discovery. Once again, you can monitor the status of the discovery by noting the count of the following items:

▶ Folders and files

▶ Windows shortcuts

▶ .INI files

▶ System configuration files

▶ Registry entries

Once the discovery is finished, snAppShot begins generating an object template. This is when the actual differences between the two discoveries are discerned and the template files are created.

Read the Completion Summary

Once the second snAppShot discovery is complete and the template files have been generated, a completion summary of what took place appears. The completion summary contains information about the application template creation, including:

- ▶ The location of the new Application object template (.AOT)

- ▶ The location of the new .FIL files

- ▶ The location of the textual version of the Application object template (.AXT)

- ▶ Listing of the steps to take to create the Application object

- ▶ Statistical totals from the second discovery

- ▶ Statistical totals from entries added to the Application object template (.AOT)

Using Express Mode

You should use express mode when you've already saved a snAppShot preference file from a previous discovery process. By choosing this file, you can skip over most of the standard or custom mode settings, which enables you to discover a new application installation much more quickly than in standard or custom modes.

To use the express mode, simply select it and perform the operations described in the following sections to create the needed files.

Choose the snAppShot Preferences File from a Previous Session

The first window that appears after you select the express mode in snAppShot is the Choose snAppShot Preferences window. From this window, you can choose to use a previously saved preference file.

If you have previously created and saved a preferences file in a previous custom mode, you can navigate to that file or enter the path to it into the text. If you have not previously created and saved a preference file, you must do so before selecting the express mode.

Read Summary Page to Verify snAppShot Discovery Settings

Once you have selected a preference file from a previous application package, click Next and a summary of the preferences are displayed in the next window. The information displayed includes:

- ▶ Application object name
- ▶ Application icon title
- ▶ Template filename
- ▶ Application files directory
- ▶ snAppShot's working drive
- ▶ Scan options
- ▶ Disks to scan
- ▶ Directories to exclude
- ▶ Files to exclude
- ▶ System text files to scan

Run the First snAppShot Discovery

The first snAppShot discovery runs when you click Next from the Preference Summary window. A screen shows the status of the discovery and a count of the items that have been discovered, including:

- ▶ Folders and files
- ▶ Windows shortcuts
- ▶ .INI Files
- ▶ System configuration files
- ▶ Registry entries

Run the Application's Installation Program

Once the first snAppShot discovery is complete, the Run Application Install button is available. When you select the Run Application Install button, a file pop-up menu appears, and you can navigate to the application install executable and execute it.

Run the Second snAppShot Discovery

Once the application install or upgrade is finished, click Next, and snAppShot runs the second discovery. Once again, you can monitor the status of the discovery by noting the count statistics of the following:

- ▶ Folders and files
- ▶ Windows shortcuts
- ▶ .INI Files

- ▶ System configuration files
- ▶ Registry entries

Once the discovery is finished, snAppShot begins generating an object. This is when the actual differences between the two discoveries are discerned and the template files are created.

Read the Completion Summary

Once the second snAppShot discovery is completed and the template files generated, a completion summary of what took place is displayed. The completion summary contains information about the application template creation, including:

- ▶ The location of the new Application object template (.AOT)
- ▶ The location of the new .FIL files
- ▶ The location of the textual version of the Application object template (.AOT)
- ▶ Listing of the steps to take to create the Application object
- ▶ Statistical totals from the second discovery
- ▶ Statistical totals from entries added to the Application object template (.AOT)

Super Express (Command-Line) Mode

You can use super express (command-line) mode to discover changes to a workstation in the fastest possible way. The super express mode of snAppShot enables you to run snAppShot from a command prompt, which enables you to discover changes to a workstation faster than the other available modes.

In order to use this mode of snAppShot, which you do exclusively from the command line, you must use a preferences file from a previous snAppShot session. To use the super express mode, perform the operations described in the following sections.

Change to the Directory Where snAppShot Is Located

The first step to use the super express (command-line) mode in snAppShot is to enter DOS and change to the directory where the snAppShot utility is located.

Enter the snAppShot Command

Once you are in the directory of the snapshot utility, enter the following command from the DOS prompt.

```
snapshot /u:<filename>
```

<filename> is the name of a snAppShot preferences file you defined and saved earlier when running snAppShot in custom or express modes.

Specify Whether to Overwrite a Previous snAppShot Discovery

Once you have executed the snAppShot command from the DOS session, a window appears that gives you the option to overwrite the existing Application object template, as shown in Figure 5.20. You must select Yes to continue.

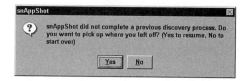

FIGURE 5.20
The snAppShot window that allows you to overwrite the previous snAppShot discovery when using the super express mode.

Once you select Yes, the Application object template creation continues the same as in the regular express mode, by displaying the pre-discovery summary screen, followed by the first discovery.

snAppShot Application Packages versus .MSI Files

Now that the creation of Application object packages using snAppShot has been discussed, it is useful to know how they compare to Microsoft Windows installer (.MSI) package files. The files involved are described as follows:

▶ *.MSI Files*—An .MSI file is a storage file containing the instructions and data required to install an application. .MSI files are used by the Microsoft Windows Installer to deploy and install applications to computers with 32-bit versions of Windows on them.

▶ *.MSM Files*—A merge module (.MSM) file, referred to as merge package file, is a single package that includes all files, Registry changes, and setup logic to install a shared component. Merge modules are contained inside .MSI files.

How .MSI Files Are Created

The information .MSI files contain depends on how they are created. The following sections describe the ways that .MSI files are typically created.

Development Tool Method

The most complete way of creating .MSI files is by using development tools to create .MSM and .MSI files, and then configuring them with the files, Registry changes, resources, and logic to perform a complete install of the application.

This method is preferred by most application developers, because it gives them the greatest control over how and what information and logic actually goes into the .MSI file.

Discovery Method

The discovery method of creating .MSI files is very similar to the way snAppShot creates its Application object templates. The discovery method works by using a double discovery process to accumulate changes made by an install. Most third-party application installs are created by this method. The following steps describe how this method is accomplished:

1. Begin with a clean PC, or one that is representative of the computers in your network.

2. Start Discover to take a picture of the representative PC's software configuration. This is the "before" snapshot.

3. Install a program on the PC on which you took the before snapshot.

4. Reboot the PC.

5. Run the new program to verify that it works.

6. Quit the program.

7. Start Discover and take an "after" snapshot of the PC's new configuration. Discover compares the before and after snapshots and notes

the changes. It creates a Microsoft installer package with information about how to install that program on such a PC in the future.

8. Clean the reference computer to prepare to run Discover again.

How Do .MSI Files Work with ZENworks for Desktops?

Now that you understand what .MSI files are and how they are created, you need to understand what role they can play in creating Application objects, instead of using .AOT or .AXT files.

The ZENworks snap-ins to ConsoleOne enable you to use .MSI files to create Application objects in exactly the same way that .AOT or .AXT files are used. Therefore, if an .MSI file is already available for an Application object, you can save yourself time and effort by simply using the .MSI file to create the Application object (discussed in the next chapter).

Using ZENworks, you can also apply .MST files along with the .MSI files to your desktops.

Creating and Using Application Objects

Now that you have an understanding of how to create an Application object template from Chapter 5, "Creating Application Packages Using snAppShot," you need to discuss how to use that template to create an actual Application object and distribute it to users. This chapter covers the following main points in taking you through the process of Application object creation and distribution:

- ▶ Creating the Application object
- ▶ Setting properties for the Application object
- ▶ Setting up Application distribution
- ▶ Distributing the Application

Creating the Application Object

The first step in using ZENworks for Desktops to distribute applications to users is to create an Application object. The Application object is an actual object in the eDirectory tree. ZENworks for Desktops uses this object to distribute the application to users based on the properties the object is created with. This section guides you through the following methods for creating Application objects:

- ▶ Creating a simple Application object without an .AOT, .AXT, or .MSI file
- ▶ Creating an application object using an .AOT/.AXT file

▶ Creating an application object using an .MSI file

▶ Creating an application object using an existing Application object

▶ Creating a Web application

▶ Creating a terminal server application

NOTE It's best to start with an .MSI, .AOT, or .AXT file, or to duplicate an existing Application object because it greatly simplifies the setup, distribution, and management of applications on user workstations. You create .AOT and .AXT files using snAppShot, which is a component of Application Launcher.

Creating an Application Object Using an .AOT/.AXT File

Creating an Application object with an .AOT or .AXT file usually creates more complex Application objects. The objects make changes to Registry settings, .INI files, text configuration files, and so on.

An example of when to use an .AOT or .AXT file is illustrated in the GroupWise Application object template created in Appendix B, "Using snAppShot to Create an Application Object Package." Installing GroupWise makes several changes to the Registry and modified existing .INI files. Therefore, it is better to use a template to create the GroupWise object.

To use an .AOT or .AXT template file to create an Application object, follow these steps:

1. Open ConsoleOne and browse the eDirectory tree to find the container you want. Right-click in the container in which you want to install the Application object. Then select Create.

2. From the Create menu, select Application. This launches the Create Application Object wizard.

3. From the Create Application Object wizard, select Create Application Object with .AOT or .AXT File, and then select Next, as shown in Figure 6.1.

4. Find the .AOT or .AXT file, select it, and then click Open. A window appears that displays the path to the .AOT or .AXT file. From this window, click Next.

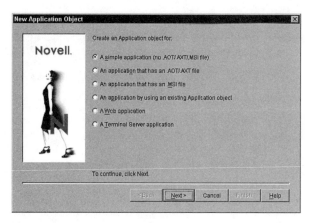

FIGURE 6.1
Choosing how to create the Application Object from the wizard.

5. Type the object name of the Application object in the Object Name text box.

6. Check (and change, if necessary) the target and source directories of the Application object (see Figure 6.2), and then click Next.

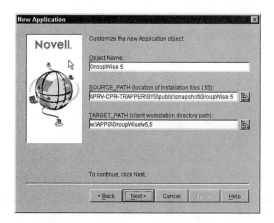

FIGURE 6.2
Choosing the target and source directories from the Application object wizard.

7. Review the information about the Application object (click the Back button to make any changes).

8. You can select Display Details After Creation to access the property pages of this Application object. This is recommended to ensure that the Application object was correctly created.

9. You can also select Create Another Application Object After This One if you want to create another object.

10. Once you have made your selections from this window, click Finish. The Application object is created.

Creating an Application Object Using an .MSI File

ZENworks for Desktops also enables you to create and administer an Application Object from an .MSI file. This makes it possible for you to use your existing .MSI files to roll out applications to users without having to create a fresh object or .AOT file.

Creating an Application object with an .MSI file is very similar to creating one with an .AOT or .AXT template file. Use the following steps:

1. Open ConsoleOne, browse the eDirectory tree, and right-click in the container in which you want to install the Application object. Then select Create.

2. From the Create menu, select Application. This launches the Create Application Object wizard.

3. From the Create Application Object wizard, select Create Application Object With .MSI File, and then select Next.

4. Browse for the .MSI file, select it, and then click Open. A window appears that displays the path to the .MSI file. From this window, click Next.

5. Type the name of the Application object in the Object Name text box and then click Next.

6. Review the information about the Application object (click the Back button to make any changes).

7. You can select Display Details After Creation to access the property pages of this Application object. This is recommended to ensure that the Application object was correctly created.

8. You also can select Create Another Application Object After This One if you want to create another object.

9. Once you have made your selections from this window, click Finish. The Application object is created.

Objects created from .MSI files are not managed exactly the same way other Application objects are. Application objects created from an .MSI file can be managed in the following ways (discussed in more detail later in this chapter):

▶ *View Package Information*—Enables you to view specific information about the MSI package.

▶ *Set Properties for MSI Package*—Enables you to modify the public properties of the MSI package.

▶ *Set Transform File List*—Enables you to create a list of transform files to be applied to the MSI object prior to distribution.

▶ *Set Fault Tolerance Options*—Normal fault-tolerance and load-balancing options for applications can also be applied to Application objects that were created from an .MSI file.

Creating a Simple Application Object without an .AOT, .AXT or MSI File

The process of creating an Application object without an .AOT or .AXT file is usually employed to create simple Application objects that do not make any changes to Registry settings, such as .INI files, text configuration files, and so on.

A good example of when to use the process of creating an Application object *without* an .AOT or .AXT file is when creating an Application object for a corporate calendar program. Many corporations have small home-grown calendar applications that contain information specific to their business. These programs rarely modify the Registry or change system .INI files, and therefore are great candidates for this option.

To create a simple Application object, use the following steps:

1. Open ConsoleOne, browse the eDirectory tree, and right-click in the container in which you want to install the Application object. Select create.

2. From the Create menu, select Application. This launches the Create Application Object wizard.

3. From the Create Application Object wizard, choose Create Application Object Without .AOT or .AXT file, and then choose Next.

4. From this window, type the name of the Application object in the Object Name dialog box.

5. Use the browse button to specify the location of the executable in the Path to Executable text box.

6. You can select Display Details After Creation to access the property pages of this Application object. This is recommended to ensure that the Application object was correctly created.

7. You can select Create Another Application Object After This One if you want to create another object.

8. Once you have made your selections from this window, click Finish. The Application object is created.

Creating an Application Object Using an Existing Application Object

You should use the Duplicate an Existing Application Object method when you want to duplicate an application, perhaps to allow for different properties and distribution options.

A good example of when to use this option is if you are setting up application fault tolerance and need several nearly identical Application objects. The fastest way to accomplish this is to create the primary Application object, and then create as many duplicate Application objects as needed. You can then adjust each duplicated Application object as necessary (for example, specify different application source [.FIL] locations for each).

To duplicate an existing Application object, follow these steps:

1. Open ConsoleOne, browse the eDirectory tree, and right-click in the container in which you want to install the Application object. Then select Create.

2. From the Create menu, select Application. This launches the Create Application Object wizard.

3. From the Create Application Object wizard, choose Duplicate an Existing Application Object, and then click Next.

4. Find the eDirectory tree and identify the reference Application object by its Distinguished Name. Once the reference application is selected, click Next.

5. Specify a custom source path (where the .FIL files are stored) and target path (where the files are copied during a distribution; usually a workstation's **c:** drive).

6. Review the new, duplicated Application object's summary and click Back to make changes.

7. You can select Display Details After Creation to access the property pages of this Application object. This is recommended to ensure that the Application object was correctly created.

8. You also can select Create Another Application Object After This One if you want to create another object.

9. Once you have made your selections from this window, click Finish. The Application object is created.

Creating a Web Application

ZENworks for Desktops allows you to create an Application object for an application that is stored and executed on the Web through a URL. This feature will be an integral component for companies wanting to create an internal as well as an external Web presence.

A good example of when you might want to create a Web Application object is if you have a corporate servlet that tracks login information. Every time a user logs in, the servlet executes and gathers and stores information about the login process.

Another example of how a Web application could be used is if you had a corporate statement or newsletter that you wanted every employee to read. You could create a Web application with a URL that pointed to that page and it would be displayed to users in their browser as they logged in.

Use the following steps to create a Web Application object:

1. Open ConsoleOne, browse the eDirectory tree, and right-click in the container in which you want to install the Application object. Then select create.

2. From the Create menu, select Application. This launches the Create Application Object wizard.

3. From the Create Application Object wizard, choose Create a Web Application, and then click Next.

4. From this window, type the name of the Application object in the Object Name dialog box, and then click Next.

5. Specify the URL for the Web application, and then click Next.

6. Add any customizations necessary for the Web application. Click Next.

7. Review the new, duplicated Application object's summary and click Back to make changes.

8. You can select Display Details After Creation to access the property pages of this Application object. This is recommended to ensure that the Application object was correctly created.

9. You can also select Create Another Application Object After This One if you want to create another object.

10. Once you have made your selections from this window, click Finish. The Application object is created.

Creating a Terminal Server Application

ZENworks for Desktops allows you to create an Application object for an application that is to be stored and executed on a Citrix MetaFrame or Microsoft terminal server. This feature is extremely useful if you implement terminal servers on your network.

Use the following steps to create a terminal server Application object:

1. Open ConsoleOne, browse the eDirectory tree, and right-click in the container in which you want to install the Application object. Then select create.

2. From the Create menu, select Application. This launches the Create Application Object wizard.

3. From the Create Application Object wizard, choose Create a Terminal Server Application, and then click Next.

4. From this window, type the name of the Application object in the Object Name dialog box. Click Next.

5. Next, specify the session type (ICA/RDP), the server name, and whether to open the desktop or execute an application on the terminal server. Click Next.

6. Add any customizations necessary for the terminal server application. Click Next.

7. Review the new, duplicated Application object's summary and click Back to make changes.

8. You can select Display Details After Creation to access the property pages of this Application object. This is recommended to ensure that the Application object was correctly created.

9. You can also select Create Another Application Object After This One if you want to create another object.

10. Once you have made your selections from this window, click Finish. The Application object is created.

Setting Properties for the Application Object

Once you have created the Application object, you need to set the Application object's properties to define how it will behave. The following sections cover using ConsoleOne to define the identity, distribution behavior, run behavior, availability, fault tolerance, and existence of the Application Object.

Setting Up the Application Object Identification

The first step in setting up the Application object in ConsoleOne is to access the Identification property page to control the application icon, description, folders, contacts, and notes that are used to define the application. Use the following steps to select which set of options you want to modify:

1. Right-click the Application object and click Properties.

2. Click the Identification tab.

3. Click the down arrow on the Identification tab to access the available Identification property pages, as shown in Figure 6.3, and then click OK.

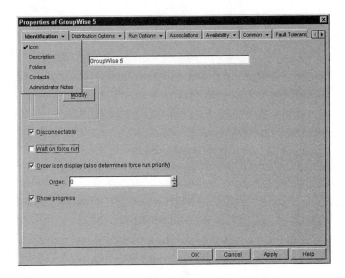

FIGURE 6.3
The Application Identification options tab in ConsoleOne.

From the Application object's Identification property tab, you should access the individual property panels to configure the application identity options described in the following sections.

Setting Application Icon Properties

First, select the icon property panel from the Identification tab. A panel similar to the one shown in Figure 6.4 is displayed and you can configure the following options for the Application object.

Configure the Application Icon Title

Type the title you want to use for the application in the Application Icon Title box. The application icon title, which is mandatory, can be different from the Application object name (the name that eDirectory* uses to identify the application) and might contain periods and other special characters. You can also use the Description property page for longer descriptions of the application. The title you select here is displayed to users when they access the Application object (for example, it's the name that appears in the Start menu if the application is set to appear there).

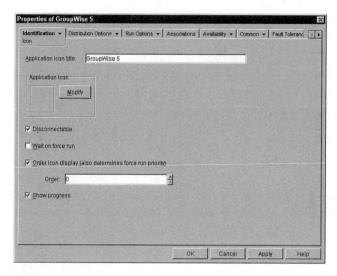

FIGURE 6.4
The Application icon property panel in ConsoleOne.

TIP If icon titles do not appear in their entirety, you might need to increase your icon spacing in Windows. After you have adjusted the icon spacing in Windows, exit Application Launcher or Application Explorer and restart for the changes to take effect. You can also use the Description property page for longer descriptions of the application.

Configure the Application Icon Title
Next you should use the Application Icon option to assign an icon for the Application object. The icon you choose appears in Application Launcher or Application Explorer, depending on what you specified on the Applications property page. If you do not specify an icon, a default Application Launcher icon is used.

Configure the Disconnectable Option
The disconnectable option enables you to control what happens to the icon when the user disconnects from the network. If this option is set, the icon remains present when the user disconnects; otherwise, it does not appear.

Configure the Wait on Force Run Option
The Wait on Force Run option enables you to specify whether the icon appears before the application has been run, if the force run option is set.

If you enable this option, the icon won't appear until the force run is complete.

Configure the Order Icon Display

From this window, you can set the order icons and set the force run sequence. This option performs two very useful functions. First, it organizes the icons in Application Launcher and Application Explorer. Second, it dictates the order in which Application objects that are set as force run are used.

To set ordering, enter a numeric value into the Icon Order text box. All Application objects you want to order must have a numeric value. The value of zero gives the icon the highest priority and thus the highest prominence in the list. The maximum value is 999. If you do not order Application objects, they are ordered alphabetically (the default order).

For example, suppose that you have 10 icons (applications A, B, C, D, E, F, G, H, I, and J) that you want to organize in Application Launcher. You specify an order number of 0 for application G, 1 for application F, 2 for application E, and 3 for application D. You specify an order number of 4 for applications C, B, H, and I. You do not order the remaining applications, A and J.

The result is that the first four applications are ordered with G being the first in the list followed by F, E, and D. After this, applications C, B, H, and I are gathered together and arranged alphabetically. The last two icons, A and J, come at the end of the list and are arranged alphabetically (the default order).

If users associated with these Application objects run Application Launcher, they will see a list of icons according to this order. If these applications have all been set to force run, they will run in this order as soon as Application Launcher has loaded itself into memory.

NOTE Ordered and force run applications run in sequential order without waiting for the last force run application to terminate.

Configure the Show Progress Option

The last thing you can configure from the icon property panel is the Show Progress option. You should select this option if you want an easy-to-read progress bar to be displayed to users the first time they distribute an application to their workstations.

TIP Turn off this option if you are distributing only a small change to the application, such as a Registry modification. Turn it on if you are distributing a large application and want to give the user a general idea of how long the distribution will take. By default, this option is on.

Setting Application Description

The second setting available for Application object identification is the capability to enter text into the Description property panel to give users more complete information than the application icon caption allows. Select the description property panel from the Identification tab. A panel similar to the one shown in Figure 6.5 is displayed and you can set the description for the Application object.

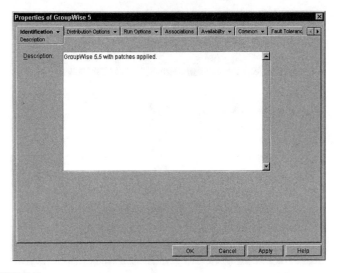

FIGURE 6.5
The description property panel for Application objects in ConsoleOne.

Once the description is set, users can right-click an Application object in Application Launcher or Application Explorer to see these details. The descriptive name of the application and the more lengthy description both appear here.

An example of when to use the description option for Application objects is when you have additional information about the application that users need. This might include information such as which new features are available in the application.

NOTE The text you type in the Description property page is the same text the user sees if you have enabled the Prompt User Before Distribution option on the Distribution property page.

Setting Up Application Folders

The next setting available for Application object identification is the Folders property panel. The Folders property panel lets you specify the folder object you want the application to reside in for the Application Launcher and Start menu. Select the Folders property panel from the Identification tab. A panel similar to the one shown in Figure 6.6 is displayed and you can set up the application folder for the Application object.

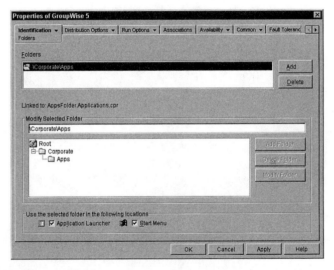

FIGURE 6.6
The folders property panel for Application objects in ConsoleOne.

Once you are at the Folders property panel, you can determine which folders the application icon will reside in by using the following steps:

1. From the Folders property panel, click the Add button.

2. Navigate the eDirectory tree and select the application folder object you want the Application to reside in.

3. In the Modify Selected Folder window, shown in Figure 6.6, add, delete, or modify the folder that is selected. This controls the location where the application appears in the Start menu and Application Explorer window.

4. Select whether you want the application to appear in the folder for the Application Launcher, Start menu, or both.

You can select multiple application folder objects for the application to reside in by following the previous steps. You might want to do this if a difference exists in behavior or availability defined in different application folders. For example, you have an application folder for accounting, development, and sales but you only want the application to appear for accounting and sales. You handle this by adding the accounting and sales folders, but not the development folder, to the application. That way the application does not appear in the developer's Start menu, but it does appear for the accountants and sales persons.

Contact Setting for Applications

From the pull-down list under Identification for Application objects, you can also specify a contact list for help if a problem occurs when deploying the application. To create the contact list, simply click the Add button and then type in the username or select the user object by browsing the eDirectory tree.

Adding Administrator Notes to Applications

From the pull-down list under Identification for Application objects, you can also specify administrator notes for users to view when deploying the application. This can be very useful in describing to users why the application is being deployed, when it remains available, and other important information. To create administrator notes, simply type in the message you want users to see when they view the information about applications available through the Application Launcher.

Viewing MSI Package Information for MSI Objects

Application objects that were created from an .MSI file enable you to select package information from the Identification drop-down menu. The package information panel for MSI Application objects displays the following information about the MSI package:

▶ The path to the MSI package

▶ The version of the MSI package

▶ The vendor who created the MSI package

▶ The locale (language) the MSI package is in

▶ Any help link that is associated with the MSI package

Setting Distribution Options for Application Objects

Once you have set up the Application objects identification, the next step in setting up the distribution options for the Application object in ConsoleOne is to configure the applications shortcuts, Registry settings, files, .INI settings, text files, distribution scripts, and pre-install schedule. Use the following steps to select which set of options you want to modify:

1. Right-click the Application object and click Properties.

2. Select the Distribution tab.

3. Click the down arrow on the Distribution tab, and a screen similar to the one in Figure 6.7 is displayed.

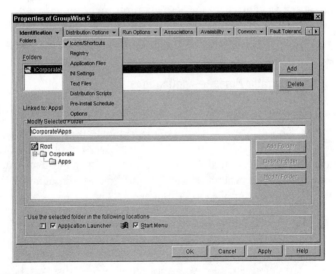

FIGURE 6.7
The distribution property panel in ConsoleOne.

From the Application object's Distribution property tab, access the individual property panels to configure the application distribution options described in the following sections.

NOTE If this Application object has been distributed previously, note that many of the changes on distribution will not go into effect until you change the Version Stamp value discussed in this chapter in the section, "Use Version Stamp to Trigger Redistribution." Changing the Version Stamp value signals Application Launcher to redistribute the application.

Configuring Application Icons/Shortcuts

The top panel accessible from the Distribution tab is the Icons/Shortcuts panel. The Icons/Shortcuts property panel enables you to add, change, or delete the Program Groups, Program Group Items, and Explorer shortcut icons that appear in Windows Explorer (Windows98, Windows NT 4.*x*, and Windows 2000/XP) when the application distributes to workstations.

You have to specify the following settings for Explorer shortcuts items:

▶ *Icon Option*—Allows you to specify the following creation options for the icon: Create always; Create only if it does not already exist; Delete the icon if it exists.

▶ *Icon Name*—Name that identifies the group icon.

▶ *Program Group*—Specifies the program group to store the item in.

▶ *Shortcut Option*—Allows you to specify the following creation options for the shortcut: Create always, Create only if it does not already exist; Delete the shortcut if it exists.

▶ *Target File*—Specifies the location of the file to execute when the item is selected.

▶ *Parameters*—Specifies parameters to be added to the command line when executing the target file.

▶ *Start In*—Specifies the location used to start the target file in.

▶ *Icon Filename*—Specifies the name of the file that stores the icon to be displayed for the item or shortcut.

▶ *Icon Index*—Specifies the index of the icon inside the icon file specified in the Icon Filename option.

▶ *Run*—Specifies whether to start the application in a normal, maximized, or minimized window.

▶ *NT/2000/XP Separate Memory*—Available for program group items because they are only supported on Windows 98.

One example of when you might modify the icons and shortcuts for an Application object is if you wanted to use special icons for all applications that users run on their workstations. Using the Icons/Shortcuts property page for this Application object, you can change icons of other applications that might not have anything to do with this Application object.

Configuring Application Registry Settings

The next panel that's accessible from the Distribution tab is the Registry Settings property panel. This panel enables you to add, change, and delete Registry keys and values when the Application object distributes to the workstation. Several Registry types are supported, including binary format, default strings, **DWORD** values, expand strings (**REG_EXPAND_SZ**), and multivalue strings (**REG_MULTI_SZ**). You can import and export Registry settings, either as .AOT or .AXT files, or using the standard Registry (.REG) format.

For each Registry setting you create, you can specify the following options:

▶ Create always

▶ Create only if it does not already exist

▶ Create only if it does already exist

▶ Delete the Registry entry

▶ Track distribution per user

▶ Distribute the change always

NOTE You should make certain you need to track changes before checking the track distribution per user box. Tracking too many items can waste resources and it can be difficult to wade through the data to gather the information you do need.

Configuring Application Files

The next panel accessible from the Distribution tab is the Application Files property panel. This panel is used to add, change, or delete application files and directories. You can also import new template information about files and directories.

From the Application Files window, you click add and then select a file or directory. If you are adding a directory, you will be prompted to enter a directory name and specify whether the directory should be deleted first. If you are adding a file, you will be prompted to enter a source and target path and specify whether the target file should be deleted first.

For each file entry you create, you can specify the following options:

- ▶ Copy always
- ▶ Copy only if it does not already exist
- ▶ Copy only if it does already exist
- ▶ Copy if newer
- ▶ Copy if newer and exists
- ▶ Copy if newer version
- ▶ Request confirmation
- ▶ Copy if different
- ▶ Track distribution per user
- ▶ Distribute the change always
- ▶ The file is a shared file

Configuring .INI File Settings for Applications

The next panel accessible from the Distribution tab is the .INI Settings property panel. This panel enables you to add, change, and delete .INI files, sections, and values when the Application object distributes to the workstation. Not only can you order the changes within the .INI file, you can also import or export .INI files and settings using the .AOT or .AXT file format or the standard .INI file format.

For each .INI entry you create, you can specify the following options:

- ▶ Create always
- ▶ Create only if it does not already exist
- ▶ Create only if it does already exist
- ▶ Create or add to existing section
- ▶ Create or append to existing value

▶ Delete the .INI entry

▶ Delete or remove from existing value

▶ Track distribution per user

▶ Distribute the change always

.INI file configuration changes can be useful if you want to add a specific version stamp that can be read later by the application to determine its current version. For example, Figure 6.8 shows that a specific version for the GroupWise Application object of 5.5 is made to the GW.INI file in the windows directory when the application is distributed. The next time GroupWise runs, it can use the version stamp to determine its current revision.

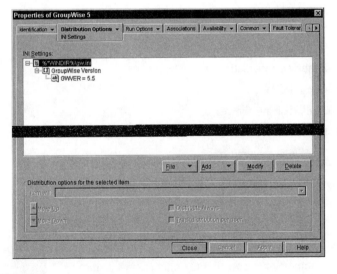

FIGURE 6.8
The .INI settings property panel for Application objects in ConsoleOne.

Configuring Text File Options

The next panel accessible from the Distribution tab is the Text Files property panel. This panel enables you to add, change, or delete workstation text files (such as CONFIG.SYS and AUTOEXEC.BAT).

Once you add a file to be modified, you can specify an entry by selecting the file and clicking on the Add button. The Edit Text File window will allow you to specify whether to simply add the text to the file, remove the text from the file, or find and replace the text in the file. If you choose to add text, you can specify whether to add the text at the beginning or the end of the file. If you choose to delete text, you can specify whether to simply search for the text in the file or search for an entire line in the file. If you choose find and replace, you can specify whether to search for text, search by line and replace text.

For each text file change, you can specify whether the workstation will need to reboot if the change is made.

One example of when to use the Text Files properties page to modify the Application object is when users are experiencing problems due to an incorrect text string found in their workstation's CONFIG.SYS file. Rather than visit and change each workstation or run the risk of users incorrectly and inconsistently implementing a change, you can set up a text file that finds, deletes, modifies, or adds text strings to the text file of your choice. The text file implements the changes the next time the application runs.

NOTE If you set the Prompt User for Reboot setting on the Distribution property page to Always, that setting overrides the setting you make here.

Configuring Application Distribution Scripts

You can set up distribution scripts that are executed automatically each time the application is distributed to a workstation. Unlike environment parameters, scripts can overwrite existing drive mappings and printer ports.

The two types of distribution scripts are the *Run before* script and the *Run after* script. Run before distribution scripts are executed before the application is distributed. Run after distribution scripts are executed after the application is closed and before the network resources are cleaned up.

Distribution scripts enable you to provide dynamic mappings beyond those defined, run other applications, log in to other servers or eDirectory trees, and perform other tasks that must be done before and after an application is distributed. The scripts support the same commands and syntax as the Novell client. However, ZENworks for Desktops allows you to specify your own script engine and file type extension. This allows you to create much more extensive and powerful scripts by using another script engine, such as a Perl parser.

To set up distribution scripts, use the following steps:

1. Right-click the Application object and click Properties.

2. Select the Distribution tab and select Distribution Scripts from the drop-down list.

3. Create the Run Before and Run After scripts in the text boxes shown in Figure 6.9.

4. Specify the location of the Script Engine.

5. Enter or select a file extension for the script file.

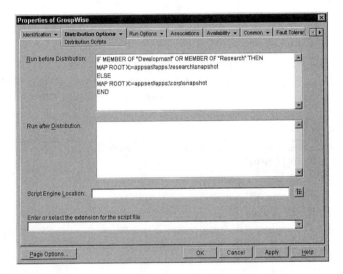

FIGURE 6.9
The distribution scripts property panel in ConsoleOne.

NOTE On Windows NT/2000/XP, distribution scripts run in the secure system space, which means that users do not see any of the script commands or the command results. Therefore, you should not use any commands that require user interaction because the script will be halted at that point.

Configuring a Pre-Install Schedule for Application

The next option to control distribution is setting up a pre-install schedule for local availability for the application. The pre-install can be extremely useful in deploying applications to a lot of workstations.

For example, if you have an application that needs to go out to 1,000 workstations all on the same day, having ZENworks for desktops deliver the application all at the same time could cause the network and server to be over utilized. If you know in advance that you need to deploy the application, you can set up a pre-install schedule to deliver the application to the workstations over a period of time before the day it needs to be installed. After this, all 1,000 workstations can install the application at the same time, without causing network problems, because they have a local copy of the application to work from.

To configure an application pre-install, select Pre-Install Schedule from the Distribution tab drop-down list, and the Schedule panel appears. If you want to have the application pre-installed prior to having it deployed, select the Pre-Install application box. The next step is to specify the schedule type you want to use for the pre-install.

The None option is selected by default, however, you can configure the Application object to pre-install the application to workstations based on a set of specific days or a range of days as described in the following sections.

Set Schedule by Specified Days

You can schedule application pre-installs by specifying the Specified Days option as shown in Figure 6.10. This enables you to select specific dates during which you want the application to be available for pre-install.

The application is only visible to be pre-installed to workstations on the specific dates and times you specify in this option. For example, if you select the dates June 7, 2003 and June 10, 2003, and start and end times of 8:00 a.m. and 5:00 p.m., the application is available to be pre-installed to a workstation from 8:00 a.m. to 5:00 p.m. on each of the days selected. The application is not available to be pre-installed to the workstation at any other time.

Set Schedule by Range of Days

You can set a schedule by specifying a range of days to make the application available for pre-install, as shown in Figure 6.11. An example is if you select a start date of June 12, 2003 and an end date of June 16, 2003, with a start time of 6:00 a.m. and an end time of 6:00 p.m. The Application object icon can be pre-installed to workstations from June 12th at 6:00 a.m. until June 16th at 6:00 p.m.

128

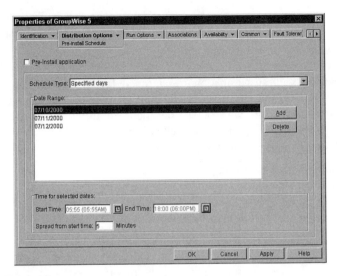

FIGURE 6.10
The pre-install schedule availability for specified days property panel in
ConsoleOne.

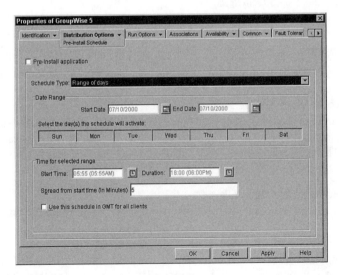

FIGURE 6.11
The pre-install schedule availability for a range of days property panel in
ConsoleOne.

Spread from Start Time

You can also specify a spread of time in which the application becomes available to users. This is useful when you don't want all users to run the application at the same time for fear that the load and traffic might bring down the network. The spread option literally "spreads out" user access times over the number of minutes specified so they don't all run the application at once.

An example of how to use the spread from Start Time option is to set it to 120 minutes; the application then becomes available, on a random basis, between the hours of 10:00 a.m. and 12 noon. This spreads the demand for the application out over a longer period of time and network traffic is minimized.

NOTE If users access applications after the spread time is expired but before the end time of the Application object, they access the application at that time and the spread variable has no effect.

GMT (Greenwich Mean Time)

The final option you have available on the scheduling panels is to specify that all application scheduling that you do with the Application property page is based on the workstation's timezone.

In other words, if your network spans different timezones and you schedule an application to run at 4:00 p.m., it would normally run at 4:00 p.m. in each timezone. However, by selecting the GMT check box, workstations run applications at the same time worldwide (according to GMT). Although, you should be aware that GMT time is not available if you are filtering out days of the week when in the Specified Days mode.

Configuring General Application Distribution Options

The next panel accessible from the Distribution tab is the Option property panel. This panel, shown in Figure 6.12, enables you to configure the following general distribution options for Application Objects.

Distribute Always

Use the Distribute Always option to force a distribution of the entire Application object every time the user runs the application or the application is set for a force run on the workstation (see the user or container object's Applications property page). This option is useful to ensure that all application settings are updated every time the application runs.

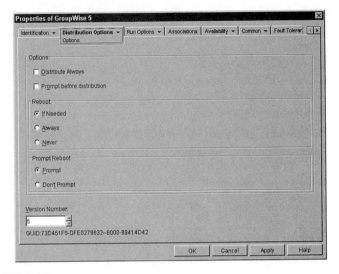

FIGURE 6.12
The Options property panel for Application objects in ConsoleOne.

You can also update settings on a case-by-case basis. For example, if you want to always distribute a particular Registry key and value, you can set the Distribute Always option on the Registry Settings property page for that particular key and value. The Distribute Always option on the Distribution property page overrides the Distribute Always option on the Registry Settings, .INI Settings, Application Files, Icons/Shortcuts, and Text Files property pages.

Prompt User Before Distribution

Next, use the Prompt Before Distribution option to display a message to users after they have clicked an Application Launcher-distributed application for the first time. This message asks them to confirm that they want to distribute the application to their workstation. This option is off by default.

TIP To better inform users, the text that you write in the Application object's Description property page is displayed in this distribution confirmation dialog box. For example, you might write a note to the user such as "This is an essential application for your workstation that takes approximately 10 minutes to distribute. Please answer Yes to distribute it now."

Prompt User for Reboot

Next, use the options in the Reboot group box to control how a workstation reboot should occur according to the following options:

▶ *If Needed*—The If Needed option (the default setting) prompts for reboot only when Application Launcher or Application Explorer needs to make changes that cannot occur while Windows is running (such as when replacing open DLLs).

▶ *Always*—The Always option prompts the user to reboot every time a distribution takes place.

▶ *Never*—The Never option does not prompt the user to reboot. In this case, the changes take effect the next time the workstation reboots.

Use Version Stamp to Trigger Redistribution

Use the version stamp option to trigger a redistribution of the application. A version stamp is simply a text string representing the version of the application that is used to customize the Application object's GUID. In fact, any change you make to the version stamp is like changing the GUID.

NOTE The version stamp might not have anything to do with the actual version of the software. It is a tool to help you upgrade applications. It helps you control the version of an Application Launcher-delivered application.

If the Run Once option is checked and you change the version stamp, the Run Once option causes the application to run again once. This is useful when upgrading application software to a new or different version.

For example, suppose you purchased new application software and want to update an Application object. By changing the version stamp number and selecting the Run Once option, the application runs once after installation even though a previous version might have already run once.

Use Application's GUID (Globally Unique Identification) for Troubleshooting

The application GUID is stamped in the workstation's Registry when ZENworks for Desktops distributes an application to a workstation. The GUID is a randomly generated number for tracking, such as {5A051144O-77C5-11D1-A663-OOA024264C3E}.

> **TIP** Use GUIDs to track and troubleshoot distributed applications. For example, if you want to ensure that a particular application has been distributed to a workstation, you can compare the GUID as recorded in the Application object's Distribution property page with the GUID that is currently stamped in the workstation's Registry.

You can make several Application objects use the same GUID by using the Synchronize Distributed GUIDs option. This is useful if you are distributing a suite of applications. You can also "regenerate" or "re-randomize" the GUIDs for those same applications.

Setting Run Options for Application Objects

Once you have set up the distribution options for an application, you need to set the run options. Setting the run options for an Application object enables you to control the behavior, environment, and licensing of an application as it is distributed to users. To access the options on the Run Options property tab, use the following steps to select which set of options you want to modify:

1. Right-click the Application object and click Properties.

2. Select the Run Options tab.

3. Click the down arrow on the Run Options tab. You'll see a screen similar to the one in Figure 6.13.

From the Application object's Run options property tab, access the individual property panels to configure the application run options described in the following sections.

Configuring Application Run Options

The top panel accessible from the run options tab is the Application panel. The Application property panel enables you to set the path, parameters, and behavior of an executable that needs to run when the application is distributed. Use this panel, shown previously in Figure 6.13, to configure the following options.

Install Only (No Executable Needed)

If you just want users to install an application, but not run it, you should check the Install Only option. An example of this is if Application object's purpose is to just update some files on the workstation. When you select the Install Only option, the software is installed but not run.

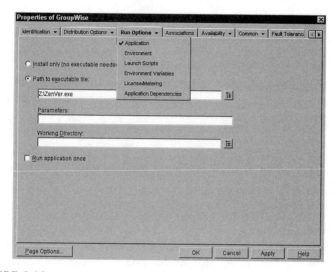

FIGURE 6.13
The run options property panel in ConsoleOne.

Set Path to Executable File

If an executable file exists that needs to be run for the application distribution, select this option. Next set the path in the Path to Executable text box to the executable that is to be run when an Application object icon is double-clicked in Application Launcher or Application Explorer. Use the Browse button to browse the file directory structure to find the executable you want. UNC pathnames are permitted. For example:

▶ server\volume:path

▶ \\server\volume\path

▶ volume_object_name:path

▶ directory_map_object_name:path

▶ driveletter:\path

NOTE If you don't want to run an application (for example, this Application object's purpose might be to just update some files on the workstation), use the Install Only option and do not specify a path.

Specify Parameters

You can specify parameters to be passed into the executable file specified in the path to the executable field. This can be extremely useful in controlling the application being executed. For example, if you wanted the application to run silently and that option is controlled by a command-line parameter, you could specify that parameter in this field to force silent execution.

Specify Working Directory

You can also specify a working directory for the application to be started in. For example, if you wanted to use a temporary location for the application to use as its base directory, you could specify a temporary directory such as `c:\temp`.

Run Applications Once

The final option you have from the object identification properties window is the run once option. It runs the application once and then removes the icon from the workstation.

You should check this option when an Application object's purpose is to install software to a workstation. It can be confusing and annoying to users if an install icon remains in the Application Launcher window or in Application Explorer after the software has already been installed.

NOTE If you selected Run Once and also specified a version stamp for this application, the application runs once until the next time you change the version stamp, whereupon the application runs one more time. This latter method is useful for upgrading applications.

Configuring Environment Options for Running Application

The next run option configurable for Application objects is the Environment option. The Environment panel, shown in Figure 6.14, is where you set up information about the environment the application runs in.

The Run section on the environment options property panel enables you to select one of the following window types with which to deploy the application:

▶ *Normal*—Simply pulls up the default window and deploys the application in it.

▶ *Minimized*—Pulls up the window and begins the application deployment, and then minimizes it so that it is out of the view of the user. This is the most commonly used option. It enables users to access the application deployment; however, it is not cluttering up their screen.

▶ *Maximized*—Pulls up and maximizes the window for application deployment. Use this option when you want the users to be very aware of the application deployment so that they wait until it is finished.

▶ *Hidden*—Hides the window that the application is deployed in from the user. Use this option for applications you don't want users to know about or when you want to seamlessly provide a silent update that doesn't affect users.

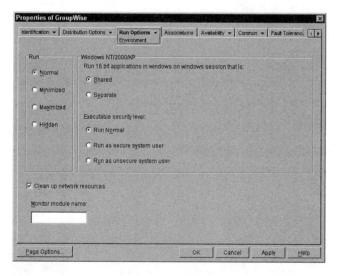

FIGURE 6.14
The environment options property panel in ConsoleOne.

The Windows NT/2000 section of the environment property panel lets you specify whether 16-bit applications are run in Shared or Separate mode. It also enables you to configure the following application security levels:

▶ *Run Normal*—This is the default for applications deployed to Windows NT/2000.

▶ *Run as Secure System User*—This option makes the application run at a secure system level. Use this option if you need the application to be installed even on workstations that have a high security level setup.

▶ *Run as Unsecure System User*—This options makes the application run at a non-secure system level. Use this option if you want workstations that have a high security level setup to be protected from applications being deployed to them.

The environment property panel also lets you select the Clean Up Network Resources option. If this is selected, any mapped drives or ports that are made by the application deployment are cleaned up when they are finished.

Configuring Application Launch Scripts

The next run option configurable for Application objects is launch scripts that are executed automatically each time the application is launched on a workstation. Unlike environment parameters, scripts can overwrite existing drive mappings and printer ports.

The two types of launch scripts are the *run before* launch script and the *run after* termination script. Run before launch scripts are executed before the application is launched. Run after termination scripts are executed after the application is closed and before the network resources are cleaned up.

Launch scripts enable you to provide dynamic mappings beyond those defined, to run other applications, to log in to other servers or eDirectory trees, to perform special termination options, and to perform other tasks that must be done before and after an application is launched. The scripts support the same commands and syntax as the Novell client. However, ZENworks for Desktops allows you to specify your own script engine and file type extension. This allows you to create much more extensive and powerful scripts by using another script engine, such as a Perl parser.

To create launch scripts, use the following steps:

1. Right-click the Application object and click Properties.

2. Select the Run Options tab and select Launch Scripts from the drop-down list.

3. Create the Run Before Launch and Run After Termination scripts in the text boxes shown in Figure 6.15.

4. Specify the location of the script engine if necessary.

5. Specify or select the extension of the script file.

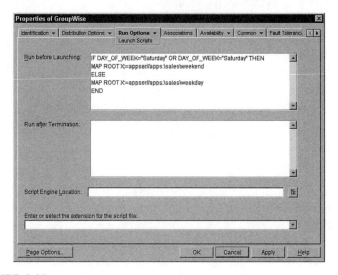

FIGURE 6.15
The application run launch scripts option property panel in ConsoleOne.

Configuring Environment Variables for Application Launch
The next run option configurable for Application objects is the environment variable option. The environment variable panel lets you add variables to be applied to the workstation environment when the application is deployed.

For example, if you have an application install that needs a temporary path variable name to be set to a specific location, you can add that variable name and path to the Application object. When the application is deployed, the path variable is inserted in the environment on the workstation, thus enabling the install to take place without user intervention.

Configuring Licensing and Metering for Applications
The next run option configurable for Application objects is the licensing/metering variable option. The licensing/metering variable panel enables you to specify that you want to use Novell licensing and

metering to run the application. If you want to use licensing, you can simply click the browse button and select the license certificate you want to use from the eDirectory tree. You can also specify that you do not want to run the application if NLS is not available.

Configuring Application Dependencies

ZENworks for Desktops allows you to define applications that the Application object is dependent on before it can be executed on a workstation. This can be a very useful feature to verify the software requirements for a workstation.

One example of when you might need to define an application dependency is if an application required a specific Windows support pack. You could create an Application object for the support pack and then use it as a dependency for any application that required it.

Another example of when you might need to define an application dependency is if you have an application upgrade that will only install on a workstation with the original software installed. You could create an Application object for the original application and use it as a dependency for the upgrade.

Other examples might include the need for an Oracle client to be installed on the workstation before the Oracle database application is run. The Application Launcher will ensure that the client is installed properly before running the database application.

ZENworks allows for the nesting of chained applications. For example, application A can depend on B, who depends on C and D, and so on. When A is launched, the Application Launcher verifies that all of the dependent applications up the chain are installed.

ZENworks allows you to define the following options for application dependencies:

- ▶ *Run Now*—Forces the application dependency object to be applied immediately to the workstation.

- ▶ *Reboot Wait*—Applies the application dependency and then forces ZENworks to wait until the workstation has been rebooted before applying the Application object.

- ▶ *Show Chain*—This option brings up a window that displays the full chain of dependent applications. This can be extremely useful in managing dependencies if you have a large number of applications.

Setting Application Object Associations

Once you have set up the run options for an application, you need to set
the Application object associations. Setting the associations for an
Application object enables you to associate the application with a user,
container, workstation, and control the behavior and visibility of the
application as it is distributed to users. To access these options, select the
Associations tab on the Application object. A screen similar to the one in
Figure 6.16 is displayed.

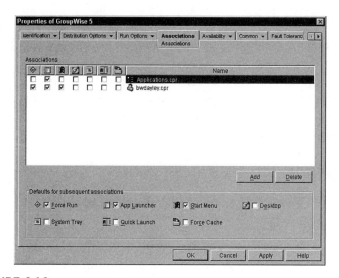

FIGURE 6.16
The Associations tab on the Application object.

From the Application object associations panel, you can click the Add
button and then navigate the tree to add objects to which you want to
associate the application. If you specify a container object, you can specify whether to associate the Application object to all users within the con-
tainter, all workstations within the container, or both users and workstations in the container.

Once the objects are added, you can check the following items for each
object in order to control the behavior and visibility of the application:

▶ *Force Run*—The force run option specifies that once the application
is available to the workstation, meaning that the user has logged in

and meets the criteria specified, the application is automatically deployed to the workstation.

▶ *App Launcher*—The App Launcher option specifies that the application should appear in the Application Launcher when the user runs it.

▶ *Start Menu*—The Start Menu option specifies that the application should appear in the Start menu on the workstation.

▶ *Desktop*—When the application is available, its icon is displayed on the desktop.

▶ *System Tray*—The Sytem Tray option specifies that when the application is available, an icon is displayed in the system tray on the workstation.

▶ *Quick Launch*—Places the icon for the application in the quick launch menu for even faster and easier distribution of the object.

▶ *Force Cache*—Forces the application to be cached to the workstation, where it can be used the next time it is run.

Setting Application Availability

Once you have set up the association options for an application, you need to set the availability options. You can use the Availability tab to modify these settings.

This feature depends on the settings you have set up for the Application Launcher on a User, Workstation, Organizational Unit, Organization, or Country object. You should be aware of those settings before trying to set up scheduling for the Application object.

A good example of how to use the advanced feature is if you want to force run a virus detection application on a user's workstation at a certain time, and only one time. You can force users to run the virus check by scheduling the appearance of the application using the Schedule property page and designating the application as Force Run.

NOTE Scheduling cannot deny access to an application outside of the schedule because file rights might still exist.

Use the following steps to select which set of options on the Availability property tab you want to modify:

1. Right-click the Application object and click Properties.

2. Select the Availability tab.

3. Click the down arrow on the Availability tab. A screen similar to the one in Figure 6.17 is displayed.

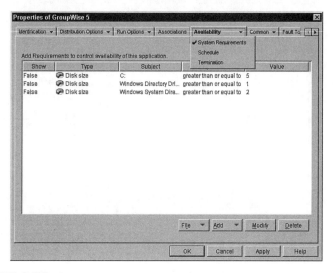

FIGURE 6.17
The Availability property tab.

From the Application object's Availability property tab, you should access the individual property panels to configure the application availability options described in the following sections.

Configuring System Requirements for Applications

The top panel accessible from the availability tab is the System Requirements panel. The System Requirements property panel enables you to choose which applications are available to workstations by making certain that the workstation meets the criteria specified. The System Requirements tab enables you to set requirements on installed applications, disk space, environment variables, memory, operating system, processor, Registry entries, and file requirements. If workstations do not meet the criteria you specify, the icons do not appear on that workstation.

For example, suppose you want a GroupWise 5.5 application icon to appear only on workstations that have at least 32MB of RAM, a Pentium processor, 5MB of free disk space on the **c:** drive, and 100MB of free disk space on a **temp** drive. You can set up those options by clicking the Add button, shown in Figure 6.18, to select and configure the requirement options described in the following sections.

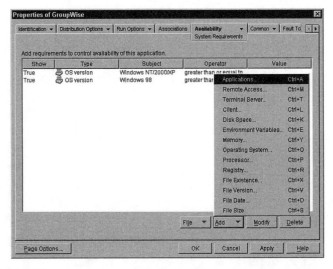

FIGURE 6.18
The system requirements property panel for Application objects in ConsoleOne.

Applications

The System Requirements tab for Application objects enables you to filter applications based on the existence of other applications on the client. To filter workstations by installed applications, click the Add button from the System Requirements panel and then select Application from the pop-up menu. A window is displayed which enables you to navigate the directory services tree to find specific applications that should or should not exist.

To filter on a specific application, simply navigate to that Application object in the eDirectory tree and then select it. Next, click the Application Object Is Installed or the Application Object Is Not Installed option. You want to use this option if an application is dependent on the existence of another one. For example if you want to deploy an application update, you can check for the existence of the original application before making it available to the workstation.

Remote Access

The System Requirements panel of Application objects enables you to filter applications based the type of remote access that they have. You can filter on whether they have a LAN connection or remote access connection.

To filter on the remote access connection type, select Remote Access from the menu shown in Figure 6.18. From the pop-up window, select LAN connection or remote access connection. Then select the criteria option of true or false.

Terminal Server

The system requirements panel for Application objects enables you to filter applications based the availability of a terminal server. This can be extremely useful for applications that require a terminal server.

To filter on terminal server availability, select Terminal Server from the menu shown in Figure 6.18. From the pop-up window, select Terminal Server Required or Terminal Server Not Required. Then select the criteria option of true or false.

Client

The System Requirements panel for Application objects enables you to filter applications based the availability of Novell client. This can be extremely useful for applications that require a Novell client connection.

To filter on terminal server availability, select Client from the menu shown in Figure 6.18. From the pop-up window, select Connection is Using Novell Client or Connection is Not Using Novell Client. Then select the criteria option of true or false.

Free Disk Space

The system requirements panel for Application objects enables you to filter applications based on the amount of free disk space available to the client. You can filter disk spaced on local drives and mapped network drives, as well as the following specific locations:

▶ Windows system directory drive

▶ Windows directory drive

▶ Temp directory drive

To filter workstations by disk space available, click the Add button from the system requirements panel and then select Disk Space from the pop-up menu. A screen similar to the one in Figure 6.19 appears. From this screen, first select the location disk, in which space is needed, from the top drop-down list. Next type the MB of disk space needed to install and run the application. Next, you can specify one of the following logical requirements:

- ▶ Less than
- ▶ Less than or equal to
- ▶ Equal to
- ▶ Greater than or equal to
- ▶ Greater than

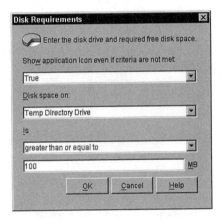

FIGURE 6.19
The disk requirements box from the system requirements panel for Application objects in ConsoleOne.

You can specify multiple locations that require disk space by performing the same steps again.

An example of when to use this is when the application requires a minimum of 5MB free on the Windows directory drive and 100MB free on the TEMP drive. If you specify these settings, the Application object icon will only appear on workstations that contain enough free disk space in all three locations.

Environment Variables

The System Requirements panel for Application objects also enables you to filter applications based on specific environment variable settings on the client. To filter workstations by environment variables, click the Add button from the system requirements screen and then select Environment Variables from the pop-up menu. A screen similar to the one in Figure 6.20 appears. From this screen, first type the name of the variable then select whether the name should exist. You can also filter on the value of the variable by typing a value and selecting a logic operation such as equal to.

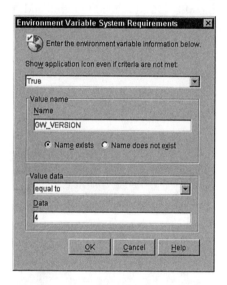

FIGURE 6.20
The environment variables box from the system requirements property panel for Application objects in ConsoleOne.

You can specify multiple environment variables to check for before displaying and installing the application by following the same process again.

One example of when to use this is when some users use Netscape as their browser and some use Internet Explorer. If you only want users who use Netscape to receive the Netscape object, you can set up a browser environment variable on the workstations and then specify that variable be present from the system requirements property panel.

Another example of when to filter on environment variables is if you wanted to apply an update to users with GroupWise 4 on their systems. You could check the version environment variable on those systems to make certain that GroupWise is installed and that its version is equal to 4.

Memory

The system requirements panel for Application objects enables you to filter applications based on the amount of memory installed on the client. To filter workstations by memory installed, click the Add button from the system requirements panel and then select Memory from the pop-up menu. A screen similar to the one in Figure 6.21 appears. From this screen, first type the MB of RAM needed to install and run the application. Next, you can specify one of the following logical requirements:

▶ Less than

▶ Less than or equal to

▶ Equal to

▶ Greater than or equal to

▶ Greater than

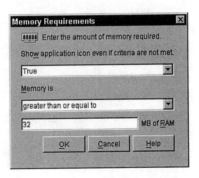

FIGURE 6.21
The memory requirements box from the system requirements property panel for Application objects in ConsoleOne.

An example of when to use this option is if the application requires 32MB of RAM; select true, memory is greater than, and then enter **32** in the text box. The Application object will not appear on workstations that do not have at least 32MB of RAM.

Display Applications on a Particular Operating System

The system requirements panel for Application objects enables you to filter applications based on the operating system installed on the client. To filter workstations by operating system, click the Add button from the system requirements panel and then select Operating System from the pop-up menu. A screen similar to the one in Figure 6.22 appears. From this screen, first select true or false for availability based on your criteria. Next, select the desired Windows platform.

Then you can specify a specific version of the operating system by specifying a version number as well as one of the following logical requirements:

▶ Less than

▶ Less than or equal to

▶ Equal to

▶ Greater than or equal to

▶ Greater than

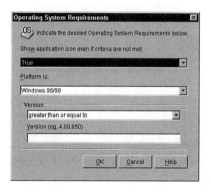

FIGURE 6.22
The operating system requirements box from the system requirements property Panel for Application objects in ConsoleOne.

An example of when to use the operating system option is if you create an Application object for an application that does not run on Windows NT 4.0 workstations. You can specify specific criteria by selecting Windows NT, typing 4.0 in the Version text box, and selecting the equal to option. Finally, select false for the availability option. The application will not show up on Windows NT 4.0 workstations.

Processor

The system requirements panel for Application objects enables you to filter applications based on the speed of the processor installed on the client. To filter workstations by processor, click the Add button from the system requirements panel and then select Processor from the pop-up menu. A screen similar to the one in Figure 6.23 appears. From this screen, first select the minimum processor needed to install and run the application from the following list:

- ▶ 386
- ▶ 486
- ▶ Pentium
- ▶ Pentium Pro
- ▶ Pentium II
- ▶ Pentium III
- ▶ Pentium 4

FIGURE 6.23
The processor requirements box from the system requirements property panel for Application objects in ConsoleOne.

Next, you can specify one of the following logical requirements:

- ▶ Less than
- ▶ Less than or equal to
- ▶ Equal to

▸ Greater than or equal to

▸ Greater than

Registry Entries

The system requirements panel for Application objects enables you to filter applications based on specific Windows Registry settings on the
client. To filter workstations by Registry settings, click the Add button
from the system requirements screen and then select Registry from the
pop-up menu. A screen similar to the one in Figure 6.24 appears. From
this screen, first navigate the Registry to find the specific Registry key to
filter on. Type the name of the Registry entry or browse to find it. Then
set the value of the entry, the data type (string or DWORD), and the logical
operation to perform on it. You can filter based on the following criteria:

▸ *Key Exists*—Filter in if key exists in the Registry, by selecting this
button.

▸ *Key Does Not Exist*—Filter in if key does not exist in the Registry, by
selecting this button.

▸ *Name*—You can specify the name of the entry that is associated
with the key.

▸ *Value Exists*—If the name box is filled in, you can specify to filter in
the application only if a name does exist for the selected key.

▸ *Value Does Not Exist*—If the name box is filled out, you can specify
to filter in the application only if a name does not already exist for
the selected key.

▸ *Value*—If a value is entered, ZENworks checks this value against
the value of the entry based on the logical operation and data type
specified in the value section.

You can specify multiple environment variables to check for before displaying and installing the application by following the same process
again.

Files

The system requirements panel for Application objects enables you to filter applications based on specific files installed on the client. To filter
workstations by files, click the Add button from the system requirements
panel and then select Files from the pop-up menu. Another pop-up
menu appears which enables you to select one of the following file filtering options:

▶ *File Existence*—The file existence option provides a window with two text boxes that enable you to specify the name of and location to the file to filter on. At the bottom, two buttons are present, which enable you to specify whether to filter if the file exists.

▶ *File Version*—The file version option provides a window with two text boxes that enable you to specify the name of and location to the file to filter on. At the bottom of this window, you can input a specific version number to filter on as well as the following logical operations: less than, less than or equal to, greater than, greater than or equal to, and equal to.

▶ *File Date*—The file date option provides a window with two text boxes that enable you to specify the name of and location to the file to filter on. At the bottom you can specify a specific date for the file based on one of the following: before, on or before, on, on or after, and after.

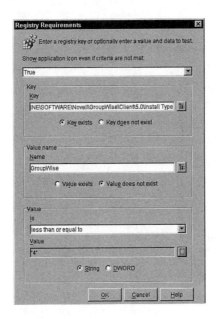

FIGURE 6.24
The Registry settings box from the system requirements property panel for Application objects in ConsoleOne.

Configuring Availability Schedule for Application

Once you have configured the system requirements for application availability, you can move on to setting up a schedule for availability for the application. Select Schedule from the Availability tab drop-down list and the schedule panel appears. The None option is selected by default; however, you can configure the Application object to be available only to workstations based on a set of specific days or a range of days as described in the following sections.

Set Schedule by Specified Days

You can schedule application availability by specifying the Specified Days option as shown in Figure 6.25. This option enables you to select specific dates during which you want the application to be available.

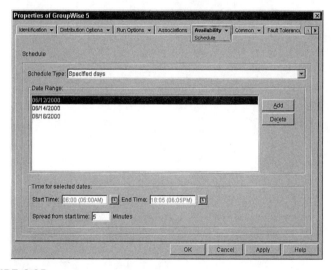

FIGURE 6.25
The schedule availability for specified days property panel in ConsoleOne.

The application is only visible to users during the specific dates and times you specify in this option. For example, if you select the dates June 7, 2003, June 10, 2003, July 2, 2003, and July 7, 2003, and start and end times of 8:00 a.m. and 5:00 p.m., this makes the application available from 8:00 a.m. to 5:00 p.m. on each of the days selected. The application is not available on any other days or at any other time. You select no more than 350 specific dates for this option.

NOTE When scheduling applications, you can also force them to run at the scheduled time (in addition to merely displaying them). Because the Force Run option is available on a per-association basis, you must select it from the Applications property page located on a User, Group, Organization, or Organizational Unit object. If the association is not set up for a Force Run, the application icon is displayed according to the location specified by the association.

Set Schedule by Range of Days

You can set a schedule by specifying a range of days to make the application available as shown in Figure 6.26. For example, you select a start date of June 12, 2003 and an end date of June 16, 2003, with a start time of 6:00 a.m. and an end time of 6:00 p.m. The Application object icon would be visible to workstations from June 12th at 6:00 a.m. until June 16th at 6:00 p.m.

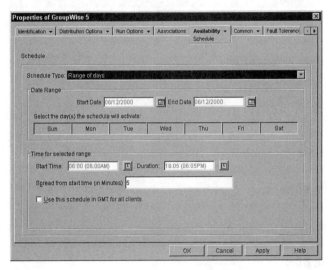

FIGURE 6.26
The schedule availability for a range of days property panel in ConsoleOne.

Another useful way to use the range of days option is to make applications available only on certain days of the week within a given range of dates. You do so by combining start and end dates and times with the Days Available buttons.

For example, suppose you select the dates June 2, 2003 and July 2, 2003, and start and end times of 6:00 a.m. and 6:00 p.m. You also select

the Tuesday and Thursday buttons. This combination makes applications
available on all Tuesdays and Thursdays that fall within the given date.
Applications are available on Tuesdays and Thursdays from 6:00 a.m.
until 6:00 p.m.

Spread from Start Time

You also can specify a spread of time in which the application becomes
available to users. This is useful when you don't want all users to run the
application at the same time for fear of load and traffic bringing down the
network. The spread option literally "spreads out" user access times over
the number of minutes specified so they don't all run the application at
once.

For example, consider a spread from start time option set to 120 minutes; the application becomes available, on a random basis, between the
hours of 10:00 a.m. and 12 noon. This spreads the demand for the application out over a longer period of time and network traffic is minimized.

NOTE If users access applications after the spread time is expired but before the end
time of the Application object, they access the application at that time and the spread
variable has no effect.

GMT (Greenwich Mean Time)

The final option you have available on the scheduling panels is to specify
that all application scheduling that you do with the Application property
page is based on the workstation's time zone.

In other words, if your network spans different timezones and you
schedule an application to run at 4:00 p.m., it would normally run at
4:00 p.m. in each timezone. However, by selecting the GMT check box,
workstations run applications at the same time worldwide (according to
GMT). Although, you should be aware that the GMT time is not available
if you are filtering out days of the week when in the Specified Days
mode.

Configuring Application Termination Options

The final option you have available from the Availability tab is to set termination options for application availability. To configure the termination
behavior, select Termination from the drop-down menu on the
Availability tab. A panel similar to the one in Figure 6.27 appears.

CHAPTER 6 Creating and Using Application Objects

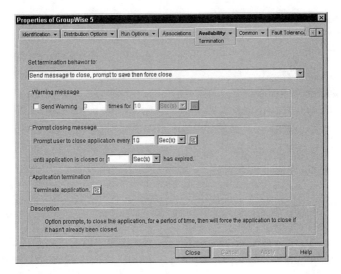

FIGURE 6.27
The termination property panel for Application objects in ConsoleOne.

From this panel, you can configure the following options that control the behavior terminating the application once it has been executed at the workstation.

None
This option (default) enables users to close the application on their own without any intervention from ZENworks. If you require the application to be closed for any reason (such as updates or database indexing), don't use this option because you will not be able to force users to close the application.

Send Message to Close Application
This option prompts users, at a specified interval, to close the application on their own until the application closes. For example, if you set an interval of five minutes, ZENworks sends a message (if one is active) to the user every five minutes until the application is closed or the message has been sent the configured amount of times.

To set this option:

1. Specify the number of times to send the message.

2. Specify the time interval between messages in the text box provided.

3. Click the message button; a message window is displayed. From this message window, you can select to use the default message, no message, or a custom message. The Custom Message option enables you to type a message to the users.

4. Choose OK.

Send Message to Close Then Prompt to Save Data

This option gives users a specified period of time to close the application on their own (this action is optional). When that period of time expires, the Application Launcher attempts to close the application. If users have not saved data, they are prompted to save it. Users can choose not to close the application. If users have no unsaved data, the application closes. Once the application has closed, users are not able to re-open it.

To set this option:

1. Select the check box next to Send warning and specify the warning interval and period in the text boxes provided (optional). If you want to specify a custom message, click the message button. A message window is displayed. Select Use Custom and then write one in the message text box.

2. In the next group box, specify the prompt message time interval in the text boxes provided. If you want to specify a custom message, click the message button. A message window is displayed. Select Use Custom and then write one in the message text box.

3. Choose OK.

Send Message to Close, Prompt to Save, and Then Force Close

This option prompts users to close the application on their own. When that period of time during which users are prompted expires, ZENworks for Desktops can close the application that is prompting users, at specified intervals, to save their work. If users have still not closed within a specified period of time, the application is forced to close.

To set this option:

1. Select the check box next to Send warning and specify the warning interval and period in the text boxes provided (optional). If you want to specify a custom message, click the message button and a message window is displayed. Select Use Custom and then write one in the message text box.

2. In the next group box, specify the prompt message time interval and period in the text boxes provided. If you want to specify a custom message, click the message button; a message window is displayed. Select Use Custom and then write one in the message text box.

3. In the last group box, click the message button and write a note to users explaining why the application terminated and perhaps when it will be available again.

4. Choose OK.

Send Message to Close Then Force Close with Explanation

This option prompts users to close the application on their own. When that period of time during which users are prompted expires, the application is forced to close.

To set this option:

1. Select the check box next to Send warning and specify the interval and period in the text boxes provided (optional). If you want to specify a custom message, click the message button and a message window is displayed. Select Use Custom and then write one in the message text box.

2. In the last group box, click the message button and write a note to users explaining why the application terminated and perhaps when it will be available again.

3. Choose OK.

Setting Common Options for Application Objects

Once you have set up the availability options for an application, you need to set some common options to control some general behavior and configure the Application object. To access the options on the Common property tab, use the following steps to select which set of common options you want to modify:

1. Right-click the Application object and click Properties.

2. Select the Common tab.

3. Click the down arrow on the Common tab. A screen similar to the one in Figure 6.28 is displayed.

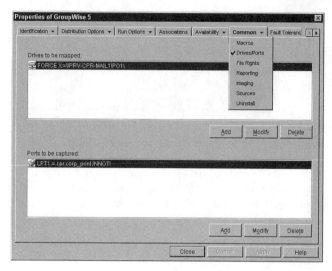

FIGURE 6.28
The common options property tab list in ConsoleOne.

From the Application object's Common options property tab, you should access the individual property panels to configure some common options for the application as described in the following sections.

Configuring Application Drives and Ports

The first advanced option available for Application objects from the Common tab pull-down menu is the Drives/Ports property panel. The Drives/Ports panel enables you to specify drives and ports that need to be mapped when the application launches on a workstation.

To add a drive to be mapped for the application launch, click the Add button under the Drives to be mapped window. The drive mapping box, as shown in Figure 6.29, appears. From this box, you can perform the following options:

▶ Specify an option (Drive, Search Drive 1 or Search Drive 16)

▶ Specify a letter

▶ Specify a network path

▶ Specify if it should be a root mapping

▶ Specify if it should overwrite existing mappings

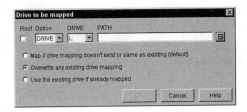

FIGURE 6.29
The drive mapping box for common options in ConsoleOne.

To add a port to be captured for the application launch, click the Add button under the Ports to be captured window. The port capturing box appears, as shown in Figure 6.30. From this box, you can perform the following options:

▶ Specify a port to capture

▶ Specify a network printer or print queue

▶ Specify to use notify flag

▶ Specify to use form feed flag

▶ Specify to use banner flag

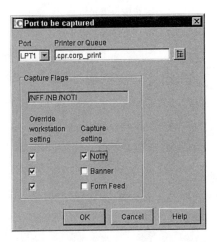

FIGURE 6.30
The port-capturing box for common options in ConsoleOne.

Configuring File Rights for Application Launch

The next advanced option available for Application objects from the Common tab pull-down menu is the File Rights property panel. The File Rights panel enables you to grant rights to files, directories, and volumes. This is used when this Application object is associated with a User object or with a Group, Organizational Unit, Organization, or Country object with which the user is already associated.

Use the following procedure to grant file rights to users when Application object is associated with them:

1. Right-click the Application object.

2. Click the File Rights button.

3. Click Add and specify the volume or directory to which users need access when they run the Application object.

4. Highlight the volume or directory and specify Supervisor, Read, Write, Create, Erase, Modify, File Scan, and Access Control rights as necessary. Click OK.

5. Associate this Application object with a User, Group, Organizational Unit, Organization, or Country object to grant the rights.

Configuring Application Reporting

The next advanced feature available from the Common tab pull-down menu is the Reporting option. When an application is distributed to the workstation, the Application Launcher records if the application was properly distributed. A successful distribution is recorded as well. Finally, errors are recorded along with the reasons for the failure in the distribution.

This record of distribution is recorded on a local file, and results in an event being sent to the centralized database that is also used for hardware and software inventory. These distributions can be set up through the Reporting property panel in ConsoleOne.

To access the Reporting Property panel, follow these steps:

1. Right-click the Application object and click Properties.

2. Select the Common tab.

3. Click the down arrow on the Common tab and select the Reporting option.

4. Once at the Reporting property panel, you can make changes to the Application object as shown in Figure 6.31.

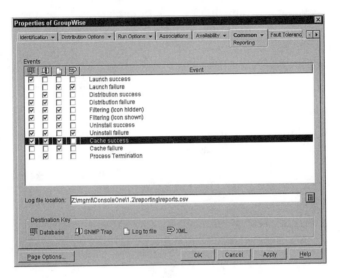

FIGURE 6.31
The reporting property panel for Application objects in ConsoleOne.

From the Reporting property panel, you can select from the four following destination keys for various events that occur during application deployment:

▶ *Enable Database Reporting*—Select the database box to enable reporting of the event to the database.

▶ *Enable Log File Reporting*—Specify a location in the text box for where reporting should log events.

▶ *Enabling SNMP Traps*—Select the Send SNMP Traps box if you want the SNMP trap engine to be notified of application distribution events.

▶ *Enable XML Reporting*—Select the XML Reporting box if you want the application event to be sent via XML to the Web-management console. Agents that collect these XML messages and place them in a database are available on the Companion CD.

You can specify these event keys for the following list of events:

- ▶ Launch success
- ▶ Launch failure
- ▶ Distribution success
- ▶ Distribution failure
- ▶ Filtering (icon hidden)
- ▶ Filtering (icon shown)
- ▶ Uninstall success
- ▶ Uninstall failure
- ▶ Cache success
- ▶ Cache failure
- ▶ Process termination

Configuring Launch Macros

One way to automate Application objects is to use the Macros property panel to set up special macros that can be used during object distribution and launch. These macros enable you to set up Application objects even when the user has a different system setup than what is expected by the administrator.

To access the Macro Property panel:

1. Right-click the Application object and click Properties.
2. Select the Common tab.
3. Click the down arrow on the Common tab and select the Macros option.
4. From the Macros property panel, you can add special macros to the Application object, as shown in Figure 6.32.

The following sections describe the special macros that can be added to an Application object for use in distribution and launching.

String Macros

The first type of macro available for Application objects is the string macro. The string macro can retain a value that remains static during application distribution and launching.

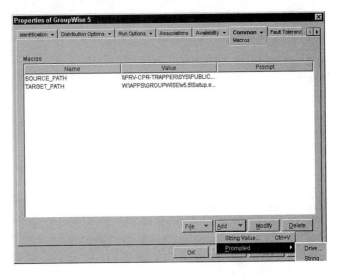

FIGURE 6.32
The Macros property panel for Application objects in ConsoleOne.

To set up a string macro, access the Macros property panel, using the steps described previously, from within ConsoleOne to select Add, String Value. You can set up the following options for the string macro:

▶ *Value Name*—Name set up for the macro for install scripts, and so on.

▶ *Value Data*—You can specify a value for the macro.

Prompted Drive Macros

The next type of macro available for Application objects is the prompted drive macro. The prompted drive macro enables you to prompt the user for a drive that will be used for application distribution and launching.

For example, users might want to put an application on a different drive than what was described in the Application object. Prompted macros enable you to request that the user be prompted for the information. By using the prompted macros feature, you can request the destination drive from the user so that the resulting distribution goes to the specified drive.

To set up prompted drive macros and access the Macros property panel, use the preceding steps from within ConsoleOne. Select Add, Prompted, Drive. A window similar to the one shown in Figure 6.33 is displayed. From the prompted macro window, you can set up the following options:

▶ *Prompt Text*—Textual information to be displayed for the user when prompting for the macro.

▶ *Macro Name*—Name set up for the macro for install scripts, and so on.

▶ *Default Value*—You can specify a default value for the drive macro for users to use if they have no need to specify otherwise. The available options are Windows System Directory Drive, Windows Directory Drive, Temp Directory Drive, or letters A...Z.

▶ *Minimum Disk Space*—You can specify a minimum amount of disk space required in setting the macro.

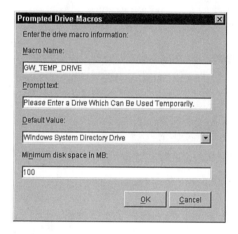

FIGURE 6.33
The prompted drive macro information window for Application objects in ConsoleOne.

Prompted String Macros

The next type of macro available for Application objects is the prompted string macro. The prompted string macro enables you to prompt the user for a string that is used for application distribution and launching.

For example, you want to ask the user for the user ID they use to access a corporate database; the macro can then be used by the application install to access the database and retrieve information necessary for the install.

To set up prompted string macros, access the Macros property panel using the preceding steps from within ConsoleOne to select Add,

Prompted, String; now you can set up the following options for the prompted string macro:

▶ *Prompt Text*—Textual information to be displayed to the user when prompting for the macro.

▶ *Macro Name*—Name set up for the macro for install scripts, and so on.

▶ *Default Value*—You can specify a default value for the macro for users to use if they have no need to specify otherwise.

▶ *Minimum Disk Space*—You can specify a minimum amount of disk space required in setting the macro.

▶ *Maximum String Length*—You can use this option to specify the maximum number of characters allowed for string macros.

Configuring Application Object Imaging

The next advanced feature available from the common pull-down menu is the object imaging option. ZENworks enables you to create an image of the application by selecting the location of the image file, as shown in Figure 6.34, and then clicking the Create Image button. That image can later be applied to a newly imaged workstation as part of the imaging process discussed in Chapter 14, "Imaging a Workstation."

Configuring Application Sources

Another advanced feature available from the Common tab pull-down menu is the Sources option. The Sources option enables you to specify network volumes and directories that ZENworks for Desktops uses to find application packages for the application during distribution and launching.

You can add volumes or directories to the list by clicking the Add button and typing the UNC path, or using the Browse button and navigating the eDirectory tree.

Configuring Application Uninstall

One of the most powerful features in ZENworks for Desktops application distribution is the capability to uninstall applications that were previously delivered. This provides you with control over which applications users have.

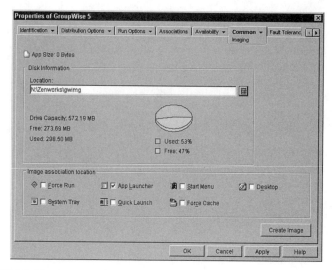

FIGURE 6.34
The imaging property panel for Application objects in ConsoleOne.

Use the following steps to access the application uninstall options panel for Application objects and configure the uninstall behavior:

1. Right-click the Application object and click Properties.

2. Select the Common tab.

3. Click the down arrow on the Common tab and select the Uninstall option as shown in Figure 6.35.

From the uninstall options panel, you can set the following options:

▶ *Enable Uninstall*—Determines whether the application can be uninstalled.

▶ *Enable User to Perform Manual Uninstall*—Determines whether users are enabled to uninstall the application.

▶ *Prompt User Before Uninstall*—Prompts the user prior to performing an application uninstall, allowing the user to save any work being done by the application.

▶ *Terminate Application Before Uninstall*—Forces the application to be terminated prior to uninstalling. This option should be used for any application that requires access to files, directories, or Registry settings that are removed by the uninstall.

▶ *Uninstall Application if Not Used Within x Days*—Enables you to specify a number of days the application remains available to users. If the user does not use the application within that number of days, the application is removed.

The following sections describe the options available to specifically control how the uninstall is performed on files, shortcuts, .INI files, and Registry entries.

Files Uninstall

From the Application Uninstall panel, you can specify the precise criteria of how files are uninstalled. Click the Files tab; a screen similar to the one in Figure 6.35 is displayed. From this screen, you can specify to uninstall files with any of the following attributes set:

▶ Copy always

▶ Copy if exists

▶ Copy if does not exist

▶ Copy if newer

▶ Copy if new and exists

▶ Copy if newer version

▶ Request confirmation

▶ Copy if different

Shortcuts Uninstall

From the application uninstall panel, you can specify how shortcuts are uninstalled. Click the shortcuts tab; a screen similar to the one in Figure 6.36 is displayed. From this screen you can specify to uninstall shortcuts with any of the following attributes set:

▶ Create always

▶ Create if does not exist

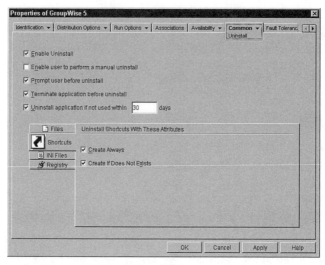

FIGURE 6.35
The files uninstall property panel for Application objects in ConsoleOne.

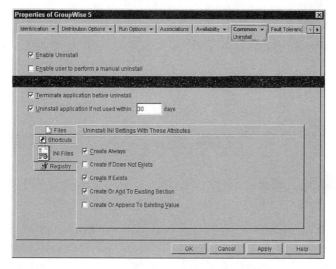

FIGURE 6.36
The shortcuts uninstall property panel for Application objects in ConsoleOne.

.INI Files Uninstall

From the application uninstall panel, you can specify how .INI files are uninstalled. Click the .INI files tab; a screen similar to the one in Figure 6.37 is displayed. From this screen you can specify to uninstall .INI files with any of the following attributes set:

- ▶ Create Always
- ▶ Create if Exists
- ▶ Create if does not exist
- ▶ Create or add to existing section
- ▶ Create or append to existing value

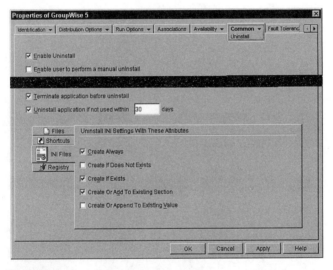

FIGURE 6.37
The .INI files uninstall property panel for Application objects in ConsoleOne.

Registry Uninstall

From the application uninstall panel, you can specify how Registry entries are uninstalled. Click to show the Registry tab and a screen similar to the one in Figure 6.38 is displayed. From this screen, you can specify how the uninstall of Registry entries with any of the following attributes set will be handled:

- ▶ Create always
- ▶ Create if does not exist
- ▶ Create if exists

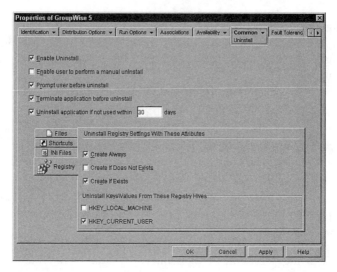

FIGURE 6.38
The Registry uninstall property panel for Application objects in
ConsoleOne.

Configuring Properties for MSI Objects

If the Application object was created from an .MSI file, there will be a
properties option available from the common pull-down menu. This
option enables you to configure any public property that is configured
inside the MSI package.

Configuring these options enables you to control more tightly how the
application is distributed to users. The properties can be anything configurable for an MSI package, for example an environment variable or a destination path.

Use the following steps to reconfigure a property in the .MSI file:

1. Click the Add button from the properties panel; a window appears.
2. Click the down arrow to display a list of property names. All properties that are configurable are displayed in this list.

3. Select the property you want to configure and add a value to the Value Data area.

4. Click OK. The property change is displayed on the properties panel along with the value you set.

Configuring Transform Files for MSI Object

If the Application object was created from an .MSI file, there will also be a transforms option available from the common pull-down menu. This option enables you to configure a list of transform files that will be applied to the MSI package before it is distributed to users.

Adding transform files to this list enables you even tighter control on the MSI Application object. These transform files modify the behavior of the MSI package install and therefore enable you more flexibility for application distribution. The transform file must be created using one of the approved methods.

Use the following steps to add a transform file to be applied to an MSI package prior to install:

1. Click the Add button from the transforms panel.

2. Type the path to the transform file, or click the browse button and navigate the eDirectory tree to the file.

3. Once the transform file is selected, click OK. The transform file is displayed on the transform panel.

Setting Up Application Fault Tolerance

Another powerful feature in ZENworks for Desktops application distribution is the capability to provide fault tolerance and load balancing to application delivery. The fault-tolerance panel enables you to control the availability of applications to users.

Use the following steps to access the fault-tolerance options panel for Application objects and configure the uninstall behavior:

1. Right-click the Application object and click Properties.

2. Select the fault-tolerance tab.

The following sections describe setting up application fault-tolerance and load-balancing options from the fault tolerance panel.

Configuring Application Fault Tolerance Options

The first option available from the drop-down menu under the fault-tolerance tab is to set up fault tolerance. The fault-tolerance feature enables you to specify alternative forms of the Application object to make the application available even if a problem with the current one exists.

From the fault-tolerance options panel, you can enable fault tolerance and then set up the following fault-tolerance options.

Use Source List

You can define a list of application package sources to use if the current Application object is unavailable for any reason. To add other application package source locations, click the Add button. A window displays the sources that have been defined for this Application object (see "Configuring Sources" earlier in the chapter). Select the sources you want to use and click OK to add them to the source section of the fault tolerance panel.

Use Application Objects

You can also define Application objects to be used as backup Application objects if the current object is unavailable. To add Application objects to the list, simply click the Add button. Then navigate the eDirectory tree to add the backup Application objects.

Configuring Application Object Load Balancing

The next option available from the drop-down menu under the fault tolerance tab enables you to set up load balancing. The load-balancing feature enables you to specify alternative forms of the Application object to balance the use for a number of users. This increases the reliability and availability of applications for busy networks.

From the load-balancing options panel, shown in Figure 6.39, you can enable load balancing for the application and then set up the following load-balancing options.

Use Source List

You can define a list of application package sources to distribute the use of the current Application object. To add application package source locations, click the Add button. A window displays the sources that have been defined for this Application object (see "Configuring Sources" earlier in the chapter). Select the sources you want to use and click OK to add them to the source section of the load-balancing panel.

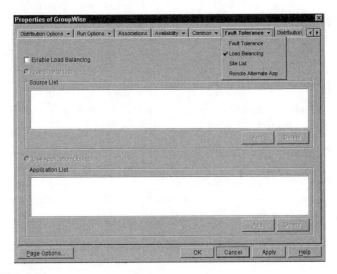

FIGURE 6.39
The fault-tolerance load-balancing property panel for Application objects in
ConsoleOne.

Use Application Objects
You can also define Application objects to be used as load-balancing
options for the current object. To add Application objects to the list, click
the Add button. Navigate the eDirectory tree to add the backup
Application objects.

Configuring a Site List for Application Objects
The next option you can define is additional sites for the Application
object. If you need your application to be highly available for users, you
should create multiple copies of the Application object and link them to
the original object by clicking the link button in this window. That way
you can maintain a list of compatible application sources to use for fault
tolerance and load balancing.

Configure Remote Failover
The final option you can define is an application to failover to if you are
remote and unable to execute the current one. To add a failover
Application object, simply click on the browse button and locate the
remote backup. You can also select Always Use the Remote Failover
Application When Remote if you want all remote users to use the failover
application.

An example of when to use this feature is if you have an application that requires a high-speed connection such as a database application. Normally the user, when connected, would launch this application over the LAN connection. You can make an Application object that will run the same database application on a Terminal Server. Then you can hook the Terminal Server version into the failover field. When the user is connected over a slow link, the system will automatically connect the user to a terminal services version of the application. This way, your users get to their applications no matter where they are connected!

Setting Up MSI-Specific Options for Application Objects

ZENworks for Desktops provides special options for MSI Application objects in addition to the standard ones mentioned earlier in this chapter. The following sections discuss those options and how to configure them.

Configuring and Viewing the Package Information

The first MSI-specific option for Application objects is the package information panel located under the Identification tab of the Application Object Properties window (see Figure 6.40). The following information is provided about the .MSI Application object:

- ▶ *Package Path*—This option is configurable and points to the location of the .MSI file.

- ▶ *Version*—Displays the version of the application.

- ▶ *Vendor*—Displays the application's manufacturer name.

- ▶ *Locale*—Displays the language the application is written to.

- ▶ *Help Link*—Displays the Web address that the vendor intended to be used to support the application.

Configuring the Transform List

The first MSI-specific option for Application objects is the transforms list located under the MSI tab of the Application object, shown in Figure 6.40. You can add multiple transform (.MST) files to be applied the Application object. This allows you to add to the MSI object without having to create a new one.

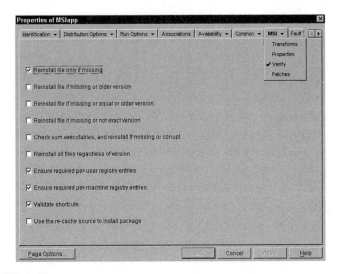

FIGURE 6.40
The MSI tab menu for Application objects in ConsoleOne.

Configuring the MSI Properties

The next MSI-specific option for Application objects is the properties list located under the MSI tab of the Application object, shown in Figure 6.40. The properties list allows you to add and customize properties of the MSI Application object. The properties available depend on the vendor that created the .MSI file. They include things like readme or copyright files, macro data, environment variables, and so on.

To add a property to an MSI Application object, click the Add button. Then select the property value name from the drop-down menu. Finally, set the correct value of the property and click OK. The property will now appear in the properties list.

Configuring the MSI Verify Options

The next MSI-specific set of options for Application objects is the verify options panel located under the MSI tab of the Application object, shown in Figure 6.40. From this panel you can customize the methods ZENworks will use, during application distribution, when verifying different aspects of the MSI application install. The following is a list of the verification settings for MSI Application objects:

- ► Reinstall file only if missing (default)
- ► Reinstall file if missing or older version
- ► Reinstall file if missing or equal or older version
- ► Reinstall file if missing or not exact version
- ► Check sum executables, and reinstall if missing or corrupt
- ► Reinstall all files regardless of version
- ► Ensure required per-user Registry entries (default)
- ► Ensure required per-machine Registry entries (default)
- ► Validate shortcuts (default)
- ► Use the re-cache source to install package

Configure the MSI Patches List

The final MSI-specific option for Application objects is the patches list located under the MSI tab of the Application object, shown in Figure 6.40. You can add multiple patch (.MSP) files to be applied the Application object. This allows you to add updates/patches to the MSI object without having to create a new one.

Setting Up Terminal Server-Specific Options for Application Objects

ZENworks for Desktops provides special options for Terminal Server Application objects in addition to the standard ones mentioned earlier in this chapter. The following sections discuss those options and how to configure them.

To access the Terminal Server options, select the Thin Client tab as shown in Figure 6.41.

Configuring Session Options for a Terminal Server Application Object

The first Terminal Server-specific option for Application objects is the options panel located under the Thin Client tab, shown in Figure 6.41, of the Application object properties window.

From the options tab, you must first specify whether the client will use an ICA or RDP session. Next you need to specify a name of the terminal server. You can specify a user login name and password to access it. If you do not specify the login name, the terminal server prompts the users for their login. You also can enable compression and/or encryption.

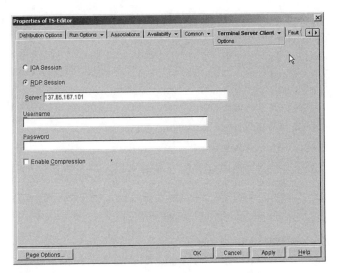

FIGURE 6.41
The Thin Client tab for Application objects in ConsoleOne.

Configuring Window Options for a Terminal Server Application Object

The next Terminal Server-specific option for Application objects is the window panel located under the Thin Client tab, shown in Figure 6.41, of the Application object properties window.

From the window tab, you can define the behavior and look of the Terminal Server session. You can define either to open the desktop or to open an executable file. If you select Open this Executable File, you have to provide the location of the file in the field provided. You can also define the width and height of the session window.

Setting Up Web-Specific Options for Application Objects

ZENworks for Desktops provides a special option for Web Application objects in addition to the standard ones mentioned earlier in this chapter. If you select the Web URL property panel from the Run Options tab of the Application objects properties window, you can configure the location of the Web application. You can also click the Test the URL button to check the behavior in the local browser.

Setting Up Application Distribution

ZENworks for Desktops has a powerful application distribution engine that enables you to distribute your applications throughout your network. Once an Application object has been created in eDirectory, you only need to set up the application distribution environment to apply the application to several workstations on your network. This chapter covers using ConsoleOne to set up application users to receive applications and application foldering, as well as automating Application object distribution.

Setting Up Application Foldering

The first step in setting up the application environment is to set up application foldering. ZENworks for Desktops offers powerful foldering capabilities that enable users to organize the applications that you deliver to them, using Application Launcher. These folders appear in the Application Launcher, Application Explorer browser view, and on the Start menu.

> **NOTE** If two folders have the same name, their contents are merged.

The following are the four types of folders available to users in Application Launcher:

▶ *Application Folder Object*—An Application Folder object is an independent object to which you associate Application objects. By linking many Application objects to one Application Folder object, you can manage the folder pathnames of many Application objects from one object. See the section "Create Application Folder Object and Associate with Application Objects" for more information.

▶ *Custom Folder*—Custom folders are set up on the Application object's Folders property page and thus belong exclusively to the Application object. A custom folder cannot be shared with another Application object. You can name Custom folders any way you please and set up folders within folders (sub-foldering). Custom folders override any System folders that exist as the result of Application object to container associations. See the section "Create Custom Folders for Application Object" for more information.

▶ *Personal Folder*—Personal folders enable users to create and name their own folders and place Application Launcher-delivered applications in them. See the section "Enable Users to Create Personal Folders" for more information.

▶ *System Folder*—System folders appear in Application Launcher or Explorer when you associate an Application object with a User, Group, Organizational Unit, Organization, or Country object, and you have not created any Custom folders for that Application object or associated the Application object with a Linked folder.

To set up application foldering to manage Application objects, you need to perform the tasks outlined in the following sections.

Create Application Folder Object and Associate with Application Objects

The first step in setting up application foldering is to create a Folder object that can be linked to Application objects. Use the following steps from within ConsoleOne to create an Application Folder object:

1. Right-click the Organization Unit, Organizational, or Country object under which you want to create a Folder object.

2. Choose Create, Application Folder, and then click OK.

3. Name the folder, select Define Additional Properties, and then choose OK.

Custom folders are tied to one Application object. Linked folders, however, can contain many Application objects. All folders appear in Application Launcher or Explorer browser view and also in the Start menu.

Once the application folder has been corrected, use the Folders property panel on a Folder object to create custom or linked folders in which to organize Application objects. To set up the folder for applications, use the following steps to access and modify the Folders property panel from within ConsoleOne:

1. Right-click the Application Folder object and select Properties.

2. Click the Folders tab; a screen similar to the one in Figure 7.1 appears.

3. Click Add, Folder and then name the folder. Repeat this process to add more folders.

4. With a folder highlighted, click Add, Application, browse to the Application object you want to add, and then choose OK. Repeat this process for all the Application objects you want to place in this folder.

5. Check the Application Launcher and/or Start menu boxes depending on whether you want to display the folders in Application Launcher/Explorer browser view or on the Start menu.

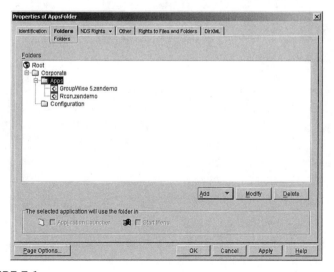

FIGURE 7.1
The folders property panel for application folders in ConsoleOne.

Create Custom Folders for Application Object

The next step in setting up application foldering is to use the Folders property panel for the Application object to create custom folders in which to organize Application objects, as described earlier in this chapter. A custom folder is tied to one Application object; however, you can have multiple custom folders per Application object.

Using custom folders, you can achieve "sub-foldering" or place folders within folders. This is essential when you have numerous Application objects available to users. Custom foldering enables you to organize Application objects and control which users see which applications.

TIP Suppose you have created a Folder object that contains several folders that are linked to several Application objects. You now want to clear these folder-application links and start over. You can delete the Folder object, which converts all of the linked folders to custom folders, which are then saved in all the relevant Application objects. In this case, you have to open each Application object and delete the Custom folders in them. A quicker method is to delete the folders and the linkages to Application objects from the Folder object, but don't delete the Folder object itself. When the Folder object is empty, you can decide if you want to start over with new folders and links to Application objects, or you can delete the Folder object.

Customize Application Launcher Configurations per User or Container

Once you have created the Folder objects, you need to customize the Application Launcher configurations. ZENworks for Desktops enables you to customize the behavior of the Application Launcher at a User, Group, Organizational Unit, Organization, or Country object level.

Use the following steps to configure the Application Launcher for an object in ConsoleOne:

1. Right-click the object and select Properties.

2. Click the Application Launcher tab as shown in Figure 7.2.

3. From this screen, select the View/Edit object's custom configuration from the drop-down menu.

4. Click the Edit button to bring up the Launcher configuration window as shown in Figure 7.2.

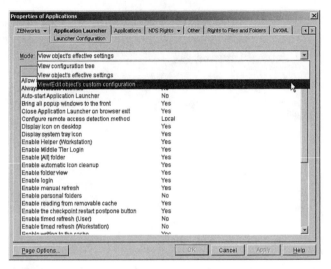

FIGURE 7.2
The Launcher Configuration panel for Application Folder objects.

From the Launcher Configuration window, you can set up the Application Launcher options for users, the Application Launcher, Application Explorer, and workstations as described in the following sections.

Setting Up User Application Launcher Options

From the Users tab of the Launcher Configuration window, you can specify configurations that dictate how users view and work with Application Launcher and Application Explorer desktop software (see Figure 7.3). From this screen, you can set the following options that define how the Application Launcher behaves for users.

Allow Users to Exit (Default=Yes)

The Allow Users to Exit option determines whether users can exit Application Launcher or Explorer.

Assume, for example, you are running software at a conference where workstations are available for the attendees of the conference to use. If you do not want users to exit Application Launcher and change settings on the hard disk drive, you set this option to No.

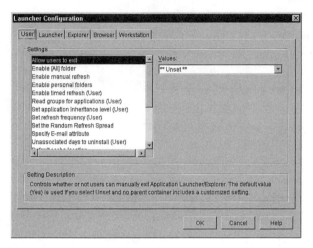

FIGURE 7.3
The Launcher Configuration property page for user objects in ConsoleOne.

Enable (All) Folder
The folder view in Application Launcher might be confusing to some
users. By setting Enable (All) Folder to No, users see only the application
icons available to them in Application Launcher.

Enable Manual Refresh (Default=Yes)
The Enable Manual Refresh option lets users refresh Application
Launcher or Application Explorer manually. This displays any
Application objects that were delivered since the last refresh.

Enable Personal Folders (Default=No)
If Enable Personal Folders is set to Yes, users can create their own folders
and move the icons around in them as they see fit. However, the icons
must originate from an application associated with the user. A user cannot add a new, unassociated Application object using personal folders.

WARNING Use caution when offering the option to create personal folders. Users
might forget where they have placed applications and call you for help. Not allowing personal folders might be a way to exert more strict control and thus reduce support calls.

Enable Timed Refresh (User) (Default=No)
The Enable Timed Refresh option refreshes the application icons automatically without the user having to choose View, Refresh or having to

press F5 to manually refresh icons. The Timed Refresh setting affects settings such as the Force Run feature.

Read Group Objects for Applications (User) (Default=Yes)

If a Group object has been associated with Application objects, users who are members of that Group can run Application objects by virtue of their membership. Although this is a convenient way of indirectly associating users with applications, it can also decrease performance. If you want to increase performance, set this option to No.

Set Application Inheritance Level (User) (Default=1)

The Set Application Inheritance Level option specifies how many parent Organization or Organizational Unit objects up the eDirectory tree Application Launcher, or Application Explorer, to search for applications.

For example, if a user object's Distinguished Name is `user1.dev.la.acme` and this option is set to a value of `2`, Application Launcher or Application Explorer looks at the Organization or Organizational Unit object `dev` and `la` for Application objects, but ignores `acme`. A value of `-1` instructs Application Launcher or Application Explorer to search all the way up the eDirectory tree.

Set Refresh Frequency (User) (Default=43200 Seconds)

The Set refresh frequency option lets you specify the refresh frequency in seconds.

For example, if you set the refresh to 300 seconds, Application Launcher or Application Explorer updates applications from the network automatically every five minutes and might even run some applications depending on how you have set them up.

NOTE A short timed refresh interval is very useful in situations where you want changes to refresh quickly. However, a short timed refresh interval can cause higher network traffic. The Refresh Icons and Timed Refresh options are not connected in any way except that they both control refresh. One option does not have to be selected for the other to work.

Set Random Refresh Spread

The Set Random Refresh Spread option enables you to specify a time range, in seconds, before the first refresh occurs.

For example, if you set the refresh spread to 300 seconds, Application Launcher or Application Explorer will choose a random number within the five-minute interval before initiating application updates from the network. This way, each workstation will randomly pick a different value within the interval, thus spreading your load on the server.

Specify E-mail Attribute (Default=Mailbox ID)

This option enables you to specify the eDirectory attribute that you want to use to display an e-mail name in the Help Contacts tab (when the user right-clicks an application icon and chooses Properties). If users have problems with applications, they can contact people by e-mail to get help. The e-mail name that appears is pulled from the eDirectory attribute you specify here.

Unassociated Days to Uninstall

The Unassociated Days to Uninstall option enables you to specify the number of days to wait until after the user has been unassociated with an application before uninstalling the application. The range can be from 0 to 730 days.

You can use this option if you do not want users to be immediately cut off from an application, but you also do not want them to have continual access; an example of this is when a user is transitioning to a new job inside your company and still needs access to their old applications for a few weeks.

Auto-Start Application Launcher

The Auto-start option enables you to control whether the Application Launcher is automatically started when a user logs in; an example of this might be if you have a new application that needs to go out to users in a specific container. You can associate the application with the container and then specify this option so that the Application Launcher runs and the application is delivered to users when they log in to the container.

Enable Reading from Removable Cache

The Enable Reading from the Cache option enables you to allow workstations to read Application objects from a removable cache.

Enable Writing to the Cache

The Enable Writing to the Cache option enables you to allow workstations to write to the disconnected NAL cache. Disabling this option forces the workstation to wait until the NAL cache has reconnected before writing to it.

Enable the Checkpoint Restart Postpone Button

The Enable the Checkpoint Restart Postpone Button option enables you to specify whether you want Application Launcher/Explorer to display a

Postpone button that will enable the users to postpone the distribution of an application to their workstation. This can be extremely useful when you are trying to distribute a large application across a slow network link.

If you enable the Postpone button, it will be displayed only when Application Launcher/Explorer detects that the user's workstation is running in remote mode. If the user clicks the Postpone button, the application distribution is postponed until they can get to a faster network location.

The setting values are Yes, No, and Unset. The default value of Yes is used if you select Unset and no parent container includes a customized setting.

Always Evaluate Referrals

The Always Evaluate Referrals option forces ZENworks for Desktops to always check the validity of protocol referrals, thus increasing the reliability of application deployment to users.

Enable Automatic Icon Cleanup

The Enable Automatic Icon Cleanup option enables you to force removal of application icons when the Application Launcher exits. If this option is enabled, all application icons are automatically cleaned up when the user exits the Application Launcher or when Application Launcher exits automatically.

Remote Access Detection

The Remote Access Detection option enables you to control how the Application Launcher will detect whether the user is at a remote or local location. This option allows you to set the following methods for remote access detection:

▶ *Always Assume User Will Be Local*—Assumes user is local and uses the local setting for the application.

▶ *Always Assume User Will Be Remote*—Assumes user is remote and uses the remote setting for the application.

▶ *Prompt*—Prompts the users to specify whether they are using a remote or local connection.

▶ *Autodetect Using Max Interface Speed*—Uses the maximum interface speed for the connection to determine whether the user is using a local or remote connection.

   This is based on the maximum speed of the card as reported to Windows and not on the speed of the current connection.

▶ *Detect Using Network ID*—You can specify a mask of the IP address that you will use to determine whether the user is connected remotely. This is useful when you have your remote users coming in over a dialup connection that is always assigned an IP address with a particular subnet.

Bring All Popup Windows to the Front (Default=Yes)

This option forces all pop-up windows displayed by the Application Launcher to be pushed to the front of the window. If this option is not set, these dialog boxes can end up being behind other windows.

Enable Middle Tier Login (Default=Yes)

This option allows a menu item to exist in the Application Launcher so the users can log in to the Middle Tier if they don't already have a Middle Tier session.

Setting Up Application Launcher Window Options

From the Window tab of the Launcher Configuration window, you can specify configurations that dictate how the Application Launcher window behaves. From this screen, shown in Figure 7.4, you can set the following options that define availability and behavior of the Application Launcher window.

Enable Folder View (Default=Yes)

For users to see the folders you have created, you must make certain that this option is enabled. If Enable Folder View is set to No, users see only the application icons available to them in Application Launcher.

Enable Login

Setting the Enable Login option to Yes activates the Login option found on Application Launcher's File menu. The user can use this option to run the GUI Login software and log in to the network. This option is not available with Application Explorer.

NOTE When this option is selected and the user is not logged in, Application Launcher searches for the Login executable in the path and, if found, displays a Login icon in Application Launcher. If the login executable cannot be found, or if the user is already logged in, the Login option is grayed. Ensure that Application Launcher can find the login program (LOGIN.EXE or LOGINW32.EXE) on the client workstation before you select the Login option.

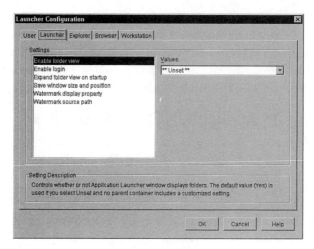

FIGURE 7.4
The window configuration property panel for the Application Launcher in
ConsoleOne.

Expand Folder View on Startup (Default=No)
The Expand Folder View on Startup option enables you to specify when
the user or container can view folders. The Expand Folder View on
Startup option expands the entire tree of folders when the Application
Launcher starts.

Save Window Size and Position (Default=Yes)
The Save Window Size and Position options enable you to set whether to
save window size and position settings on a local drive. By setting this
option to Yes, Application Launcher is displayed in the same position for
every user.

Watermark Display Property
The Watermark Display Property option enables you to specify how the
watermark should be positioned inside of the Application Launcher window. The watermark is displayed as background wallpaper inside the
Application Launcher window. You can specify to use the default, which
centers the watermark, or tiled, which tiles the watermark inside the
window.

Watermark Source Path
The Watermark Source Path option enables you to determine the path to
the watermark file that you want to display in the Application Launcher

window. This can be useful when you want to display different watermarks for different containers, users, or workstations. For example, you could set up a different watermark for Windows 98, Windows 2000, and Windows XP workstations by creating three different workstation containers and assigning each a different source path.

Setting Up Application Explorer Options

From the Explorer tab of the Launcher Configuration window, you can specify configurations that dictate how the Application Explorer behaves. From the screen shown in Figure 7.5, you can set the following options that define the availability and behavior of the Application Explorer.

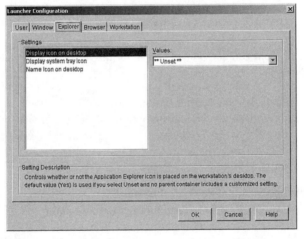

FIGURE 7.5
The launcher configuration property panel for the Application Explorer in ConsoleOne.

Display Icon on Desktop (Default=Yes)
The Display Icon on Desktop option enables you to specify whether you want the Application Explorer icon to appear on the user desktop. When enabled, an Application Explorer icon appears on the desktop.

Display System Tray Icon (Default=Yes)
The Display System Tray Icon option enables you to specify whether you want the Application Explorer icon to appear on the user system tray.

When enabled, users can launch Application Explorer from the icon on their system tray.

Name Icon on Desktop (Default=Application Explorer)

The Name Icon on Desktop option enables you to change the name of the icon that opens the Application Explorer browser view. For example, you could name it something such as Corporate Applications.

Setting Up Browser Application Launcher Options

From the Browser tab of the Browser Configuration window, you can control how the browser view behaves. The following sections cover the options you'll find on the Browser tab.

Close Application Launcher on Browser Exit (Default=No)

When the user launches an application's browser view (via the MYAPPS.HTML page on the Middle Tier server), the `naldesk` executable is automatically launched on the workstation. If this option is set to No (the default), the `naldesk` executable remains active and will maintain a connection to the Middle Tier server, even when the user closes the browser. If this option is set to Yes, then the `naldesk` is terminated when users close IE.

NOTE If users are not already logged into the Middle Tier, when they launch the browser they will be prompted for the eDirectory login name and password. Users are prompted each time they open the browser to MYAPPS.HTML if this flag is set to Yes.

Setting Up Workstation Application Launcher Options

From the Workstation tab of the Launcher Configuration window, you can specify configurations that dictate how workstations view and work with Application Launcher and Application Explorer desktop software. From the screen shown in Figure 7.6, you can define how the Application Launcher behaves for workstations.

Enable Helper

The Enable Helper option enables the helper DLL by loading and adding it to the WM scheduler for the workstations.

CHAPTER 7   Setting Up Application Distribution

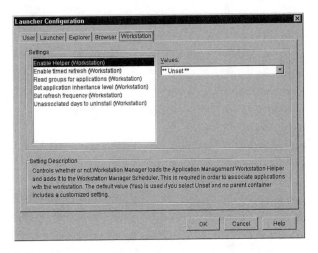

FIGURE 7.6
The launcher configuration property page for workstation objects in ConsoleOne.

Enable Timed Refresh

The Enable Timed Refresh option refreshes the application icons automatically without the user having to choose View, Refresh or pressing F5 to manually refresh icons. The Timed Refresh setting also affects settings such as the Force Run feature.

Read Groups for Applications

If a Group object has been associated with Application objects, users who are members of that Group can run Application objects by virtue of their membership. Although this is a convenient way of indirectly associating users with applications, it can also decrease performance. If you want to increase performance, set this option to No.

Set Application Inheritance Level

The Set Application Inheritance Level option specifies how many parent Organization or Organizational Unit objects up the eDirectory* tree Application Launcher, or Application Explorer, should be searched for applications.

For example, if a user object's Distinguished Name is user1.dev.la.acme and this option is set to a value of 2, Application Launcher or Application Explorer looks at the Organization or Organizational Unit object dev and

1a for Application objects, but ignores acme. A value of -1 instructs Application Launcher or Application Explorer to search all the way up the eDirectory tree.

Set Refresh Frequency

The Set Refresh Frequency option enables you to specify the refresh frequency in seconds.

For example, if you set the refresh to 300 seconds, Application Launcher or Application Explorer updates applications from the network automatically every five minutes and might even run some applications depending on how you have set them up.

Unassociated Days to Uninstall

The Unassociated Days to Uninstall option enables you to specify the number of days to wait until after the user has been unassociated with an application before the application is uninstalled. The range can be from 0 to 730 days.

You can use this option when you do not want users to be immediately cut off from an application, but you also do not want them to have continual access. This might happen when, for example, a user is transitioning to a new job inside your company and still needs access to his old applications for a few weeks.

Setting Up Users to Receive Applications

Once you have set up application foldering, you need to set up users to receive applications via ZENworks for Desktops. This section covers using ConsoleOne to set up User objects to receive applications by using the following methods:

- ▶ Associating users' objects with an Application object
- ▶ Making Application Explorer and Application Launcher available to users
- ▶ Setting Application Launcher configurations

Associate a User, Group, Workstation, or Container Object to Application Objects

The first step in setting up users to receive applications is to use the Applications property panel to associate a User, Group, Workstation, Organizational Unit, Organization, or Country object to one or more Application objects. You can also use the Associations panel for Application objects to individually add users or containers; however, unless you associate applications using one of these two methods, applications are not available to users.

You should design your application associations to make it as easy as possible to administer. For example, separating applications into company, division, group, and then users levels would enable you to make the fewest associations as possible and would also reduce the cost of future administration.

In addition to associating applications with other objects, use the Applications property panel to specify where and how users access applications on their workstations. For example, you can display application icons in Application Launcher, Application Explorer, Windows Explorer, Start menu, the Desktop, and the system tray (or in all of these areas). You can also force applications to launch when Windows starts.

NOTE The default method of access is App Launcher, meaning that users see the application only in the Application Launcher and Application Explorer browser view (depending on what you have made available).

To specify who sees an application and where it is displayed on workstations, use the following method:

1. Right-click the User, Group, Organizational Unit, Organization, or Country object, and then click Properties.

2. Click the Applications tab.

3. Click Add, browse and select the Application object, and then click OK. From container objects, you can add application associations for users or workstations located within the container.

4. Select an Application object and then specify how and where you want the application to work. Check the appropriate check box and then click OK, as shown in Figure 7.7.

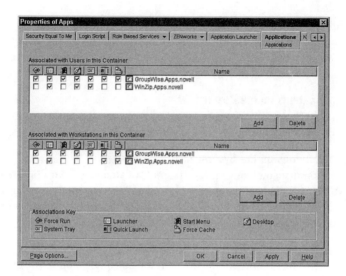

FIGURE 7.7
The application property panel for user, group, or container objects in ConsoleOne.

The following sections describe the options from the Applications panel that specify how the application is available to users.

Force Applications to Run
The Force Applications to Run option runs applications immediately when Application Launcher or Application Explorer starts and when the application is available. You can use this option in conjunction with several other Application object settings to achieve unique behaviors.

For example, if you set an application as Run Once (on the Application object's Identification property page) and Force Run (on the User, Group, or container object's Applications property page), the application runs immediately one time (if available).

Put Applications in the Application Launcher or Explorer Browser View
This option displays application icons in Application Launcher and Application Explorer (browser view), depending on which one you make available to your users.

Put Applications on the Start Menu

When Application Explorer is enabled, the Start Menu option displays icons on the Windows98 or Windows NT/2000/XP Start menu under Novell Application Launcher.

Put Applications on the Desktop

When Application Explorer is enabled, this option displays icons on the Windows 98 or Windows NT/2000/XP desktop area.

Put Applications on the System Tray

This option displays icons on the system tray, an area on the Windows 98 or Windows NT/2000/XP taskbar where small icons, representing applications, are placed for easy access. Application Explorer can display or remove applications on the system tray at any time.

Set Application for Quick Launch

The Quick Launch option puts the icon for the application in the quick launch menu for even faster and easier distribution of the object.

TIP If you plan to add the application to the quick launch menu, you should use an icon that users can easily recognize.

Force Cache the Application

The Force Cache option forces the application to be cached to the workstation, where it can be used the next time it is run. This is extremely useful for applications that need to run more than once. For example, you could use this option for a virus scanner that runs every time the user logs into the network. The workstation would need to pull down the virus scanner object only once; from then on, it would be applied out of cache.

Make Application Launcher/Explorer Available to Users

Once you have associated the Application object with the specific users you want receiving it, you need to make Application Launcher/Explorer available to them.

Application Launcher and Explorer are types of software that run on users' Windows 98 or Windows NT/2000/XP workstations. They display the applications that you distribute to users using the Application

Launcher/Explorer snap-in. You can specify to what degree users control the options in Application Launcher/Explorer by using a User, Organizational Unit, Organization, or Country object's Launcher Configuration property page.

Application Explorer displays application icons in a special Application Explorer window, Windows Explorer, Start menu, System Tray, or Desktop. Use the Applications property page of the User, Group, Organizational Unit, Organization, or Country object to set up the different Application Explorer access points, as discussed earlier in this chapter.

The following sections discuss methods to make applications available to your users through Application Launcher/Explorer.

NOTE You can run Application Launcher or Explorer on a workstation; however, you should not run them both at the same time on the same workstation.

Manually Starting Application Launcher/Explorer

The easiest way to make Application Launcher and Explorer available to users is to have users run them manually.

Click Start, Programs, Novell ZENworks for Desktops, Application Management Window to start Application Launcher manually on a workstation with the ZENworks for Desktops client installed on it.

Click Start, Programs, Novell ZENworks for Desktops, Integrated Application Explorer to start Application Explorer manually on a workstation with the ZENworks for Desktops client installed on it.

You can also set the Launcher/Explorer to start automatically as part of the installation of the ZENworks Management Agent.

Starting Application Launcher/Explorer from a Login Profile

The most user-friendly method for making Application Launcher/Explorer available to users is to add the command to launch them to a login profile that the users will run when logging into the network. This gives the administrator more control over how and where they are run.

To make Application Explorer available to users, ensure that NALEX-PLD.EXE is in a network directory (such as `sys:\public`) where users have rights and access. The Application Explorer is installed to the `sys:\public` directory when ZENworks for Desktops is installed on a server, but you might need to copy it to the public directory on other servers that do not have ZENworks for Desktops installed on them.

To make Application Launcher available to users, follow these steps:

1. Ensure that NAL.EXE is in a network directory (such as `sys:\public`) where users have rights and access.

2. Add one of the following commands to the login script of the User object or the user's Organizational Unit:

   `#\\servername\sys\public\nal.exe`

   Or

   `@\\servername\sys\public\nal.exe`

NOTE The # command requires the external command to complete before executing the next line in the login script. The @ command enables the login script to continue processing while the external command is processed. It's recommended that you use the @ symbol for faster script execution. Do not equate NAL.EXE, a "wrapper" executable that does not stay in memory, with NALWIN32.EXE. If you use # with NALWIN32.EXE, the scripts will wait until the user exits Application Launcher.

In ZENworks for Desktops 4, the Application Launcher actually resides in `C:\Program Files\Novell\ZENworks` directory. The NAL.EXE on the server is replaced with an executable that will launch the local copy of the launcher.

Setting Up Application Launcher/Explorer As a Shell

The most powerful way for you to make applications available to users via Application Launcher is to use Application Launcher as a shell in place of Windows Explorer. This allows you to completely control which applications your users have access to on their local workstations.

Use the following steps to set Application Launcher as the Shell on a Windows 98 workstation with the ZENworks for Desktops client installed on it:

1. Copy the files specified in Table 7.1 from the source location to the destination location.

2. Open the SYSTEM.INI file in a text editor.

3. Replace the `SHELL=EXPLOR.EXE` line with the following one:

   `SHELL=C:\NOVELL\CLIENT32\NALWIN32.EXE`

4. Save the SYSTEM.INI file.

5. Reboot the workstation.

TABLE 7.1 Files to Be Copied to a Windows 98 Workstation to Create an Application Launcher Shell

FILE	SOURCE	LOCATION
NALWIN32.EXE	Z:\PUBLIC	C:\NOVELL\CLIENT32
NALRES32.DLL	Z:\PUBLIC\NLS\ENGLISH	C:\NOVELL\CLIENT32\NLS\ENGLISH
NALBMP32.DLL	Z:\PUBLIC\NLS\ENGLISH	C:\NOVELL\CLIENT32\NLS\ENGLISH
NALEXP32.HLP	Z:\PUBLIC\NLS\ENGLISH	C:\NOVELL\CLIENT32\NLS\ENGLISH
NALEXP32.CN	Z:\PUBLIC\NLS\ENGLISH	C:\NOVELL\CLIENT32\NLS\ENGLISH
NWAPP32.DLL	Z:\PUBLIC	C:\NOVELL\CLIENT32

Use the following steps to set Application Launcher as the Shell on a Windows NT/2000/XP workstation with the ZENworks for Desktops client installed on it:

1. Copy the files specified in Table 7.2 from the source location to the destination location.

   Run REGEDIT.EXE and navigate to the following setting: HKEY_LOCAL_MACHINE\SOFTWARE\Microsoft\WindowsNT\CurrentVersion\Winlogon

2. Replace the **SHELL** value of the entry with the following one:
   SHELL=C:\WINNT\SYSTEM32\NALWIN32.EXE

3. Close REGEDIT.

4. Reboot the workstation.

TABLE 7.2 Files to be Copied to a Windows NT/2000/XP Workstation to Create an Application Launcher Shell

FILE	SOURCE	LOCATION
NALWIN32.EXE	Z:\PUBLIC	C:\WINNT\SYSTEM32
NALRES32.DLL	Z:\PUBLIC\NLS\ENGLISH	C:\WINNT\SYSTEM32\ NLS\ENGLISH
NALBMP32.DLL	Z:\PUBLIC\NLS\ENGLISH	C:\WINNT\SYSTEM32\ NLS\ENGLISH
NALEXP32.HLP	Z:\PUBLIC\NLS\ENGLISH	C:\WINNT\SYSTEM32\ NLS\ENGLISH
NALEXP32.CNT	Z:\PUBLIC\NLS\ENGLISH	C:\WINNT\SYSTEM32\ NLS\ENGLISH
NWAPP32.DLL	Z:\PUBLIC	C:\WINNT\SYSTEM32

Automating Application Objects

The final step in setting up the application distribution environment is automating Application objects. Automating Application objects is the process of setting up scripting, scheduling, and macros to remove required interaction with Application object distribution. This step is optional; however, you might want to use some of the following options to make the application distribution seamless for users.

Manage Application Object Macros

One way to automate Application objects is to use the Macros property page to manage the Application object macros that you create expressly for this Application object and that are used on other property pages of the Application object. You can use all types of macros (including Application object macros) in the following Application object locations:

▶ Path to Executable (Identification property page)

▶ Command Line (Environment property page)

▶ Working Directory (Environment property page)

▶ Mapping Path (Drives/Ports property page)

▶ Capture Port Path (Drives/Ports property page)

▶ Registry Settings Property Page: Key, Name, Value (String only)

▶ .INI Settings Property Page: Group, Name, Value

▶ Application Files Property Page: Source/Target, Directory

▶ Text Files Property Page: Find and Add String

▶ Icons/Shortcuts Property Page: All locations

> **TIP** You can put macros within macros. For example:
> %TARGET_PATH%=%*WINDISK%\Program Files
> EMAIL_ADDRESS=%CN%@acme.com.

To access the Macros property page, use the following steps from within ConsoleOne:

1. Right-click the Application object and click Properties.

2. Click the Common tab and select Macros from the drop-down menu.

3. Click Import. Browse and highlight the Application Object template (.AOT or .AXT) file that you created with snAppShot, and then click Open.

   Or click Add and then String to create a new macro template entry. Name the macro and include a value, and then click OK.

   Or click Add Then Prompted and then either String or Drive to create a new macro template entry. Name the macro and include a default value and prompt string, and then click OK.

> **TIP** For best results, use a UNC pathname for the source path rather than a mapped drive. If you use a mapped drive letter as the source drive, some files might not copy correctly.

Prompted Macros

One way to automate Application objects is to use the Macros property page to set up special prompted macros. Sometimes the user has a different system setup than what the administrator expects.

For example, users might want to place an application on a different drive than what was described in the Application object. Prompted macros enable the administrator to request that the users be prompted for the information. By using the prompted macros feature, the administrator can request the destination drive from the users so that the resulting distribution goes to the specified drive.

To set up prompted macros, access the Macros property panel. Select Add, Prompted, String from within ConsoleOne. A window similar to the one shown in Figure 7.8 is displayed. From the prompted macro window, you can set up the following options for the macro:

▶ *Prompt text*—Textual information to be displayed to the user when prompting for the macro.

▶ *Macro name*—Name setup for the macro for install scripts, and so on.

▶ *Default value*—You can specify a default value for the macro.

▶ *Minimum disk space*—You can specify a minimum amount of disk space required in setting the macro.

▶ *Maximum string length*—You can use this option to specify the maximum number of characters allowed for string macros.

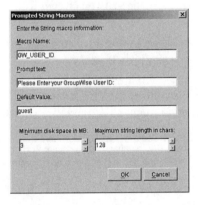

FIGURE 7.8
The prompted string macro property window for Application objects in ConsoleOne.

Special Windows Macros

Another way to automate application distribution is by using special Windows macros. A special Windows macro is one that defines Windows 98 and Windows NT/2000/XP directories. The typical paths are based on default installations and might not match your specific setup. On

Windows 98 workstations, macros behave differently if User Profiles are enabled.

The following macros are very helpful for redirecting application files that expect Windows directories to be in a particular location:

```
%*WinDir% Windows directory, typically c:windows or c:winnt
%*WinSysDir% Windows system directory, typically
➥c:\windows\system or c:\winnt\system32
%*WinDisk% Drive letter (plus colon) for Windows directory,
➥typically c:
%*WinSysDisk% Drive letter (plus colon) for Windows system
➥directory c:
%*WinSys16Dir% Windows NT** 16-bit system directory
➥(c:\winnt\system)
%*TempDir% Windows temporary directory (c:\windows\temp)
```

> **NOTE** The asterisk character (*) is required syntax for these macros. Don't confuse these asterisk characters with the Novell trademark asterisk.

Login Script Variables

Another way to automate application distribution is by using login script variables. Application Launcher supports the familiar or traditional login script variables; however, not all login script variables are supported.

Table 7.3 displays a list of supported login script macros and what they mean. Alternative macro names are shown in parentheses.

TABLE 7.3   Login Script Macros

LOGIN SCRIPT MACRO	DEFINITION
DAY	Numeric day of the month. For example: 01, 10, 15, and so on.
FILESERVER (FILE_SERVER)	Name of the NetWare file server of eDirectory* monitored connection. For example: APPS_PROD.
FULL_NAME	Full name attribute of the User object. For example: Jane Doe.
HOUR24 (24HOUR)	Time of the day according to a 24-hour clock. For example: 02, 05, 14, 22, and so on.

TABLE 7.3 Continued

LOGIN SCRIPT MACRO	DEFINITION
HOUR (HOURS)	Hour of the day. For example: 0 = 12, 13 = 1, and so on.
LAST_NAME	Last name of the current user (also known as the user's eDirectory Surname attribute).
LOGIN_NAME	First eight bytes of the user's eDirectory object name. For example: jsmith.
MINUTE (MINUTES)	Current minute. For example: 02, 59, and so on.
MONTH	Current month number. For example: 01 for January, and so on.
NDAY_OF_WEEK	Numeric day of the week. For example: 1 for Sunday, and so on.
NETWORK (NETWORK_ADDRESS)	Workstation network address. For example: 01010120.
OS_VERSION	Version of the OS. For example: v5.00. (Win3 shows DOS version, Win 98 and NT/2000/XP shows Windows version).
OS	OS type. For example: MSDOS, WIN98, WINNT, and so on. (Win3 shows MSDOS.)
PLATFORM	Platform running. For example: WIN, W98, WNT and so on.
PHYSICAL_STATION (P_STATION)	MAC address. For example: 0000C04FD92ECA.
REQUESTER_CONTEXT	Context of the requester (for the selected tree).
SECOND (SECONDS)	Number of seconds. For example: 03, 54, and so on.
SHORT_YEAR	Short year number. For example: 97, 00, and so on.
WINVER	Windows version. For example: v3.11, v4.00, and so on.
YEAR	Full year number. For example: 1997, and so on.

eDirectory Attribute Macros

Another useful tool in automating application distribution is using eDirectory attribute macros. Application Launcher supports macros that pull information from the attributes of the currently logged-in user, the current Application object, or from the attributes of other eDirectory objects.

An example of using eDirectory attribute macros is a GroupWise* Application object that runs OFWIN.EXE with a command-line parameter:

`/@U-@USERNAME@`

USERNAME can be replaced with a macro that uses a user's eDirectory* common name (CN):

`/@U-@%CN%@`

If the eDirectory object name is the same as the e-mail login for GroupWise, every user who runs the application has the correct user-name passed into GroupWise.

Table 7.4 displays variables that are defined by an attribute in an eDirectory object that can be used as eDirectory attribute macros.

TABLE 7.4 eDirectory Attribute Macros

ATTRIBUTE MACRO	EDIRECTORY OBJECT ATTRIBUTE
%CN%	Common Name (user's object name or login name)
%DN%	User's Full Distinguished Name (used with Application Launcher only)
%Given Name%	Given Name
%Surname%	Last Name
%Full Name%	Full Name
%Telephone Number%	Telephone
%Home Directory%	Home Directory
%Email Address%	E-mail Address
%Mailbox ID%	Mailbox ID

Environment Variables

Another useful tool in automating application distribution is using environment variables. The following are some examples of environment variables that Application Launcher supports:

▶ %NWLANGUAGE%

▶ %TEMP%

▶ %PATH%

NOTE The value of the variable must not exceed the length of the Application object name; otherwise, the variable fails.

Schedule Application Pre-Install

Another useful tool in automating application distribution is to schedule application pre-install. Earlier in this chapter, you read about using the Pre-Install property panel for Application objects to set schedules of when the application will be pre-installed to the workstation. Set up large application distributions to be pre-installed in advance so that the objects are locally available to users. This provides you with the following safeguards:

▶ Low network bandwidth can't inhibit deployment of the application.

▶ You know for certain that all workstations are set up and ready to deploy the application.

▶ You don't need to stagger workstation installs over a period of time, making the transition much easier for users.

Schedule Application Availability

Another useful tool in automating application distribution is scheduling application availability. Earlier in this chapter, you read about using the Scheduling property panel for Application objects to set schedules of when the application is available. You can use this to help automate when users can access the Application object.

Create Application Scripts

Another useful tool available to automate application distribution is the use of the Scripts property page to set up scripts that are executed automatically each time the application is launched and closed. Unlike environment parameters, scripts can overwrite existing drive mappings and printer ports.

The two types of application scripts are the startup script and the post-termination script. *Run before launching* (or startup) scripts are executed after the environment is set and before the application is launched. *Run after termination* (or post-termination) scripts are executed after the application is closed and before the network resources are cleaned up.

The following are some examples of how you can use application scripts:

- ▶ To provide extra mappings beyond those defined on the Drives/Ports property page

- ▶ To provide a mapping to override another mapping

- ▶ To run other applications

- ▶ To log in to other servers or eDirectory* trees

- ▶ To terminate applications under certain circumstances

The following are examples of script syntax:

```
#ipconfig.exe /renew
```

This example runs the ipconfig application to renew the DHCP configuration, pausing the script processing until Calculator returns control.

```
@ ipconfig.exe /renew
```

This example runs the ipconfig application to renew the DHCP concurrently with the remainder of the script processing.

To create Application object scripts, use the steps listed in the "Creating Pre-Install Scripts and Launch Scripts for Application Objects" section, earlier in this chapter.

TIP Clean-up commands (for cleaning up the changes made by the pre-launch script) should be placed in the post-termination script. The post-termination script is run after Application Launcher detects that the application has terminated.

The following is a list of scripting commands that Application Launcher
does not support:

- CLS
- DISPLAY
- EXIT
- FDISPLAY
- INCLUDE
- LASTLOGINTIME
- NO_DEFAULT
- NOSWAP
- PAUSE
- PCCOMPATIBLE
- SCRIPT_SERVER
- SET_TIME
- SWAP
- WRITE

The following is a list of actions that Application Launcher scripting does
not perform:

- Output anything to the screen
- Display errors
- Pause

Distribute the Applications

Once you have created the Application object, have set up the properties
for the object, and have set up the distribution options, the final step is
to actually distribute the Application object to the users. To do this, do
nothing. That is what ZENworks for Desktops application distribution is
all about. Once you have it set up, ZENworks for Desktops automatically
distributes the application according to your Application object settings.

Setting Up User Policies

This chapter discusses the use and creation of user policies. User policies are associated with users and affect their working environment.

You can create User Policy Packages in ZENworks for Desktops 4 for any of the Windows 32 environments, namely Windows 98/NT/2000/XP. The support for Windows 95 is available only with the ZENworks 3.x version; Windows 3.1 support is available only with the ZENworks 2 version.

Relationship of User Policies to Users

Users are associated with user policies through associations with policies in any of three ways: 1) policies can be associated with the user object directly; 2) policies can be associated with a parent container of the user object; and 3) policies can be associated with a group to which the user is a member.

When a user logs into the tree, a ZENworks for Desktops 4 agent (Workstation Manager Service) walks up the tree looking for the first User Policy Package it can find that is associated with the user. Like all agents associated with ZENworks for Desktops 4, the order that the tree is searched is dependent on standard Novell Directory Services behavior and any search policies in the tree.

When a policy is being searched from the tree, the Workstation Manager agent walks the tree until it finds the root of the tree or a search policy that limits the searching. All of the applicable user policies are merged and then the culmination is applied to the workstation. If any policy conflicts exist (such as two user policies affecting the same parameter), the parameter setting in the first policy is applied.

The remote control policy can be created for both the user and the workstation. In the instances when a remote control policy exists for both the user and the workstation, the remote control subsystem takes the most restrictive combination of the policies. For example, if one policy says to prompt the user for permission and the other does not, the system prompts the user.

General and Platform-Specific Policy Advantages

ZENworks 4 gives you easier administration by selecting policies in one place (the general page) and applying to all types of workstations that your users access. At the same time, you do not lose the ability to have unique policies for each platform, because the general policies can be overridden by a platform-specific policy (alternate platform page).

Regardless of the users who are logged into the system, each workstation finds the policies associated with it for that user, whether the policies come from the general policies or from the platform specific set, and executes the administrative configurations for that workstation.

On some occasions, you might want to associate a particular, unique policy to a set of users who are housed in containers along with other users of the same type. You can then create a group of users and associate specific policies to those users by associating the policy package to the user group. Consequently, these users receive the policies from this group rather than from the container.

Creating a User Policy Package

In order to create a policy that affects users who are logging into the tree through workstations, you need to create a User Policy Package. To create a User Policy Package, do the following:

1. Start ConsoleOne.

2. Browse to the container where you want to have the policy package. Make sure you have the container where you want the policy package selected in ConsoleOne. Remember that you do not have to create the policy package in the container where you are doing the associations. You can associate the same policy package to many containers in your tree.

3. Create the policy package by right-clicking and choosing New, Policy Package or by selecting the Policy Package icon on the toolbar.

4. Select the User Package object in the wizard panel and press Next.

5. Enter the desired name of the package in the Policy Package Name field and select the container where you want the package to be located. The container field is already filled in with the selected container so you should not have to browse to complete this field. If you do need to browse, press the Browser button next to the field and find the container where you want the policy object stored. Press Next.

6. Select the Define Additional Attributes field in order to go into the properties of your new object and activate some policies. Press Finish.

7. Check and set any policies you desire for this User Policy Package and press OK.

The following subsections describe each of the fields and property pages that are available in the User Policy Package.

Policies Property Page

All of the user policies are activated within the policies property page. Initially, the page is on the general policies. As other platforms are selected, additional policies are displayed. You can select which platform to display by clicking the word *Policies* in the tab. This activates a drop-down menu that allows you to select which platform-specific page you want to display, (see Figure 8.1).

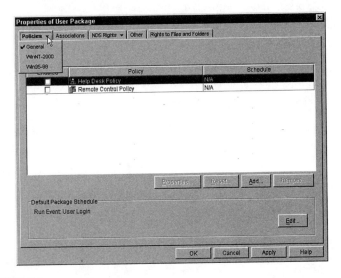

FIGURE 8.1
User Policy Package policies property page with drop-down menu.

The following sections discuss briefly each of the policy pages; subsequent sections cover the specifics of each policy.

General Policies
When you first go into the properties of the User Policy Package, you are presented with the Policy Property page. The policy page first displays the general category. All of the policies that are activated in the general category are active for all platforms supported by ZENworks for Desktops and associated with the logged in user.

Figure 8.2 shows a snapshot of the initial property page of the User Policy Package.

As you can see from Figure 8.2, only the Remote Control Policy and the iPrint Policy are available to all of the platforms supported by ZENworks for Desktops 4. The Remote Control Policy and iPrint Policy are discussed later in this chapter.

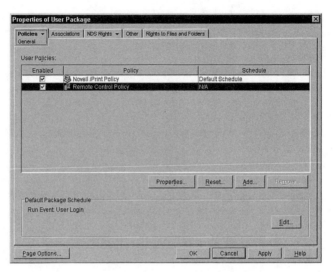

FIGURE 8.2
User Policy Package policies general property page.

In order to activate a policy, you simply need to check it. You can then go into the details of the policy and set additional configuration parameters on that specific policy.

Win95-98 Policies

Within the policies tab, you can select the Windows 95-98 policy page. This page displays the policies that are available for your Windows 98 users. These policies include the Windows Desktop Preferences policy, Remote Control policy, iPrint Policy, and the User Extensible policies. See Figure 8.3 for a sample of the Win95-98 policies page.

As you can see, the Remote Control policy is under the general and the Win95-98 policies page. When you select a policy in the Win95-98 page it supercedes any selections made on the General tab. The policies are not merged; only the platform-specific policy is used instead of the policy set in the general category. Also, only the policies selected in the platform-specific tab are used in place of the general policies. For example, if the remote control policy is selected in the General tab and is not selected in the Win95-98 tab, when an associated user logs into a Windows 98 system, the general remote control policy is activated for that user.

CHAPTER 8 Setting Up User Policies

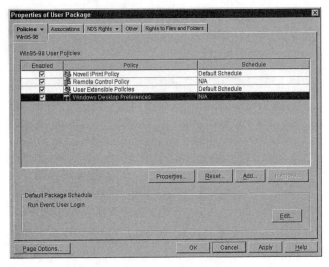

FIGURE 8.3
User Policy Package Win95-98 policies property page.

WinNT Policies

Within the policies tab you can select the Windows NT policy page. This page displays the policies for Windows NT users. These policies include the Novell iPrint policy, Dynamic Local User policy, Windows Desktop Preferences policy, Remote Control policy, and the User Extensible policies. See Figure 8.4 for a sample of the WinNT policies page.

As with the Win95-98 properties page, you can see the Remote Control policy is under the general and the WinNT policies page. When you select a policy in the WinNT page, it supercedes any selections made on the General tab for that platform. The policies are not merged; only the platform-specific policy is used instead of the policy set in the general category. Also, only the policies selected in the platform-specific tab are used in place of the general policies. For example, if the remote control policy is selected in the general tab and is not selected in the WinNT tab, when an associated user logs into a Windows NT system, the general remote control policy is activated for that user.

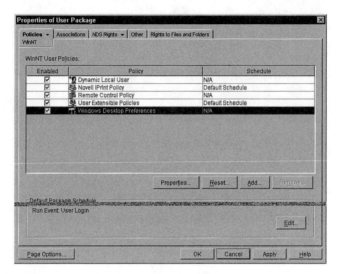

FIGURE 8.4
User Policy Package WinNT policies property page.

Win-2000 Policies

Within the policies tab you can select the Windows 2000 policy page. This page displays the policies for your Windows 2000 users. These policies include the Dynamic Local User policy, Windows Desktop Preferences policy, Novell iPrint policy, Remote Control policy, User Extensible policies, and the Windows Group Policy. See Figure 8.5 for a sample of the Win2000 policies page.

Note that the Remote Control policy is under the general and the Win2000 policies page. When you select a policy in the Win2000 page, it supercedes any selections made on the general tab for that platform.

WinXP Policies

Within the policies tab you can select the Windows XP policy page. This page displays the policies that are available for your Windows XP users. These policies include the Dynamic Local User policy, Novell iPrint policy, Windows Desktop Preferences policy, Remote Control policy, and the Windows Group Policy. See Figure 8.6 for a sample of the WinXP policies page.

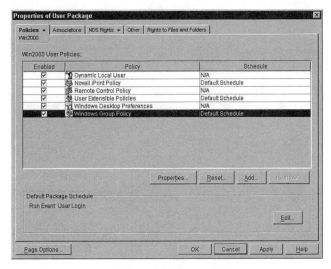

FIGURE 8.5
User Policy Package Win2000 policies property page.

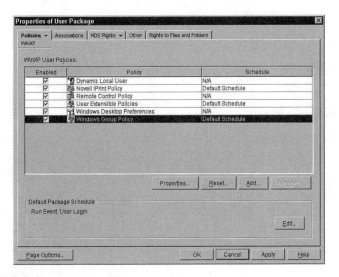

FIGURE 8.6
User Policy Package WinXP policies property page.

You can see the Remote Control policy is under the general and the WinXP policies page. When you select a policy in the WinXP page it supercedes any selections made on the General tab for that platform.

Win2000 Terminal Server Policies

Within the policies tab, you can select the Windows 2000 Terminal Server policy page. This page displays the policies that are available for your Windows 2000 Terminal Server users. These policies include the Dynamic Local User policy, Novell iPrint policy, Windows Desktop Preferences policy, Remote Control policy, User Extensible policies, and the Windows Terminal Server Policy. See Figure 8.7 for a sample of the Win2000 Terminal Server policies page.

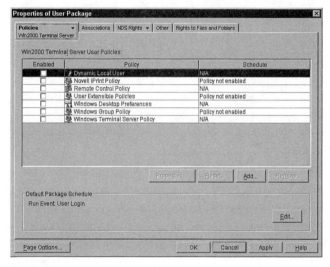

FIGURE 8.7
User Policy Package Win2000 Terminal Server policies property page.

You can see the Remote Control policy is under the general and the Win2000 Terminal Server policies page. When you select a policy in the Win2000 Terminal Server page, it supercedes any selections made on the general tab for that platform, as described in earlier sections.

WinXP Terminal Server Policies

Within the policies tab, you can select the Windows XP Terminal Server policy page. This page displays the policies for your Windows XP Terminal Server users. These policies include the Dynamic Local User policy, Novell iPrint policy, Windows Desktop Preferences policy, Remote Control policy, User Extensible policies, and the Windows Terminal Server Policy. See Figure 8.8 for a sample of the WinXP Terminal Server policies page.

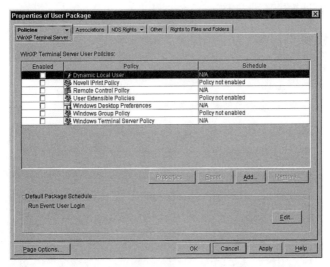

FIGURE 8.8
User Policy Package WinXP Terminal Server policies property page.

You can see the Remote Control policy is under the general and the WinNT Terminal Server policies page. When you select a policy in the WinXP Terminal Server page it supercedes any selections made on the general tab for that platform, as described in previous sections.

Associations Property Page

The Associations Page of the Windows User Policy Package displays all of the locations in the tree (containers) where the policy package has been associated. These associations do not necessarily reflect where the policy package is located in the directory. The Windows users who are in or below those containers have this policy package enforced. Choosing the Add or Remove buttons allows you to add or remove containers in the list that are associated with this policy.

NDS Rights Property Pages

The NDS Rights property page is made up of three sections. You can get to each of the pages by clicking on the small triangle to the right of the page name, and then selecting the desired page to be displayed.

These pages allow you to specify the rights that users have to this object. The following subsections discuss briefly each of these pages. These NDS Rights pages are displayed for every object in the tree.

Trustees of This Object Page

On this page you can grant objects rights as trustees of the User Policy Package. These trustees have rights to this object or to attributes within this object.

When you assign a container as a trustee of an object, everyone in that container or subcontainer has some rights to this object. To view the details of any trustee assignment (in order to modify the assignment), you need to choose the Assigned Rights button.

When you choose the Assigned Rights button, you are presented with a dialog box that allows you to select either [All Attribute Rights] (meaning all of the attributes of the object) or [Entry Rights] (meaning the object, not implying rights to the attributes).

From within the assigned rights dialog box, you can set the rights for the object on this package. You can set those rights on the object as well as any individual property in the object. The rights that are possible are the following:

▶ *Browse*—Although not in the list, this right shows up from time to time (especially in the effective rights screens). This represents the capability to view this information through public browse capabilities.

▶ *Supervisor*—This right identifies that the trustee has *all* rights, including delete, for this object or attribute.

▶ *Compare*—This right provides the trustee with the capability to compare values of attributes.

▶ *Read*—This right allows the trustee to read the values of the attribute or attributes in the object.

▶ *Write*—This right provides the trustee with the capability to modify the contents of an attribute.

▶ *Add Self*—This right allows the trustee to add himself as a member the list of objects of the attribute. For example, if this right were given to an attribute that contains a list of linked objects, the trustee could add himself (a reference to their object) into the list.

If you want to add the object as a trustee to an attribute, choose the Add Property button to bring up a list of properties or attributes that are available for this object.

From this list, you can select a single attribute. This attribute is then displayed in the Assigned Rights dialog box. From there you can select the attribute and then set the rights you want the trustee to have for that property. A user does not require object rights in order to have rights on a single attribute in the object.

Remember that rights flow down in the tree. If you give user rights at a container level, those rights continue down into that container and any sub-containers until that branch is exhausted or until another explicit assignment is given for that user in a sub-container or on an object. An explicit assignment changes the rights for the user at that point in the tree. You can also use inherited rights filters to restrict the flow of rights down into the tree.

Inherited Rights Filters Page

This page allows you to set the IRF (Inherited Rights Filter) for this object. This filter restricts the rights of any user who accesses this object, unless that user has an explicit trustee assignment for this object.

You can think of the IRF as a filter that lets only items checked pass through unaltered. Rights that bump up against an IRF filter are blocked and discarded if the item is *not* checked. For example, consider a user who has write privileges inherited at some point above the current container (they were explicitly granted that right at some container at or above the one we're in). This user runs into an IRF for an object or attribute that has the write privilege revoked (that is, unchecked). When the user got to that object, their write privilege would be gone for that object. If the object were a container, the user would lose write privileges for all objects in that container or sub-container.

You can effectively remove supervisor privileges to a portion of the tree by setting an IRF with the supervisor privilege turned off. You must be careful not to do this without someone being assigned as the supervisor of that branch of the tree (given an explicit supervisor trustee assignment at the container where the IRF is done) or you'll make that part of the tree permanent (that is, you can't ever delete any objects in that branch of the tree).

ConsoleOne helps prevent you from performing this action. It shows an error dialog box that keeps you from doing this without having first given an explicit supervisor assignment on the same container.

The Effective Rights Page

The Effective Rights property page allows you to query the system to discover the rights that selected objects have on the object you are administering.

Within this page, you are presented with the Distinguished Name (DN) of the object whose rights you want to observe. Initially, this is your currently logged in user running ConsoleOne. You can use the Browse button to the right of the trustee field and browse throughout the tree to select any object.

When the trustee object is selected, you can then move to the properties table on the lower half of the screen. As you select the property, the box to the right changes to reflect the rights that the trustee has on that property. These rights may be via an explicit assignment or through inheritance.

Other Property Page

This page might not be displayed for you, depending on your rights to the plug-in that now comes with ConsoleOne.

WARNING This page is particularly powerful. People who do not have an intimate knowledge of the schema of the object in question and its relationships with other objects in the directory should avoid using this page.

The intention of this property page is to give you generic access to properties that you cannot modify or view via the other plugged-in pages. The attributes and their values are displayed in a tree structure, allowing for those attributes that have multiple types (are compound types that consist of, say, an integer and a distinguished name, or postal code that has three separate address fields).

Every attribute in eDirectory is defined by one of a specified set of syntaxes. These syntaxes identify how the data is stored in eDirectory. For this page, ConsoleOne has developed an editor for each of the syntaxes currently available in eDirectory. When an attribute is displayed on this page, the editor displays the data and modifies when the user clicks the specific attribute.

For example, if the syntax for an attribute were a string or an integer, an in-line editor is launched, thus allowing the administrator to modify the string or the integer value on the screen. More abstract syntaxes such as octet-string require that an octet editor be launched, thus giving the administrator access to each of the bytes in the string, without interpretation of the data.

The danger with this screen is that some applications require that there be a coordination of attribute values between two attributes within the same object or across multiple objects. Additionally, many applications assume that the data in the attribute is valid, because the normal user interface checks for invalid entries and does not allow them to be stored in the attribute. If you should change a data value in the other page, no knowledge of related attributes, objects, or valid data values are checked because the generic editors know nothing about the intention of the field. Should you change a value without making all the other appropriate changes, some programs, and the system, could be affected.

Rights are still in effect in the Other property page. You cannot change any attribute values that are read-only, or change any values that you do not have rights to modify.

Rights to Files and Folders Property Page

This page in the property book is present in all objects in the directory. This property page allows you to view and set rights for this object for specific files and folders on that volume.

You must first select the volume that contains the files and folders in which you are interested. You can do this by pressing the Show button on the right and then browsing the directory to the volume object. Selecting the volume object places it in the volumes view. When that volume is selected you can use the Add button to add a file or folder of interest. This brings up a dialog box allowing you to browse to the volume object. Clicking on the volume object moves you into the file system. You can continue browsing that volume until you select the file or directory you are interested in granting rights.

Selecting the file or folder in the lower pane displays the rights that the object has been granted on that file or folder. To modify the rights, simply choose them to turn them on or off.

You can also see the effective rights that the object has on the files by pressing the Effective Rights button. This displays a dialog box, allowing you to browse to any file in the volume. The object's effective rights are displayed (in bold). These effective rights include any explicit and inherited rights from folders higher in the file system tree. Remember that anyone with supervisor rights to the server or volume automatically has supervisor rights in the file system.

Understanding iPrint Policy

The iPrint Policy option is available across all platforms and on the general policy page. It allows you to configure an iPrint client that can be placed on the workstation, allowing it to use Internet printing capabilities.

Client Install Page

This page allows you to specify the path on a server where the iPrint client is. Setting this option on the iPrint policy will cause the iPrint client to automatically be installed on the workstation. You can also specify the language and the version number of the software.

Settings Page

This page allows you to specify any set of printers you want to automatically install and configure on the receiving workstation.

Using Remote Control Policy

The Remote Control Policy option is available across all platforms and on the general policy page.

A Remote Management Policy is activated for this policy package by selecting the check box on the Remote Management Policy. The Remote

Management Policy is then activated for all users associated with the User Policy Package.

The Remote Management Policy controls the features of the Remote Management subsystem that ships with the ZENworks for Desktops 4. The Remote Management system is comprised of two parts:

- ▶ Remote Management Session Manager, which makes the connection and is used by the administrator

- ▶ Remote Management Agents, which are installed on the user's workstation

The remote control agent is part of the full ZENworks management agent and is installed as part of the agent installation process. You can run SETUP.EXE in the `public\zenworks` folder or get the MSI version of this from the Novell Cool Solutions and update sites.

The Remote Management system makes a peer-to-peer connection between the administrator's workstation and the remote workstation. You can do this using either the IPX or the TCP/IP protocol. In this policy, you can specify the preferred protocol for the connection. This protocol is attempted first, but if the connection cannot be made, the alternative protocol is used.

Remote controlling a workstation via ZENworks for Desktops 4 also requires rights within the Workstation Object that represent the workstation wanting to be controlled. Without these rights, the administrator is denied access to the remote control subsystem. Both the session manager and the agents validate that the user has rights to remote control the workstation. You assign the remote control rights through the Remote Management Rights wizard, or in the Workstation object in the Remote Operators page.

ZENworks for Desktops 4 added the capability to remote control via a password, without any workstation object in the tree. When launching remote control from the Tools menu of ConsoleOne, the dialog box that appears requires the IP address of the workstation and a password. This password must match the password entered by the user through the Security menu of the remote control agent (on the tray) of the workstation. The password use of remote control must be configured in the policy.

Remote Management Page

The Remote Management page identifies the features that you want to be activated with the Remote Management system. The following sections describe configuration options available under each of the tabs of the Remote Management policy window.

General Tab

The first tab of the remote management panel allows you to set the following general system functions:

▶ *Enable Diagnostics*—This allows the agent on the workstations to perform a diagnostics report. Select the workstation and then right-click and select Actions, Diagnostics of the menu. The Diagnostics utility performs some basic queries on the system and returns the information about the workstation. This information includes memory, environment, and processes running. Additionally, it would include NDS and Netware connection information, client information, network drives, and open file list, as well as printers, Network protocols, and network services active. You can also view the various event and error logs that have been recorded on that workstation.

▶ *Enable Password-based Remote Management*—This field allows the operator to establish password-based remote management with the workstation.

▶ *Terminate Session When Workstation User Logs In and Requires to Be Prompted for Permission*—Terminates any ongoing remote management session with the workstation when a new user, whose permission for starting a remote management session is required, logs in.

Control Tab

The Control tab enables you to set the following remote control functions:

▶ *Enable Remote Control*—When this option is enabled, the remote control subsystem can be activated. Without this setting, no one can remote control the workstations.

▶ *Prompt User for Permission to Remote Control*—This option displays a dialog box on the user's machine when a remote control session is started. The user can accept or deny the remote control request. The dialog box tells the user who wants to remote control their machine and asks if this is approved. If the user denies the remote control session, the session is terminated and the administrator cannot remote control the workstation.

▶ *Give User Audible Signal When Remote Controlled*—This option provides the user with a tone periodically while the remote control session is active. You can also set the number of seconds between each beep.

▶ *Give User Visible Signal When Remote Controlled*—This option displays a dialog box on the user's desktop while the remote control session is active. The dialog box indicates that the workstation is being remote controlled and who is controlling the workstation. You can set the number of seconds that you want to have between flashing the name of the user who is initiating the remote control session.

▶ *Allow Blanking User's Screen*—This option causes the screen on the remote desktop to be blank, preventing the user from seeing what the administrator is doing. When you enable the blanking of the screen, the keyboard and mouse are automatically locked.

▶ *Allow Locking User's Keyboard and Mouse*—When the administrator remote controls the workstation the keyboard and the mouse on the remote workstation are deactivated. The user can move the mouse or keyboard, but they will not function and any input from them will be ignored.

View Tab

The View tab enables the remote view functions. Remote view is the capability of the administrator to view the remote Windows screen of the target machine but not control the mouse or keyboard of the machine.

▶ *Enable Remote View*—When this option is enabled, the remote view subsystem can be activated. Without this setting, no one can remote view the workstations.

▶ *Prompt User for Permission to Remote View*—This option displays a dialog box on the user's machine when a remote view session is started. The user can accept or deny the remote view request. The dialog box notifies the user who it is that wants to remote view their machine and asks if this is approved. If the user denies the remote view session, the session is terminated and the administrator cannot remote view the workstation.

▶ *Give User Audible Signal When Remote Viewed*—This option provides the user with a tone periodically while the remote view session is active. You can also set the number of seconds between each beep.

▶ *Give User Visible Signal When Remote Viewed*—This option displays a dialog box on the user's desktop while the remote view session is active. The dialog box displays that the workstation is being remote viewed and who is viewing the workstation. You can set the number of seconds that you want to have between flashing the name of the user who is initiating the remote view session.

File Transfer Tab

The File Transfer tab enables the file transfer system. This allows you to send files to the remote workstation.

▶ *Enable File Transfer*—When this option is enabled, the file transfer subsystem can be activated. Without this setting, no one can send files to the workstations in question.

▶ *Prompt User for Permission to Transfer Files*—This option displays a dialog box on the user's machine when a file transfer session is started. The user can accept or deny the file transfer request. Within this dialog box, the user is told who wants to perform the file transfer from his machine and asks if this is approved. If the user denies the file transfer session, the session is terminated and the administrator cannot send the files to the workstation.

Remote Execute Tab

The Remote Execute tab describes the feature enabling of the remote execute system. This allows you to remotely execute a program on the remote workstation. The output of the program is not displayed on the administrative console.

▶ *Enable Remote Execute*—Enables the administrator to execute applications or files on the remotely managed workstation.

▶ *Prompt User for Permission to Remote Execute*—This option displays a dialog box on the user's machine when a remote execute session is started. The user can accept or deny the remote execute request. If the user denies the remote execution session, the session is terminated and the administrator cannot execute the program on the workstation.

NAT Tab

The NAT tab allows you to enable remote management operations across a NAT network boundary. The following options are configurable for remote management operations across NAT:

- ▶ *Accept Connections Across NAT*—This option enables the administrator to connect across NAT to perform remote management operations.

- ▶ *Prompt User for Permission to Remote Execute*—This option displays a dialog box to be displayed on the user's machine identifying the remote connection across NAT request. The user can accept or deny the remote connection request. If the user denies the remote connection request, the connection is terminated.

Desktop Preferences Policy

This policy is an option across all platforms. It allows you access to the ZAW/ZAK features that are exposed by the Microsoft Windows system. Within the ZENworks for Desktops 4 system, these ZAW/ZAK policies are divided into their logical parts: Desktop Preferences, User System Policies, and Workstation Policies. This policy allows the administrator to set the desktop preferences for any Windows system to which the user is currently connected. This policy follows the users as they move from workstation to workstation.

Microsoft provides tools called `poledit` for version prior to Windows 2000 and `gpedit` with Windows 2000 on. These tools allow an administrator to construct some Registry settings (ZAW/ZAK features) and have those settings saved in a file. These files can then be applied to any workstation by having the system look for these files on the server. The problem here is that these policy files must be located on every server that any user might use as an initial connection. With ZENworks for Desktops 4, this information is stored in these policies and into Novell Directory Services, thus making it always accessible to every user who connects to the system without having to place these policy files on every server.

Editing policies is discussed in more detail later in the chapter when group policies are discussed.

The Desktop Preferences policies allow the administrator to set Control Panel features as well as roaming profile configurations.

Roaming Profile Page

The settings for any particular desktop such as the desktop icons, screen colors, taskbar selections, and so on, are stored in profiles. These profiles can, with this Roaming Profile feature, be placed into the file system on the network. By doing this, when users who have profiles saved on the network log into any workstation, their profiles are retrieved from the network and brought to that workstation. This allows a consistent look and feel for the workstation to be presented to the users regardless of which actual workstation they are using. Any changes to the desktop, or preferences, are stored on the network and therefore reflected the next time that the user logs into any workstation. Figure 8.9 shows the Roaming Profile page.

In the Roaming Profile page, the administrator can set whether roaming profiles are available. If they are available, you want to also check the Enable Storage of Roaming Profiles check box. This option allows the profiles to be stored on a network server for access from any workstation.

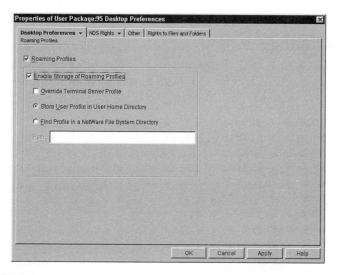

FIGURE 8.9
Roaming Profile page of a Windows Desktop Preferences policy of the User Policy Package.

The Override Terminal Server Profile option means that this user profile will override any profiles that they receive via the Terminal Server system available for NT servers.

Once the enabling of storage has occurred, you have the choice of either allowing the profiles to be stored in the user's home directory or in a specified file system directory. When you specify that the profiles be stored in the user's home directory, a subdirectory called Windows 95 Workstation Profile is created in the home directory. Within that directory, the profile information is stored and maintained.

If you identify a specific directory, all users who log into the workstation with that policy store the desktop information directly into that directory, and have the profiles shared with all users who log into that workstation. This is why storage into a specific directory is recommended for mandatory profiles only.

The NDS Rights, Other, and Rights to Files and Folders pages are described in the "Creating a User Policy Package" section earlier in this chapter.

The Settings Page

By clicking each of the icons presented in the Settings page of the Windows Desktop Preferences policy, the administrator can configure the properties of each of these Control Panel items.

The standard scenario is that the agent searches the tree for this policy and applies it during the user login process. You can change this schedule in the policy package to be another scheduled time or event. To ensure that these preferences are always applied when the user logs into the tree, regardless of the schedule in the policy, you need to check the Always Update Workstation During NDS Authentication check box.

Accessibility Options

By clicking this icon, you are presented with a tabbed dialog with the capability to set the following properties:

▶ Keyboard page allows you to set the standard Windows 95/98 Accessibility Options for StickyKeys, FilterKeys, and ToggleKeys.

▶ Sound page allows you to set the SoundSentry and ShowSounds.

▶ Mouse page allows you to configure the mouse keys.

▶ General page allows you to configure Automatic reset, Notification, and SerialKey devices.

Console

This icon brings up the property page that allows you to configure the properties of the console window (such as a DOS box) for the Windows 95/98 system. The Console Windows properties allow you to set the following:

▶ From the Options tab, you can set the console options such as Cursor Size, Display Options, Command History sizes and buffers, QuickEdit Mode, and Insert Mode.

▶ From the Layout tab, you can configure the Screen Buffer Size, Window Size, and the Window Position.

▶ From the Colors tab, you can set the console colors for the text and backgrounds.

From this policy, you cannot set the font properties of the Console window.

Display

Clicking this icon brings up the property page that allows you to make the following configurations:

▶ The Background tab enables setting of the wallpaper. You can specify that no wallpaper be presented or specify a filename of the .BMP file to be displayed for the wallpaper.

▶ The Screen Saver page enables you to determine whether a screen saver should be available. You can specify a particular .SCR or .EXE file to be executed for the screen saver. In addition to the screen saver program, you can specify if the screen should be password protected. Also on this page you can specify the capability to use the energy saving features of your monitor.

▶ The Appearance tab enables you to specify the color scheme that you want applied for this user. You can set the color scheme to any of the following choices: Windows Standard, Brick, Desert, Eggplant, High Contrast Black, High Contrast White, Lilac, Maple, Marine (high color), Plum (high color), Rainy Day, Red White and Blue (VGA), Rose, Slate, Spruce, Storm (VGA), Teal (VGA), or Wheat.

▶ The Plus page enables you to set some basic features of the Plus! Package. You can use large icons, show window contents while dragging, show smooth edges of screen fonts, show icons using all possible colors, and stretch the desktop wallpaper to fit the screen.

Keyboard

This icon allows you to specify character repeat rates and the cursor blink rate on the user's machine.

Mouse

This icon brings up the property page of the mouse system for the user. From this property page, you can set the following features:

▶ The Buttons tab provides you with the following features: button configuration for left- or right-handed mouse and double-click speed.

▶ The Pointers tab allows you to configure the mouse cursor to be used: 3D Bronze, 3D-White, Conductor, Dinosaur, Hands 1, Hands 2, Magnified, Old Fashioned, Variations, Windows Animated, or Windows Default.

▶ The Motion property tab gives you the capability to set the pointer speed, snap to default, and the pointer trail speed.

Sounds

This icon allows you to specify the sound scheme as one of the following for these users: No Sounds, Jungle Sound Scheme, Windows Default, Musica Sound Scheme, Robotz Sound Scheme, or Utopia Sound Scheme.

User Extensible Policies

This policy option is available across all platforms.

Microsoft has required that software packages that bear the Windows approved logo provide capabilities to be configured through .POL files. The `poledit` program allows you to edit these "extensible policies" and include them in the system .POL file. ZENworks also allows the policies that are stored in NDS to accept these additional extensible polices and provide them to all of the users who are associated with these policies.

The User Extensible policy allows you to import these special .ADM files into the NDS tree and have them administered and dispersed to the users associated with the policy package. Once these .ADM files have been imported into the tree, they can be administrated and associated to users in the NDS tree. These settings are applied like the User System Policies.

User Extensible Policies Page

When you first bring up the User Extensible Policies dialog box, you are presented with the User Extensible Policies page. An example of this page is displayed in Figure 8.10.

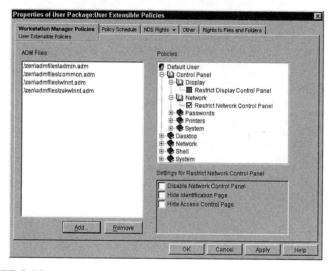

FIGURE 8.10
User Extensible Policies page of the User Extensible Policies policy.

This page is split into three areas: ADM files, Policies, and the policy-specific window in the bottom-right corner.

The files in the ADM file list are the policies that are applied to the users associated with this policy. To add a policy file to the list, use the Add button. You are presented with a file dialog box where you can browse and select the file. Remember that this file should reside on the server, as it is stored there for retrieval by the policy managers. When you browse and select a file, make sure it is on the server, and that the drive that you use is mapped correctly for all users who are associated with the policy. You can enter a UNC path in the filename field of the dialog box and thereby get a UNC path for the ADM file; however if you browse and then select, the program puts a drive letter into the path, thus necessitating that each user has the same drive mapping.

When this policy is initialized, four .ADM files are automatically pulled in by the plug-in into ConsoleOne. These include ADMIN.ADM, COMMON.ADM, WINNT.ADM, and ZAKWINNT.ADM. Each of these files is stored in the `ConsoleOne\bin\zen\admfiles` directory and is considered the default package.

NOTE The .ADM file must be stored on a server that users can access. The policy references the .ADM file and needs to retrieve it to apply it to the users and to allow the administrators to modify the settings. It's recommended, therefore, to use a UNC path in specifying the location of the file.

You delete the .ADM file from the applied set by selecting the file and pressing the Remove button.

NOTE Other .ADM files are available depending on which version of Windows you are running on your workstation. For example, Windows 2000 clients also include SYSTEM.ADM; there is an INETRES.ADM file for restricting Internet Explorer.

You can also modify the settings of the .ADM files by selecting the file in the ADM files windows. When you select the file, its Registry content is displayed in the Policies window. The user interface for this window mimics the `poledit` program available from Microsoft. The small window underneath the Policies box displays information about the selected Registry setting along with any categories that are available for the specific key. Selecting the key in the policies window populates the details fields.

You can browse through the ADM files and turn on, turn off, or leave as set in the Registry (unchecked and grey) for each of the keys as you would in the `poledit` program. Once you have made your changes, choose Apply or OK to update the ADM files on the server.

The NDS Rights, Other, and Rights to Files and Folders pages are described in the "Creating a User Policy Package" section earlier in this chapter.

The Policy Schedule Page

The Policy Schedule page enables you to customize (outside of the package default schedule) when you want the ADM files applied to the workstation/desktop of the user.

This page enables you to select when the package should be applied: Event, Daily, Weekly, Monthly, or Yearly.

Once you have selected when you want the package applied, you have additional fields to select in the lower portion of the screen. The following sections discuss these options.

Event

When you choose to have the ADM files applied when a certain event occurs in the workstation, you also need to select which event affects the changes.

The events that you can select include the following:

- ▶ *User Login*—This causes the policies to be applied when the user logs into the system. This happens after the user enters a username and password, but before the desktop appears and the user login scripts have started.

- ▶ *User Desktop Is Active*—This runs the policies after the user has logged into the system and all login scripts have been completed, but before the desktop is displayed. This is available with Windows NT/2000 only.

- ▶ *Workstation Is Locked*—This causes the policies to be applied when the workstation is locked (such as when the screen saver is activated and is locked awaiting a password). This is available with Windows NT/2000 only.

- ▶ *Workstation Is UnLocked*—This runs the policies when the workstation becomes unlocked, after the user has supplied the password to unlock the system. This is available with Windows NT/2000 only.

- ▶ *Screen Saver Is Activated*—This runs the policies when the screen saver is activated on an idle system.

- ▶ *User Logout*—This applies the policies when the user logs out of the system.

- ▶ *System Shutdown*—This applies the policies when a system shutdown is requested.

Daily

When you choose to have the ADM files applied daily on the workstation, you have to select when the changes are made.

This schedule requires that you select the days when you want the policy applied. You select the days by clicking on the days you desire. The selected days appear as pressed buttons.

In addition to the days, you can select the times the policies are applied. These times, the start and stop times, provide a range of time when the policies are applied.

To keep all workstations from simultaneously accessing the servers, you can select the Randomly Dispatch Policy During Time Period option. This causes each workstation to choose a random time within the time period when they retrieve and apply the policy.

Weekly

You can alternatively choose that the policies be applied only weekly.

In the weekly screen, you choose on which day of the week you want the policy to be applied. When you select a day, any other selected day is unselected. Once you have selected the day, you can also select the time range when the policy may be applied.

To keep all workstations from simultaneously accessing the servers, you can select the Randomly Dispatch Policy During Time Period option. This causes each workstation to choose a random time within the time period when they retrieve and apply the policy.

Monthly

Under the monthly schedule, you can select on which day of the month the policy should be applied, or you can select the last day of the month to handle the last day because all months obviously do not end on the same calendar date.

Once you have selected the day, you can also select the time range when the policy is applied.

To keep all workstations from simultaneously accessing the servers, you can select the Randomly Dispatch Policy During Time Period option. This causes each workstation to choose a random time within the time period when it will retrieve and apply the policy.

Yearly

Select a yearly schedule when you want to apply the policies only once a year.

On the yearly page, you must choose the day that you want the policies to be applied. You do this by selecting the Calendar button to the right of the Date field. The monthly dialog box appears. Browse through the calendar to select the date you want to choose for your policies to be applied. This calendar does not correspond to any particular year and might not take into account leap years in its display. This is because you are choosing a date for each year that comes along in the present and future years.

Once you have selected the date, you can also select the time range when the policy is applied.

To keep all workstations from simultaneously accessing the servers, you can select the Randomly Dispatch Policy During Time Period option. This causes each workstation to choose a random time within the time period when they will retrieve and apply the policy.

Advanced Settings

On each of the scheduling pages you have the option of selecting the Advanced Settings button, which allows you some additional control on the scheduled action that is placed on each user's workstation. Pressing the Advanced Setting button gives you a dialog box with several tabs to set the specific details of the schedule.

When first displayed, the Completion tab is activated. The following sections describe each field on the tabs and how it relates to the action.

Completion

The Completion tab allows you to specify what should happen on the workstation once the scheduled action has completed. You can choose any of the following:

▶ *Disable the Action after Completion*—This prevents the action from being rescheduled after completion. If you decide that the policy should be applied every hour, choosing this turns off that action. The policy will not be reapplied. This rescheduling only occurs and is reset when the user logs off and back onto the system.

▶ *Reboot After Completion*—This causes the workstation to reboot after applying the policies.

▶ *Prompt the User Before Rebooting*—This allows the user to be prompted before rebooting. The user can cancel the reboot.

Fault

This tab allows you to specify what should occur if the scheduled action fails in its completion.

The following choices are available to failed actions:

▶ *Disable the Action*—This results in the action being disabled and not rescheduled or rerun.

▶ *Retry Every Minute*—This attempts to rerun the action every minute despite any schedule specified in the policy.

▶ *Ignore the Error and Reschedule Normally*—This assumes that the action ran normally, and reschedules the action according to the policy.

Impersonation

These settings allow you to specify the account that should be used when running the action.

The following choices are available for the user type that is used to run the scheduled item:

▶ *Interactive User*—This option runs the action with the rights of the currently logged in user. This should be used if it is acceptable to run this action and not have access to the secure portions of the Registry, because most local users do not have access to the secured portions of the Registry or file system.

▶ *System*—This option runs the action in the background with administrative privileges. This impersonation level should be used only if the action has no user interface and requires no interaction with the user.

▶ *Unsecure System*—This option runs the action as a system described above, but allows user interaction. This is available only on Windows NT and 2000 and should be used carefully because NT does not normally allow a cross-over between user and system space.

Priority

This tab allows you to specify at which level you want the action to run on the workstation.

The following choices are available within the priority schedule:

▶ *Below Normal*—This schedules the actions at a priority that is below the normal user activity. This level does not interfere with the behavior of the system and gives the user a normal experience.

▶ *Normal*—This schedules the action at the same level as any user activity. This can cause the workstation to perform at a slower level because the service is competing with the user for resources.

▶ *Above Normal*—This level schedules the action at a higher priority than the user requests and results in being completed before user activity, such as mouse and keyboard input, is serviced by the system. Using this level allows the action to be completed faster; however, it can impact the user by resulting in slow performance on the client.

Time Limit

This tab of the scheduled advanced settings allows you to specify how long the service should be allowed to run before it is terminated. You can use this option to protect yourself from having the action run for long periods of time on the workstation. This terminates the action, which might cause the action to not complete properly. This tab is not normally used because you usually want the action to complete.

Dynamic Local User Policy

Often, several users within a company have access to shared Windows NT workstations, and it would be an administrative nightmare to have to keep up accounts for all users of these shared systems. Consequently, ZENworks for Desktops 4 can dynamically create accounts on the local NT workstation while the user is logging into the system. The local account is literally created at login time.

By having the system automatically create the account at the time that the user is authenticated to the Novell Directory Services tree, any of these users can log into any Windows NT workstation and have a local account automatically created on that workstation. To prevent the system from allowing any user to log into a specific workstation, you can administer the Restrict Login Policy in the Windows NT specific Workstation Policy Package. The Restrict Login Policy allows you to specify which users can log into the specific workstation. Figure 8.11 displays the dynamic local user policy page.

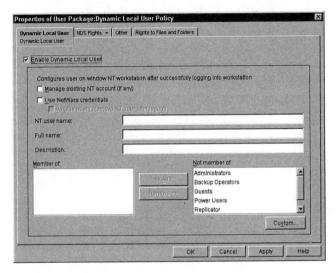

FIGURE 8.11
Dynamic Local User page of a Dynamic Local User Policy within a User Policy Package.

> **NOTE** This policy option is available on all platforms excluding Windows 95-98.

The NDS Rights, Other, and Rights to Files and Folders pages are described in the "Creating a User Policy Package" section earlier in this chapter.

Checking the Enable Dynamic Local User option allows the system to start creating accounts on the local system. The following options can be set in this policy:

▶ *Manage Existing NT Accounts (If Any)*—This option allows the ZENworks for Desktops 4 agents to manage a previously existing account for this user through the Dynamic Local User system. Any previously generated accounts are subject to the properties that you administer in this policy.

▶ *Use NetWare Credentials*—The system uses the Novell Directory Services password as the password for the local account.

▶ *Volatile User (Remove NT User After Logout)*—This check box is accessible only if you have previously checked the Use NetWare credentials box. This check box enables the system to remove the local account that was used for the dynamic user when the user logs out of the system. This feature in conjunction with the Manage Existing NT Account (If Any) option causes a previously created local account to become volatile and to be removed when that person logs out of the workstation.

▶ *NT Username*—This field is accessible only if the Use NetWare Credentials option is disabled. The system uses the specified name for the local account when any Novell Directory Services user logs into the system.

▶ *Full Name*—This field is accessible only if the Use NetWare Credentials option is disabled. The system uses the specified full name for the local account when any Novell Directory Services user logs into the system.

▶ *Description*—This field is accessible only if the Use NetWare Credentials option is disabled. The system uses the given description for the local account when any Novell Directory Services user logs into the system.

▶ *Member of/Not Member of*—These lists allow you to specify which local accounts, created or used for these users, are members of which local NT groups.

▶ *Custom*—This button allows you to create new custom groups in order to make the dynamic local users members of these groups.

If the NetWare credentials are not used for the Dynamic Local User policy—causing the NT username, full name, and description to be used—this account will always be volatile and will be created and then removed each time a user logs into and out of the workstation.

Additionally, if *any* password restrictions (including minimum password age or length or uniqueness) have been placed in the local workstation policy, the Dynamic Local User system is not activated for that workstation. A dialog box notifying the user that Dynamic Local User features have been disabled is displayed whenever anyone attempts to log into the workstation.

Windows Group Policy

The Windows Group Policy option is available on the Win2000 and WinXP platforms.

With Windows 2000 and Active Directory, Microsoft introduced the Group Policy to their servers. You can apply this policy to a set of users who are part of a container or a sub-container in Active Directory. Novell ZENworks for Desktops 4 incorporates this group policy into ZENworks by applying this policy to any group, user, or container in the tree.

The Microsoft Group Policy is nothing more than another .ADM file that is applied to all the users in the container—in Novell's case, users associated with this policy via direct association, group association, or container association.

Figure 8.12 displays a sample screen of this policy.

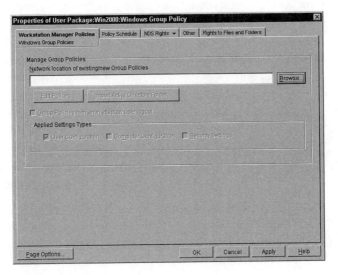

FIGURE 8.12
Group Policy of the Workstation Manager Policies page.

Network Location of Existing/New Group Policies

This allows you to specify or browse to the location of the group policy you want to edit or create.

- ▶ *Edit Policies*—If you are running on a Windows 2000 or XP workstation, the Microsoft Management Console editor appears. You can then edit the user and computer configuration settings.

- ▶ *Import Active Directory Folder*—If you want to create or access a group policy from Active Directory, this option allows you to browse to the folder where the Active Directory Group policy is and copy it to the directory specified in the Network Location field.

Group Policies Remain in Effect on User Logout

Check this box to indicate that the selected group policies remain in effect on the local desktop after the user has logged out.

Applied Settings Type

In earlier releases of ZENworks, it wasn't possible to apply computer configuration settings to a user. ZENworks for Desktops 4 allows you to apply Windows user, computer, and security settings to be selected with a user policy.

- ▶ *User*—This option enables the settings under User Configuration with the group policy.

- ▶ *Computer*—This option enables the settings under Computer Configuration (except security settings) with the group policy.

- ▶ *Security*—This option applies all security settings in the group policy.

The NDS Rights, Other, *and* Rights to Files and Folders pages are described in the "Creating a User Policy Package" section earlier in this chapter. The Policy Schedule page is described in the "User Extensible Policy," which also appears earlier in this chapter.

Windows Terminal Server Policy

The Windows Terminal Server policy option is available on the WinNT Terminal Server, Win2000 Terminal Server, and the WinXP Terminal Server platforms.

For a greater compatibility between ZENworks for Desktops 4 and other systems, ZENworks has included a new policy that allows you to administer your user's interaction and the behavior of terminal server available on Microsoft servers.

The NDS Rights, Other, *and* Rights to Files and Folders pages are described in the "Creating a User Policy Package" section, earlier in this chapter.

Figure 8.13 displays a sample page of this policy.

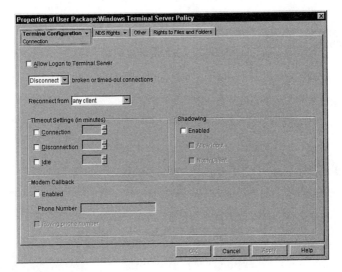

FIGURE 8.13
Terminal Server Policy of the User Extensible Policies policy.

In this policy, you can administer the various aspects of the terminal server, as follows:

▶ *Allow Login to Terminal Server*—This allows associated users the capability to log into the terminal server system.

▶ *Broken or Timed-Out Connections*—You can cause the system to disconnect these broken connections or choose to reset the connection.

▶ *Reconnect From*—This allows you to choose whether the reconnection should be done from any available client on the terminal server or from the previous client (the one that timed out).

▶ *Timeout Settings*—Here, you can set the time in minutes for each of the connection times, disconnect timeout, and idle timeout times.

▶ *Shadowing*—These fields allow you to enable or disable shadowing on the terminal server along with the options to allow input and to notify the client when shadowing is enabled.

▶ *Modem Callback*—This allows you to enable modem callback and administer the phone numbers to use.

Login Page

From the login page, you can specify the initial client configuration, including the workstation directory on the terminal server. Additionally you can specify whether to connect client printers at login and indicate the Terminal Server Home directory and profile paths.

## CHAPTER 9

Setting Up a Workstation Policy Package

This chapter discusses the use and creation of workstation policies. Workstation policies are associated with workstations and workstation groups, and affect their working environment.

Relationship of Workstation Policies to Workstations

Workstations are associated with Workstation Policies through associations with policies in any of three ways: 1) policies can be associated with the workstation object directly; 2) policies can be associated with a parent container of the workstation object; and 3) policies can be associated with a workstation group to which the workstation is a member.

The ZENworks for Desktops 4 Workstation Manager agent is activated on a workstation at user login time for Windows 98 systems, and on Windows NT/2000/XP systems, it is activated when the service is started. Once the ZENworks for Desktops 4 Workstation Manager agent is activated, it logs into the tree as the workstation and walks up the tree looking for the first Workstation Policy Package it can find that is associated with the workstation. Like all ZENworks for Desktops 4 agents, the order that the tree is searched is dependent on standard Novell Directory Services behavior and any search policies in the tree. All of the applicable workstation policies are merged and then the culmination is applied to the workstation. If any conflicts occur with the policies (such as two workstation policies affecting the same parameter), the parameter setting in the first policy is applied.

The remote control policy can be created for both the user and the workstation. In the instances when a remote control policy exists for both the user and the workstation, the remote control subsystem takes the most restrictive combination of the policies. For example, if one policy says to prompt the user for permission and the other does not—the system prompts the user.

Advantages of Platform Specific Policies

ZENworks for Desktops 4 enables the administration of specific policies for each platform that is supported in the system. By having a policy that is categorized for each type of platform, the administrator can make unique policies for each system. Regardless of the users who are logged into the system, each workstation finds the policies associated with it and executes the administrative configurations for that platform.

Occasions exist when you might want to associate a particular, unique policy to a set of workstations that are held in containers along with other workstations of the same type. You can then create a group of workstations and associate specific policies to those workstations. Consequently, these workstations receive the policies from this group rather than from the container.

Setting Up a Workstation Policy Package

In order to have a Workstation Policy Package, you must first create the policy package. To create a Workstation Policy Package, do the following:

1. Start ConsoleOne.

2. Browse to the container where you want to have the policy package. Remember that you do not have to create the policy package

in the container where you are doing the associations. You can associate the same policy package to many containers in your tree.

3. Create the policy package by right-clicking and choosing New, Policy Package or by selecting the Policy Package icon on the toolbar.

4. Select the Workstation Policy Package object in the wizard panel and press Next.

5. Enter the desired name of the package in the Policy Package Name field and select the container where you want the package to be located. The container field is already filled in with the selected container so you should not have to browse to complete this field. If it is not filled in, press the browser button next to the field to find the container where you want the policy object stored. Press Next.

6. Select the Define Additional Attributes field in order to go into the properties of your new object and activate some policies. Press Finish.

7. Check and set any policies you desire for this Workstation Policy Package and press OK.

The following subsections describe each of the fields and property pages that are available in the Workstation Policy Package.

Policies Property Page

All of the policies are activated within the Policies property page. Initially the page is on the general policies. As other platforms are selected additional policies are displayed. You can select which platform to display by clicking the small triangle to the right of the word Policies in the tab. This activates a drop-down menu that enables you to select which platform-specific page you want to display.

The following sections discuss briefly each of the policy pages; subsequent sections cover the specifics of each policy.

General Policies

When you first go into the properties of the Workstation Policy Package, you are presented with the Policy Property page. The policy page first displays the general category. All policies activated in the general category are active for *all* workstation platforms supported by ZENworks for Desktops 4 and associated to the workstation.

Figure 9.1 shows a snapshot of the initial property page of the Workstation Policy Package.

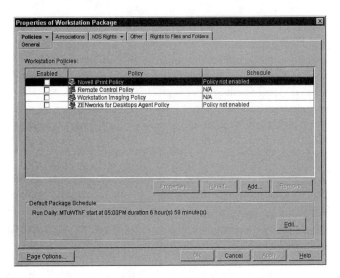

FIGURE 9.1
Workstation Policy Package policies general property page.

As you can see in Figure 9.1, four policies are available to all of the platforms supported by ZENworks for Desktops 4. They include the Novell iPrint Policy, the Remote Control Policy, the Workstation Imaging Policy, and the ZENworks for Desktops Agent Policy. These, as well as all of the other policies, are discussed later in this chapter.

In order to activate a policy, you simply need to select it. You can then go into the details of the policy and set additional configuration parameters on that specific policy.

Windows NT Policies

Within the policies tab you can select the Windows NT policy page. This page displays the policies that are available for Windows NT workstations, including the Computer Extensible Policies, the Novell iPrint Policy, the Remote Control Policy, the Workstation Imaging Policy, the Workstation Inventory, and the ZENworks for Desktops Agent Policy. See Figure 9.2 for a sample of the Windows NT policies page.

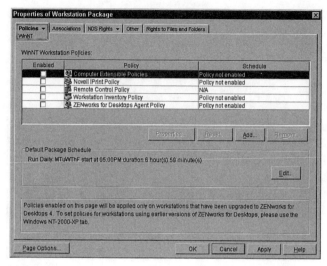

FIGURE 9.2
Workstation Policy Package, Windows NT policies property page.

As you can see, the same policies appear on the General and on the Windows NT policies page. When you select a policy in the Windows NT page, it overrides any selections made on the General tab for that platform. The policies are not merged, and only the platform-specific policy is used. For example, if the Workstation Import policy is selected in the General tab and in the Windows NT tab, agents on a Windows 2000 system use the Windows NT Workstation Import policy rather than the policy in the General tab.

Windows 2000 Policies

Within the policies tab you can select the Windows NT policy page. This page displays the policies that are available for Windows 2000 workstations, including the Computer Extensible Policies, the Novell iPrint Policy, the Remote Control Policy, the Windows Group Policy, the Workstation Imaging Policy, the Workstation Inventory, and the ZENworks for Desktops Agent Policy. See Figure 9.3 for a sample of the Windows 2000 policies page.

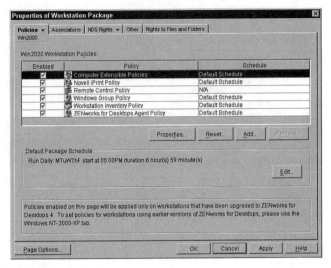

FIGURE 9.3
Workstation Policy Package, Windows 2000 policies property page.

As you can see, the same policies are on the General and the Windows 2000 policies page. When you select a policy in the Windows 2000 page, it supercedes any selections made on the General tab. The policies are not merged, and only the platform-specific policy is used. For example, if the Workstation Import policy is selected in the General tab and in the Windows 2000 tab, agents on a Windows 2000 system use the Windows 2000 Workstation Import policy rather than the policy in the General tab.

Windows XP Policies

Within the policies tab, you can select the Windows XP policy page. This page displays the policies that are available for Windows XP workstations. These policies include the Computer Extensible Policies, the Novell iPrint Policy, the Remote Control Policy, the Windows Group Policy, the Workstation Imaging Policy, the Workstation Inventory, and the ZENworks for Desktops Agent Policy. See Figure 9.4 for a sample of the Windows XP policies page.

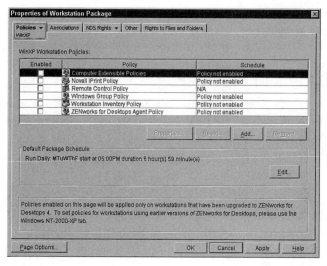

FIGURE 9.4
Workstation Policy Package, Windows XP policies property page.

As you can see, the same policies are on the General and the Windows XP policies page. When you select a policy in the Windows XP page, it supercedes any selections made on the General tab. The policies are not merged, and only the platform-specific policy is used. For example, if the Workstation Import policy is selected in the general tab and in the Windows XP tab, agents on a Windows 2000 system use the Windows XP Workstation Import policy rather than the policy in the General tab.

WindowsNT-2000-XP Policies
The WindowsNT-2000-XP tab provides backward-compatibility for workstations using previous versions of ZENworks. If you need to set policies for workstations that are using versions of ZENworks previous to ZENworks for Desktop 4, you need to set these policies using the WindowsNT-2000-XP tab.

Associations Property Page

The Associations page of the Workstation Policy Package displays all of the locations in the tree (containers) where the policy package has been associated. These associations do not necessarily reflect where the policy package is located in the directory. The agents that are associated with users or workstations that are in or below those containers have this policy package enforced. Choosing the Add or Remove buttons enables you to add or remove containers in the list that are associated with this policy.

NDS Rights Property Pages

The NDS Rights Property page is made up of three sections. You can get to each of the pages by clicking on the small triangle to the right of the page name, and then selecting the desired page to be displayed.

These pages enable you to specify the rights that users have to this object in the directory. The following subsections discuss briefly each of these pages. These NDS Rights pages are displayed for every object in the tree.

Trustees of This Object Page

On this page, you can assign objects rights as trustees of the Workstation Policy Package. These trustees have rights to this object or to attributes within this object.

If `user admin.novell` has been added to the trustee list, this user has some rights to this object. To get into the details of any trustee assignment (in order to modify the assignment), you need to choose the Assigned Rights button.

When you press the Assign Rights button, you are presented with a dialog box that enables you to select [All Attribute Rights] (meaning all of the attributes of the object) or [Entry Rights] (meaning the object, not implying rights to the attributes).

From within the Assigned Rights dialog box, you can set the rights the object can have on this package. You can set those rights on the object as well as any individual property in the object. The rights that are possible are the following:

▶ *Browse*—Although not in the list, this right shows up from time to time (especially in the effective rights screens). This right represents the capability to view this information through public browse capabilities.

▶ *Supervisor*—This right identifies that the trustee has *all* rights, including delete, for this object or attribute.

▶ *Compare*—This right provides the trustee with the capability to compare values of attributes.

▶ *Read*—This right enables the trustee to read the values of the attribute or attributes in the object.

▶ *Write*—This right provides the trustee with the capability to modify the contents of an attribute.

▶ *Add Self*—This right enables the trustee to add him or herself as a member to the list of objects of the attribute. For example, if this right were given on an attribute that contains a list of linked objects, the trustee could add him or herself (a reference to their object) to the list.

If you want to add the object as a trustee to an attribute, you need to press the Add Property button to access a list of properties or attributes that are available for this object.

From this list, you can select a single attribute. This attribute is then displayed in the Assigned Rights dialog box. From there, you can select the attribute and then set the rights you want the trustee to have for that property. A user does not require object rights in order to have rights on a single attribute in the object.

Remember that rights flow down in the tree, and if you give a user or an object rights at a container level, those rights continue down into that container and any sub-containers until that branch is exhausted, or until another explicit assignment is given for that user in a sub-container or on an object. An explicit assignment changes the rights for the user at that point in the tree. You can also use inherited rights filters to restrict this flow of rights down into the tree.

Inherited Rights Filters Page

This page enables you to set the IRF (Inheritance Rights Filter) for this object. This filter restricts the rights of any user who accesses this object, unless that user has an explicit trustee assignment to this object.

You can think of the IRF as a filter that lets only items checked pass through unaltered. Rights that bump up against an IRF filter are blocked and discarded if the item is *not* checked. For example, consider a user who has write privileges inherited at some point above the current container (they were explicitly granted that right at some container at or above the one they're in). This user runs into an IRF for an object or attribute that has the write privilege revoked (that is, unchecked). When the user gets to that object, his write privilege is gone for that object. If the object is a container, the user loses write privileges for all objects in that container or sub-container.

You can effectively remove supervisor privileges from a portion of the tree by setting an IRF with the supervisor privilege turned off. You must be careful to not do this without someone being assigned as the supervisor of that branch of the tree. Otherwise, you won't be able to delete any objects in that branch of the tree. ConsoleOne helps prevent you from performing this action by giving you an error dialog box. You cannot put an IRF on the [Entry Rights] of the object without having first given an explicit supervisor assignment on the same container.

Effective Rights Page

The Effective Rights property page enables you to query the system to discover the rights that selected objects have on the object you are administering.

Within this page you are presented with the Distinguished Name (DN) of the object whose rights you want to observe. Initially, this is your currently logged-in user running ConsoleOne. You can use the browse button to the right of the trustee field to browse throughout the tree and select any object.

When the trustee object is selected, you can then move to the properties table on the lower half of the screen. As you select the property, the rights box changes to reflect the rights that the trustee has on that property. These rights may be via an explicit assignment or through inheritance.

Other Property Page

This page might not be displayed for you, depending on your rights to the plug-in that now comes with ConsoleOne. This page is particularly powerful. People who do not have an intimate knowledge of the schema of the object in question and its relationships with other objects in the directory should avoid using this page. The intention of this property page is to give you generic access to properties that you cannot modify or view via the other plugged-in pages. The attributes and their values are displayed in a tree structure, enabling those attributes that have multiple types (are compound types that consist of, say, an integer and a distinguished name or postal code that has three separate address fields).

Every attribute in eDirectory is defined by one of a specified set of syntaxes. These syntaxes identify how the data is stored in eDirectory. For this page, ConsoleOne has developed an editor for each of the syntaxes that are currently available in eDirectory. When an attribute is displayed on this page, the editor displays the data and then modifies it should the user click the specific attribute.

For example, if the syntax for an attribute were a string or an integer, an in-line editor is launched, enabling the administrator to modify the string or the integer value on the screen. More abstract syntaxes, such as octet-string, require that an octet editor be launched, thus giving the administrator access to each of the bytes in the string, without interpretation of the data.

The danger with this screen is that some applications require that there be a coordination of attribute values between two attributes within the same object or across multiple objects. Additionally, many applications assume that the data in the attribute is valid, because the normal user interface checks for invalid entries and does not allow them to be stored in the attribute. If you should change a data value in the other page, no knowledge of related attributes, objects, or valid data values are checked, because the generic editors know nothing about the intention of the field. Should you change a value without making all the other appropriate changes, some programs *and* the system could be affected.

Rights are still in effect in the Other property page and you are not enabled to change any attribute values that are read-only or that you do not have rights to modify.

Rights to Files and Folders Property Page

This page in the property book is present in all objects in the directory. This property page enables you to view and set rights for this object on the volumes and specific files and folders on that volume.

You must first select the volume that contains the files and folders in which you are interested. You can do this by pressing the Show button on the right and then browsing the directory to the volume object. Selecting the volume object places it in the volumes view. When that volume is selected you can use the Add button to add a file or folder of interest. This brings up a dialog box enabling you to browse to the volume object; then clicking on the volume object moves you into the file system. You can continue browsing that volume until you select the file or directory to which you are interested in granting rights.

Selecting the file or folder in the lower pane displays the rights that the object has been granted on that file or folder. To modify the rights, simply select the rights that you want to have explicitly granted for the object.

You can also view the effective rights that the object has on the files by pressing the Effective Rights button. This displays a dialog box, enabling you to browse to any file in the volume. The object's effective rights are displayed (in bold). These effective rights include any explicit and inherited rights from folders higher in the file system tree. Remember that anyone who has supervisor rights to the server or volume objects automatically gets supervisor rights in the file system.

Computer Extensible Policies

Microsoft requires that software packages that bear the Windows approved logo be capable of being configured through .POL files. The `poledit` program enables you to edit these extensible policies and include them in the system .POL file. ZENworks also enables the policies that are stored in eDirectory to accept these additional extensible polices and provide them to all of the users who are associated with these policies.

The User Extensible policy enables you to import these special .ADM files into the eDirectory tree and administer and disperse them to the users associated with the policy package. Once these .ADM files have been imported into the tree, they can be administrated and associated to users in the eDirectory tree. These settings are applied like the User System Policies.

The NDS Rights, Other, and Rights to Files and Folders pages are described in the "Setting Up a Workstation Policy Package" section.

Computer Extensible Policies Page

When you first bring up the Computer Extensible Policies page, you are presented with the Computer Extensible Policies page. An example of this page is displayed in Figure 9.5.

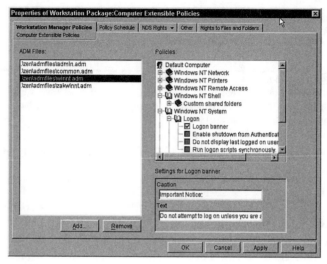

FIGURE 9.5
Computer Extensible Policies page of the User Extensible Policies policy.

This page is split into three areas: ADM files, Policies, Policy specific window in the bottom-right corner.

The files in the ADM file list are the policies that are applied to the users associated with this policy. To add a policy file to the list, simply press the Add button. You are presented with a file dialog box where you can browse and select the file. Remember that this file should reside on the server, as it is stored there for retrieval by the policy managers. When you browse and select a file, make sure it is on the server, and that the drive that you use is mapped correctly for all users who are associated with the policy. You can enter a UNC path in the filename field of the dialog box and thereby get a UNC path for the ADM file; however, if you browse and then select, the program puts a drive letter into the path, thus necessitating that each user have the same drive mapping.

When this policy is initialized, four .ADM files are automatically pulled in by the plug-in into ConsoleOne. These include ADMIN.ADM, COMMON.ADM, WINNT.ADM, and ZAKWINNT.ADM. Each of these files is stored in the `ConsoleOne\1.2\bin\zen\admfiles` directory and they are considered the default packages.

NOTE Other .ADM files are available depending on which version of Windows you are running on your workstation. For example, Windows 2000 clients also include SYSTEM.ADM; there is an INETRES.ADM file for restricting Internet Explorer.

NOTE The .ADM file must be stored on a server on which users have access. The policy references the .ADM file and needs to retrieve it to apply it to the users and to enable the administrators to modify the settings. It's recommended, therefore, that you use a UNC path to specify the location of the file.

You delete the .ADM file from the applied set by selecting the file and pressing the Remove button.

You can also modify the settings of the .ADM files by selecting the file in the ADM files windows. When you select the file, its Registry content is displayed in the Policies window. The user interface for this window mimics the `poledit` program available from Microsoft. The small window underneath the Policies box displays information about the selected Registry setting along with any subsetting categories. Double-click the key in the policies window to populate this details field.

You can browse through the ADM files and turn them on, turn them off, or leave them as set in the Registry as you can in the `poledit` program. Once you have made your changes, press Apply or OK to update the ADM files on the server.

Policy Schedule Page

The Policy Schedule page enables you to customize (outside of the package default schedule) when you want the ADM files applied to the user's workstation/desktop.

This page enables you to select when the package should be applied: Event, Daily, Weekly, Monthly, or Yearly.

Once you have selected when you want the package applied, you have additional fields to select in the lower portion of the screen. The following sections discuss the various options.

Event

When you choose to have the ADM files applied on an event that occurs in the workstation, you have the additional need to select which event affects the changes.

You can select from one of the following events:

▶ *User Login*—This causes the policies to be applied when the user logs into the system. This happens after the users enter their username and password, but before their desktop is shown and the user login scripts have started.

▶ *User Desktop Is Active*—This runs the policies after the user has logged into the system and all login scripts have been completed but before the desktop is displayed. This is available with Windows servers only.

▶ *Workstation Is Locked*—This causes the policies to be applied when the workstation is locked (such as when the screen saver is activated and is locked awaiting a password). This is available with Windows servers only.

▶ *Workstation Is Unlocked*—This runs the policies when the workstation becomes unlocked, after the user has supplied a password to unlock the system. This is available with Windows servers only.

▶ *Screen Saver Is Activated*—This runs the policies when the screen saver is activated on an idle system.

▶ *User Logout*—This applies the policies when the user logs out of the system.

▶ *System Shutdown*—This applies the policies when a system shutdown is requested.

Daily

When you choose to have the ADM files applied daily on the workstation, you need to indicate when the changes are made.

This schedule requires that you select the days when you want the policy applied. You select the days by clicking on the days you desire. The selected days appear as pressed buttons.

In addition to the days, you can select the times the policies are applied. These start and stop times provide a range of time where the policies are applied.

To keep all workstations from simultaneously accessing the servers, you can select the Randomly Dispatch Policy During Time Period option. This causes each workstation to choose a random time within the time period when they will retrieve and apply the policy.

You can have the policy also reapplied to each workstation within the timeframe every specified hour/minute/second by clicking the Repeat the Action Every Field and then specifying the time delay. This results in a scheduled action being run on every associated user's workstation for the selected repeat time.

Weekly

You can alternatively choose that the policies be applied only weekly.

In this screen, you choose which day of the week you want the policy to be applied. You can select only one day at a time. Once you have selected the day, you can also select a time range.

To keep all workstations from simultaneously accessing the servers, you can select the Randomly Dispatch Policy During Time Period option. This causes each workstation to choose a random time within the time period when they retrieve and apply the policy.

Monthly

Under the monthly schedule, you can select which day of the month the policy should be applied or you can select Last day of the month to handle the last day because all months obviously do not end on the same calendar date.

Once you have selected the day, you can also select the time range.

To keep all workstations from simultaneously accessing the servers, you can select the Randomly Dispatch Policy During Time Period option. This causes each workstation to choose a random time within the time period when they will retrieve and apply the policy.

Yearly

Select a yearly schedule when you want to apply the policies only once a year.

On this screen you must choose the day that you want the policies to be applied. You do this by selecting the calendar button to the right of the Date field. This brings up a monthly dialog box where you can browse through the calendar to select the date you want. This calendar does not correspond to any particular year and might not take into account leap years in its display. This is because you are choosing a date for each year that will come along in the present and future years.

Once you have selected the date, you can also select the time range for the policy.

To keep all workstations from simultaneously accessing the servers, you can select the Randomly Dispatch Policy During Time Period option. This causes each workstation to choose a random time within the time period in which they will retrieve and apply the policy.

Advanced Settings

On each of the scheduling pages you have the option of selecting the Advanced Settings button. It affords you some additional control on the scheduled action that is placed on each user's workstation.

When first displayed, the Completion tab is activated. The following sections describe each field on the tabs and how they relate to the action.

Completion

The Completion tab enables you to specify what should happen on the workstation once the scheduled action has completed. You can choose any of the following by selecting the check box next to the appropriate items:

- ▶ *Disable the Action After Completion*—This stops the action from being rescheduled after completion. If you chose to apply the policy every hour, choosing this turns off that action. The policy is not reapplied. This rescheduling only occurs and is reset when the user logs off and back onto the system.

- ▶ *Reboot After Completion*—This causes the workstation to reboot after applying the policies.

- ▶ *Prompt the User Before Rebooting*—This enables the user to be prompted before rebooting. The user can cancel the reboot.

Fault

This tab enables you to specify what should occur if the scheduled action fails in its completion.

The following choices are available to failed actions:

- ▶ *Disable the Action*—This results in the action being disabled and not rescheduled or rerun.

- ▶ *Retry Every Minute*—This attempts to rerun the action every minute despite the schedule that might have been specified in the policy.

- ▶ *Ignore the Error and Reschedule Normally*—This assumes that the action ran normally and reschedules the action according to the policy.

Impersonation

These settings enable you to specify the account that should be used when running the action. The following choices are available for the user type that is used to run the scheduled item:

▶ *Interactive User*—This runs the action with the rights of the currently logged in user. This should be used if it is acceptable to run this action and not have access to the secure portions of the Registry, as most local users do not have access to the secured portions of the Registry or file system.

▶ *System*—This runs the action in the background with administrative privileges. This impersonation level should be used only if the action has no user interface and requires no interaction with the user.

▶ *Unsecure System*—This runs the action as a system described above but enables user interaction. This is only available on Windows servers and should be used with care because normally Windows NT does not allow a cross-over between user and system space.

Priority

This tab enables you to specify at which level you want the action to run on the workstation. The following choices are available within the priority schedule:

▶ *Below Normal*—This schedules the actions at a priority that is below the normal user activity. This level does not interfere with the behavior of the system and it gives the user a normal experience.

▶ *Normal*—This schedules the action at the same level as any user activity. This can cause the workstation to perform at a slower level because the service is competing with the user for resources.

▶ *Above Normal*—This level schedules the action at a higher priority than the user requests and results in being completed before user activity is serviced.

Time Limit

This tab of the scheduled advanced settings enables you to specify how long the service should be allowed to run before it is terminated. This can be used to protect yourself from having the action run for long periods of time on the workstation. Terminating the action, though, might prevent the action from completing properly. Therefore, because you usually want the action to fully complete, this tab is not normally used.

Novell iPrint Policy

The Novell iPrint Policy is new with ZENworks for Desktops 4 and replaces all previous ZENworks print policies with a single effective, easy-to-use policy. You can control printer access using the iPrint Policy by taking the time to design a set of Workstation Policy Packages specifically organized to provide the correct workstations with access to the correct printers.

The iPrint policy, shown in Figure 9.6, allows you to specify the following options that will define how workstations associated to the workstation package print on your network:

▶ *Client Install Location*—Allows you to specify the network location of the iPrint client install you want users associated with this workstation object to use.

▶ *Language*—Allows you to specify the language to use when installing the iPrint client.

▶ *Force Install*—Forces workstations to install the iPrint client.

▶ *Reboot Option*—Forces the workstation to reboot immediately after applying the client install. This allows you to ensure the installation is complete.

▶ *Printer List*—Clicking the Add button allows you to add a list of iPrint printers installed on the workstation.

▶ *Force Default*—Allows you to force the workstations to use a specific printer as the default. This can be an extremely useful administrative tool when you need to push printing to a specific printer.

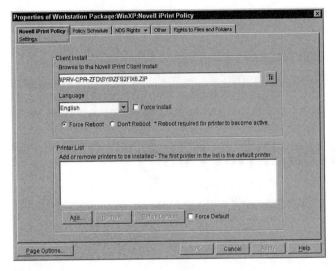

FIGURE 9.6
iPrint Policies page of a Workstation Policy Package.

Remote Control Policy

A Remote Management Policy is activated for this policy package by selecting the check box on the Remote Management Policy. Once this is selected, this Remote Management Policy is activated for all workstations associated with the Workstation Policy Package.

The Remote Management Policy controls the features of the Remote Management subsystem that is shipped with the ZENworks for Desktops 4 package and is not shipped with the ZENworks Starter Pack. The Remote Management system is comprised of two parts: Remote Management Session Manager, which makes the connection and is used by the administrator, and the Remote Management Agents, which are installed on the user's workstation. The remote control agents can be installed on the workstation when the client that is shipped with ZENworks for Desktops 4 is installed. The agents can be installed on the workstation through the remote control application objects that were added to your tree when you installed ZENworks for Desktops 4. You simply need to associate these application objects to the users or workstations and then have the ZENworks for Desktops 4 Application launcher install these agents automatically on the workstation. For more information, see Chapter 6, "Creating and Using Application Objects."

The Remote Management system makes a peer-to-peer connection between the administrator's workstation and the remote workstation. This is done using either the IPX or the TCP/IP protocol. In this policy, you specify the preferred protocol for the connection. This protocol is attempted first, but if the connection cannot be made, the alternative protocol is used.

Remote controlling a workstation via ZENworks for Desktops 4 also requires rights within the Workstation object that represent the workstation wanting to be controlled. Without these rights the administrator is denied access to the remote control subsystem. Both the session manager and the agents validate that the user has rights to remote control the workstation. The way that you assign the remote control rights is through the Remote Management Rights wizard or in the Workstation object on the Remote Operators page.

The NDS Rights, Other, and Rights to Files and Folders pages are described in the "Setting up a Workstation Policy Package" section.

Remote Management Page

The Remote Management page identifies the features that you want to be activated with the Remote Management system. Figure 9.7 shows the Remote Management page.

The following sections describe each of the options available from each tab of the Remote Management policy.

General Tab

This tab includes general system functions.

▶ *Enable Diagnostics*—This allows the agent on the workstations to perform a diagnostics report. This can be done by selecting the workstation and then right-clicking and selecting Actions, Diagnostics from the menu. The Diagnostics utility performs some basic queries on the system and returns the information about the workstation. This information includes memory, environment, and processes running. Additionally, it would include eDirectory and Netware connection information, client information, network drives, and open file list, as well as printers, Network protocols, and network services active. You can also view the various event and error logs that have been recorded on that workstation.

▶ *Enable Password-based Remote Management*—This field allows the operator to establish password-based remote management with the workstation.

▶ *Terminate Session When Workstation User Logs in and Requires to Be Prompted for Permission*—Terminates any ongoing remote management session with the workstation when a new user, whose permission for starting a remote management session is required, logs in.

▶ *Display Remote Management Agent Icon to Users*—Allows you to specify whether to display an icon in the system tray for users to access remote management, such as viewing remote management operations that are being performed on their workstation or terminating sessions.

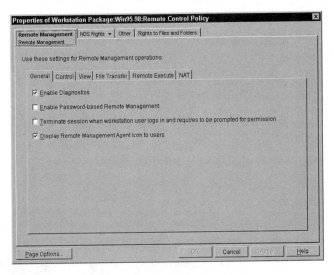

FIGURE 9.7
Remote Management Policy page, General tab of a Workstation Policy Package.

Control Tab

This tab describes the feature enabling of remote control functions.

▶ *Enable Remote Control*—When this option is enabled, the remote control subsystem can be activated. Without this setting, no one can remote control the workstations in question.

▶ *Prompt User for Permission to Remote Control*—This option causes a dialog box to be displayed on the user's machine when a remote control session is started. The user can accept or deny the remote control request. This dialog box tells the user who wants to remote control their machine and asks if this is approved. If the user denies the remote control session, the session is terminated and the administrator cannot remote control the workstation.

▶ *Give User Audible Signal When Remote Controlled*—This option provides the user a periodic tone while the remote control session is active. You can also set the number of seconds between each beep.

▶ *Give User Visible Signal When Remote Controlled*—This option displays a dialog box on the user's desktop while the remote control session is active. The dialog box displays that the workstation is being remote controlled and also displays the eDirectory name of the user who is remote controlling the workstation. You can set the number of seconds that you want to have between flashing the name of the user who is initiating the remote control session.

▶ *Allow Blanking User's Screen*—This option causes the screen on the remote desktop to be blank, thus preventing the user from seeing what the administrator is doing. When you enable the blanking of the screen, the keyboard and mouse are automatically locked.

▶ *Enable Locking User's Keyboard and Mouse*—When the administrator remote controls the workstation, the keyboard and the mouse on the remote workstation are deactivated. The user can move the mouse or keyboard, but they will not function and any input from them is ignored.

View Tab

This tab describes the feature enabling the remote view functions. Remote view is the capability of the administrator to view the remote Windows screen of the target machine but not control the mouse or keyboard of the machine.

▶ *Enable Remote View*—When this option is enabled, the remote view subsystem can be activated. Without this setting, no one can remote view the workstations in which the currently logged in user has this policy associated with their user object.

▶ *Prompt User for Permission to Remote View*—This option causes a dialog box to be displayed on the user's machine when a remote view session is started. The user can accept or deny the remote view request. Within this dialog box the user is told who wants to remote view their machine. If the user denies the remote view session, the session is terminated and the administrator cannot remote view the workstation.

▶ *Give User Audible Signal When Remote Viewed*—This option provides the user a tone periodically while the remote view session is active. You can also set the number of seconds between each beep.

▶ *Give User Visible Signal When Remote Viewed*—This option displays a dialog box on the user's desktop while the remote view session is active. The dialog box displays that the workstation is being remote viewed and also displays the eDirectory name of the user who is remote viewing the workstation. You can set the number of seconds that you want to have between flashing the name of the user who is initiating the remote view session.

File Transfer Tab

This tab describes the feature enabling of the file transfer system. This enables you to send files to the remote workstation.

▶ *Enable File Transfer*—When this option is enabled, the file transfer subsystem can be activated.

▶ *Prompt user for permission to transfer files*—This option causes a dialog box to be displayed on the user's machine when a remote view session is started. The user can accept or deny the remote view request. Within this dialog box the user is told who wants to remote view their machine. If the user denies the remote view session, the session is terminated and the administrator cannot remote view the workstation.

Remote Execute Tab

This tab describes the feature enabling of the remote execute system. This enables you to remotely execute a program on the remote workstation.

The output of the program is not displayed on the administrative console.

▶ *Prompt User for Permission to Remote Execute*—This option causes a dialog box to be displayed on the user's machine when a remote view session is started. The user can accept or deny the remote view request. Within this dialog box the user is told who wants to remote view their machine. If the user denies the remote view session, the session is terminated and the administrator cannot remote view the workstation.

NAT Tab

The NAT tab allows you to enable remote management operations across a NAT network boundary. The following options are configurable for remote management operations across NAT:

▶ *Accept Connections Across NAT*—This option enables the administrator to connect across NAT to perform remote management operations.

▶ *Prompt User for Permission to Remote Execute*—This option displays a dialog box on the user's machine identifying the remote connection across NAT request. The user can accept or deny the remote connection request. If the user denies the remote connection request, the connection is terminated.

Windows Group Policy

The Windows 2000 and Windows XP policy pages include the Windows Group Policy. This policy can be applied to a set of workstations that are part of a container of a sub-container in Active Directory.

The Windows Group Policy is nothing more than another .ADM file that is applied to all the users in the container—in Novell's case, users associated with this policy via direct association, group association, or container association.

The NDS Rights, Other, and Rights to Files and Folders pages are described in the "Setting Up a Workstation Policy Package" section.

Figure 9.8 displays a sample screen of this policy.

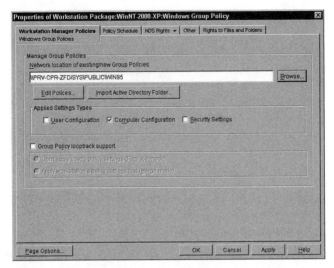

FIGURE 9.8
Windows 2000 Group Policy of the Workstation Policy Package.

This policy enables you to browse to the group policy ADM file (the default policy file for the Windows 2000 group policy is the default). You can then press the Edit button to launch the `poledit` program on the local administrator workstation in order to edit this group policy.

Workstation Imaging Policy

ZENworks for Desktops 4 has the capability to image a workstation and then to apply that image back to the original or other workstations. See Chapter 14, "Imaging a Workstation," for more detailed information on the functionality of the ZENworks for Desktops 4 imaging system.

The placement of an image associated with an Image object in the directory onto a workstation can occur three ways in ZENworks for Desktops 4.

▶ Booting the workstation with a floppy disk that communicates with the imaging agent on the server.

▶ Placing a special boot partition on an unregistered workstation that communicates with the imaging agent on the server.

▶ Placing a special boot partition on a registered workstation and setting the Put an Image On this Workstation on the Next Boot field in the workstation object.

Each of these ways results in the workstation being imaged with the image associated with the workstation or determined by the imaging agent that resides on the server. The way that the workstation finds the imaging server is when the imaging boot diskettes are created, the administrator can specify either an IP or a DNS name for the server. This information is saved on the diskettes or in the special boot partition.

The Workstation Imaging Policy comes into effect if the workstation is to be imaged and there is no image associated with the workstation object and the policy is activated.

This policy enables the administrator to create a set of rules that can govern when a particular image should be used, based on some basic information from the workstation. The imaging server follows the list of rules in the policy until one of the rules is satisfied. The rule that is satisfied results in an associated image that is then applied to the workstation.

Rules Page

This page enables the administrator to input the rules and associated images that the system uses to determine the image to place on a specific type of workstation. Figure 9.9 shows a sample of this page.

You must first press the Add button to add rules to the list. Once you have added several rules, you can then select a specific rule and change its order in the list, look at its properties, or remove the rule. When you choose the Add button, a dialog box appears, in which you add the rule to the policy.

Use the browse button next to the Use this Image field to browse to an image object in the tree that is associated with an image file on the image server. Once the image object is selected, you can identify the rule that is associated with this image. You can currently have six key/value pairs about the workstation to compare in order to determine which image to use.

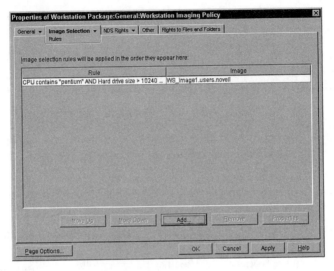

FIGURE 9.9
Rules page for a sample Workstation Imaging Policy of a Workstation
Policy Package.

In the middle of this dialog box, you can see the six potential equations
that you can generate to determine whether the image should be used.
The equation is made up of a series of True/False statements that are
combined with AND and OR logic. You construct the statement by filling
in the drop-down statements. (The resulting statement is displayed in a
more English-like view to help you understand the equation.)

The logic for the AND and OR operators is strictly left to right in the
equation. In the Rule Description box, parentheses are added to the
equation to help the administrator understand how the rule is evaluated.
You cannot insert the parentheses; they are automatically inserted and are
not under user control.

Select the key you want to examine via a drop-down dialog box. The
keys that you can choose from are the following:

▶ *Chipset*—This displays the reported processor. An example is
GenuineIntel Mobile Pentium MMX 233 MHZ.

▶ *Video*—This option captures the type of video adapter that is in the
workstation. An example of this is Trident Cyber9397 (rev 243).

▶ *Network*—This is the network adapter for the workstation. An example is "3Com."

▶ *Sound Card*—This is the sound card that has been reported. Often this field results in no sound card detected. This is because the system sends out a PCI request and, if no sound cards respond, you get this even if a sound card is present.

▶ *Hard Drive Controller*—This is the type of hard drive in the system. If the hard drive is an IDE device, the value for this field is IDE. If the hard drive is a SCSI device, you get the reported name of the device, such as `FUJITSU MHJ2181AT`.

▶ *MAC Address*—This is the MAC address of the network card. An example of this value is `00 60 80 03 C2 E7`.

▶ *IP Address*—This is the assigned IP address of the workstation. This is reported as the traditional `137.65.237.5`.

▶ *Hard Drive Size*—This reports the disk size in megabytes. Therefore an 8GB hard drive is reported as 8192MB in this field. The imaging system might not always report the full disk capacity. It's best to use a wide boundary when generating your rules. For instance, if you want to look for an 8GB drive, use the statement `Hard drive size > 8000MB`.

▶ *RAM*—This is the reported amount of RAM in megabytes. This field also might not always report the exact amount of RAM space that you would expect on your workstation. It is advisable that you use a wide boundary when generating your rules, as in the previous field.

When the workstation is booting the imaging system, it is in reality booting up the Linux operating system and running the tools that are included in the imaging system. The values for the keys described previously are values that the Linux system can report to the software. In order to discover what a system reports to Linux, you need to boot a sample workstation with the Imaging system boot disk and run the `Img` information command. This displays the information that is sent to the image server about the workstation. This information includes the data values that you put into the key comparison equations for your rules. You can also get this information from an image by opening the image in the ZENworks image editor and choosing properties on the image root. See

Chapter 14, for more detailed information on the functionality of the ZENworks for Desktops 4 imaging system.

The next step of the equation involves specifying the operator. Two types of operators exist: String and Integer operators. The Hard drive size and RAM fields are treated as integers, whereas all of the other fields are treated as strings. A case-insensitive string compare is performed to determine operator results. The string operators are contains, doesn't contain, begins with, and equals. The integer operators are =, <>, >, >=, <, and <=.

These operators perform expected comparisons between the key value supplied by the workstation to the imaging server and the value that you place into the value field of the equation. The following meanings are placed with each operator:

- ▶ *contains*—The specified value is a substring anywhere in the reported value.

- ▶ *doesn't contain*—The specified value is not equal to or contained in the reported value.

- ▶ *begins with*—The specified values are represented in the initial character of the reported value.

- ▶ *equals*—The specified value is the same as the reported value.

- ▶ = (equals)—The specified value is numerically equivalent to the reported value.

- ▶ <> (not equal)—The specified value is not equal to the reported value.

- ▶ > (greater than)—The specified value is greater than the reported value.

- ▶ >= (greater than or equal to)—The specified value is numerically equal or greater than the reported value.

- ▶ < (less than)—The specified value is less than the reported value.

- ▶ <= (less than or equal to)—The specified value is numerically less than or equal to the reported value.

The next field in the operation is where you enter the value that you want to compare. The far right field enables you to extend the operation to additional key/value comparisons. Your choices currently are AND and OR.

The Boolean operators are evaluated strictly from left to right. For example if the following rules were entered into the policy:

1. `Hard drive size >= 600MB AND`

2. `RAM < 16MB OR`

3. `RAM > 31MB`

The resultant evaluation would be (`Hard drive < 60MB AND RAM < 16 MB`) `OR` (`RAM > 31MB`). This would result in giving the image to any system that has a disk smaller than 200MB with less than 16MB of RAM. This would also give the image to any system that has more than 31MB of RAM regardless of the size of the hard drive.

You can view the precedence of the equation; complete with parentheses, on the bottom half of the screen as you introduce new key/value pairs into your rule.

Once your set of key/value pairs have been entered and you have reviewed your equation at the bottom of the screen, you press the OK button to include the rule into the imaging system. You are returned to the original Rules page with the rule that you had entered placed on the screen.

Once again, from this page, after you have entered some rules you can then specify the order in which the rules are evaluated. After selecting a rule you can move that rule in the order by pressing either the Move Up or the Move Down buttons. As the imaging server is evaluating the rules, the first rule that results in a **TRUE** evaluation results in that imaging being supplied to the workstation.

Workstation Inventory Policy

The ZENworks for Desktops 4 Workstation Inventory Policy page allows you to configure how workstations associated with this Workstation Policy Package are inventoried.

See Chapter 13, "Using ZENworks Workstation Inventory," for more detailed information about the inventory system with ZENworks for Desktops 4.

With the Workstation Inventory policy you identify where the collector of the inventory information is located, whether hardware or software scanning is done, and the capability to customize the scan list to identify programs without an identifying header. The NDS Rights, Other, and Rights to Files and Folders pages are described in the "Setting Up a Workstation Policy Package" section earlier in this chapter.

Figure 9.10 displays the Workstation Inventory page of the Workstation Inventory Policy.

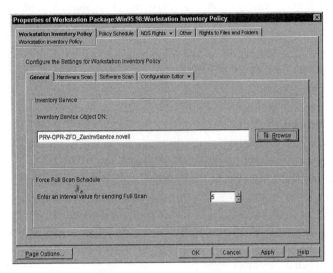

FIGURE 9.10
Workstation Inventory Policy within a Workstation Policy Package.

Within the inventory policy, the administrator can administer the following parameters:

▶ *Inventory Service*—This field represents the service object in the tree that represents the service module running on a server in the network. This server agent is responsible for receiving the information from the workstations and processing it, either by placing it in a local Sybase database, or forwarding it on to the next level of the inventory database hierarchy (see Chapter 12, "Creating a Server Policy Package"). All workstations that have this policy associated with them send their scanned information to the specified server agent.

▶ *Hardware Scanning*—This field allows you to enable DMI, WMI, and custom scanning as well as configure the custom attributes to scan for.

▶ *Software Scanning: Enable software scan*—This field turns on ZENworks for Desktops 4 agents to perform a software scan in addition to the standard hardware scan.

▶ *Software Scanning: Custom Scan Editor button*—Pressing this button brings up a dialog box that enables you to configure information about files found on a workstation. You can store the Vendor Name, Product Name, Product Version, File name, and File size in this list. When a file does not have header information, it is found in this table (by filename and size) and reported as the specified program. You can export and import these file lists into the eDirectory policy object.

▶ *Configuration Editor*—Allows you to import, export, and modify custom scanning configuration settings, such as ZIP file extensions to scan for, vendor and product rules, and asset information.

Policy Schedule Page

This schedule determines when the hardware and software inventories for associated workstations are run. See the "Computer Extensible Policy" section for a description of this page.

ZENworks for Desktops Agent Policy

The ZENworks for Desktops Agent is one of the most dynamic features of ZENworks for Desktops 4 because it enables you to maintain workstations that do not have the Novell Client installed on them. The ZENworks for Desktops Agent policy, shown in Figure 9.11, enables you to configure the following settings, which the agent running on workstations associated with the Workstation Policy Package will use:

▶ *Webserver IP Address or DNS Name*—Specifies the IP address or DNS name for the Web server that is running on the middle tiered server that the ZENworks for Desktops agent will use to connect the workstation to the network.

▶ *eDirectory Refresh Rate*—Specifies the amount of time in minutes that the ZENworks for Desktops agent will wait before checking eDirectory for changes in objects of policies. The default is 540 minutes. Each time the agent refreshes eDirectory information, traffic is generated on your network, so if you have a large number of workstations connecting through the agent you might need to make this a larger number.

▶ *Enable Login*—Allows you to specify whether the Novell Login windows is displayed when workstations running the ZENworks for Desktops agent are started.

▶ *Enable Volatile Cache*—When checked, this option allows volatile user information that has been cached on a workstation to stay cached on the workstation for the specified period of time. The default time is five days. Because volatile users are not created or removed at every login or logout, this makes login times much faster and makes it possible for a user to continue using the workstation even when the workstation is disconnected from the network and the user is not a registered user on the workstation.

▶ *Resident Workstation Welcome Bitmap*—Specifies the name of a bitmap file, located in the `\WINNT` directory of the workstation, that appears on the welcome screen when you start Windows NT/2000/XP. The default is blank (no bitmap).

▶ *Welcome Caption*—This field allows you to specify the caption that is displayed in the header of the welcome screen when you start Windows NT/2000/XP.

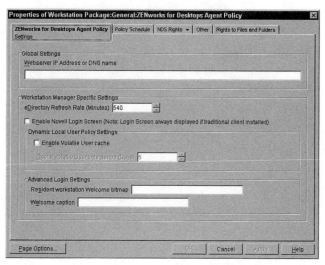

FIGURE 9.11
ZENworks for Desktops Agent Policy within a Workstation Policy Package.

Scheduled Action Policy

The Scheduled Action policy is a plural policy that enables you to specify one or more actions to perform on workstations associated with the Workstation Policy Package based on the policies schedule. Because it is a plural policy, you can create as many Scheduled Action policies for each platform in the Workstation Policy Package as you need.

For example, if you needed all of your DNS/DHCP clients to refresh their IP configuration every day at 8:00 a.m., you could create a Scheduled Action policy that runs the `IPCONFIG` utility twice, once with the `/release` parameter and once with the `/renew` parameter. Then, you would set the policy schedule to run daily at 8:00 a.m.

You create a Scheduled Action policy by going to the package you desire and pressing the Add button on the policies tab. This will bring up a dialog box that lists the available plural policies. Schedule Action policy will be one of them. Enter a policy name and press OK to add the policy to the package.

From the Scheduled Action Policy window Actions tab, shown in Figure 9.12, you can configure the following for each action by clicking the Add or Properties button:

▶ *Name*—Full pathname to the application that will be executed on the workstation.

▶ *Working Directory*—The working directory the policy will use when applying the action.

▶ *Parameters*—Command-line parameters that are added to the command line when the action is executed.

▶ *Priority*—Specifies the priority assigned to this action when compared to the priority of the user's access to the workstation. You can specify a priority of Action Default, Above Normal, Normal, and Below Normal. Setting the priority to Above Normal helps ensure that the action is performed quickly on the workstation no matter what the user is doing. Setting the priority to Below Normal will impact the user on the workstation less. For example, you should take into account this priority balance when scheduling actions. You might want to create one Scheduled Action policy for high priority actions and one for low priority ones.

▶ *Termination Time*—Specifies the amount of time in minutes that the application can run on the workstation before the policy will force its termination. The default is 1 minute. This can be extremely useful in protecting users from experiencing too big of a performance hit by the scheduled action. It can also be useful when ensuring that all of the actions in the policy can run.

You can also disable an individual action by selecting it and clicking the Disable button, as shown in Figure 9.12. This allows you to keep the action and its setting available for future use but not execute it the next time the policy schedule is reached.

The final setting you have on the Actions tab of the Scheduled actions policy is the Run Items in Order Listed option, shown in Figure 9.12. This option forces the actions to run one at a time in the order that they are listed in the Actions list. This can be extremely useful when you need to run a set of actions in a specific order. The Move Up and Move Down buttons allow you to change the order of the actions, if necessary.

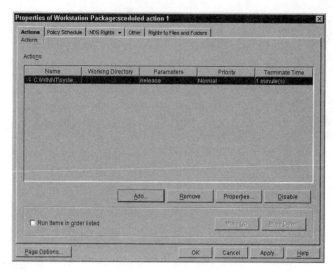

FIGURE 9.12
Scheduled Action Policy within a Workstation Policy Package.

## CHAPTER 10

Creating a Container Policy Package

In addition to user and workstation policies, you can also create a Container Policy Package. This package is associated with a container and affects the understanding of policies below the container level. This chapter discusses the Container Policy Package.

What Is a Container Policy Package?

A Container Policy Package contains a set of policies that are associated only with containers. These policies are expected to affect the behavior of other ZENworks for Desktops 4 user and workstation policies and are therefore only associated with containers.

ZENworks for Desktops 4 agents work in a standard way to search out policies within a tree, starting at either the User or the Workstation object depending on the application of the policy. Once the User or Workstation object is located, the ZENworks for Desktops 4 agents seek out a Container Policy Package. The first Container Policy Package that is found as the agent is walking up the tree is used to modify the behavior of the search for all other policies. Once the Container Policy Package is discovered, the agents use the information in the package to seek other user or Workstation Policy Packages.

Setting Up a Container Policy Package

In order to have a Container Policy Package affect policies, you must first create it. To create a Container Policy Package, do the following:

1. Start ConsoleOne.

2. Browse to the container where you want to create the policy package.

NOTE Remember that you do not have to create the policy package in the container where you are doing the associations. You can associate the same policy package with many containers in your tree.

---

3. Create the policy package by right-clicking and choosing New, Policy Package or by selecting the Policy Package icon on the toolbar.

4. Select the Container Policy Package object in the wizard panel and press Next.

5. Enter the desired name of the package in the policy package name field and select the container where you want the package to be located. The container field is already filled in with the selected container, so you should not have to browse to complete this field. If not, press the Browse button next to the field, browse to and select the container where you want the policy object stored, and then press Next.

6. Select the define additional attributes field in order to go into the properties of your new object and activate some policies, and then click Finish.

7. Check and set any policies you desire for this Container Policy Package, and then click OK.

The following sections describe each of the tabs, panels, and options available on the Properties of Container Package window.

The Policies Tab

The Policies tab on the Properties of Container Package page lists the set of available and active policies (see Figure 10.1). Because no platform-specific policies currently exist in the container package, only the General panel of the Policies tab is available.

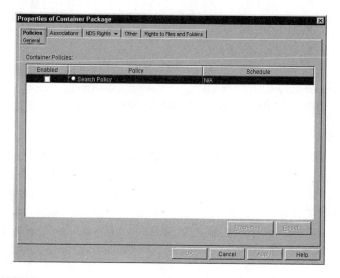

FIGURE 10.1
The Policies tab on the Properties of Container Package page, showing the General panel.

Once you have created a container package, you can now activate policies. By clicking a policy within the policy package, that policy becomes active. An active policy is designated by a check in the check box (refer to Figure 10.1). The details of any particular policy can be modified by selecting the policy and pressing the Properties button. The Reset button resets the selected policy to its system defaults.

The Associations Tab

·The Associations tab on the Properties of Container Package page displays all of the locations in the tree (containers) where the policy package has been associated. These associations do not necessarily reflect where in the directory the policy package is located. The agents that are associated with users or workstations that are in or below those containers have this policy package enforced. Pressing the Add or Remove buttons enables you to add or remove containers in the list that are associated with this policy.

The NDS Rights Tab

The eDirectory Rights tab on the Properties of Container Package page is made up of three panels. You can get to each of these panels by clicking on the small triangle to the right of the tab's name, and then selecting the desired panel to be displayed.

These panels allow you to specify the rights that users have to this object in the directory. The following subsections discuss briefly each of these panels. These eDirectory Rights panels are displayed for every object in the tree.

Trustees of This Object Panel

On this panel, you can assign objects rights as trustees of the Container Policy Package. These trustees have rights to this object or to attributes within this object.

If the user `admin.novell` has been added to the trustee list, this user has some rights to this object. To get into the details of any trustee assignment (in order to modify the assignment), you need to press the Assigned Rights button.

When you press the Assigned Rights button after selecting the user you want to modify, you are presented with a dialog box that enables you to select either all attribute rights (meaning all of the attributes of the object) or entry rights (meaning the object, not implying rights to the attributes).

From within the Assigned Rights dialog box, you can set the rights the object has on this package. You can set those rights on the object as well as any individual property in the object. The attribute rights that are possible are the following:

▶ *Browse*—Although not in the list, this right shows up from time to time (especially in the effective rights screens). This right represents the capability to view this information through public browse capabilities.

- ▶ *Supervisor*—This right identifies that the trustee has all rights, including delete, for this object or attribute.

- ▶ *Compare*—This right provides the trustee with the capability to compare values of attributes.

- ▶ *Read*—This right enables the trustee to read the values of the attribute or attributes in the object.

- ▶ *Write*—This right provides the trustee with the capability to modify the contents of an attribute.

- ▶ *Add self*—This right enables the trustee to add themselves as a member to the list of objects of the attribute. For example, if this right were given on an attribute that contains a list of linked objects, the trustee could add himself or herself (a reference to their object) into the list.

If you want to add the object as a trustee to an attribute, you need to press the Add Property button to bring up a list of properties or attributes that are available for this object.

From this list, you can select a single attribute. This attribute is then displayed in the Assigned Rights dialog box. From there, you can select the attribute and then set the rights you want the trustee to have for that property. A user does not require object rights in order to have rights on a single attribute in the object.

TIP Remember that rights flow down in the tree. If you give a user or an object rights at a container level, those rights continue down into that container, and any sub-containers, until that branch is exhausted, or until another explicit assignment is given for that user in a sub-container or on an object. An explicit assignment changes the rights for the user at that point in the tree. Inherited rights filters can also be used to restrict this flow of rights down into the tree.

Inherited Rights Filters Panel

This panel allows you to set the IRF (Inherited Rights Filter) for this object. This filter restricts the rights of any user who accesses this object, unless that user has an explicit trustee assignment for this object.

You can think of the IRF as a filter that lets only items checked pass through unaltered. Rights that bump up against an IRF are blocked and discarded if the item is not checked. For example, consider a user who has write privileges granted at some container at or above the one at issue in this example. That user runs into an IRF for an object or attribute that has the write privilege revoked (that is, unchecked). When the user gets to that object, his write privilege would be gone for that object. If the object is a container, the user loses write privileges for all objects in that container or sub-container.

You can effectively remove supervisor privileges from a portion of the tree by setting an IRF with the supervisor privilege turned off. You must be careful not to do this without someone being assigned as the supervisor of that branch of the tree (that is, given an explicit supervisor trustee assignment at the container where the IRF is done), or you make that part of the tree permanent and unchangeable (that is, you are never able to delete or modify any objects in that branch of the tree).

ConsoleOne helps prevent you from performing this action by giving you an error dialog box that keeps you from putting an IRF on the entry rights of the object with the supervisor right filtered away, without having first given an explicit supervisor assignment on the same container.

The Effective Rights Panel

The Effective Rights panel allows you to query the system to discover the rights that selected objects have on the object you are administering. Within this panel you are presented with the Distinguished Name (DN) of the object whose rights you want to observe. Initially, this is your currently logged in user running ConsoleOne. You can press the Browse button to the right of the trustee field and browse throughout the tree to select any object.

When the trustee object is selected, you can then move to the properties table on the lower half of the screen. As you select the property, the rights box to the right changes to reflect the rights that the trustee has on that property. These rights can be via an explicit assignment or through inheritance.

The Other Tab

The Other tab on the Properties of Container Package page might not be displayed for you, depending on your rights to the plug-in that now comes with ConsoleOne. The intention of this property page is to give you generic access to properties that you cannot modify or view via the other plugged-in pages. The attributes and their values are displayed in a tree structure, allowing for those attributes that have multiple types (such as compound types consisting of, say, an integer and a distinguished name, or a postal code with three separate address fields).

WARNING This page is particularly powerful. Users who don't have an intimate knowledge of the schema of the object in question and its relationships with other objects in the directory should avoid using this page.

Every attribute in eDirectory is defined by one of a specified set of syntaxes. These syntaxes identify how the data is stored in eDirectory. For this page, ConsoleOne has developed an editor for each of the different syntaxes that are currently available in eDirectory. You can invoke the editor to modify an object that is displayed on this page by clicking on a specific attribute.

For example, if the syntax of an attribute were a string or an integer, an in-line editor is launched. This allows the administrator to modify the string or the integer value on the screen. More abstract syntaxes such as octet-string require that an octet editor be launched giving the administrator access to each of the bytes in the string, without interpretation of the data.

The danger with this screen is that some applications require that there be a coordination of attribute values between two attributes within the same object or across multiple objects. Additionally, many applications assume that the data in the attribute is valid, because the normal user interface checks for invalid entries and does not allow them to be stored in the attribute.

If you should change a data value in the other page, no knowledge of related attributes or objects or valid data values are checked, because the generic editors know nothing about the intention of the field. Should you change a value without making all the other appropriate changes, or without putting in a valid value, some programs and the system could be affected.

Rights are still in effect in the Other property tab, and you are not allowed to change any attribute values that are read-only or that you do not have rights to modify.

The Rights to Files and Folders Tab

This tab on the Properties of Container Package page is present in all objects in the directory and enables you to view and set rights for an object onto the volumes and specific files and folders on that volume. You must first select the volume that contains the files and folders in which you are interested. To use the options on this tab, do the following:

1. Press the Show button on the right and then browse the directory to the volume object. Selecting the volume object places it in the volumes view.

2. When that volume is selected, you can then go to the Add button to add a file or folder of interest. This brings up a dialog box enabling you to browse to the volume object.

3. Clicking the volume object moves you into the file system. You can continue browsing that volume until you select the file or directory to which you are interested in granting rights.

4. Selecting the file or folder in the lower pane displays the rights that the object has been granted on that file or folder.

5. To modify the rights, simply select the rights that you want to have explicitly granted for the object.

You can also see the effective rights that the object has on the files by pressing the Effective Rights button. This displays a dialog box, enabling you to browse to any file in the volume and view the object's effective rights (in bold). These effective rights include any explicit plus inherited rights from folders higher in the file system tree.

NOTE Remember that the person with supervisor rights to the server or volume objects automatically gets supervisor rights in the file system.

Understanding the Search Policy

A search policy governs the behavior of the ZENworks for Desktops 4 agents as they search for user and workstation policies. With all of the ZENworks for Desktops 4 agents, there can be some significant walking of the tree as it searches for the policies of the identified user and workstations, especially if the tree is deep. This is the reason why ZENworks for Desktops 4 has this search policy.

Often the performance of your network searching with ZENworks for Desktops 4 is not an issue until you cross a partition boundary. When you cross a partition boundary, the system must make a connection and authenticate to another server. This is particularly time-consuming should the system need to cross a WAN link.

The search policy tells the ZENworks for Desktops 4 agent how far up the tree it should search and what order (object, group, container) should be followed to find the policies.

TIP The search order is significant, because often the first policy found governs the behavior of the system.

The Search Level Tab

This tab on the Search Policy window (see Figure 10.2) enables the administrator to identify how far up the tree the ZENworks for Desktops 4 agents should travel in their search for policies.

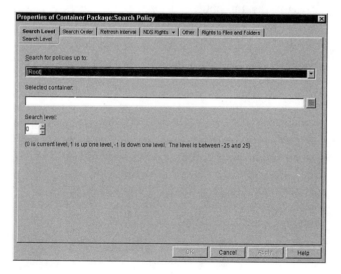

FIGURE 10.2
The Search Level tab on the Search Policy window within a Container Policy Package.

The following fields can be administered in the search level features on the Search Level tab:

▶ *Search for policies up to*—This field enables you to specify the container in the tree at which searching will complete. The choices that can be made through the drop-down list may be any of the following:

    ▶ *[Root]*—Search up to the root of the tree.

    ▶ *Object container*—Search up to the container that holds the object that is associated with the policy. For example, if you were searching for a User Policy Package, the object container would be the context of the user object.

    ▶ *Partition*—Search up the tree to a partition boundary. Crossing a partition boundary causes connections to other systems in the tree. This option is available for performance considerations.

    ▶ *Selected container*—This searches up to the specified container. When this option is chosen, the selected container field is activated and you can browse in this field to the desired container.

▶ *Search level*—This field enables you to specify an additional level of container beyond that given in the search for policies up to field. A search level value of **0** causes searches to be limited to the specified container. A search level of a positive numerical value enables searching the number of containers specified. Should the search level be a negative number, the search proceeds at the specified level minus the number specified. For example, if the object container value were selected, the object is in the `Provo.Utah.Novell` container, and the search level is **0**, the searching stops at the `Provo.Utah.Novell` container. If the search level is **2**, the searching continues to the Novell container. If the search level is **-1**, no policy will be found because the object container is already above the search level.

At first it might not be apparent why a negative search level exists, but this value does have a purpose. Suppose that your tree is set up as `Organization.Region.Company`, whereby the organization is the container that is given to each organization in the company, and the region represents the area of the company. Now suppose that you want policies to be effective only for each organization. You could set up one single search policy at the `Region.Company` level with a selected container as `Region.Company` and a search level of -1. This would enable each organization to have a customized policy and ensure that no one organization's policies impact another's, because the search would stop at the organization level.

The Search Order Tab

This tab enables the administrator to identify the order that the agents should look for policies. The default order is always object, group, and then container. This policy enables the administrator to change this order.

You can modify the search order by selecting the item in the search order list and then using the up or down arrows to rearrange the list. Pressing the Remove button removes the selected order. Pressing the Add button adds that search order item, if any have been previously deleted.

TIP Because the first policy that is found has the greatest significance in the behavior of the system, you should be sure that you have the order set (from top to bottom) in the way that you want to find that first policy.

You should be aware of when it is a good idea to use the search order policy. Because many ZENworks for Desktops 4 features stop walking up the tree when a policy is found, it would be wise to make policies search in order of object, container, and then group. This is because the proximity of these objects in the tree is always going to be closer to the partition on the server. The object is, obviously, always the closest in the tree to the workstation or user object. The container is the next closest in the tree-walking scenario because the container must be known in order for the object to be found in the tree. Consequently, the container is very close in the local replica to the object. Groups, however, can be stored in any container and they could be in a completely different part of the tree than the object.

Therefore, the amount of tree walking with a group can potentially be significant. Any significant walk of the tree has a corresponding performance cost, and you should consider this as you manage your tree and search policies.

The Refresh Interval Tab

The Refresh Interval tab on the Search Policy window enables the administrator to identify whether the policy manager should refresh the set of policies from eDirectory and how often to check eDirectory for new or changed policies. The policy manager in ZENworks for Servers is an agent that resides on the server and is responsible for getting ZENworks for Servers policies and enforcing them on the server. An option on the Refresh Interval tab gives this refresh interval configuration to this agent. If the check box is disabled, meaning the agent should not refresh from eDirectory, the agent gets the policies only at initialization time, or should the server or the agent be restarted. If the check box is enabled, the agent checks for any changes or new policies every time the interval has passed.

This same behavior is also available in Workstation Manager, the agent that enforces policies on the workstation. It also looks for new policies and scheduled actions, and only does that at boot time and at identified intervals.

NOTE The workstation manager interval is specified in the Workstation Policy Package under the NT/2000 client configuration and 95/98 client configuration policies.

## CHAPTER 11

Creating a Service Location Policy Package

In addition to user, workstation, and container policies, a Service Location Policy Package also exists. This package is associated with a container and identifies where agents associated with objects below the associated container may locate services they need, such as the database to record events or workstation inventory. This chapter discusses the Service Location Policy Package.

What Is a Service Location Policy Package?

A Service Location Policy Package contains a set of policies only associated with containers. These policies are expected to identify the location of resources other ZENworks for Desktops 4 agents, throughout the network, need. These resources are associated through the container to all agents working on behalf of the objects in the container or sub-container.

For example, if you have set up a Service Location Policy Package associated with container A, and activated a database location policy specifying the database is located on server A, all of the workstation agents on the PCs whose workstation objects are located in or below container A, look in the tree and walk up the tree to find the Service Location Policy Package associated with container A.

In this policy, they would find the database where they should store their events or inventory information located on server A, because the database location policy in the Service Location Policy Package would be active. The agents would then contact the database on server A and send it their information.

Setting Up a Service Location Policy Package

To create a Service Location Policy Package, do the following:

1. Start ConsoleOne.

2. Browse to the container where you want to have the policy package.

NOTE Remember: You do not have to create the policy package in the container where you are performing the associations. You can associate the same policy package to many containers in your tree.

3. Create the policy package by right-clicking and choosing New, Policy Package or by selecting the Policy Package icon on the toolbar.

4. Select the Service Location Policy Package object in the wizard panel and press Next.

5. Enter the desired name of the package in the Policy Package Name field and select the container where you want the package to be located. The container field is already filled in with the selected container, so you should not have to browse to complete this field. If it's not filled in, press the Browse button next to the field, and then select the container where you want the policy object stored. Press Next.

6. Select the Define Additional Attributes field. You can activate some policies in your new object. Press Finish.

7. Check and set any policies you desire for this Service Location Policy Package, and then press OK.

The following sections describe the options available in the Service Location Policy Package.

Policies Tab

All the user policies are activated within the Policies tab on the Location Policy page. Initially, the Policies tab displays the General panel. In the Service Location Policy Package, no platform-specific policies currently exist. Therefore, no drop-down menu is present on the Policies tab. The Policies tab lists the set of available policies (see Figure 11.1).

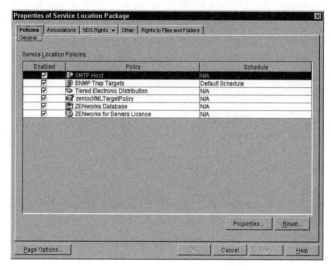

FIGURE 11.1
The Policies tab of the Service Location Package page.

Once you have created a Service Location Policy Package, you can activate policies. By clicking on a policy within the policy package, that policy becomes active. You can modify the details of any particular policy by selecting the policy and then pressing the Properties button.

The Reset button on the policies page resets the selected policy to the system defaults.

Associations Tab

The Associations tab of the Service Location Policy Package page displays all of the locations in the tree (containers) where the policy package has been associated. These associations do not necessarily reflect where the policy package is located in the directory. The agents associated with users or workstations in or below those containers have this policy package enforced.

The Add and Remove buttons enable you to add or remove containers in the list that are associated with this policy.

NDS Rights Tab

The NDS Rights tab is made up of three panels. You can get to each of these panels by clicking on the small triangle to the right of the tab's name, and then selecting the desired panel.

These panels enable you to specify the rights that users have to this object in the directory. The following sections discuss briefly each of these panels, which are displayed for every object in the tree.

Trustees of This Object Panel

Here you can assign objects rights as trustees of the Service Location Policy Package. These trustees have rights to this object or to attributes within this object.

If the `user admin.novell` has been added to the trustee list, this user has some rights to this object. To view the details of any trustee assignment (in order to modify the assignment), you need to:

1. Select the user you want to modify and then press the Assigned Rights button. You are presented with a dialog box.

2. In the dialog box, you can select All Attribute Rights (meaning all of the attributes of the object) or Entry Rights (meaning the object, not implying rights to the attributes).

3. From within the Assigned Rights dialog box, you can set the rights the object has on this package. You can set those rights on the object as well as any individual property in the object. The possible attribute rights are as follows:

   ▶ *Browse*—Although not in the list, this right shows up from time to time (especially in the Effective Rights screens). This enables you to view this information through public browse capabilities.

   ▶ *Supervisor*—This right identifies that the trustee has all rights, including delete, to this object or attribute.

   ▶ *Compare*—This provides the trustee with the capability to compare values of attributes.

▶ *Read*—This right enables the trustee to read the values of the attribute or attributes in the object.

▶ *Write*—This right provides the trustee with the capability to modify the contents of an attribute.

▶ *Add Self*—This right enables trustees to add themselves as members of the list of objects of the attribute. For example, if this right were given on an attribute that contains a list of linked objects, a trustee could be added into the list.

4. If you want to add the object as a trustee to an attribute, you need to select the Add Property button to bring up a list of properties or attributes that are available for this object.

5. From this list, you can select a single attribute. This attribute is then displayed in the Assigned Rights dialog box.

6. From the Assigned Rights dialog box, you can select the attribute and then set the rights you want the trustee to have for that property.

NOTE A user does not require object rights in order to have rights on a single attribute in the object.

Remember that rights flow down in the tree. If you give a user or an object rights at a container level, those rights continue down into that container and any sub-containers until that branch is exhausted or another explicit assignment is given for that user in a sub-container or on an object. An explicit assignment changes the user's rights at that point in the tree. You can also use inheritance rights filters to restrict the flow of rights down into the tree.

Inherited Rights Filters Panel

This panel enables you to set the IRF (Inherited Rights Filter) for this object. This filter restricts the rights of any user who accesses this object, unless that user has an explicit trustee assignment for this object.

You can think of the IRF as a filter that lets only checked items pass through unaltered. Rights that bump up against an IRF are blocked and discarded if the item is not checked. For example, consider a user who has write privileges inherited at some point above the current container (explicitly granted at some container at or above the one in question). That user runs into an IRF for an object or attribute that has the write privilege revoked (that is, unchecked). When the user gets to that object, his write privilege would be gone for that object. If the object is a container, the user loses write privileges for all objects in that container or sub-container.

You can effectively remove supervisor privileges from a portion of the tree by setting an IRF with the supervisor privilege turned off. You must be careful not to do this without someone being assigned as the supervisor of that branch of the tree (given an explicit supervisor trustee assignment at the container where the IRF is done). Otherwise, you'll never be able to delete or modify any objects in that branch of the tree.

ConsoleOne helps prevent you from performing this action by giving you an error dialog box that keeps you from putting an IRF on the entry rights of the object, without having first given an explicit supervisor assignment on the same container.

Effective Rights Panel

The Effective Rights panel enables you to query the system to discover the rights that selected objects have on the object you are administering.

Within this panel, you are presented with the Distinguished Name (DN) of the object whose rights you want to observe. Initially, this is your currently logged in user running ConsoleOne. You can press the Browse button to the right of the trustee field and browse throughout the tree to select any object.

When the trustee object is selected, you can then move to the properties table on the lower half of the screen. As you select the property, the rights box changes to reflect the rights that the trustee has on that property. These rights can be gained via an explicit assignment or through inheritance.

Other Tab

This tab might not be displayed for you, depending on your rights to the plug-in that now comes with ConsoleOne. The intention of this tab is to give you generic access to properties you cannot modify or view via the other plugged-in pages.

The attributes and their values are displayed in a tree structure, allowing for those attributes that have multiple types, such as compound types consisting of an integer and a distinguished name, or postal codes that have three separate address fields.

WARNING The options on this tab are particularly powerful. People who do not have an intimate knowledge of the schema of the object in question and its relationships with other objects in the directory should avoid these options.

Every attribute in eDirectory is defined by one of a specified set of syntaxes. These syntaxes identify how the data is stored in eDirectory. For this tab, ConsoleOne has developed an editor for each of the different syntaxes currently available in eDirectory. When an attribute is displayed on this tab, the editor displays the data and then modifies it should the user click the specific attribute.

For example, if the syntax for an attribute were a string or an integer, an in-line editor is launched. This editor enables the administrator to modify the string or the integer value on the screen. More abstract syntaxes, such as octet-string, require that an octet editor be launched, thus giving the administrator access to each of the bytes in the string, without interpretation of the data.

The danger with this screen is that some applications require that there be a coordination of attribute values between two attributes within the same object or across multiple objects. Additionally, many applications assume that the data in the attribute is valid, because the normal user interface checks for invalid entries and does not enable them to be stored in the attribute. If you should change a data value on the Other tab, no knowledge of related attributes, objects, or valid data values are checked, because the generic editors know nothing about the intention of the field. Should you change a value without making all the other appropriate changes or without putting in a valid value, some programs and the system could be affected.

Rights are still in effect on the Other tab, and you are not allowed to change any attribute values that are read-only or that you do not have rights to modify.

Rights to Files and Folders Tab

This tab is present in all objects in the directory. It enables you to view and set rights of the files and folders on the volume in question. To set such rights, use the following steps:

1. First select the volume that contains the files and folders in which you are interested. You can do this by pressing the Show button, and then browsing the directory to the volume object.

2. Selecting the volume object places it in the volumes view. When that volume is selected, you can then choose the Add button to add a file or folder of interest.

3. This brings up a dialog box enabling you to browse to the volume object; clicking the volume object moves you into the file system. You can continue browsing that volume until you select the file or directory to which you are interested in granting rights.

4. Selecting the file or folder in the lower pane displays the rights that the object has been granted on that file or folder. To modify the rights, simply click on or off the rights that you want to have explicitly granted for the object.

5. You can also see the effective rights that the object has on the files by pressing the Effective Rights button. This displays a dialog box that enables you to browse to any file in the volume. The object's effective rights are displayed (in bold). These effective rights include any explicit and inherited rights from folders higher in the file system tree.

NOTE Remember that anyone who has supervisor rights to the server or volume objects automatically gets supervisor rights in the file system.

SMTP Host Policy

Several of the features in ZENworks for Desktops 4 include the capability to e-mail information and events to identified users. In order to send the e-mail, the agents must contact the SMTP server in your environment, communicate, and send the e-mail through that system. This policy enables you to specify the IP address of the SMTP host that the agents associated with this policy (through inheritance) use.

NOTE For more information on the topics in this section, see Chapter 6, "Creating and Using Application Objects."

The SMTP Host tab, accessed from the Service Location Object window in ConsoleOne, enables the administrator to identify the IP address of the SMTP mail server in their environment (see Figure 11.2).

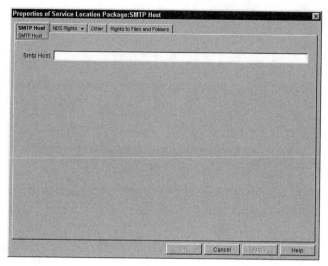

FIGURE 11.2
SMTP Host tab of the SMTP Host policy page.

Just place your cursor on the SMTP Host field and enter the IP address of the SMTP mail host. You must enter the IP address and not the DNS name.

SNMP Trap Target Policy

In ZENworks for Desktops 4, the Application Launcher has been enhanced to send an SNMP message to a central server that stores these messages and enables you to print reports on the traps. These traps can identify whether an application was successfully distributed; if not, it identifies the potential problem with the distribution.

> **NOTE** This policy used to be in the Container Policy Package in previous versions of ZENworks for Desktops.

The SNMP trap targets policy identifies the location of the service accepting and recording the SNMP messages from the Application Launcher. In previous versions of ZENworks for Desktops, you had to place the database service as an SNMP trap target policy in order to receive Application

Launcher events. This is no longer necessary, as the Application Launcher can write directly to the database.

Figure 11.3 displays the SNMP Trap Policy tab on the SNMP Trap Targets page, accessed from the Service Location Object window in ConsoleOne. The service on the workstation walks the tree to find this policy and uses the service location stored in this policy as the destination of the SNMP messages.

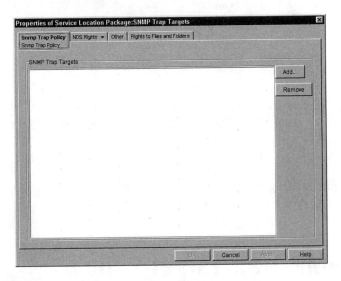

FIGURE 11.3
The SNMP Trap Policy tab of the SNMP Trap Targets policy page.

Once you have opened the policy page, you can add as many trap targets as you desire. The service on the workstation sends the SNMP message to all of the specified trap targets. Use the Add button to specify whether the destination can be achieved with an IP address, an IPX address, or a DNS name. After selecting the type, a dialog box comes up for you to enter either the address or the DNS name of the target service.

The XML Targets Policy Tab

The XML Targets Policy tab of the XML Targets policy page (see Figure 11.4) allows you to specify the URL(s) used to view information exported from ZENworks application management in XML format. XML provides ZENworks with an extremely flexible way to create useful, platform-independent reports. The XML Targets Policy tab can be accessed from the Service Location Object window in ConsoleOne.

Click the Add button to add any URL you want, so you can view exported XML reports from application management.

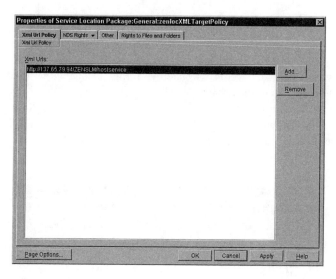

FIGURE 11.4
The XML Target Policy tab of the zenlocXML TargetPolicy page.

ZENworks Database Policy

Many of the agents in the system want to record information into the ZENworks database installed on your system. Previously, agents (such as the Application Launcher agent) would insert their event information into the database indirectly through SNMP messages. Now, in ZENworks for Desktops 4, the Application Launcher agent and other agents write directly to the database and do not rely on the SNMP system to record events.

In order for these agents to determine on which database they should place their information, they walk the tree, from the object representing the system they are supporting, until they find a Service Location Policy Package with an active ZENworks database policy.

The database policy then refers to a ZENworks database object in the directory (created at installation time), which, in turn, contains the server or the IP address of the server supporting the database. The system uses other information in the database object as well.

ZENworks Database Page

This page enables you to browse to the database objects in the directory that represent the databases you want to use for inventory and application management. All agents associated with this policy then write their log information into these databases. Figure 11.5 shows a snapshot of the Inventory Management tab, which can be accessed from the Service Location Object window in ConsoleOne. From this tab, you can click the browse button and navigate to the ZENworks inventory database you want to use for this service location policy.

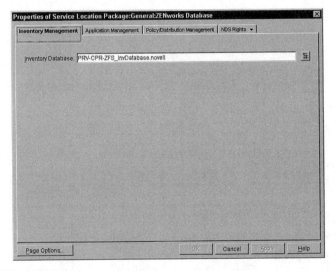

FIGURE 11.5
The Inventory Management tab of the ZENworks Database page.

Application Management Tab

You can also specify the location of the application management database for the service location. From the ZENworks Database page, click the Application Management tab (refer to Figure 11.5), and then click the Browse button to navigate to the ZENworks application management database object you want to use for this service location.

Objects associated with this service location object use the inventory or application management databases you assign to store and retrieve data.

NOTE For more information about ZENworks databases, see Chapter 2, "Installing ZENworks for Desktops 4."

## CHAPTER 12

Creating a Server Policy Package

In addition to User, Workstation, Service Location, and Container policies is the Server Policy Package. This package is associated with a container or a server and includes policies that are used by agents that reside on the server. This policy package is used by both ZENworks for Desktops 4 and ZENworks for Servers products, although some policies are effective only for Desktops 4 and others for Servers. This chapter discusses the Server Policy package.

What Is a Server Policy Package?

A Server Policy Package contains a set of policies that are associated with agents that run on servers. These policies are expected to give policy information and configuration behavior to these agents and can be associated with the server, a group of servers, or a container.

The agents follow the expected walking of the tree to locate their server policy package. Namely, they find the search policy and then use the order specified in the search policy, or they use the default. The default is to search for a Server Policy Package associated with the server, and then the group of servers, and lastly the container. The first policy package is the one that the agents use.

Setting Up a Server Policy Package

To create a Server Policy Package do the following:

1. Start ConsoleOne.

2. Browse to the container where you want to have the policy package. Remember that you do not have to create the policy package in the container where you are doing the associations. You can associate the same policy package to many containers in your tree.

3. Create the policy package by right-clicking and choosing New, Policy Package or by selecting the Policy Package icon on the toolbar.

4. Select the Server Policy Package object in the wizard panel and press Next.

5. Enter the name of the package in the Policy Package Name field and select the container where you want the package to be located. The container field is already filled in with the selected container so you should not have to browse to complete this field. If it's not filled in, press the browser button next to the field and browse to and select the container where you want the policy object stored. Press Next.

6. Select the Define Additional Attributes field in order to activate some policies. Press Finish.

7. Check and set any policies you desire for this Server Policy Package and press OK.

The following subsections describe each of the fields and property pages that are available in the Server Policy Package.

The Policies Property Page

All of the policies for users are activated within the policies property page. Initially, the page is on the general policies. As other platforms are selected additional policies are displayed. You can select which platform to display by mousing over the small triangle to the right of the word Policies. This activates a drop-down menu that enables you to select which platform specific page you want to display.

The following sections briefly discuss each of the policy pages; subsequent sections cover the specifics of each policy.

General Policies

When you first go into the properties of the Server Policy Package, you are presented with the Policies Property page. The policy page first displays the general category. The policies activated in the general category are active for all server platforms supported by ZENworks for Desktops 4 and associated to the server.

Figure 12.1 shows a snapshot of the initial property page of the Server Policy Package.

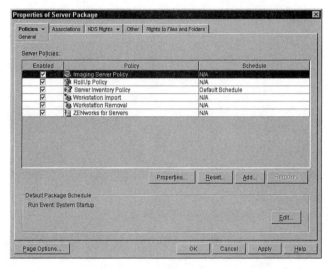

FIGURE 12.1
Server Policy Package policies general property page.

As you can see in Figure 12.1, four policies are available to all of the platforms supported by ZENworks for Desktops 4. They are Imaging Server Policy, Workstation Import Policy, Workstation Removal Policy, and RollUp Policy. These, as well as all of the other policies, are discussed later in this chapter.

In order to activate a policy, you simply need to select it. You can then go into the details of the policy and set additional configuration parameters on that specific policy.

Windows Policies

Within the policies tab you can select the Windows Servers policy page.
This page displays the policies that are available for your Windows
Servers. These policies include Imaging Server Policy, Workstation
Import, Workstation Removal, and RollUp Policy. See Figure 12.2 for a
sample of the Windows policies page.

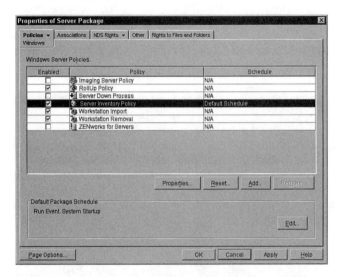

FIGURE 12.2
Server Policy Package Windows polices property page.

As you can see, the same policies appear in the General and the
Windows policies pages. When you select a policy in the Windows page
it supercedes any selections made on the General tab. The policies will
not be merged; only the platform-specific policy is used. For example, if
the Workstation Import policy is selected in the General tab and the
Workstation Removal policy is selected in the Windows tab, agents on a
Windows Servers system use the general import policy and the Windows
removal policy is activated.

NetWare Policies

Within the policies tab you can select the NetWare policy page. This
page displays the policies that are available for NetWare servers. These
policies include Imaging Server Policy, Workstation Import, Workstation

Removal, and RollUp Policy. See Figure 12.3 for a sample of the NetWare
policies page.

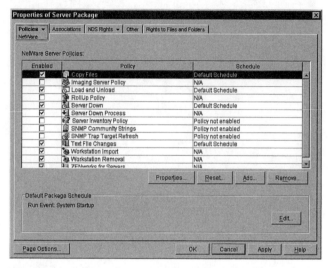

FIGURE 12.3
Server Policy Package NetWare polices property page.

As you can see, the same policies appear in the General and the NetWare
policies pages. When you select a policy in the NetWare page, it
supercedes any selections made on the General tab. The policies will not
be merged; only the platform specific policy is used. For example, if the
Workstation Import policy is selected in the General tab and the
Workstation Removal policy is selected in the NetWare tab, agents on a
NetWare system use the general import policy and the NetWare removal
policy is activated.

Linux Policies
Within the policies tab you can select the Linux policy page. This page
displays the policies that are available for Linux servers. These policies
include Imaging Server Policy, Workstation Import, Workstation
Removal, and RollUp Policy. See Figure 12.4 for a sample of the Linux
policies page.

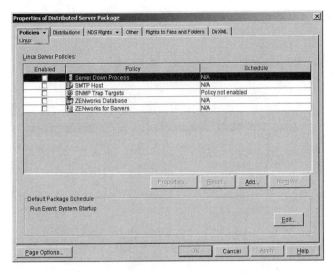

FIGURE 12.4
Server Policy Package Linux polices property page.

As you can see, the same policies appear in the General and the Linux policies pages. When you select a policy in the Linux page, it supercedes any selections made on the General tab for that platform. The policies will not be merged; only the platform specific policy is used. For example, if the Workstation Import policy is selected in the General tab and the Workstation Removal policy is selected in the Linux tab, agents on a Linux system use the general import policy and the Linux removal policy is activated.

Solaris Policies

Within the policies tab, you can select the Solaris policy page. This page displays the policies available for Solaris servers. These policies include Imaging Server Policy, Workstation Import, Workstation Removal, and RollUp Policy. See Figure 12.5 for a sample of the Solaris policies page.

As you can see, the same policies appear in the General and the Solaris policies pages. When you select a policy in the Solaris page, it supercedes any selections made on the General tab. The policies will not be merged; only the platform specific policy is used. For example, if the Workstation Import policy is selected in the General tab and the Workstation Removal policy is selected in the Solaris tab, agents on a Solaris system use the general import policy and the Solaris removal policy is activated.

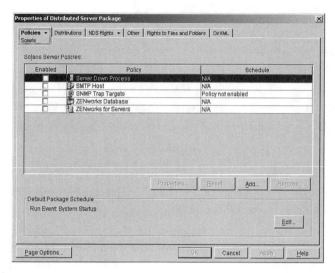

FIGURE 12.5
Server Policy Package Solaris polices property page.

Associations Property Page

The Associations Page of the Server Policy Package displays all of the locations in the tree (containers) where the policy package has been associated. These associations do not necessarily reflect where the policy package is located in the directory. The agents that are associated with users or workstations that are in or below those containers have this policy package enforced. The Add and Remove buttons enable you to add or remove containers in the list that are associated with this policy.

NDS Rights Property Pages

The NDS Rights property page is made up of three pages. You can get to each of the pages by clicking on the small triangle to the right of the page name, and then selecting the desired page to be displayed.

These pages enable you to specify the rights that users have to this object in the directory. The following subsections briefly discuss each of these pages. These NDS Rights pages are displayed for every object in the tree.

Trustees of This Object Page

On this page, you can assign objects rights as trustees of the Server Policy Package. These trustees have rights to this object or to attributes within this object.

If the **user admin.novell** has been added to the trustee list, this user has some rights to this object. To view the details of any trustee assignment (in order to modify the assignment), you need to press the Assigned Rights button.

When you press the Assign Rights button, you are presented with a dialog box that enables you to select [All Attribute Rights] (meaning all of the attributes of the object) or [Entry Rights] (meaning the object, not implying rights to the attributes).

From within the Assigned Rights dialog box, you can set the rights the object has on this package. You can set those rights on the object as well as any individual property in the object. The rights that are possible are the following:

- ▶ *Browse*—Although not in the list, this right shows up from time to time (especially in the Effective Rights screens). This represents the capability to view this information through public browse capabilities.

- ▶ *Supervisor*—This identifies that the trustee has *all* rights, including delete, for this object or attribute.

- ▶ *Compare*—This provides the trustee with the capability to compare values of attributes.

- ▶ *Read*—This enables the trustee to read the values of the attribute or attributes in the object.

- ▶ *Write*—This provides the trustee with the capability to modify the contents of an attribute.

- ▶ *Add Self*—This right enables the trustee to add himself or herself as a member of the list of objects of the attribute. For example, if this right were given on an attribute that contains a list of linked objects, the trustee could add himself or herself (that is, a reference to their object) to the list.

If you want to add the object as a trustee to an attribute, you need to press the Add Property button to view a list of properties or attributes available for this object.

From this list you can select a single attribute. This attribute is then displayed in the Assigned Rights dialog box. From there you can select the attribute and then set the rights you want the trustee to have for that property. A user does not require object rights in order to have rights on a single attribute in the object.

Remember that rights flow down in the tree. If you give a user or an object rights at a container level, those rights continue down into that container, and any sub-containers until that branch is exhausted, or another explicit assignment is given for that user in a sub-container or on an object. An explicit assignment changes the rights of the user at that point in the tree. You can also use inheritance rights filters to restrict this flow of rights down into the tree.

Inherited Rights Filters Page

This page enables you to set the IRF (Inheritance Rights Filter) for this object. This filter restricts the rights of any user who accesses this object, unless that user has an explicit trustee assignment for this object.

You can think of the IRF as a filter that lets only checked items pass through unaltered. Rights that bump up against an IRF filter are blocked and discarded if the item is not checked. For example, consider a user with write privileges inherited at some point above the current container (they were explicitly granted that right at some container at or above the one they're in). This user runs into an IRF for an object or attribute that has the write privilege revoked (that is, unchecked). When this user gets to that object, their write privilege will be gone for that object. If the object is a container, the user will lose write privileges for all objects in that container or sub-container.

You can effectively remove supervisor privileges to a portion of the tree by setting an IRF with the supervisor privilege turned off. You must be careful not to do this without someone being assigned as the supervisor of that branch of the tree (given an explicit supervisor trustee assignment at the container where the IRF is done). Otherwise, you'll make that part of the tree permanent (that is, you will never be able to delete any objects in that branch of the tree).

ConsoleOne helps keep you from performing this action by showing an error dialog box that keeps you from putting an IRF on the [Entry Rights] of the object without having first given an explicit supervisor assignment on the same container.

Effective Rights Page

The Effective Rights property page enables you to query the system to discover the rights that selected objects have on the object that you are administering.

Within this page, you are presented with the Distinguished Name (DN) of the object whose rights you want to observe. Initially, this is your currently logged in user running ConsoleOne. You can press the browse button to the right of the trustee field and browse throughout the tree to select any object.

When the trustee object is selected, you can then move to the properties table on the lower half of the screen. As you select the property, the rights box to the right changes its text to reflect the rights that the trustee has on that property. These rights can be granted via an explicit assignment or through inheritance.

Other Property Page

This page might not be displayed for you, depending on your rights to the plug-in that now comes with ConsoleOne. This page is particularly powerful. People who do not have an intimate knowledge of the schema of the object in question and its relationships with other objects in the directory should avoid using it. The intention of this property page is to give you generic access to properties that you cannot modify or view via the other plugged-in pages. The attributes and their values are displayed in a tree structure, allowing for those attributes that have multiple types (are compound types that consist of, say, an INT and a distinguished name, or postal code that has three separate address fields).

Every attribute in eDirectory is defined by one of a specified set of syntaxes. These syntaxes identify how the data is stored in eDirectory. For this page, ConsoleOne has developed an editor for each of the different syntaxes that is currently available in eDirectory. When an attribute is displayed on this page, the editor is invoked to display the data and then modify it should the user click the specific attribute.

For example, if the syntax of an attribute were a string or an integer, an in-line editor enables the administrator to modify the string or the integer value on the screen. More abstract syntaxes, such as octet-string, require that an octet editor be launched, thus giving the administrator access to each of the bytes in the string, without interpretation of the data.

The danger with this screen is that some applications require that there be a coordination of attribute values between two attributes within the same object or across multiple objects. Additionally, many applications assume that the data in the attribute is valid, because the normal user interface checks for invalid entries and does not allow them to be stored in the attribute. If you should change a data value in the other page, no knowledge of related attributes or objects or valid data values are checked because the generic editors know nothing about the intention of the field. Should you change a value without making all the other appropriate changes, or without putting in a valid value, some programs and the system could be affected.

Rights are still in effect in the Other property page and you are not allowed to change any attribute values that are read-only or that you do not have rights to modify.

Rights to Files and Folders Property Page

This page in the property book is present in all objects in the directory. This property page enables you to view and set rights for this object on the appropriate volumes.

You must first select the volume that contains the files and folders to which you are interested. You can do this by pressing the Show button and then browsing the directory to the volume object. Selecting the volume object places it in the volumes view. When that volume is selected you can then go to the Add button to add a file or folder of interest. This brings up a dialog box enabling you to browse to the volume object; clicking on the volume object moves you into the file system. You can continue browsing that volume until you select the file or directory you are interested in granting rights.

Selecting the file or folder in the lower pane displays the rights that the object has been granted on that file or folder. To modify the rights, you simply click on or off the rights that you want to have explicitly granted for the object.

You can also see the effective rights that the object has on the files by pressing the Effective Rights button. This displays a dialog box, enabling you to browse to any file in the volume. The object's effective rights are displayed (in bold). These effective rights include any explicit and inherited rights from folders higher in the file system tree. Remember that whoever has supervisor rights to the server or volume objects automatically has supervisor rights in the file system.

Imaging Server Policy

ZENworks for Desktops 4 can image a workstation and then apply that image back to the original workstation or to other workstations. See Chapter 14, "Imaging a Workstation," for more detailed information on the functionality of the ZENworks for Desktops 4 imaging system.

The placement of an image associated with an image object in the directory onto a workstation can occur three ways in ZENworks for Desktops 4.

▶ Booting the workstation with two floppy disks that communicate with the imaging agent on the server.

▶ Placing a special boot partition on an unregistered workstation that communicates with the imaging agent on the server.

▶ Placing a special boot partition on a registered workstation and setting the Put an Image On This Workstation On the Next Boot field in the workstation object. (In this case, the image is determined by an image association or the rules in the Workstation Imaging Policy; see Chapter 9, "Setting Up a Workstation Policy Package," for more details.)

Each of these ways results in the workstation being imaged with the image associated with the workstation, or determined by the imaging agent that resides on the server. The workstation finds the imaging server from the information the administrator specifies—either from an IP or a DNS name for the server. This information is saved on the disks or in the special boot partition.

The imaging policy becomes effective when the workstation is not associated with a workstation object. Because no image is associated with the specific workstation, the imaging server must determine, based on rules, which image to place on the workstation.

This policy enables the administrator to create a set of rules that can govern when a particular image should be used, based on some basic information from the workstation. The imaging server follows the list of rules in the policy until one of the rules is satisfied. The rule that is satisfied results in an associated image that is then applied to the workstation.

The NDS Rights, Other, and Rights to Files and Folders pages are described in the "Setting Up a Server Policy Package" section.

Imaging Partition

The Imaging Partition page allows you to disable the ZENworks imaging partition if it exists. This is useful when you want to disable imaging because it there is no active imaging occurring on the workstation. For example, you have a one-time image that is applied to a workstation annually in January. You need the partition to remain intact, but you can disable it the rest of the year.

PXE Settings

Now that ZENworks for Desktops ships with PXE-enabled software, you can also set the PXE settings for deploying any images. Novell now recommends that the Linux partition on the workstation be removed. Customers should move to the PXE method of image deployment. You can determine whether the PXE menu should appear automatically when PXE is launched and you set the values that appear on the menu.

A PXE menu will display, for example, whether to receive or to take an image.

Rules Page

This page enables the administrator to input the rules and associated images that the system uses to determine the image to place on a specific type of workstation. Figure 12.6 shows a sample of this page.

You must first press the Add button to add rules to the list. Once you have added several rules, you can then select a specific rule and change its order in the list, look at its properties, or remove the rule. When you press the Add button, the following screen is displayed (see Figure 12.7).

You first press the browse button next to the Use this Image field to browse to an image object in the tree that is associated with an image file on the image server. Once the image object is selected, you can identify the rule that is associated with this image. You can have six key/value pairs at one time.

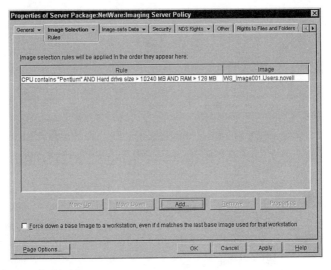

FIGURE 12.6
Rules page for a sample Imaging Server Policy of a Server Policy Package.

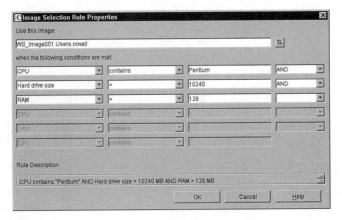

FIGURE 12.7
Add rule dialog box for a sample Imaging Server Policy of a Server Policy
Package.

In the middle of the dialog box, note the six potential equations that you
can generate to determine whether the image should be used. The equation is made up of a series of True/False statements that are strung
together with **AND** and **OR** logic. You construct the statement by filling in

the drop-down statements. (The resulting statement is displayed in a more English-like view.)

The logic of the **AND** and **OR** operators is strictly left to right in the equation. In the Rule Description box parentheses are added to the equation to help the administrator understand how the rule is evaluated. You cannot insert the parentheses; they are automatically inserted as part of the explanation of the equation and are not under user control.

You first select the key you want to examine by selecting the key via a drop-down dialog box. The keys that you can choose from are the following:

▶ *Chipset*—This displays the reported processor. An example is Genuine Intel Mobile Pentium MMX 233 MHZ.

▶ *Video*—This captures the type of video adapter that is in the workstation. An example of this would be Trident Cyber9397 (rev 243).

▶ *Network*—This is the network adapter for the workstation. An example would be 3Com.

▶ *Sound Card*—This is the sound card that has been reported. Often this field results in no sound card being detected. This is because the system sends out a PCI request; if no sound cards respond, you get this even though a sound card is present.

▶ *Hard Drive Controller*—This is the type of hard drive in the system. If the hard drive is an IDE device, the value for this field is IDE. If the hard drive is a SCSI device, you get the reported name of the device, such as `FUJITSU MHJ2181AT`.

▶ *MAC Address*—This is the MAC address of the network card. An example of this value is `00 60 80 03 C2 E7`.

▶ *IP Address*—This is the assigned IP address of the workstation. This is reported as the traditional `137.65.237.5`.

▶ *Hard Drive Size*—This reports the disk size in number of megabytes. Therefore, an 8GB hard drive would be reported as 8192MB. The imaging system might not always report the full disk capacity. Use a wide boundary when generating your rules. For instance, if you want to look for an 8GB drive, use the statement `Hard drive size > 8000 MB`.

▶ *RAM*—This is the reported amount of RAM in megabytes. This is reported as 64MB. This field also might not always report the exact amount of RAM space that you would expect on your workstation. It is advisable that you use a wide boundary when generating your rules. If you want to look for 16MB RAM, for example, use the statement `RAM > 15MB`.

When the workstation is booting the imaging system, it is in reality booting up the Linux operating system and running the tools that are included in the imaging system. The values for the keys described previously are values that the Linux system can report to the software. In order to discover what a system reports to Linux, you need to boot a sample workstation with the Imaging system boot disk and run the `Img` information command. This displays the information that is sent to the image server about the workstation. This information is the data values that you put into the key comparison equations for your rules. You can also get this information from an image by opening the image in the ZENworks image editor and choosing properties on the image root. See Chapter 14, for more detailed information on the functionality of the ZENworks for Desktops 4 imaging system.

The next part of the equation specifies the operator. Two types of operators exist: string and integer operators. The hard drive size and RAM fields are treated as integers, whereas all of the other fields are treated as strings where a case-insensitive string compare is done to determine operator results. The string operators are contains, doesn't contain, begins with, and equals. The integer operators are =, <>, >, >=, <, and <=.

These operators perform expected comparisons between the key value supplied by the workstation to the imaging server and the value that you place into the value field of the equation. The following meanings are placed with each operator:

▶ *Contains*—The specified value is a substring anywhere in the reported value.

▶ *Doesn't Contain*—The specified value is not equal to or contained in the reported value.

▶ *Begins With*—The specified values are represented in the initial character of the reported value.

▶ *Equals*—The specified value is the same as the reported value.

▶ = (equals)—The specified value is numerically equivalent to the reported value.

▶ <> (not equal)—The specified value is not equal to the reported value.

▶ > (greater than)—The specified value is greater than the reported value.

▶ >= (greater than or equal to)—The specified value is numerically equal to or greater than the reported value.

▶ < (less than)—The specified value is less than the reported value.

▶ <= (less than or equal to)—The specified value is numerically less than or equal to the reported value.

The next field in the operation is where you enter the value that you want to compare. The far right field enables you to extend the operation to additional key/value comparisons. Your choices currently are **AND** and **OR**.

The Boolean operators are evaluated strictly from left to right. For example, if the following rules were entered into the policy, the resultant evaluation would be (hard drive < 600MB AND RAM < 16MB) OR (RAM > 31MB).

1. Hard drive size >= 600MB AND

2. RAM < 16MB OR

3. RAM > 31MB

This would result in giving the image to any system that has a disk smaller than 200MB with less than 16MB of RAM. This would also give the image to any system that has more than 31MB of RAM regardless of the size of the hard drive.

You can view the precedence of the equation, complete with parentheses, on the bottom half of the screen as you introduce new key/value pairs into your rule.

Once your set of key/value pairs has been entered and you have reviewed your equation at the bottom of the screen, you press the OK button to include the rule into the imaging system, and you are returned to the original Rules page with the rule that you had entered on the screen.

Once again, from this page, after you have entered some rules you can then specify the order in which the rules are evaluated. After selecting a rule you can move that rule in the order by pressing either the Move Up or the Move Down buttons. As the imaging server is evaluating the rules, the first rule that results in a TRUE evaluation results in that image being supplied to the workstation.

Multicast

This page allows you to specify whether the imaging server determines whether the workstation should take part in a multicast session prior to checking the image selection rules within this policy. If the check box is checked, the imaging server will check the image selection rules prior checking its multicast sessions.

NOTE This check box will have no effect on workstations configured to serve as session masters, because that role takes priority over any other imaging setting.

Image-Safe Data Page

The Image-Safe data page is composed of three pages. These pages represent information and data that is placed or retrieved from the system regardless of the image that is used. The following depicts the pages that are available by selecting the small triangle drop-down menu on the tab.

The Image-Safe Data agent can be placed on the workstation. This agent has the responsibility of moving data between a special sector on the disk that is used to store configuration information such as IP address or DHCP configuration along with workgroup information. This information on the disk is not affected by an image taken or placed on the drive.

When the Image-Safe Data agent runs on the workstation it makes sure that the information in the special sector and the operating system are synchronized properly. For example, following an image placement, the agent moves the data from the disk into the operating system, setting up the DHCP and computer name. On a workstation that has not just been imaged the agent moves the information from the operating system into the sector on the disk so the data can be restored should a new image be placed on the drive. Should the agent not run, the workstation would be an exact mirror of the image (with the same IP and computer name configuration).

The Image-Save Data configuration page enables the imaging server to pass this configuration information to the agent via this disk sector.

IP Assignment Log Page

The IP Assignment Log page displays the IP addresses that the imaging server has assigned to any imaged or re-imaged workstations. The set of available IP addresses can be set in the IP Configuration page.

The IP Assignment page displays the log of the assigned addresses.

This page can also be used to place an IP address back into the pool of available addresses. If you have an address that you want to place back into the pool, you can select it in the log list and then press the Remove button.

WARNING When you remove a specific IP address it might not be properly represented in the IP Configuration range and therefore cannot be reused.

If you have specified a range to be the set of IP addresses that you will make available for workstations, when the imaging server uses a portion of the range (at the ends), the range is refreshed on the configuration page. For example, if the range 123.65.234.1 ... 123.65.234.100 were in the configuration and IP address 123.65.234.1-10 were assigned, the range would be changed to 123.65.234.11 ... 123.65.234.100. Consequently, when you go to the log page and free up IP address 123.65.234.10, the range is not reconfigured and the freed IP address is not reassigned. You must manually go to the configuration page and modify the range to include the addresses that you have freed.

IP Configuration Page

The IP Configuration page enables you to specify whether the workstations that are imaged by the imaging server will obtain their IP address from a DHCP server or via a static assignment that is done as part of the imaging process.

If you select the DHCP option, the windows system gets the IP addresses from a DHCP server. If, however, you select that you want to specify an IP address, the other fields on the page are activated.

To specify a static IP address, you must first enter the subnet mask and default gateway that you want all of your imaged workstations (imaged via the image server using this particular policy) to receive. You must also specify the range of IP addresses that are used by the imaging server and assigned uniquely to each of the imaged workstations. You specify the set of IP addresses by using the Add and Add Range buttons.

When the imaging server receives a request for an image, the IP address information is transmitted and assigned to the workstation. That address is then logged in the imaging server and not reused for another workstation.

To remove any address or ranges from the possible set, select the item and press the Remove button. These addresses will no longer be in the pool of available addresses for the imaging server to assign.

Windows Networking Page

In the Windows Networking page, you can specify the computer name for the workstation and the workgroup for the system.

The computer name prefix that you enter in the field (maximum of seven characters) is prepended to a randomly generated set of characters and numbers to construct the final 15-character computer name for the workstation.

The Make the Computer a Member of the Following field enables you to specify the workgroup that you want for the workstation. You select which you prefer by selecting the field and entering the workgroup name.

DNS Settings

This page allows you to specify the DNS suffix and name servers used by this policy. Simply type the suffix you want to use and then click the Add button to specify the addresses of name servers. It is important to use the correct suffix and name servers for the ZENworks for Desktops imaging engine to process imaging operations on a workstation.

Security Page

As part of the imaging system, you can request that the workstation have an image taken of itself and placed onto the server. This is done by checking some fields in the workstation object (See Chapter 14, for more details), which causes the workstation to take an image of itself on its next reboot.

When the workstation takes an image of itself, or when an image is taken when a request is made through the Linux boot system, the image is transmitted to the image server. This image server then receives the .ZMG file and places it in the path that was specified. To protect the system from overwriting any files or by having users place the image files into inappropriate directories, the imaging server takes the information in the security page and restricts the placement of the image files.

When you check the Allow Imaging to Overwrite Existing Files When Uploading option, you are enabling the system to overwrite any files that have the same name as the one specified by the user, with the name of the image file.

The Restrict Uploads to the Following Directories check box activates the requirement that all requested uploads must specify one of the directories identified. If the directory portion of the destination path, specified by the user, does not match one of the directories specified in the list on this page, the request to store the uploaded image is refused. To add paths to the list of accepted destinations, press the Add button and enter in the path that is acceptable.

Paths in the directories can be one of the following formats:

```
Driveletter:path
Volume\path
NTShare\path
```

The system does not, for example, take any UNC path. When the user enters the location of the file, this information transmits to the imaging server, and the server compares the directory portion of the path given with all of the strings in this list. If a match occurs (that is, the directory is listed), the operation is accepted and the image is taken and stored; otherwise, the operation fails and the image is not taken.

Workstation Import Policy

In previous versions of ZENworks for Desktops when a workstation registered with the tree, it would place a cookie into the container of the user. Then the administrator had to execute an import program on their workstation to take these registration records and create workstation objects. These workstation object DNs were then communicated back to the workstation via the same registration/reboot process. If your system was very large, it could become very uncomfortable having to keep running the import program. Often administrators got creative and scheduled the import process to run as a scheduled action on their workstations.

In ZENworks for Desktops 4, this is no longer necessary. A service that now runs on a NetWare or Windows server automatically receives these requests and immediately creates the workstation object. Once the object is created it returns the DN to the workstation. The workstation no longer needs to perform a reboot in order to get its registered workstation DN. In order to perform these actions, the import service must be running on the server and must be accessible using the DNS name of `zen-wsimport` through the local host file on each workstation or via a DNS service. Additionally, the import service must have rights in the directory to be able to create the workstation objects. The pages in this policy enable you to grant these create rights to the import service, to specify how to name the workstation objects and in which container to place the objects, and to limit the number of requests that can be satisfied (to keep the system from overloading a server).

The import service can also be configured to ignore the first N requests from a workstation before it creates a workstation object. This can be useful if the workstation needs to pass through several hands to get properly configured and tested before it is actually given to the final user. This is to help this process settle before the workstation object is actually created.

NOTE Your desktops do not import automatically if the workstations are finding a ZENworks 2 search policy in the tree. They must see either no search policy or a ZENworks for Desktops 4 search policy in order to activate the automatic workstation import and other ZENworks for Desktops 4 features. See Chapter 3, "Setting Up ZENworks for Desktops 4 in Your Tree," and the section, "Setting Up the Workstation in the Tree" for more information.

The following sections describe each of the pages found in the Workstation Import process. The NDS Rights, Other, and Rights to Files and Folders pages are described in the "Setting Up a Server Policy Package" section.

Containers Page

This page enables you to grant rights to the import service to containers where they must create workstation objects. When you add a container to the list, the system grants rights to the policy object. When the import service needs to perform an import it logs in as the policy being used, enabling it to obtain rights to create workstation objects in the specified container.

The process of adding and removing containers is familiar. You press the Add button and then you are presented with a dialog box that enables you to browse through the tree to select the container you desire. Once selected, the container is added to the list and the import service is given a trustee assignment to that container and given the rights to Browse and Create objects.

To remove a container from the list, select the desired container and press the Remove button. This removes the trustee assignment that was given to the service and deletes it from the displayed list.

Platforms Page

The Platforms page enables you to specify the naming of the workstation objects, the location of the object in the tree, and any workstation groups of which you want the workstation objects to be a member. This can be specified for each of the following categories: General, WinNT/2000 (including Windows XP), or Win 9x (for example, Windows 95/98).

Each of the pages within these categories is identical, with the exception that on the non-general pages you have the additional field: Enable Platform Settings to Override General Settings. When this field is checked, the platform-specific configuration parameters are used rather than the general ones. This chapter discusses the general pages because they apply to all of the other platform pages.

Figure 12.8 displays the first general page that is available.

Each page has three tabs that enable you to configure separate options of the import policy. These tabs are Location, Naming, and Groups. Each of the following subsections discusses these tabs.

Location Tab

This page enables you to identify the container in the tree that should hold the workstation object when it is created during the import process. Figure 12.8 displays this screen.

The Allow Importing of Workstations flag enables you to import workstations from this user. Once this flag is activated, the other fields of the page are usable.

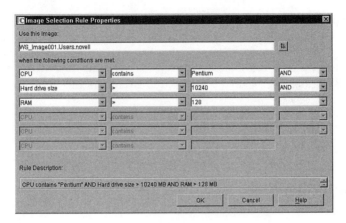

FIGURE 12.8
General page of a sample Workstation Import Policy of a Server Policy
Package.

The Create Workstation Objects in drop-down box allows the administrator various options for locating the container in which to place the
workstation objects. The options are as follows:

▶ *Server Container*—This option is new to ZENworks for Desktops 4
and when selected tells the system to place the workstation objects
in the same container as the server that is running the import
process.

▶ *User Container*—This signals that the container that holds the user
object, of the user who had logged into the system when the registration of the workstation occurred, is the container that also holds
the workstation object. Remember it is the first user who connects
to the system (after the number of ignored connections has passed)
that has the association to the workstation. You can specify a path
relative to the user's container. The path field is constructed by
entering a relative path. This relative path is constructed by a series
of dots and container names. For each dot in the path, the system
moves up one level from the associated object container. For example, the path of ..Workstations tells the system to go up two levels
and then in a container called Workstations at that level. If you
want an alternative user, you must run the un-registration tool
described in Chapter 14.

▶ *Associated Object Container*—This signals that the container that has the policy package associated with it is used as the starting container to place the workstation object. If a path is specified, the associated container is used as the base and the path is considered a relative path. The path field is constructed by entering a relative path, as described previously.

▶ *Selected Container*—This identifies that the specified path is an absolute container path in the tree. The Path field is required with this selection and must identify the specific container that will hold the workstation object.

Workstation Naming Page

On this page, you can describe how the import process should use the information in the registration to craft the name of the workstation object.

The Workstation Name field displays the final combination of registration information that is combined into the name. In the previous example, the workstation object name is the computer name followed by the MAC address. This is confirmed by the fact that the workstation name field has Computer+MAC Address. If the computer name was `Rtanner` and the MAC address of the NIC card were `12345`, the workstation object name would be `Rtanner12345`.

The Add Name Fields and Place Them in Order field displays the various components that form the workstation name. Each line that is displayed in this field represents a value that is part of the name. The order of the lines from top to bottom represents the order that they appear in the name. The options that can be placed in the names are as follows:

▶ *<User Defined>*—This represents an administrator defined string. When this field is chosen, the administrator is prompted to enter a string into the dialog box. This string is placed into the name. This can be any combination of standard ASCII visible characters including white space characters.

▶ *Computer*—This represents the computer name that was given to the computer usually during installation of the operating system.

▶ *Container*—This represents the name of the container into which the workstation object is placed. This name is then included in the workstation name.

▶ *CPU*—This value represents the CPU type of the machine. The possible values are 386, 486, and PENTIUM.

▶ *DNS*—This represents the DNS (Domain Name Services) name of the computer.

▶ *IP Address*—This represents the IP address of the machine when it is first registered with the tree. In previous versions of ZENworks for Desktops this was retrieved through the Network Address request and a preferred protocol set to IP.

▶ *MAC Address*—This represents the address of the machine when it is first registered with the tree. In previous versions of ZENworks for Desktops this was referred to as the network address.

▶ *OS*—This represents the operating system type of the machine. The expected values would be WINNT, WIN95, for example.

▶ *Server*—This represents the name of the current server. If the user login has not occurred, and the preferred server has not been done, this server could simply be the first server that responded with a connection. In WINNT systems, where the registration is running as part of a service, this server is the first server to respond to the request for the connection and not necessarily the preferred server of the user.

▶ *User*—This is the login name of the user who was connected to the tree when the registration process first executed.

As an example, assume that a workstation had been registered with the following values:

```
CPU = PENTIUM
DNS = zen.novell.com
MAC address = 00600803c2e7
IP address = 137.65.61.99
OS = WINNT
Server = ZENSERVER
User = rtanner
Computer = RonComputer
```

Then, if you were to administer the workstation import policy with the following naming attributes, the corresponding workstation name would be created, assuming pieces that are in quotes are a user-defined string:

```
UserOS = rtannerWINNT
DNSCPU = zen.novell.comPENTIUM
User" "MAC Address = rtanner 00600803c2e7
```

You must remember that these values are only used at workstation object creation time. Once the object is created its name never changes. So if you replace the NIC card, although the address of the workstation changed, the name of the workstation does not change; if the name includes the NIC address, the workstation retains the name with the old NIC address.

Workstations Groups

The Workstation Groups page enables you to specify into which groups you want to place the workstation object when it is created. By placing the workstation object into a specific group you can automatically provide policies or rights to the workstation by group associations.

In the Workstation Groups page you can add and remove groups in the list and the workstation will be placed in as a member of each group. The following describes the behavior of each button on the screen:

▶ *Add*—Press this button to add a group to the list. A dialog box enables you to browse the tree to identify the group. You browse the tree in the right pane and select the group in the left pane. Once a group is selected it is added and displayed to the list.

▶ *Remove*—This button is activated when a group in the window is highlighted (by pressing the left mouse button) when the cursor is over the desired group. When a group is selected and this button is pressed, the group is removed from the list.

▶ *Remove All*—This button removes all groups from the list and cleans the set from consideration.

Remember that this policy is only activated when a new workstation is imported into the tree. If a workstation that was created with this policy is associated with a group and you go into the import policy and change the group memberships, the workstations that have already been created retain their group memberships. Only the new workstations created after the change are affected.

Limits Page

On the Limits page you can have some control over when a workstation automatically registers and how the import service on the server behaves. The intention of these fields is to ensure that the performance of the service does not consume a significant amount of processing on the server.

The first portion of the page, the User Login Number field, enables you to configure how many times the workstation must be used (a user logs into the network via that desktop) before it is registered into the tree. This option is useful when your desktops must pass through several hands (that may connect to the tree) before they get to the final user destination. Each time the workstation is used and a user is connected to the tree (or the Workstation Manager agents connect to the tree), the workstation communicates with the workstation import and requests a workstation object. If the number of login times has not been consumed, the service reports that one is not created, and the workstation continues. This repeats until the number of login times has occurred, whereupon the service creates the workstation object and returns the DN of the workstation object to the workstation. The desktop then records this DN in its Registry.

The user login count is kept in the workstation Registry and is transmitted to the import server, which checks it against the policy. If the count is greater than the policy, the import is performed. This count on the workstation is not reset if the policy changes.

Limiting the number of workstations imported enables the administrator to throttle the number of workstations that are created. This keeps your NDS from overloading with a tremendous amount of objects and having to synchronize them around your tree. Imposing this limit forces the service to only create the specified number of workstations in an hour. As soon as the maximum has been reached within the hour, the workstations are told to proceed without a workstation object. The next time they log into the network, and the maximum has not been exceeded, the service creates a workstation object for them.

Workstation Removal Policy

Along with the capability to automatically create workstations in the tree, ZENworks for Desktops 4 provides an automated way to remove expired workstation objects from the tree. This is to keep the tree from being cluttered with workstations that are no longer associated with any physical device.

Each time a workstation is used and it has been registered in the tree, a service visits the workstation object and timestamps the last visit into the workstation object, along with refreshing several other pieces of information in the workstation object. This timestamp is what the Workstation Removal service is looking at when it determines whether the workstation should be removed.

The following pages enable the administrator to configure how the system removes these expired workstation objects. The NDS Rights, Other, *and* Rights to Files and Folders pages are described in the "Setting Up a Server Policy Package" section.

Containers Page

This page enables you to grant rights to the removal service to containers where they must remove workstation objects. When you add a container to the list, the system grants rights to the policy object. When the removal service needs to perform and delete a workstation object it logs in as the policy being used, enabling it to obtain rights to remove workstation objects in the specified container.

These containers are the only ones that the service monitors for stale workstation objects.

The process of adding and removing containers is familiar. You press the Add button and then you are presented with a dialog box that enables you to browse through the tree to select the container you desire. Once selected, the container is added to the list and the import service is given a trustee assignment to that container, and given the rights to Browse and Delete objects.

To remove a container from the list, select the desired container and press the Remove button. This removes the trustee assignment that was given to the service and deletes it from the displayed list.

Limits Page

This page enables you to specify how stale a workstation object must be before it is considered for removal. Figure 12.9 shows a snapshot of a sample limits page.

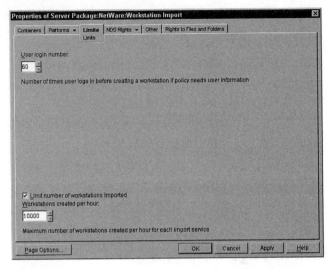

FIGURE 12.9
Workstation Removal Policy; Limits page.

You can use the up and down buttons to specify the number of days the workstation should not be connected with a device before it is considered for deletion. Once the timestamp in the workstation object is older than the specified number of days on this page, the removal service deletes the object from the directory.

Schedule Page

This page enables you to identify how often and when the workstation removal service should run on the server.

On this page, you can identify the following configuration schedules:

- ▶ *Year*—This is the year to begin the launch of the removal service.
- ▶ *Date*—This is the calendar date with the above year when the removal service will be launched.
- ▶ *Start Time*—This is the time of day when the removal service is available to run.
- ▶ *Duration*—This enables you to specify how long, after the start time, the removal service should run.

▶ *Repeat Interval*—This enables you to specify how often after the initial start date the removal service should re-run and be made available.

▶ *Limit Number of Workstations Removed*—This enables you to specify in the session value the maximum number of workstations that should be removed while the removal service is available. When this maximum is reached, the service quits removing workstations until the next specified execution time. This is to keep from consuming a significant amount of processing cycles for DS to refresh the partitions where the removal has occurred.

The service, when started, calculates based on the start date and how often it should come alive (interval) and which day it should work. If today's the day, the service begins its workstation removal work. This is done so that even if the server needed to be rebooted, the service would still properly calculate the day it should run and not rely on being up the number of days in the interval.

Using the Roll-Up Policy

The Roll-Up Policy dictates to the services that are running on a specific server where they should roll-up or transmit the inventory information that they have received from the various workstations. By doing this, the system provides the capability to receive local inventory information and then move it up in the tree hierarchy, consolidating inventory information from various remote locations, and constructing a more centralized database of inventory information (see Chapter 13, "Using ZENworks Workstation Inventory," for more detailed information).

When the inventory system is installed into the network, the system creates service objects that govern the behavior of the agents that are working on each of the inventory servers. These agents also respond to this policy to understand to which service agent they should transmit their inventory information. All service agents that are associated with this policy transmit their inventory information to the same target agent.

The NDS Rights, Other, *and* Rights to Files and Folders pages are described in the "Setting Up a Server Policy Package" section.

Figure 12.10 shows a sample of this page.

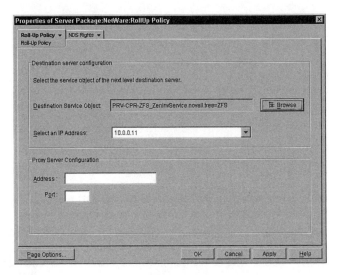

FIGURE 12.10
Inventory Roll-up Policy of a Server Policy Package.

As you can see in Figure 12.10, the policy simply requests the object DN of the service where the associated agents should transmit their inventory information. The local agents can keep a copy of the inventory data, if they are a designated database gathering location, but they still transmit an additional copy if they are configured to do so.

In this policy, you press the browse button to the right of the field and browse the tree to select the service object of the inventory agent that you want to receive the information.

The roll-up policy is only read by the service manager agent upon startup and then every 1000 minutes (this is not configurable). So if the policy change needs to be immediately effective, the service manager agent on the server must be stopped and restarted.

Using the Wake-on-LAN Policy

The Wake-on-LAN policy allows you to manage which managed workstations are controlled by the Wake-on-LAN service. The Wake-on-LAN service allows you to wake up a managed workstation or a set of managed workstations when activity on the LAN is detected. From the

Wake-on-LAN policy page, you can specify objects from the following list of targets:

- ▶ *Containers*—All workstations in a Country, Locality, Organization, or Organizational Unit.

- ▶ *Workstation*—A specific workstation object.

- ▶ *Workstation Group*—All workstations associated with a specific workstation group object.

## CHAPTER 13

Using ZENworks Workstation Inventory

ZENworks for Desktops includes powerful workstation inventory software that allows you to gather complete hardware and software inventory for all managed workstations on your network. Once workstations have been imported, you can use the inventory software to collect, store, and report information about the client workstations on your network. This information can be useful in making business decisions on how to manage workstations. The following are some examples of business decisions that can be made from workstation inventory information:

- ▶ Which workstations need new applications
- ▶ Which workstations need updated hardware and drivers
- ▶ Which workstations should receive an application object
- ▶ Which workstations are running the corporate software standard
- ▶ Which workstations conform to the corporate hardware standard

The following sections describe the workstation inventory process, how to set up inventory in your environment, and which tasks can be performed once it has been properly installed and configured.

Understanding Workstation Inventory

To better help you understand how to make the most of the workstation inventory feature of ZENworks for Desktops, you need to know how the process works and which components are involved. The following sections describe the inventory process, the servers that are involved, and the roles they play in various inventory database designs.

Understanding the Inventory Process

The inventory process is the act of acquiring hardware and software information from the workstation, relaying that information to the inventory server, and then storing it into a database for later retrieval. The following sections describe how workstations are scanned, how inventory data is rolled up to the database, what information is collected, and the files and directories involved.

Workstation Scanning

Workstation scanning is done by an application that runs on the workstation. The inventory scanner and all necessary components were installed on the workstation when the ZENworks Management Agent was installed. That application scans the workstation and collects data based on the configurations of the inventory settings. If the workstation is Desktop Management Interface (DMI)-compliant or Web-based Management Interface (WMI)-compliant, the scanner can also query the DMI and WMI service layers to collect data.

Once the scanner has collected information about the workstation, it stores it in an .STR file in the scan directory of the inventory server. The scanner tracks the changes in the scan data by storing it in the HIST.INI file, located in the ZENworks installation directory. Any errors that the scanner reports are stored in the ZENERRORS.LOG file, located in the ZENworks installation directory.

Workstation inventory scanning uses the following steps to update the inventory server and eDirectory:

   1. The inventory policies in eDirectory define the inventory settings, such as scanning time, whether to include software scanning of workstations, and the location of the scan directory.

2. The scanner reads the settings in the inventory policies and uses them to collect the workstation inventory information.

3. The scanner stores the scan data of each workstation as an .STR file in the scan directory (**SCANDIR**) at the server.

4. The scanner also stores a minimal subset of workstation inventory information of the workstation, in the eDirectory workstation object.

5. The selector, running on the inventory server, validates the .STR file and places the file in the enterprise merge directory (**ENTMERGEDIR**). If a database is attached, the selector places the files in the database directory (**DBDIR**).

6. If a database is attached to the server, the server updates the database with the inventory information of the .STR file.

7. You can then view the inventory information, query the database, and generate inventory reports in ConsoleOne.

Inventory Data Roll Up

Now that you understand how the inventory scan process works, you need to understand how that information is rolled up to other servers and databases that are higher in the tree. In many networks, one server is not enough to collect and store inventory data for every workstation in the tree. For this reason, you can configure multiple servers to collect inventory data and roll that information up to other servers.

ZENworks uses the following steps to roll up scanned data once it has been collected on a server:

1. Once the selector validates the .STR file and places the file in the enterprise merge directory (**ENTMERGEDIR**) for roll-up of scan data, the sending server uses a roll-up policy to identify the server to which it will transmit the scan data. It also reads the roll up schedule to determine the specified time for rolling up the data.

2. The sending server compresses the .STR files as a .ZIP file and places the .ZIP file in the enterprise push directory (**ENTPUSHDIR**). The sender then sends the .ZIP file to the receiver on the next-level server.

3. The receiving server on the next-level receives the .ZIP file and places the file in **ENTPUSHDIR**. If this server has a database attached to it or if the server is a root server, the compressed files are placed in the database directory (**DBDIR**).

4. The receiving server extracts the .ZIP file containing the .STR files into a temp directory (**DBDIR\TEMP**) and updates the database with the inventory information of the workstation .STR file.

5. The network administrator can then view the inventory information, query the database, and generate inventory reports in ConsoleOne.

What Software Information Is Recorded

The scan program scans the workstation software for Desktop Management Interface (DMI) software as well as WMI (Web-based Management Interface) systems. Even if both of these are not present, the scanner will contact the hardware directly and then continue to scan the drive for installed software. The software scan performs the following functions based on its setup and configuration:

▶ Checks for the existence of the software at the workstations and servers.

▶ Gathers information about the application file.

▶ Reports the information about the scanned software (such as software vendor, software title, file size, and so on).

▶ Checks for the software specified in the inventory policy associated with the workstation object.

▶ Customizes the software scanning based on the software list configured (discussed later).

▶ Collects configuration file information and reports details and contents of the system files.

▶ Reports information about the installed drivers.

Inventory Files and Directories

Workstation inventory uses several files and directories during the scanning and roll up processes. You should be aware of the following files used during the scanning and roll up process:

▶ *HIST.INI*—Located in the Windows **TEMP** directory on the workstation. Contains the history of the scan data for each workstation.

▶ *.STR*—Formatted: *macaddress_gmt_sequencenumber*.**STR**. Located in the **SCANDIR** directory on the inventory server. Created by the scanning program. Contains all inventory information scanned from the workstation.

▶ *.ZIP*—Formatted: *scheduletime_inventoryservername_siteID_*
sitename.**ZIP**. Located in the **EntPushDir** and **DBDir** directories.
Contains the compressed scan data for several workstations, up to
1000 .STR files, collected by a receiving inventory server. Used to
transmit the data from one server to another.

▶ *.PRP*—Formatted: scheduletime_inventoryservername.PRP. Located
in the .ZIP files. Identifies the information for roll up from the
enterprise push directory to the next-level server. The properties
file contains the schedule time, inventory server name, and signa-
ture that helps to authenticate the .ZIP file.

Once the scan program runs and the hardware and software information
about the server is recorded, that information is stored on the inventory
servers in the following directory locations:

▶ **ScanDir**—Contains the .STR files. This is the raw data collected by
the scan programs run at the workstation.

▶ **DBDir**—Contains the .STR files for workstations that have been
scanned on the network. The .STR files in the **DBDir** directory are
used to update the workstation objects in the database.

▶ **EntMergeDir**—Stores the .STR and files created and transferred by
the workstation scan programs.

▶ **EntPushDir**—Stores the .STR and .ZIP files used to roll up inventory data in an enterprise tree.

Understanding Inventory Database Server Types

Now that you understand how the scan process works, you need to
understand what happens to the data that is scanned by the workstations. That data is stored in directories and databases located on inventory servers. The following sections describe the types of servers used in
the inventory process.

Root Server

The root server acts as the highest point in the inventory tree. A root
server by default must have a database attached to it. The root server can
collect data from intermediate servers, leaf servers, or from workstations
attached to it. A root server can be configured only to receive data, not to
roll it up to another level.

Intermediate Server

The intermediate server acts as a staging server to receive data from a lower server in the tree and send it to another intermediate server or to a root server. By default, the intermediate server does not have a database, nor does it have workstations. However, you can configure the intermediate server to have both workstations and a database attached to it. The intermediate server typically receives data from a leaf server or another intermediate server and then rolls it up higher in the tree, eventually to the root server.

Leaf Server

The leaf server gathers inventory information from workstations. By default, the leaf server must have workstations attached, but does not have a database attached to it. The leaf server simply gathers data and rolls it up higher in the tree. Typically the data is rolled up to an intermediate server, but a leaf server can also roll data up to a root server.

Stand-Alone Server

The stand-alone server acts as a single point of inventory data collection for workstations. The stand-alone server must have both a database and workstations attached to it. The data collected by a stand-alone server cannot be rolled up to another server, nor can information collected by a leaf server be rolled up to a stand-alone server. Typically the stand-alone server is used in small networks where only one inventory server is needed to collect data.

Understanding Inventory Server Roles

Now that you understand the types of servers that are used for workstation inventory, you need to know the roles they can provide. Depending on their types, each server can be configured to perform one or both of the following two roles.

Workstations Attached

The first role servers can perform is to have workstations attached. Setting this option means that this server accepts data from the scan programs being run at the workstations. At least one server on the network must be performing this role, but usually most of the servers configured for workstation inventory will be performing the role of collecting data from the workstations. Leaf servers and stand-alone servers always have this option set, but you can configure root server and intermediate servers to have workstations attached as well.

Database Attached

The next role a server can perform is to have a database attached to it. Setting this option means that the server is configured to enter the information scanned by the workstation, either locally or up from a server below, into a local database. This means that a database must be running on the server to accept the information from ZENworks. Root servers and stand-alone servers always have this option set, but you can configure intermediate servers and leaf servers to have a database as well.

Workstation Inventory Design

Now that you understand the types of servers and the roles they play in workstation inventory, you need to design an inventory tree that matches your network. The following sections describe some common designs for generic networks.

Stand-Alone Inventory

The stand-alone inventory is the simplest design. Only one server is involved. That server acts as the collection and storage service for inventory data scanned from workstations. It has an inventory database installed on it and workstations attached.

This type of design is perfect for smaller networks with 5,000 or fewer workstations. It is easy to maintain and configure; however, it is not scalable.

Centralized Inventory

The centralized inventory design, shown in Figure 13.1, is for large networks where all servers are connected on a LAN. In this approach allowance is made for a larger number of users by adding a number of leaf and intermediate servers for workstation scanners to send their data to.

The centralized inventory approach is still fairly easy to maintain; however, roll up policies must be configured for the intermediate and leaf servers.

Centralized Inventory

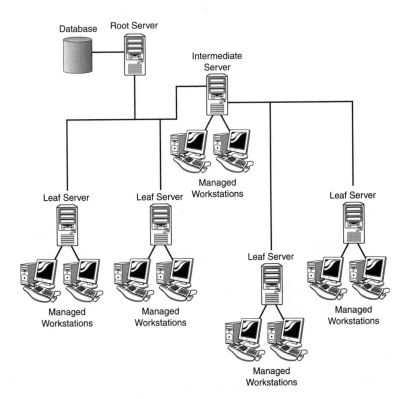

FIGURE 13.1
The centralized workstation inventory design.

Distributed Inventory

The distributed inventory design, shown in Figure 13.2, is for large networks where several remote sites are connected through a WAN. In this approach allowance is made for a larger number of users by creating several root servers, one at each remote site, and then leaf and intermediate servers for workstation scanners to send their data to.

The distributed inventory approach is still much more difficult to maintain because you need to manage several inventory trees. However the distributed approach overcomes problems that can occur, rolling up large numbers of workstations from remote offices.

Distributed Inventory

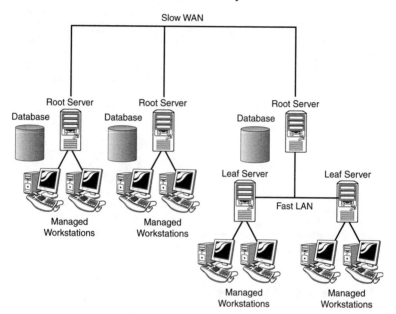

FIGURE 13.2
The distributed workstation inventory design.

Enterprise Inventory

The final type of inventory design is the enterprise inventory design shown in Figure 13.3. Most enterprise networks take this approach in one form or another. In the enterprise design, accommodations for the large number of users, yet a single management point, is made by creating a single root server and then interlacing intermediate and leaf servers at strategic locations in the network to insure optimal performance.

The best way to achieve an optimal enterprise design is to follow the steps outlined in the following sections.

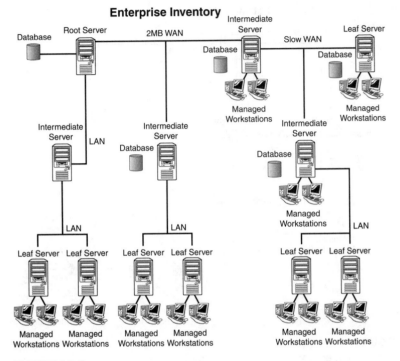

FIGURE 13.3
The enterprise workstation inventory design.

List the Sites in the Enterprise

The first step in designing an enterprise workstation inventory tree is to describe the entire network of your company by doing the following:

- ▶ List the various sites in your company (buildings, cities, countries, and so on).

- ▶ List the physical links between the various sites.

- ▶ Identify the type of links in terms of bandwidth and reliability.

Determine the Ideal Place for Root Server

Once you have listed the sites in your enterprise network, you need to determine the best place to put the root server. The inventory information stored in the inventory database of the root server consists of all lower-level sites on the network as well as the root server site.

The location of the root server determines the behavior and scalability of your inventory tree. You should consider the following factors when determining its location:

▶ The root server should be on the site with high network bandwidth.

▶ A console administrator can collect workstation inventory information from any of the sites connected on high-speed links from the root server, or from the root server level site.

▶ A database server of suitable configuration can be provided for the inventory server. For a network with 250,000 workstations, the recommended configuration for the root server is 25GB of disk space and 1GB RAM.

Determine Requirements for Other Databases

Now that you have determined the location of the root server, you need to determine if you need to maintain database servers at different sites. You might want to maintain additional databases if sites or sub-trees are managed for inventory at different locations over a slow link.

You should also consider specific reasons to have a separate database for a single site or a set of sites. Your company might have organizational needs that require the database server to be on different sites.

NOTE For a majority of enterprises, there is no need to have any other database besides the enterprise-wide single database. All site-specific reports can be generated from this database easily.

If you determine that another database is required, consider the following to determine the appropriate location and setup:

▶ Identify the sites that need a database. Additionally, you need to examine whether the database will cater to the local site or a site of sites (sub-tree). Then identify the sites that require data in each inventory database.

▶ All the sites served by a single database should typically access this database instead of the database at root server for inventory management. This reduces the load on the database at the root server.

▶ Database administrators should be available for these sites.

Identify the Route for Inventory Data

Once you have determined any additional databases needed, you need to identify the routes for inventory data for all sites to the nearest database. From those routes, you then need to determine the final route to the database on the root server.

The route plan can become complex, so to help devise a route plan, follow these guidelines:

▶ Each route can have an intermediate server at a staging site. The Intermediate Server receives and transmits the data to the next destination. These are application-layer level routes for inventory data. There can be various network-layer level routes between two adjacent servers, which is determined and managed by the routers in the network.

▶ The route answers the basic question: To which site will the inventory data travel from a particular site so that it eventually reaches the database at the root server, which is its final destination?

▶ There can be multiple routes. Choose the fastest and most reliable route. To determine the route, consider the physical network links.

▶ Routes identified once and made operational can be changed later; although there might be some cost in terms of management and traffic generation. If no intermediate database is involved, you can change the route by changing the eDirectory-based policy only.

▶ Put intermediate servers on sites where the link parameters change substantially. Criteria to consider is difference in bandwidth, unreliability of the links, and need for different scheduling.

▶ Availability of servers on the intermediate site for staging the inventory data should be considered in deciding the sites for intermediate servers. Provide enough disk space on these servers to store all the inventory data on the disk until the roll-up policy asks to send them to the next destination.

▶ Workstations should not be connected to the inventory server over a WAN, as the scanning of workstations should not happen across a WAN.

Identify Servers on Each Site for Inventory, Intermediate, and Database

Once you have planned the routes that the data will take to the root server, you need to identify servers on each site to perform the roles necessary to achieve the route. Specifically you need to identify servers to act as inventory, intermediate, and database server.

A single server can have different roles if it has sufficient resources. For example, an inventory server can be a leaf server with a database. You can also designate a server as an intermediate server with a database, which receives inventory from the workstations and also has an inventory database.

When considering the roles of the server, consider the following factors:

▶ The number of workstations attached to the server also determines the load.

▶ Take an average of 50KB inventory data from each workstation to calculate the load.

▶ Any inventory server that has workstations attached to it requires 100KB per workstation.

▶ The server that has the inventory database requires 200KB per workstation.

▶ An intermediate server that rolls up data requires 5KB for roll-up of 50KB scan data.

Create the Tree of Servers for Workstation Inventory

Once you have determined the roles that inventory servers will take at each site, you need to create the tree of servers that will be used for workstation inventory.

Once you have the inventory server tree designed, make certain that the following are true:

▶ The root of the tree is the root server.

▶ Servers on each site of the tree represent all the sites in the company.

▶ At least one server exists per site.

▶ Assuming that workstations to be scanned exist on each site, there is an inventory server role on each site.

▶ Optionally, database and intermediate servers exist at the appropriate sites.

Create an Implementation Plan

Once you have designed your inventory server tree, you need to create an implementation plan. The implementation plan should cover the phased deployment of inventory throughout the network.

To help with creating an implementation plan, use the following guidelines:

▶ Start the deployment from the root server site and flow it down to the servers of other sites that connect to the root server.

▶ Use the number of workstations on each site and server as the main criteria for deployment.

▶ Deploy the product on approximately 5,000 workstations per day.

Setting Up Workstation Inventory

Now that you understand how workstation inventory works, you need to know how to set it up and configure it for your network. Once you have installed the appropriate components and you have your workstation inventory tree design completed, you are ready to begin configuring your network to start scanning workstation data and storing it into the inventory database. The following sections describe the configuration process necessary to implement your tree design.

Configuring the Settings for the Inventory Service Object

The first step in configuring workstation inventory is to configure the settings for the inventory service object. The inventory service object controls how, when, and where the inventory server collects inventory scan data. The following sections discuss how to configure the inventory service object.

Configuring the Inventory Service Object Properties

The first thing you must configure for the inventory service object is the roll, scan data time, and path in the Inventory Service object properties page.

From within ConsoleOne, right-click the inventory service object, click Properties, and then click the Inventory Service Object Properties tab as shown in Figure 13.4. From the Inventory Service Object property page, you can configure the options discussed in the following sections.

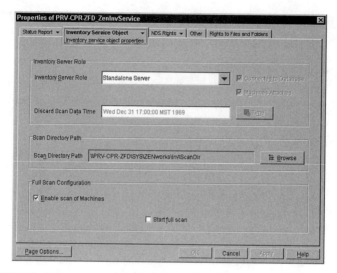

FIGURE 13.4
The Inventory Service Object Properties tab for Inventory Service objects in ConsoleOne.

Modify the Role for the Inventory Service Object
Based on the servers that you have deployed for scanning inventory, you must specify the role of the server. You can select Root Server, Intermediate Server, Leaf Server, or Stand-alone Server based on your inventory configuration.

Discard Scan Data Files at the Specified Date and Time
Set the time at which you want any scan data files (.ZIP files) to be discarded. The scan data files are removed from the server at the time specified in this field. This can be useful in keeping your servers from running out of disk space.

Modify the Path for the Scan Files
When you install ZENworks for Desktops, you specify the volume on the server for storing the scan data files. If required, you can modify the volume or the directory of the Scan Directory (SCANDIR) setting from the Inventory Service Object property page.

To modify the setting, type the location of the new SCANDIR directory path on the server format of the Scan Directory Path, as follows:

`\\server_name\volumename\path`

NOTE You cannot modify the server name specified in the SCANDIR path. If you modify the directory, the directory must already exist.

Enable Scanning of Workstations

You must select the Enable Scanning of Workstations option in order to scan the workstations associated with the policy. By default, the scanners collect only hardware information of the workstations.

Enforce Full Scan

When scanning the workstation for the first time the Scanner collects the complete inventory of the workstation. A complete inventory scan of the workstation is referred as a *full scan*.

After the workstation is inventoried, the next time the scanner runs, it compares the current inventory data to the history data that it maintains. If any changes to the workstation exist, the Scanner creates a *delta scan*, which collects the changes in inventory since the last scan was reported. The delta scan setting is the default scan operation for each successive scan after the first scanning of the workstation.

If the status log reported by the inventory component indicates that the scanning on the workstation is not successful, you can force a full scan. This policy's settings are applicable for all workstations associated with it. To override this policy, you set this option for an individual workstation.

Configuring the Inventory Service Sync Schedule

Once you have configured the settings on the Inventory Service Object Properties page, you need to configure the sync schedule for the inventory service. The Inventory Sync Service runs on all inventory servers that have inventoried workstations attached to them. The Inventory Sync Service is loaded by the Inventory Service Manager. It removes the redundant or obsolete inventoried workstations from the Inventory database.

Use the following steps in ConsoleOne to configure the Inventory Sync Service Schedule to schedule the Inventory Sync Service to run:

1. Right-click the Inventory Service object and select Properties from the pop-up menu.

2. Select Inventory Service Object tab, Inventory Service Sync Schedule, as shown in Figure 13.5.

3. Modify the schedule settings to schedule Inventory Sync Service to run at the appropriate time.

4. Click the OK button to apply the settings and close the window.

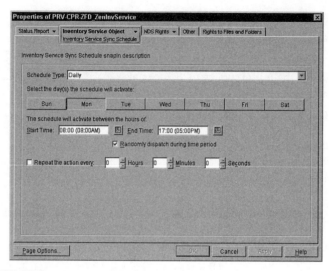

FIGURE 13.5
The Inventory Service Sync Schedule tab for Inventory Service objects in
ConsoleOne.

Configuring the Roll-Up Policy of Scan Data

If your workstation inventory tree design includes multiple levels, you
need to configure roll-up of scan data in your inventory setup. You need
to specify the details, such as the next-level server for roll-up in the Roll-
Up Policy that is contained in the Server Policy Package. Use the steps
discussed in the following sections to create and configure a role-up policy for scan data.

Create a Server Package That Contains the Roll-Up Policy for Identifying the Next-Level Server for Roll-Up

1. In ConsoleOne, right-click the Policy Packages container. Click
   New, click Policy Package, and then click Server Package.

2. Type the name for the Server Package, and click Next. Click Finish.

Enable the Roll-Up Policy in the Server Package and Associate the Server Package

1. In ConsoleOne, right-click the Server Package, and then choose
   Properties, Policies. Choose one of the following sub-tabs: General,
   NetWare, Windows, Linux, or Solaris.

2. Check the check box under the Enabled Column for the Roll-Up
   Policy.

3. Click Properties. The Roll-Up Policy tab should be displayed.

4. Browse to select the DN of the Inventory Service object. Click OK.

5. Next, select the IP address of the inventory server you want to assign the roll-up policy to. You can also specify a proxy server address and port.

6. Click the OK button to assign the roll-up policy.

Schedule the Roll-Up Time

1. In ConsoleOne, right-click the Server Package. Choose Properties, Policies. Then choose one of the following sub-tabs: General, NetWare, Windows, Linux, or Solaris.

2. Choose Roll-Up Policy row, Properties, Roll-Up Policy tab, Roll-Up Schedule. Modify the settings for scheduling the roll-up time. Click OK.

> **NOTE** While scheduling the roll-up of data in the Inventory Policies, the roll-up frequency should be at least one day. It is likely that if the roll-up frequency is too often, for example less than one hour, there might be some performance degradation of the Inventory server.

Configuring the Policies for the Database

The installation program creates the database object for Sybase and configures the database server. However, you need to set up the associations for the database server.

If you are maintaining the inventory database in Oracle or MS SQL Server, you need to perform the tasks in the following sections before making the associations.

Configure the Database Server Options of the Database Object

1. In ConsoleOne, right-click the Database object. Choose Properties, ZENworks Inventory Database.

2. Browse for the DN of the server or type the server IP address.

3. Use these values for the following options: Database (Read-Write) User Name: *MW_DBA*; Database(Read-Write) Password: *<inventory password>*; Database(Read Only) User Name: *MW_READER*; Database(Read Only) Password: *<inventory password>*; Database(Write Only) User Name: *MW_UPDATER*; Database(Write Only) Password: *<inventory password>*.

4. Click OK.

Ensure That the JDBC Driver Properties Are Correct As Per Your Database Configuration.

1. In ConsoleOne, right-click the Database Object. Choose Properties, and then click Jdbc Driver Information.

2. Click Populate Fields and set the default settings for an Oracle database as shown in Table 13.1.

3. Click Populate Now.

4. Click OK.

TABLE 13.1   Database Settings for a Sybase Database, an Oracle Database, and an MS SQL Server Database

DATABASE SETTINGS	FOR A SYBASE DATABASE	FOR AN ORACLE DATABASE	FOR AN MS SQL SERVER
Driver	Com.sybase. jdbc.SybDriver	oracle.jdbc. driver. OracleDriver	com.microsoft. jdbc.sqlserver. SQLServerDriver
Protocol	Jdbc:	jdbc:	jdbc:
SubProtocol:	Sybase:	oracle:	microsoft:
SubName:	Tds:	thin:@	sqlserver:11
Port:	2638	1521	1433
Flags:	?ServiceName= mgmtdbs&JCONNECT_ VERSION=4		
SID Service Name (Service ID of the Oracle database)	-	Orcl	

Once you have completed the steps for creating the inventory database in Oracle or MS SQL, or if you are simply using the Sybase database, use the following steps to associate the server.

Create the Service Location Package to Associate the Database Object with this Package.

You must set up the ZENworks database policy to establish the location of the database; otherwise, no information can be logged to the database. To establish the service location of the database, use the following steps:

1. In ConsoleOne, right-click the Policy Packages container. Click New, Policy Package, Service Location Package. Click Next.

2. Type the name for the Service Location Package. Click Next.

3. Click Finish.

Configure the Service Location Policy and Associate the Database with the Policy

1. In ConsoleOne, right-click the Service Location Package. Choose Properties, and then click the Policies tab.

2. Check the check box under the Enabled column for the ZENworks database policy.

3. Click Properties.

4. Browse to the DN of the ZENworks Database object and click OK to accept the object. Click OK again to close the ZENworks Database properties window.

5. Select the Associations tab, and then click the Add button.

6. Browse to select the container under which the Database Object is present. Click OK twice.

Configuring the Inventory Policies for Workstations

Once you have configured the server database and service location policies, you need to configure the inventory policies for the workstation. In the Workstation Inventory Policy, you configure the following settings for scanning workstations:

- ▶ Scanning time at the workstations
- ▶ Inventory server to which the workstations send scanned data
- ▶ Include software scanning of workstations
- ▶ List software applications for scanning

Use the following steps to configure the Workstation Inventory Policy. First, you need to create a policy package for the workstations:

1. In ConsoleOne, right-click the Container. Click New, Policy Package. Click Workstation Package, and then click Next.

2. Type the name for the Workstation Package. Click Next. Click Finish.

Enable and Associate the Workstation Inventory Policy

1. In ConsoleOne, right-click the Workstation Package. Click Properties, Policies. Click one of the following sub-tabs: Win95-98, WinNT, Win2000, or WinXP.

2. Check the Enable the Workstation Inventory Policy. Click OK.

3. Click the Associations tab, and then choose Add.

4. Select the container object under which the workstations are registered. Click OK twice.

Specify the Inventory Server to Which the Scanner Will Send the Workstation Scan Data

1. In ConsoleOne, right-click the Workstation Package. Choose Properties, Policies. Then click one of the following sub-tabs: Win95-98, WinNT, Win2000, or WinXP.

2. Select the Workstation Inventory Policy row, Properties, and then the Workstation Inventory tab.

3. Configure the Workstation Inventory Policy as described in the next section.

4. Click OK.

Schedule the Time for Activating the Scanning at the Workstations

1. In ConsoleOne, right-click the Workstation Package, and then click Properties, Policies. Choose one of the following sub-tabs: Win95-98, WinNT, Win2000, or WinXP.

2. Click the Workstation Inventory Policy row, Properties. Select the Policy Schedule tab.

3. Modify the settings for scheduling the scan of the workstations. Click OK twice.

Ensure That Scanning Is Enabled

1. In the Inventory Service Object property page, you enable the scan of the workstations associated with the selected Inventory server.

2. From ConsoleOne, right-click the Inventory Service object (`servername_ZenInvService`), and then click Properties. Choose the Inventory Service Object Properties tab.

3. Check Enable Scan of Workstations. Click OK.

Once you have finished configuring the workstation inventory policies for workstations, make the following checks in your environment to make certain that the inventory scanning process can complete properly:

▶ If you have configured the inventory server as a Windows NT/2000 server and Windows 98 workstations are present that will send their scan data to that Windows NT/2000 server, you must do the following for the scanners to collect data:

   ▶ If eDirectory users are present who are also Windows NT/2000 domain users, ensure that the users logged in are valid users of the Windows NT/2000 domain in the existing share created by ZENworks.

   ▶ If users are logged into a different domain, ensure that the users are trusted users of the domain in the existing share created by ZENworks.

   ▶ If eDirectory users are present who are not users of any Windows NT/2000 domain, ensure that the users do not log in to eDirectory during workstation start up. However, these users can log in to eDirectory later.

Configuring the Workstation Inventory Policy

The Workstation Inventory Policy allows you to configure which inventory service that workstations associated with this workstation policy package use. It also allows you to enable and configure hardware and software scanning.

To configure the Server Inventory Policy for a workstation policy package, follow these steps:

1. Right-click the package and select Properties from the drop-down menu.

2. Select the Policies tab for the operating system you want to configure. ZENworks for Desktops 4 allows you to select Win95/98, WinNT, Win2000, WinXP, or general.

3. Enable the Workstation Inventory Policy by checking the box next to it.

4. Select the Workstation Inventory Policy and click the Properties button to bring up the Workstation Inventory Policy Properties window.

The following sections discuss how to configure the Workstation Inventory Policy from this window.

Configure General Settings for the Workstation Inventory Policy

The first step in configuring the Workstation Inventory Policy is to configure which inventory service that workstations associated with this policy will use. Select the General tab in the Workstation Inventory Policy panel as shown in Figure 13.6 and configure the following settings:

- ▶ Inventory Server Object DN—Use the browse button to navigate through the eDirectory tree and locate the correct roll-up schedules and locations configured for servers associated with this Workstation Policy Package.

- ▶ Force Full Scan Schedule—Once you have selected the Inventory Server Object, you need to specify, in the Force Full Scan Schedule field, the number of delta scans that will occur before a full scan is required.

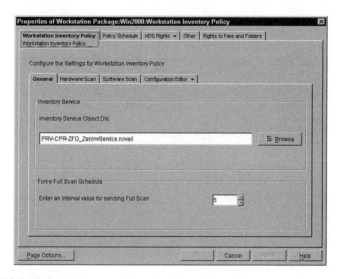

FIGURE 13.6
General settings in the Workstation Inventory Policy panel.

Configure Hardware Scan

Next, you need to configure hardware scanning by selecting the Hardware Scan tab, shown in Figure 13.7, and setting the following options:

- ▶ Enable DMI Scan—Enables ZENworks to collect hardware inventory data from Windows workstations using the Desktop Management Interface (DMI) 2.0 specification.

▶ Enable WMI Scan—Enables ZENworks for Desktops 4 to collect hardware inventory data from Windows workstations using the Web-based Management Interface (WMI) 1.5 specification.

▶ Enable Custom Scanning—Allows you to enable custom hardware scanning and specify a custom scan executable to be run on inventoried workstations.

▶ Custom Attribute Editor—Allows you to specify a list of custom hardware attributes that should be scanned during the workstation scanning process.

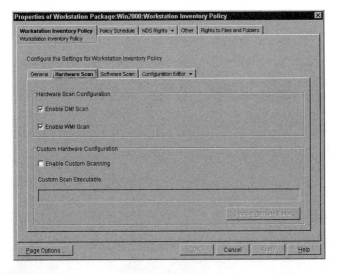

FIGURE 13.7
Hardware inventory settings for the Workstation Inventory Policy.

Configure Software Scan

Next, you need to configure software scanning. From the Software Scan tab, shown in Figure 13.8, you can enable the following software inventory options:

▶ Enable Software Scan—Enables software scanning on workstations associated with this Workstation Policy Package.

▶ Product Identification Numbers—Scans for product identification numbers of applications that are installed on inventoried workstations. The product identification number can be extremely useful in sorting and organizing inventory software reports.

▶ Product Location—Allows you to specify software scanning to include scanning of the full path of the product executable installed on the inventoried workstations.

▶ Perform Custom Scanning only—Allows you to specify software scanning to scan only for the software defined by the custom scan editor.

▶ Custom Scan Editor—You can click on the Custom Scan Editor button to bring up the Custom Scan Editor window discussed later in this chapter.

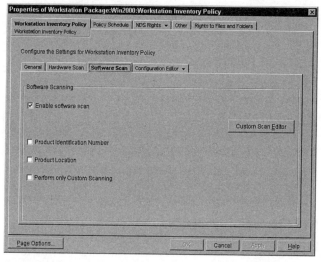

FIGURE 13.8
Software Scan settings for the Workstation Inventory Policy for a Workstation Policy Package.

Configure the Configuration Editor

Once you have enabled and configured software scanning, you can modify the .INI file that ZENworks for Desktops 4 uses when reporting software inventory. Do this by selecting the Configuration Editor tab, shown in Figure 13.9. You can edit the SWRules file by clicking on the Set Default button to open the default file and then modifying the entries. ZENworks will use this file when you create inventory reports.

If you are modifying the Workstation Inventory policy for Windows, the Configuration Editor tab will have a drop-down arrow allowing you to modify the entries in the .INI files for Zipped Names. This allows you to specify the manufacturer of software being used to zip files as well as the identifiers that they are using for the zipped files.

You can also modify the entries in the .INI file for Asset Information. You can specify the DMI classnames and attributes for things such as a workstation model, model number, serial number, and computer type.

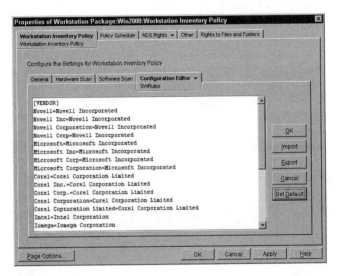

FIGURE 13.9
Configuration Editor for the Workstation Inventory Policy for a Workstation Policy Package.

Workstation Inventory Tasks

Once you have installed, configured, and started the workstation inventory process for you network, you should be aware of several tasks. The following sections describe common tasks that you need to be aware of and use to maintain your workstation inventory.

Optimizing Database Performance

One important task you should be familiar with is improving the database performance by improving database cache size. You can improve the performance of the Inventory database maintained in Sybase on NetWare or Windows NT/2000 servers. The default database cache size is 32MB; however, this database cache size might not be adequate for large databases with more than 10,000 workstations.

You should change the database cache size to an optimum size. A good rule of thumb is a database cache size that is 1/4 of the database size. You must also consider server memory size while assigning a cache size. For example, if you have 256MB RAM, a cache size of 64MB is recommended.

Use the following steps to change the database cache size on a NetWare server:

1. Close all connections to the Inventory database.

2. Quit the Sybase server.

3. Open the MGMTDB.NCF in SYS:\SYSTEM directory.

4. Modify the -c parameter. For example, using -c 64M sets the cache size to 64MB.

5. Save the file.

6. On the server console, load the Inventory database. Enter MGMTDBS.

Use the following steps to change the database cache size on a Windows NT/2000 server:

1. Run the file, NTDBCONFIG.EXE, from the installation directory on the database server.

2. Modify the -c parameter.

3. Save the file.

4. Restart the server so that the Inventory database service (Adaptive Service Anywhere - ZENworks for 4Desktops 4) starts.

Backing Up the Inventory Database

Another inventory task you should be aware of is backing up the inventory database. ZENworks for Desktops provides an option to back up the Inventory database from the server. It's a good idea to back up the database on a weekly basis. However, if you are tracking the inventory of workstations frequently, increase the frequency of your backups.

The Database Backup tool can be run from ConsoleOne by choosing Tools, ZENworks Inventory, Configure DB, ZENworks Database object. Then click OK. Then choose Tools, ZENworks Inventory, Database

Backup. Specify where to back up the database and then click the Start Backup button.

Use the following steps to restore the database:

1. If the Inventory database server is up, stop the database storing service. At the database server console, enter the following:

   StopSer Storer

2. Quit from the Sybase database.

3. At the database server prompt of NetWare servers, enter **q** to stop the Sybase database.

4. On Windows NT/2000, stop the Sybase service (Adaptive Service Anywhere - ZENworks for 4Desktops 4).

5. Copy the backup files, overwriting the working database files.

6. Restart the database server.

NOTE The backup tool creates a .LOG file located in ZENworks database directory on NetWare and Windows NT/2000 servers. The log records the status of the backup operation. This file increases in size every time a backup is created. Remove the existing contents of the file if you do not need the details.

These steps work for the Sybase database only. For detailed instructions on backing up the oracle database, refer to the online ZENworks for Desktops documentation.

Customizing Software Scanning

Another important task you should be familiar with is how to customize software scanning. You can customize the list of software applications that you want to scan by specifying the software scan settings in the Workstation Inventory Policy page.

By default, the scanner does not scan for software applications at the workstation. You must enable the software scan option in the Workstation Inventory policy. You should use the Custom Scan Editor to configure the list of applications for scanning. The Custom Scan Editor provides you with a powerful tool to optimize software scanning for your network. Use the Custom Scan Editor to specify the vendor, product name, product version, filename, and file size of the software you want to scan for on servers. This allows you to selectively inventory only software that is important to track reducing the size of inventory reports as well as network and server utilization.

Use the following steps to configure custom application scanning for workstations:

1. In ConsoleOne, select the Workstation Inventory Policy and click Properties. Select the Software Scan tab of the Workstation Inventory Policy page and ensure that the Enable software scan option is checked.

2. Click the Custom Scan Editor button to bring up the Custom Scan Editor, shown in Figure 13.10.

3. Click the Add button to add a custom application to be scanned for.

4. Fill in the details of the application: vendor name, product name, product version, filename, and file size (in bytes).

5. Click OK.

6. To save the application entry in eDirectory, click OK in the Custom Scan Editor dialog box.

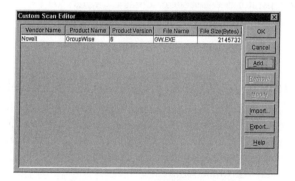

FIGURE 13.10
Custom Scan Editor dialog box for software scanning in the Workstation Inventory Policy.

You can also add application entries to the Custom Scan table by importing a file with the list of application entries. Use the following steps:

1. Open a text editor.

2. Create a file. The format of the custom scan file is as follows:

```
total_number_of_application_entries_in_Custom_Scan_file>
;total_number_of_columns_in_the_application_entry
vendor_name;product_name;product_version;file_name;file_
size(in Bytes)
vendor_name;product_name;product_version;file_name;file_
size(in Bytes)
```

3. Save the application as a text file with any extension you prefer.

4. In ConsoleOne, select the Workstation Inventory Policy and click Properties. Ensure that the Enable Software scan operation is checked.

5. Click Custom Scan Editor.

6. Click Import. To save the application entry in eDirectory, click OK in the Custom Scan Editor dialog box.

You should keep the following guidelines in mind if you decide to create your own custom scan files:

▶ The default total number of columns in the application entry is 5.

▶ The separator between the columns is a semicolon (;).

▶ Fill in all the columns for each application entry.

▶ Do not use comma (,) in the file size parameter.

Exporting the Inventory Data to CSV Format

ZENworks for Desktops includes a tool that allows you to customize inventory data you want from the inventory database and export it to a file. Once you select the inventory components that you need and further filter the data, the export program exports the data into a Comma Separated Value (CSV) file format.

All workstations satisfying the filter you specify in the selected database are exported to a CSV file. If you save the settings, you can later reload the configuration file to export the data. The following sections describe how to set the filters and queries and export the data from either a client or a server.

Exporting Inventory Data from ConsoleOne

You can run the Data Export tool from ConsoleOne by choosing Tools, ZENworks Inventory, Configure DB, ZENworks Database Object. Click

OK. Then choose Tools, ZENworks Inventory, Data Export to open the Data Export tool.

Once the tool is open, use the following steps to export the inventory data to a CSV file:

1. Select to Create a New Database Query to open the Defined Query dialog box shown in Figure 13.11. This option lets you add a new query that defines the inventory fields such as hardware, software, network, and others that you want to export. You can also specify the criteria to limit the workstations and the database to be included in the query. Based on the inventory components and criteria you specify, the inventory data from the database is exported to a CSV file. Click Next.

2. Specify the scope of the query to be Workstations Servers or both.

3. Form the query and specify the filter conditions as described in the following section by clicking on the Edit Query button shown in Figure 13.11. Click Next.

4. Configure the database fields that you want be exported for the workstations that match the criteria you specified in Step 3. The fields can be added and removed by navigating the Database Fields and Selected fields lists, shown in Figure 13.12, and using the arrow button to add and remove entries. Click Next.

5. View the summary data export settings. Click Save Configuration to save the configurations settings to an .EXP file, specify the filename for the .EXP file, and then click Save. The configuration file (.EXP) contains the settings such as the inventory components you selected, and also the query formed for filtering the workstation data export. You create an .EXP file so that you can reload the configuration settings and generate the .CSV files any time you need to. Click Next.

6. Click Perform the Query from this Computer to run the data export processing from the workstation computer. This option accesses the inventory database on the specified database server and exports the data to a .CSV file. Click Finish.

7. Specify the .CSV filename. Click OK.

This process generates the .CSV file in the specified directory. You can then open the .CSV file in any CSV-supported viewer to view the exported data.

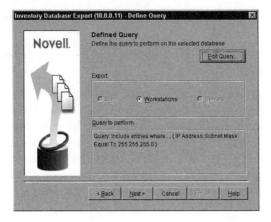

FIGURE 13.11
Defined Query dialog box in the ZENworks Inventory Data Export tool of
ConsoleOne.

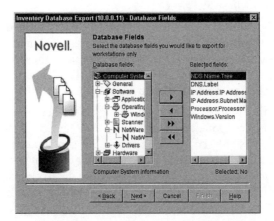

FIGURE 13.12
Database Fields dialog box in the ZENworks Inventory Data Export tool of
ConsoleOne.

Forming a Query and Setting Filter Conditions

The following sections discuss setting the appropriate query values on
the Define Query window shown in Figure 13.13.

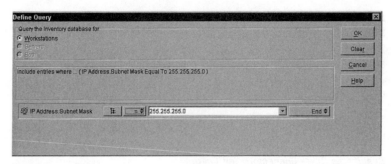

FIGURE 13.13
Define Query dialog box in the ZENworks Inventory Data Export tool of
ConsoleOne.

Select the Attributes of the Inventory Components

Click the Browse Attribute button to select component attributes in the
Select Attribute window shown in Figure 13.14. For example, to specify
the version of Bios as a component in the data export, select Bios as the
component, and select Version as the component attribute.

Components are as follows: Software, Hardware, Network System, DMI,
and General Information.

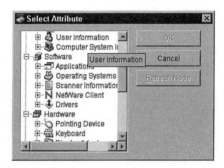

FIGURE 13.14
Select Attribute dialog box in the ZENworks Inventory Data Export tool of
ConsoleOne.

Select the Operator

Relational operators show the relationship between the component and
the value. Use the Matches option to specify the wildcard characters in
the Value field.

Specify the Values for the Inventory Attributes

Description values are the possible values of an inventory component. For example, 6.0 is a possible value for the DOS-Version attribute. Description values are not case-sensitive. Use the wildcard character % to substitute any number of characters, or the ? character to substitute one character in the Value field.

The list of description values displayed for an Inventory component is taken from the inventory database corresponding to the component.

Specify the Query Connectors and Controls

The connectors and controls available for building filter conditions include the following:

- ▶ **AND:** The expressions before and after the AND must be true.

- ▶ **OR:** Either the expression before the OR or the expression after the OR must be true.

- ▶ **Insert Row:** Lets you build the filter condition for this current row.

- ▶ **Delete Row:** Deletes the row.

- ▶ **New Group:** Lets you form a new filter condition group and specify the criteria for it. This group is combined with the previous group by using the relational operator specified between the groups.

- ▶ **End:** Ends the filter condition.

Exporting Inventory Data from the Server

Accessing the inventory database from a server is recommended if you are exporting data from a large database or if you have specified complex queries for filtering the workstation.

Use the following steps to run the Data Export program from the server:

1. Ensure that you have generated the data configurations files. Then perform Steps 1 through 5 of the "Exporting Inventory Data from ConsoleOne" section of this chapter. Also ensure that you save the settings in the .EXP file.

2. Click Perform the Query on a Remote Server to run the data export program from any server that has Workstation Inventory components installed. Click Finish.

3. From the server console, run DBEXPORT.NCF on NetWare servers or DBEXPORT.BAT on Windows NT/2000 servers, by typing DBEXPORT configuration_filename.exp csv_filename.csv where

`configuration_filename.EXP` is an existing file that contains the data export settings. The data exported from the database is stored in the `csv_filename.csv` file. The corresponding .CFG file for the .EXP file should be in the same folder as the .EXP file. The .CFG file contains the list of the database attributes to be exported.

4. Choose the Inventory sites.

5. If you want to export the data from all database sites, satisfying the filter conditions, type 0.

6. To choose the database sites, type the numbers corresponding to the site names in the displayed list.

7. To select multiple site databases, separate the site numbers corresponding to the site names by commas.

   The data export displays the number of workstations that satisfy the query and filter conditions for export.

8. Open the .CSV file in Microsoft Excel, or any other CSV-supported viewer to view the exported data.

Viewing Inventory Data

Another important inventory task you should be familiar with is viewing the information in the workstation inventory. The following sections describe how to view information about managed workstations.

Viewing Minimal Inventory Information from an eDirectory Object

Workstation inventory scanners store a subset of the scan data directly into the workstation object in eDirectory. You can view that information by right-clicking the Workstation object and selecting Properties, ZENworks Inventory tab, Minimal Information.

The minimal view, shown in Figure 13.15, displays the following information about that workstation: asset tag, BIOS type, computer model, computer type, disk information, IP address, IPX address, last scan date, MAC address, memory size, model number, NIC type, Novell client, OS type, OS version, processor, serial number, subnet mask, and video type.

Viewing the Workstation Inventory Summary of a Managed Workstation

If the minimal inventory information does not show all you need, you can see the complete listing from ConsoleOne by clicking Tools, ZENworks Inventory, Configure DB. Right-click the workstation object, and then choose Actions, Inventory.

The summary view, shown in Figure 13.16, allows you to view the entire listing of the inventory scan data for the workstation object.

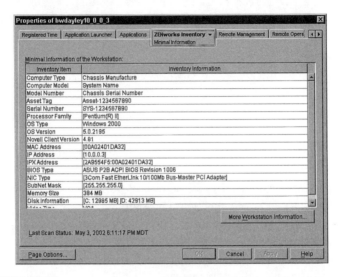

FIGURE 13.15
Minimal view of inventory data for a workstation object in ConsoleOne.

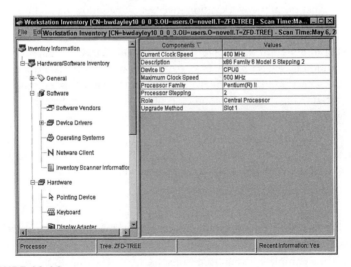

FIGURE 13.16
Summary view of inventory data for a workstation object in ConsoleOne.

Viewing the Workstation Inventory Summary of a Managed Workstation Formed by Query

If the entire listing for the workstation object is too much for you, you can view only the information that you requested by performing a query. Use the following steps to view the information that was formed by a query:

1. In ConsoleOne, click a container.
2. Choose Tools, ZENworks Inventory, Configure DB.
3. Choose Tools, ZENworks Inventory, Inventory Query.
4. From the Inventory Query dialog box, shown in Figure 13.17, specify the criteria for the query. Set the Find in, Search Entire Database, Find Type, Attributes, Operator, Value, and Save options for the query.
5. Click Find.

A query is run on the database and the results are displayed for you to view.

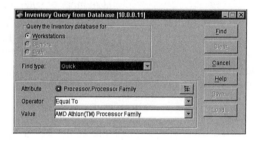

FIGURE 13.17
Inventory Query dialog box for the ZENworks inventory database in ConsoleOne.

Creating Inventory Reports

Another inventory task that is useful is running inventory reports. You can run reports from a predefined list to gather inventory information from the inventory database. Once you run the report, it can be printed or exported as desired.

Use the following steps to generate the inventory report:

1. In ConsoleOne, click a server object.
2. Click Tools, ZENworks Reports.
3. Click the report you want to generate. See Table 13.2 for a list of reports and their descriptions.

4. Specify the selection criteria. See Table 13.2 for a list of reports and their criteria.

5. Click the Run Selected Report button.

A status box appears displaying the progress of the report generation. When the report is generated, it appears in the viewer. Use the buttons on the toolbar to page through, print, or export the report.

TABLE 13.2 Report Types and Criteria for Inventory Reports

NAME (SIMPLE/COMP)	CRITERIA*	DESCRIPTION
Scan Time Listing(S)	Last Scan Date	Data and time of the last Inventory scan on each workstation
Operating System Listing(S)	OS Type, OS Version	List of all the workstations with an OS Type, an OS Version, and the total number of such workstations
BIOS Listing(S)	BIOS Install Date	List of all the workstations with a BIOS release date, and the total number of such workstations
Processor Family Listing(S)	Processor Family	List of all the workstations with a processor family (such as Pentium* Pro), and the total number of such workstations
Processor Current Clock Speed(S)	Lower Bound, Upper Bound	List of all the workstations within a range of processor speed (such as 200-1000 MHz), and the total number of such workstations
Processor Maximum Clock Speed(S)	Lower Bound, Upper Bound	List of all the workstations within a range of maximum processor speed (such as 200-1000 MHz), and the total number of such workstations
Video Adapter Listing(S)	Video Architecture	List of all the workstations with a video adapter (such as MGA 2064W), and the total number of such workstations
Network Adapter Listing(S)	Adapter Name	List of all the workstations with a network adapter (such as 3Com* Fast EtherLink*) and the total number of such workstations

TABLE 13.2   Continued

NAME (SIMPLE/COMP)	CRITERIA*	DESCRIPTION
Software Listing(S)	Software Name and Version	List of all the workstations with a software name, version and the total number of such workstations
Software Summary Listing(S)	Software Name and Version	Lists of the total number of workstations with a particular software and version
Application Software Inventory Report	DN of Workstation	Software information including product name, version and vendor on each workstation
Asset Management Report	DN of Workstation	BIOS, computer description, processor, and OS Description for each workstation
System Internal Hardware Report	DN of Workstation	Memory, processor, display details, physical disk drive, and modem for each workstation
Networking Information Report	DN of Workstation	OS Description, MAC Address, NIC Type, IP Address, and Network Drive mappings for each workstation
Storage Devices Inventory Report	DN of Workstation	Hard disk, removable disk, logical drives, disk and CD-ROM details for each workstation
System Software Inventory Report	DN of Workstation	OS description, display drivers, pointing device drivers, network adapter drivers and NetWare Client details for each workstation
System Peripherals Inventory Report	DN of Workstation	Computer description, display details, keyboard, pointing device and network adapter details for each workstation

* The IP Address, DN, Distinguished Tree, and DNS name can be used as criteria for all workstation inventory reports.

View the Workstation Inventory Status Logs

Another valuable task that you should frequently perform is to view the status and scan logs generated by workstation inventory. The following sections list the logs, what they contain, and how to access them.

Workstation Scan Log

The workstation scan log monitors information from scan programs and the database storage process on the server. It contains the scanned workstation name, time of scan, inventory component, message type, and status message.

To access the workstation scan log from within ConsoleOne, select the container; then choose Tools, ZENworks Inventory, Workstation Scan Log. The Workstation Scan Log, shown in Figure 13.18, displays a listing of inventory scans that have occurred on the configured inventory database.

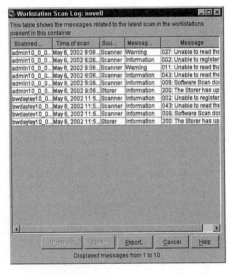

FIGURE 13.18
Workstation Scan Log for the ZENworks Inventory database in ConsoleOne.

Roll-Up Log

The roll-up log contains information collected from data sending servers, data receiving servers, and the database storage process. The roll-up log contains information about where the roll-up initiated from, roll-up start time, inventory component, message type, and status message.

To access the roll-up log from within ConsoleOne, select the container for the Inventory Service Object and then click Tools, ZENworks Inventory, Roll-Up Log.

Workstation Scan Status

The workstation scan status monitors information from the scan programs and the database storage process. It contains the time of scan and status message.

To access the workstation scan status from within ConsoleOne, right-click the workstation object and click Properties, ZENworks Inventory tab, Scan Status. The Scan Status tab, shown in Figure 13.19, displays the time of each scan as well as status messages that occurred during the scan. You can use the up and down arrows to navigate through the status messages.

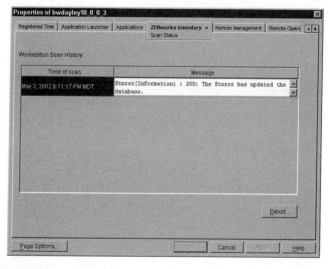

FIGURE 13.19
Scan Status of inventory scans that have occurred on a workstation object in ConsoleOne.

Status of Inventory Components on Server

The status of inventory components on the server contains information gathered from the sending server, receiving servers, the selector on the server, the database storing process, the service manager, and the roll-up scheduler. It shows the time of log, source, message type, and a textual message.

To access the status of inventory components on the server from within
ConsoleOne, right-click the Inventory Service object and then click
Properties, Status Report, Server Status.

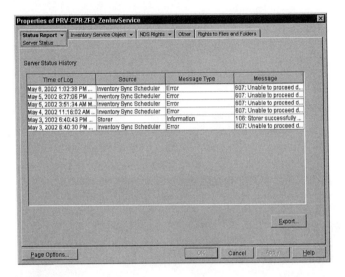

FIGURE 13.20
Inventory Server status window for a ZENworks Inventory Service object in
ConsoleOne.

Roll-Up Status

The roll-up status contains information gathered from the sending server,
receiving servers, and the database storing process. It shows the roll-up
start time and message.

To access the roll-up status from within ConsoleOne, right-click the
Inventory Service object. Then choose Properties, Status Report, Roll-Up
Status.

## CHAPTER 14

Imaging a Workstation

One significant feature added to ZENworks for Desktops 4 is the capability to create and deploy images of workstations throughout the network. Using this feature, you can provide an additional level of support and service to users of workstations by being able to take an image of a golden workstation for your organization and then apply that image to any workstation in the network. This can be used to initially set up workstations in your organization and to restore a workstation to properly functioning status should problems occur that are best repaired by getting the workstation to a known, beginning state.

Workstation Imaging System

The ZENworks for Desktops 4 system for imaging workstation is made up of the following components: Linux operating system, Linux imaging software, Imaging server agents, and the Windows workstation image-safe data agent. In addition to these components, objects in eDirectory, and some administrative tools in ConsoleOne, are there to get the job done.

There might be a Linux partition placed on a workstation (minimum of 15MB) that can hold the Linux OS and the imaging engine. It's ideal to place this partition on workstations that you might want to image on the fly (from ConsoleOne) because, when requested, the workstation gets notified of this work and then performs the imaging task. If no work exists for the imaging system to perform, the partition boots into the normal operating system. See the section on placing a Linux partition on a workstation for potential issues and instructions.

The ZENworks for Desktops 4 imaging system is designed to function in an automatic mode (although it does have a manual mode). The expectation is that you use the system to deploy images to your workstations in the network in order to set up initial systems or repair systems and get them back online as quickly as possible. Consequently, the system assumes that a workstation that is contacting the imaging server, but is not registered in the tree, is requesting an image; and a registered workstation is contacting the imaging server to determine whether any work (indicated by flags in the workstation object) is to be done.

The ZENworks for Desktops 4 product ships with the ZENworks Preboot Services product. This allows you to have PXE (Pre-Execution Environment) support right out of the box! Now you don't have to have a Linux partition on the workstation. Instead, you can boot PXE. The PXE Server provided in ZfD4 will then send the device the Linux Kernel. The imaging system will contact the imaging server for work and proceed to send and apply the image.

Linux Operating System

ZENworks for Desktops 4 uses the free Linux operating system to take and apply images to workstations. The imaging process begins by booting the workstation with some boot floppies that contain the Linux operating system and several drivers to handle most network cards. If the boot disks cannot support your network card, you need to look for those resources on the Internet. The following sites might have the driver you're looking for:

```
cesdis1.gsfc.nasa.gov/linux/drivers/index.html
www.linuxvoodoo.com/drivers/cards/nics/index.html
www.scyld.com/network/index.html
```

Linux Imaging Software

This is the Linux software application that actually takes and applies the image. This software is automatically started with the boot disks and is launched when the workstation is told to take or receive an image.

This software is *not* writing bits and bytes on the sectors, but it has knowledge of the various supported file system types, and reads and writes the files. The supported file system types are FAT16, FAT32, NTFS 4 (Windows NT), and NTFS 5 (Windows 2000/XP). Because the imaging software is reading files, it also writes files. This means that if you take the manual approach to restoring the image and the partition is not empty then you have a mingling of currently existing files with the files from the restore—causing a very unexpected behavior (OS and driver files are intermixed, and so on).

Something else to note is that the images always have the suffix of .ZMG and are not compressed. You must have enough room on the destination server to store the entire image or the image transfer will fail and the partial image will be deleted.

The imaging software can function in one of two modes: automatic and manual. In the automatic mode the imaging software contacts the imaging server agent and requests any work. This work can be to take or receive an image (this is set in the workstation object). If an image must be taken or received, the imaging software begins the process. If no work must be done, the imaging software completes and the workstation reboots to the native operating system.

If the imaging software is in manual mode, the software does not automatically communicate with the agent, but places prompts on the workstation screen that enable you to perform specific partitioning and imaging tasks including taking or receiving an image. See the "Advanced Imaging" section in this to learn about the commands you can perform in the manual mode. When the imaging software is done, the user must manually request the reboot to the native operating system.

Imaging Server Agents

This is the agent that runs on the server and is responsible for communicating with the imaging software that is running on the workstation. These agents tell the workstation whether to take the image or to receive an image and are responsible for walking the eDirectory tree to find the image. This agent is affected by the Imaging Server Policy in the Server Policy Package. It is responsible for receiving information from the workstation and processing the rules in the policy in order to find an image object that should be applied to the workstation.

Once the image is determined, this agent gets the image file and transmits that image to the Linux image software residing on the workstation. It is also responsible for receiving any images that the workstation is sending it and storing them on the server in the specified and approved locations.

The image server is loaded on the NetWare server as `imgserv.nlm` and the NT/2000 version is a service DLL with the same name. The imaging server has a status screen that tells you some information on the number of requests and images it has received and served. It, unfortunately, does not have any information on the screen on currently receiving or delivering work. You can load the service with a debug option and get it to write a log file called ZIMGLOG.XML on the server.

Windows Workstation Image-Safe Data Agent

This agent resides on the Windows workstation and is responsible for receiving image-safe data from the disk and placing that into the Windows Registry. It also makes sure that the information in the Windows Registry is synchronized on the disk.

A special sector on the disk is reserved for placing information that is preserved despite having an image applied to the workstation. This way, a workstation keeps its IP address (or DHCP settings), computer name, workstation object, domain, and group names.

eDirectory Objects

Several objects are introduced to the tree in order to support ZENworks for Desktops 4 imaging. These objects are the following:

- ▶ *Workstation Imaging Policy*—This policy is in the Workstation Policy Package and determines, for the associated workstations, the image to be used when a re-image is requested. See Chapter 9, "Setting Up a Workstation Policy Package," for more information about this policy.

- ▶ *Imaging Server Policy*—This policy is in the Server Policy Package and determines the image used when an image is requested for a non-registered workstation. See Chapter 12, "Creating a Server Policy Package," for more information about this policy.

- ▶ *Image Object*—This is an eDirectory object that represents an image taken of a workstation and stored on the imaging server. See the following section to learn more about the Image object.

- ▶ *Workstation Object: Imaging Configuration*—These are some configuration parameters that are part of the workstation object. In this page, you can configure whether the workstation should take or receive an image on the next reboot.

Image Object

The administrator creates the Image object in the directory and associates it with an image file (.ZMG) taken by the ZENworks for Desktops 4 imaging system. To properly configure an Image object, you must do the following:

1. Take an image of a workstation and store that image on an imaging server. See the section that follows about creating a workstation image.

2. Launch ConsoleOne and browse to the container where you want the Image object to reside.

3. Create an Image object by selecting the container and then choosing the File, New, Object menu and selecting Workstation Image object from the list of objects.

4. Once the object is created, go into the object's properties by either selecting additional properties in the create process or by right-clicking the object and choosing Properties.

5. Select the Image Files tab and specify whether you want to use a base file image or set up scripted imaging. If you select standard imaging, you must administer the location of the .ZMG files by pressing the browse button in the Base Image File field. You then need to browse to the imaging server and then to the file system on that server to specify the .ZMG file. If you select scripted imaging, you can specify an imaging command in the text window that appears (see "Advanced Imaging" later in this chapter).

6. Choose the file set to bring as part of the image by selecting the set in the Use File Set parameter at the bottom-left side of the screen. You can have up to 10 file sets. See following section, "Modifying an Image," for more details.

7. If you are using standard imaging, you can also append additional images to this image by pressing the Add button and placing them in the Add on Image File field. These additional images are included with the base image and placed on the workstation when it is imaged. These images can be Application Object images (see Chapter 6, "Creating and Using Application Objects," for more information).

8. Press OK to save the administrative changes and get out of ConsoleOne.

Administrative Tools

Several tools exist that are available to perform the imaging operation. First are the snap-ins into ConsoleOne that enable you to create image objects and launch tools to create the imaging boot disks and to view and manipulate an image file.

The boot disk creator and the Image Explorer program are both Windows programs that are launched from the Tools menu of ConsoleOne. The boot disk creator creates the Linux disks needed to boot the workstations to communicate with the imaging server and to take and put the images.

The Image Explorer enables you to view the contents of the image file and to mark files in the image to be included in various sets of files, as well as remove and add files from/to the image. See the "Modifying an Image" section later in the chapter for more details.

Setting Up Workstations for Imaging

The ZENworks for Desktops 4 imaging engine that performs the actual workstation imaging is a Linux application. Therefore, the workstation must be booted to Linux temporarily while the imaging is performed. For a workstation to use the ZENworks engine, you need to prepare a bootable device that has the following components:

- ▶ *Linux Kernel*—Either a bootable device or partition with Linux installed.

- ▶ *Imaging Engine*—ZENworks for Desktops Imaging Software.

- ▶ *Network Drivers*—Drivers to access the network to communicate with the ZENworks for Desktops imaging server.

You can use any of the following methods to prepare workstations to be imaged:

- ▶ Preboot services (PXE)
- ▶ Boot disks
- ▶ Boot CD
- ▶ Linux partition on a workstation

Using Preboot Services with ~~Cool !~~
Imaging

When a workstation with Preboot Services (PXE) is booted, it searches the network for PXE. Once it locates the server where PXE is installed, it uses a DHCP request to query the server and determine whether there is any imaging work to do. If ZENworks determines that there is imaging work to do, it then downloads the following files to boot the workstation to Linux and performs the imaging operations: LINUX.1, LINUX.2, and LOADLIN.EXE. These files aren't downloaded if ZENworks determines that there is no work to be done.

PXE is an industry-standard protocol that allows a workstation to boot up and execute a program from the network before the workstation operating system starts. For more information, see "Preboot Services" at the following Web site:

http://www.novell.com/products/zenworks/

Creating Boot Disks

All imaging starts by booting the workstation up with the ZENworks for Desktops 4 Imaging boot disks. To create these disks, you need to do the following:

1. Get two *newly* formatted floppy disks. The system does not work properly if you create image disks on previously used floppies without reformatting them first.

2. Launch ConsoleOne.

3. Launch the boot disk creator program (`sys:\public\zenworks\imaging\zimgboot.exe`) by going to the Tools menu and selecting the correct option (Tools, ZENworks Utilities, Imaging, Create or Modify Boot Diskettes).

4. Within the Boot Disk Creator program, choose the options that you want. Figure 14.1 shows a sample of the Boot Disk Creator window.

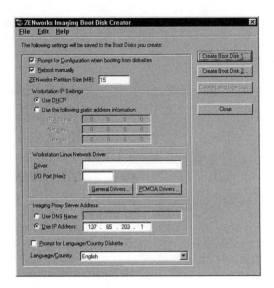

FIGURE 14.1
ZENworks Imaging Boot Disk Creator.

You can make the following choices in the program:

▶ *Prompt for Configuration When Booting From Diskettes*—After
the boot process is done, this prompts the screen for the configuration information that is included on this screen (such as
reboot manually, proxy address, use DHCP, and so on). This
enables you to change these values from the specified defaults
given in this screen. You just press Enter when running the
imaging program on the workstation, because you want to
keep the defaults that you specify on this screen.

▶ *Reboot Manually*—Requires that the user request the reboot
(Ctl+Alt+Del) manually at the completion of the imaging process
(either take an image or receive an image) rather than having the
program automatically reboot the workstation when done.

▶ *ZENworks Partition Size*—Enables you to specify how many
megabytes you want any Linux partition to be on the workstation, if you decide to create the partition.

▶ *Workstation IP Settings: Use DHCP*—Tells the Linux system to
use DHCP to get the workstation's IP address to connect to
the imaging server.

▶ *Workstation IP Settings: Use the Following Static Address Information*—Enables you to specify the address instead of using DHCP. This is the address used by the workstation to connect to the imaging server.

▶ *Workstation Linux Network Driver: Driver:*—Specifies the special driver to use for your network card. The Linux boot disks are configured for most of the common network cards. The known network cards are automatically detected and the appropriate driver is loaded. Should you not have a card that is part of the default set, you need to include additional drivers on the disk.

▶ *Workstation Linux Network Driver: I/O Port*—Identifies the I/O port for access to your network card. In most cases, this field can be blank because it is auto-detected. If not, you need to enter the port number (for example, 300) of the interrupt for the network card.

▶ *Workstation Linux Network Driver: Drive Buttons*—These buttons bring up a driver window, which enables you to browse to the file system and find a Linux driver and then select it to be included on the disks. The driver selected in the field is attempted first, followed by the list of alternative drivers in the button lists, followed by the default drivers.

▶ *Imaging Proxy Server Address: Use DNS Name*—Enables you to select and enter the DNS name of the imaging server. Choose this option only if you have DNS enabled and have entered a record in the DNS system for this server. Enter the full DNS name, such as `imgsrvr.novell.com`.

▶ *Imaging Proxy Server Address: Use IP Address*—This flag identifies that the system should use the IP address to connect to the imaging server rather than DNS. The address specified should be the address of the server that is running the imaging service.

▶ *Prompt for Language/Country Diskette*—Requests that the system should prompt for the language disk at boot time. If this is on, the system waits for the language disk to be inserted before it finishes. This is not necessary if you are using the default English system.

▶ *Language/Country*—Chooses the country language. This results in these language files being placed on the system and used in the workstation imaging system.

5. Put a first floppy into the disk drive and press the Create Diskette 1 button. This writes a compressed file with the Linux boot system and portions of the imaging engine.

6. Put a second floppy into the disk drive and press the Create Diskette 2 button. This writes a compressed file with the remainder of the Linux drives and the imaging system.

7. If you chose to have a non-English version of the imaging system, you need to insert the third formatted disk and press the Create Language Diskette button. This places the non-English language files on the floppy.

8. Press the Close button.

Now these floppies can be used to boot the workstation and begin the imaging process.

Creating a Boot CD

If you have systems that are capable of booting from CD-ROM, you can create a CD with the Linux boot system. With your CD writer software, you need to create a CD using the ISO file called BOOTCD.ISO from the `public\zenworks\imaging` directory or from the ZENworks for Desktops 4 Program CD. You also need the SETTINGS.TXT file, which holds the configuration for the boot CD, such items as prompt, size of Linux partition, and so on. You also need to include this SETTINGS.TXT file on the CD. Your CD writer software can include the SETTINGS.TXT file into the ISO image, or can write a multi-session CD. Obviously, your workstations will then need to support booting from a multi-session CD.

The SESSION.TXT file is an ASCII text file that holds key/value pairs that tell the boot system the configuration settings for the imaging engine. The following is a sample of the SETTINGS.TXT file:

```
# ZENworks Imaging settings.txt
#  denotes a comment

#PROMPT should be set to YES if you want to configure
# various parameters
#PROMPT=YES
```

```
#PARTITIONSIZE should be set to the Linux partition size
# in MB, to be created on install
PARTITIONSIZE=15

#IPADDR should be set to the desired ip address of the
# machine. To use DHCP comment out the line, or remove
# it from the file.
#IPADDR=137.65.138.128

#GATEWAY is the router address for this machine. If
# using DHCP,remove this line, or comment it out.
#GATEWAY=137.65.139.254

#NETMASK is this machine's subnet mask. If using DHCP,
# remove or comment out this line.
#NETMASK=255.255.252.0

#PROXYADDR is the address of the server running ZENworks
# Image Server nlm
PROXYADDR=137.65.203.1

#uncomment if you want to reboot manually.
#MANUALREBOOT=YES
```

Creating a Workstation Image

Depending on your situation and setup, you can create a workstation image in one of several ways.

If the workstation is registered in the directory and has a Linux partition on it (see the section following about placing a Linux partition on a workstation), you can go to the Workstation object in the tree and set a workstation flag (in the ZENworks Imaging Configuration tab) to take an image on the next boot. The next time that the workstation boots, the Linux partition boots and then the imaging engine on the workstation contacts the imaging server. The server notes that the Workstation object has the flag set and requests that the workstation send an image. When the image is completed, the flag is reset in the Workstation object and the workstation continues to boot into the native operating system.

Be sure to disable or remove any boot manager systems such as System Commander. You do not want them in the image that you take, because when they are placed onto a workstation, they overwrite the ZENworks boot system and the connectivity between the workstation and the imaging server does not occur. This keeps you from having the features of automatic execution.

If the workstation is registered in the directory but does not have a Linux partition, you need to boot from the floppies, PXE, or the CD. Once the system is booted, you can let Linux proceed in automatic mode. This contacts the image server and takes the image as described in the previous paragraph.

If the workstation is not registered in the directory and yet it has a Linux partition installed, when the workstation boots into the Linux partition it contacts the imaging server, which runs its rules attempting to discover a matching image. If one is found, it images the workstation with the matching image. If you need to, boot the workstation from the floppies to get the imaging engine into manual mode and to avoid connecting to the imaging server.

If the workstation is not registered in the directory and does not have a Linux partition, you must boot from floppies (or CD) and then type **manual** when the Linux partition is booted. Then you type **img mp** **<proxy address> <full path to image>**. Don't forget that the path must use forward slashes and must include the server. The directories in the path must already exist. This takes an image of the workstation and places it on the imaging server.

> **NOTE** Whenever you take or place an image on a workstation, the ZENworks imaging engine does *not* take an image of the Linux partition or replace it with an image being brought down. The only way to place a Linux partition on a workstation is via the bootable floppies or another imaging program.

The imaging process reads files from FAT16, FAT32, NTFS 4, and NTFS 5 systems and includes them in the image on a file-by-file basis. If the imaging system does not understand the partition type, it does a sector-by-sector copy of the partition.

Placing a Linux Partition on a Workstation

With ZENworks for Desktops 4, Novell is recommending that customers move from the Linux partition and use PXE instead.

If you still want to, you can put a Linux partition on each of your work-stations. This Linux partition is the boot partition, and upon boot-up of the workstation, contacts the imaging server to determine whether it has any requested work (based on administration in the workstation object). If it has work, the imaging engine either gets or puts an image. If it has no work, the imaging system continues the boot process, booting the workstation to the native operating system.

If you are placing a Linux partition on a previously functioning system, this process assumes that the workstation has already registered with the network, has an associated Workstation object and that the image-safe data agent has run on the workstation. Having the workstation already registered prevents the imaging server from attempting to place a new image on the workstation. However, if you are placing the Linux partition on a new workstation this process can place a new, standard image on the workstation, preparing it for use in your organization.

The ZENworks for Desktops 4 boot system does not function with such booting programs as System Commander. These systems need to be disabled or marked such that the Linux partition is automatically booted. The ZENworks for Desktops 4 boot system functions properly with the Windows boot manager by fixing the BOOT.INI file to properly boot.

> **NOTE** The imaging system has special recognition for Compaq systems and does not destroy the Compaq partition that is used to run machine configurations.

> **WARNING** Placing a Linux partition destroys the disk and all of the other partitions unless you take special care in saving the partitions or using another program to create a new partition without destroying the current partitions.

To place a ZENworks for Desktops 4 Linux imaging partition on a work-station, you need to perform the following steps. Be sure to save any data on the workstation; any time that you are messing with partitions, you must prepare yourself should a failure occur and the data is lost.

Make sure that an empty place exists on the disk that is sufficient to hold the Linux partition (the size was identified in the creation of the boot disks and is 15MB minimum). This can be leftover space or be created by some program such as Partition Magic. If sufficient free space *is* present on the hard drive, the Linux install process should consume that space only when the free partition is partition 0 (in other words, the first partition in the partition table). The following steps describe how to place the Linux partition without loss of data and without any other tools:

1. Create your ZENworks for Desktops 4 boot disks with the proper configuration, including the setting to reboot manually. See the preceding section for tips on how to do that.

2. Boot the workstation with the ZENworks for Desktops 4 Imaging boot disks. Be sure to request manual mode when the system comes up. Typing `manual` at the prompt following the boot to Linux does this. If you type nothing at the prompt in 60 seconds, the system boots to automatic mode.

3. If this is a previously functioning workstation, take an image of the workstation by entering the following command: `img makep <address/DNS of image server> <filename for image file>`. The address can be an IP address or the DNS name of the image server. The filename is the name of the image file you want to hold the image. The filename must include the following format: `//servername/dir/dir/../filename.img`. The servername is actually ignored because the address of the server that is receiving the image stores the file on its disk. (Redirection of image servers does not work in manual mode.)

4. Enter `img dump` to view the list of known partitions on the disk. Remember the numbers of the partitions.

5. Enter `/bin/install.s` to install the Linux partition on the disk. This *destroys* all data on the workstation's hard drive. It creates a new Linux partition on the disk at the specified size and place of the Linux boot system on that partition. The ZENworks boot loader is automatically installed in this process. A message should appear stating that the boot process could not fully function. This is because Linux creates logical partitions for all the partitions that are seen at boot time. You just added a new partition and it cannot create a logical partition for it. When it reboots the boot manager system automatically reinstalls itself when it is assumed that all partitions are now present.

6. Enter `img dump` to view the list of known partitions. There should be one less partition listed than in Step 4 because the Linux partition is hidden from this listing. You should also note that all the other partitions are destroyed (in other words, they have no file system type associated with them).

7. Perform a reboot of the workstation to make sure the Linux partition is functioning properly. This can be done by typing **reboot**, or by turning the workstation off and on. Make sure you have removed the Linux boot disks. This should boot to the Linux partition and show the Linux prompt (because the system has been configured to not automatically reboot).

8. If you took an image in Step 3, bring down the image that was taken by typing **image rp <address of image server> <image filename>**. The image is brought down to the disk. The image is then reduced in size sufficiently to take the remaining space on the disk. If the image is too big to be reduced, an error occurs. Installation of an image from ZENworks for Desktops 4 takes special care to not destroy or overwrite the Linux partition. When the image is successfully down, you have the same workstation data and environment with the exception of a new Linux partition.

9. Enter `img dump` to view the list of partitions again. There should be the same number as in Step 6 (one less than in Step 4) and there should now be file system types for the partitions that you have just restored.

10. Reinitialize the boot manager by running `/bin/lilo.s`. You should do this any time you bring down any image to the workstation. In automatic mode, the system performs this automatically.

11. Perform a reboot of the workstation. This can be done by typing **reboot** or by turning the workstation off and on. Make sure you have removed the Linux boot disks. This should boot to the Linux partition and get to the Linux prompt (because the system has been configured not to automatically reboot).

12. The workstation should now boot to the Linux partition that goes into automatic mode communicating with the image server. It should find no work if the workstation is registered and the image configuration flags are off. If the workstation is not registered and you did not lay down an image in Step 8, the image server goes through its rules processing (see Server Policy Package, Imaging Server Policy) and determines an image that should be placed on

this workstation. If one is found, that image is placed on the workstation. If you manually placed an image down on a workstation that had not been previously registered, the imaging server compares the name of that image file with the image determined by the imaging server. If they are the same, the imaging server does not attempt to lay down a new image. This should result in the workstation having no work and again booting to its native operating system.

Modifying an Image Cool!

Once an image has been taken on the system and stored on the imaging server, you can examine the contents of an image by running the ZENworks for Desktops 4 Image Explorer (`\zenworks\imgexp.exe`). When you launch the Image Explorer, you are placed in a Windows program. From there you go to the File menu and open the .ZMG file that holds the workstation image. Figure 14.2 shows a sample of an image in the Image Explorer.

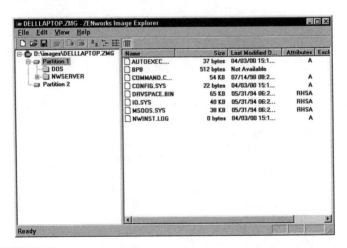

FIGURE 14.2
ZENworks Image Explorer.

As you can see in the example, you can browse the image and discover the partitions and files in the image. You can also, using the Image Explorer, look at the information gathered from the workstation such as

the hardware configuration. To look at this information, select the .ZMG
file in the image editor. Go to File, Properties or right-click and select
Properties. When you do so, the dialog box in Figure 14.3 is displayed.

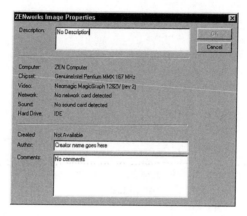

FIGURE 14.3
Image properties from an image in the ZENworks Image Explorer.

As you can see, this dialog box displays the description of the image,
including all of the hardware information on the workstation where the
image was captured. (You can use this information to help you construct
your rules in the Image server policy.) Other fields include when created,
the author, and any comments. If you want to modify any of the
Description, Author, or Comments fields, just move the cursor to these
fields and type the information you desire.   *very*
                                                              cool!!

From within the Image Explorer, you can add files or a directory of files *Cool!!*
to the image. ZENworks also allows you to create up to 10 versions of
the file set for the image. This is extremely useful for tailoring your
images once they have been created or creating an image from scratch.
For example, you might want to have two separate versions of the same
workstation images, one for the user's local workstation and one for your
remote workstation.

Use the following steps to add files and/or directories to an image object
in Image Explorer:

1. Select the partition and, optionally, the directory in the partition
   where you want to add the files or directories.

2. Choose Image, Add Files or Image, Add Directory.

3. Navigate to the file or directory you want to add to the image and click the Add button.

   The files and directories you selected will be added to the image.

Use the following steps to create a new directory in an image object from within Image Explorer:

1. Select the partition and, optionally, the directory in the partition where you want to create the directory.

2. Choose Image, Add Directory.

3. Specify the name of the directory. A new directory will be added to the image.

Image Explorer also allows you to add a Windows Registry file to an image. This is necessary to add additional Registry entries that you might need to update an image. Use the following steps to add a Registry file to an image object from within Image Explorer:

1. Select the partition and, optionally, the directory in the partition where you want to add the Registry file.

2. Choose Image, Add Registry file.

3. Navigate to the file or directory you want to add to the image and click the Add button.

The files and directories you selected will be added to the image. You can remove files from an image as well as mark files and place them into image sets. These sets consist of a group of files that can then be referenced from the imaging server (for example, place all files in set 1 from image A onto this workstation). By default, all files in the image are included in all sets.

NOTE When the imaging engine requests an image from the imaging server, it automatically requests all files from the image in set 1.

Use the following steps to exclude files from a file set:

1. Select the file in the view window of Image Explorer.

2. Right-click the file and select File Sets from the pop-up menu.

3. Select the set you want to exclude from the pop-up menu listing. The file icon will be grayed out.

You can also click Edit from the pop-up menu; a dialog box similar to the one in Figure 14.4 is displayed and you can specify which sets you want to exclude the file from. This is much faster if you need to specify multiple file sets to exclude the file from.

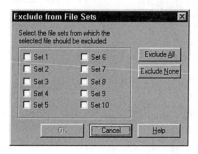

FIGURE 14.4
The Exclude from File Sets dialog box in the ZENworks Image Explorer.

When you create a Workstation Image object in the directory, and associate it with the image file, you can specify, in the object, which set of files to use. See the discussion on image objects in the previous section, "Image Objects."

Assigning an Image to a Workstation

Three ways exist in which the workstation automatically discovers the workstation image that it should place onto its hard drive.

▶ The imaging server can choose an image when an unregistered workstation boots the Linux system and contacts the imaging server. The imaging server goes through its rules to determine the image to place on the workstation. (See Chapter 12.)

▶ The imaging server can choose the image when a registered workstation boots the Linux system and contacts the imaging server and the workstation has an associated Workstation Imaging policy. (See Chapter 9.)

▶ If the administrator has configured the workstation object to be associated with a specific image in the directory, when the Linux system is booted and contacts the imaging server, the server looks into the workstation object to determine whether it should be re-imaged. If so, it determines whether a specific image file has been specified and sends that file. Otherwise, it performs as described in Step 2.

Workstation Object   *Oh so cool! !!*

In the Workstation object properties, an Image page exists. Within this image page you have a couple of settings that you can administer in relationship to the imaging system. The following settings can be applied on the Image page of the Workstation object:

▶ *Take an image of this workstation on the next boot*—This flag enables you to specify that on the next reboot of the workstation, the Linux boot system contacts the imaging server and is told to take an image of the workstation. With this field, you also get to specify the name of the image file. The image server saves the image to the specified filename.

▶ *Put an image on this workstation on the next boot*—This flag enables you to signal that the workstation should receive an image on the next boot. When the Linux boot system contacts the imaging server, it is told that it should put down an image. In addition to this field you can specify the image object that represents the image you want put down on the workstation. Press the browse button to select the image object in the directory. If no image object is specified, the image server looks for any Workstation Image Policy that can be associated with the workstation. If no Workstation Image Policy is associated with the workstation and you specify no image, no image is applied to the workstation.

After the workstation reboots and performs the requested action (make or restore an image), these flags are reset so that upon the next reboot no work is done. If the action is not successful, these flags are *not* reset; they continue to request the action upon each reboot.

Applying Application Objects to an Image

One of the most significant advancements that ZENworks for Desktops 4 has over your standard imaging systems is the capability to include all the files and software associated with an application object into a workstation image. This way, when the image is placed onto the workstation, all of the included application object files are installed with the image. When the workstation boots into the native operating system, these application object files are treated as disconnected applications and are available from the workstation. See Chapter 6, for more information regarding ZENworks Application Launcher.

In order to apply the application objects to an image, you need to perform the following steps. These steps assume that you already have an image object representing some base image and an application object in your tree.

1. Launch ConsoleOne.

2. Browse to and select properties on an application object that you want to include in an image. This application object can be included in any number of images.

3. Go to the Common tab, Imaging property page.

4. On the Imaging property page, you can identify the name of the image file by browsing to an existing file (to be overwritten) or by typing in a new filename to be created. It is recommended that you type in a UNC path so that all machines can get to this image, rather than having to have a mapped drive to the identified volume.

5. Select the Application Object flags at the bottom of the screen that tell the ZENworks Application Launcher how to handle the application.

6. Press the Create an Image button to create an image representation of the application into the specified image file.

7. Close the dialog boxes to get back to the main ConsoleOne screen.

8. Browse to and select the properties of the Workstation image object that you want to include the application object.

9. Go to the Images tab.

10. Press the Add button on the screen and enter the server name and path to the image file you want to add to the image.

11. Press OK to save all the changes and exit ConsoleOne.

Now when the image is applied to a workstation, either through the policy or through direct association, the base image and the added image are placed on the workstation.

NOTE If you update an Application object, you have to re-create the image file. You do not have to add it to the base image again as long as you kept the same image filename.

Re-imaging a Workstation

You can re-image the workstation (for example, apply a new image on top of the file system) through manual mode with the floppies or through the automatic method. Applying an image does not overwrite the Linux partition or the image-safe data on the hard drive.

You can automatically apply an image by following these steps. This procedure assumes that the workstation already has a Linux partition, that the workstation is associated with a Workstation object, and that an image exists in the tree.

1. Launch ConsoleOne.

2. Browse and select properties on the workstation object associated with the desktop.

3. Select the Images tab and select Put an Image on This Workstation on the Next Boot. Press the browse button in the Image file field to select an image to apply.

4. Press OK and exit from ConsoleOne.

5. Request that the users reboot the workstation.

Advanced Imaging

When the workstation boots the Linux partition and you request to enter manual mode, you have the following commands available. The following describes the minimal keystrokes to get the command functional.

Remember that you are running on top of the Linux operating system and that any normal Linux command is valid on the command line. This enables you the freedom to use any command to help in the setup and configuration of the workstation. For example, you can see a listing of files (`ls -FC`) or mount a drive (`mount /dev/hdc /mnt/cdrom`). Any Linux utility can be run on the workstation.

Accessing the Imaging Engine Command Menu

You can access operations available in the imaging engine from the command menu. To access the command menu, use the `img` command with no parameters; a menu appears where you select the operation you want to perform.

Information Commands

The following general-purpose commands display information about the system.

▶ `img help [mode]`—This displays a help screen to remind you about some of the commands. It does not display an exhaustive list of available commands. The optional mode parameters are `m` to display information on the make mode, and `p` to display information on the partition mode.

Example:

`img help p`

▶ `img info [zisd]`—This displays the detected hardware information. This is useful to determine the values for the rules in the policies. The engine sends this information to the imaging server. The optional `zisd` parameter lists the data currently stored in the image-safe area on the computer and the last base image that was put down to the workstation.

Example:

`img info zisd`

Automation Commands

Automatic mode images the computer automatically based on any applicable NDS or eDirectory policies and settings. In this mode, the imaging engine queries the imaging specified in the **PROXYADDR** environment variable for any work to do. The imaging server checks the relevant NDS or eDirectory policies and settings to determine which imaging tasks should be performed. The following command causes the imaging engine to connect to the imaging server and perform any actions that are specified in NDS or eDirectory:

`img auto`

This command sends a request to the imaging server to determine whether any work needs to be performed. If work must be performed, the imaging server immediately performs the work. The following codes are returned to the Linux shell upon completion: 0—no work to perform; 0—successful imaging task completed, no change to the hard drive; 1—successfully received one or more images, the hard drive has been altered; n—other error codes. Here's an example:

```
img auto
```

Partition Commands

The following commands deal with manipulation of the partitions on the workstation.

▶ `img dump`—Displays the partition information of the hard disk. This command is important because the partition numbers displayed from this command are used as parameters to other advanced imaging commands.

Example:
```
img dump
```

▶ `img dump geo`—Displays the partition information of the hard disk and the geometry of the disk. This command is important because the partition numbers displayed from this command are used as parameters to other advanced imaging commands.

Example:
```
img dump geo
```

▶ `img pa<partition number>`—Makes the specified partition the active partition. The partition number is the partition number returned from the `img dump` command.

Examples:
```
img pa2
img pa1
```

 ▶ `img pc<partition number> <partition type> [partition size] [cluster=<cluster size>]`—Creates a partition in an empty slot. The partition number is the partition number returned from the `img d` command. The command fails if the partition specified is not empty. The partition type must be one of the following: `fat12`, `fat16`, `fat32`, or `ntfs`. The partition size parameter is optional and represents the number of megabytes requested. If the size is not given, the largest partition size possible for the specified type is created. The cluster size is only supported for NTFS partition types; for the FAT partitions the cluster size is determined automatically by the size of the partition.

When a partition is created, the ZENworks imaging engine performs some low-level pre-formatting. This pre-formatting process is dependent upon the actual file system being created. It is usually a subset of the formatting process performed on new partitions by the various operating systems, but it is not enough to be recognized as a valid partition by those operating systems. It is only formatted enough to enable the imaging engine to start inserting files into the partition. At least one base image must be applied to the partition before it is recognized by the operating system.

Examples:

```
img pc2 ntfs 500 c8
img pc3 fat32
img pc4 NTFS 2000 cluster=1
```

▶ `img pd<partition number>`—Deletes the specified partition from the hard drive.

Example:

```
img pd3
```

Creating Image Commands

The following commands deal with the creation of workstation images:

▶ `img makel[partition number] <path> [comp=<comp level>] [x<partition number>]`—Makes an image of the disk and places it in the local file system. The optional partition number represents the partition where you want to store the image. This specified partition is *not* included in the image. If no partition is specified, all partitions (except the Linux boot partition) are imaged and the image is stored on the Linux partition. The path must resolve to a valid path on the system—no directories are automatically created, and any existing file with the same name is overwritten.

By specifying the partition number used to store the image, you can use an attached Jaz drive, which shows up as a partition and then stores the image of the hard drive on your removable media. The `comp` parameter specifies the amount of compression used when storing the image. Valid compression levels are from 0-9, where 0 is no compression for optimized speed and 9 indicates full compression optimized for space. Use 6 to balance between space and speed. The `x<partition number>` option excludes the partition specified from the image. You can exclude as many partitions as you need to reduce the imaging size and time.

Examples:

```
img make112 imgdump.zmg
img makel fulldump
img makel /images/wsdump.zmg comp=6 x2 x3
```

► `img makep <imaging server address> <UNCpath> [comp=<comp level>] [x<partition number]`—Takes an image of the workstation and sends that image to the specified imaging server. This imaging server address is the actual IP address (not the DNS name) of the imaging server. The UNC path is where the image is stored on that imaging server. The path must resolve to a valid path on the system—no directories are automatically created, and any existing file with the same name is overwritten. The UNC must have the format of `//server name/dir/dir.../filename` (make sure you use the forward slashes). If the suffix .ZMG is not specified, it is automatically appended to the filename. The server name is really ignored because the image is sent and stored on the imaging server specified by the IP address. The `comp` parameter specifies the amount of compression used when storing the image. Valid compression levels are from 0-9, where 0 is no compression for optimized speed and 9 means full compression optimized for space. Use 6 to balance between space and speed. The `x<partition number>` option excludes the partition specified from the image. You can exclude as many partitions as you need to reduce the imaging size and time. The server name might be used at some future release.

Examples:

```
img makep 137.65.203.1 //zen1/vol1/images/dellb.zmg
img makep 137.65.203.254 //zen2/vol2/ibmlaptop
img makep 137.65.79.123 //zen2/vol2/ntws.zmg comp=9 x2
```

Restoring Image Commands

The following commands deal with restoring images onto the workstation. These commands might destroy previous data on the workstation.

▶ img restorel[partition number] path [s<set number>]—
Restores an image from the partition and path specified onto the disk. All partitions on the hard disk, other than the Linux partition, are removed prior to the image being placed on the workstation. The optional partition number specifies the partition (as displayed in the img d command) where the image is stored. The path must resolve to a valid image file on the system. If you are restoring from a removable media drive, the partition number is the partition for the Jaz or CD-ROM drive. The path must be valid and must represent an image file on the specified partition. The optional set number enables you to specify which set of files to include from the image. The sets can be specified in the ZENworks Image Editor program. If the set number is not specified, it is assumed that it is set 1.

Examples:

```
img restorel2 myimage
img restorel theimage.zmg s2
```

▶ img restorep <proxy IP address> <UNCpath> [s<set number>]—Takes an image from the imaging server and puts it on the workstation. The proxy IP address must be the address of the imaging server where the image is stored. You cannot use a DNS name in this field. The UNC path must be a valid path that represents the image file. The path must be the format //server name/share/dir/dir.../filename or //server name/volume/dir/dir.../filename. The optional set number enables you to specify which set of files to include from the image. The sets can be specified in the ZENworks Image Editor program. If the set number is not specified it is assumed that it is set 1.

Examples:

```
img restorep 137.65.200.1 //zen9/image/delllaptop.zmg
img restorep 137.65.200.1 //any/image/delllaptop.zmg s2
```

Advanced Restoring Image Commands

These advanced image restore commands enable you to specify that the partitions on the disk should not be destroyed and how to map the partitions in the image to the partitions on the disk. Additionally, when images are restored the partitions are automatically resized to fit the archived partition. In these commands, the physical partition can remain larger than the archived partition.

▶ `img restorel[partition number] path [s<set number>] a<archive partition>:p<physical partition>`—Restores an image from the partition and path specified onto the specified partition on disk. This does not destroy the partition, but instead takes the archived partition and places its files into the specified partition. Any files already existing on the partition remain; files with the same name are overwritten. The optional partition number specifies the partition (as displayed in the `img d` command) where the image is stored. The path must resolve to a valid image file on the system. If you are restoring from a removable media drive, the partition number is the partition for the Jaz or CD-ROM drive. The path must be valid and must represent an image file on the specified partition. The optional set number enables you to specify which set of files to include from the image. The sets can be specified in the ZENworks Image Editor program. If the set number is not specified it is assumed that it is set 1.

The `a<archive partition>:p<physical partition>` option enables you to create a mapping between the two drive spaces. You can take archived partition 1 and place it on physical partition 2, for example. You must specify at least one partition mapping to keep from having the default, wipe all partitions, behavior. You can specify as many mappings as are needed and you can map multiple archive partitions onto a single physical partition. An archive partition cannot be mapped to more than one physical partition.

Examples:

```
img restorel2 myimage a1:p2
img restorel3 theimage.zmg s2 a1:p2 a2:p2
```

▶ `img restorep <proxy IP address> <UNCpath> [s<set number>] a<archive partition>:p<physical partition>`—Takes an image from the imaging server and puts it on the workstation into the specified partition. The proxy IP address must be the address of the imaging server where the image is stored. You cannot use a DNS name in this field. The UNC path must be a valid path that represents the image file. The path must be the

format //server name/share/dir/dir.../filename or //server
name/volume/dir/dir.../filename. The optional set number
enables you to specify which set of files to include from the image.
The sets can be specified in the ZENworks Image Editor program.
If the set number is not specified it is assumed that it is set 1.

The a<archive partition>:p<physical partition> option
enables you to create a mapping between the two drive spaces. You
can take archived partition 1 and place it on physical partition 2,
for example. You must specify at least one partition mapping to
keep from having the default, wipe all partitions, behavior. You can
specify as many mappings as are needed and you can map multiple
archive partitions onto a single physical partition. An archive partition cannot be mapped to more than one physical partition.

Examples:

```
img restorep 137.65.200.1 //zen9/image/delllaptop.zmg
a2:p1
img restorep 137.65.200.1 //any/image/dtop.zmg s2 a2:p2
a3:p2
```

ZENPartition Commands

You can use the ZENPartition mode to enable, disable, or remove the installed ZENworks for Desktops imaging partition from the workstation. This
allows you to control the behavior of ZENworks imaging on the workstation.

The following are the commands available for the ZEN partition mode:

▶ zenPartition enable—Enables the ZENworks imaging partition.

▶ zenPartition disable—Disables the ZENworks imaging partition
  to stop imaging on the workstation.

▶ zenPartition remove—Removes the ZENworks imaging partition
  from the workstation to permanently stop imaging on it.

Example:

```
img zenPartition enable
```

Multicast Commands *Oh yes!!*

You can also set up the ZENworks Imaging system to perform image
multicasting. You can set up a single workstation to act as the master and
send its hard drive contents to all the participating slave workstations.

You start the multicast session by entering the following on all workstations that are participating on the session:

```
img session <session name> [option]
```

The following options are available for the `img session name`:

- **name**—Specifies the name of the multicast session that each computer joining the session will use.

- **master¦client**—Specifies whether this client will be the session master or just a client. If you do not use this parameter, the system will wait until a master is found.

- **clients=<count>**—Specifies the number of computers that must be registered with the master before imaging will begin. Once imaging has begun, computers attempting to register with the session are denied.

- **t=<minutes>**—Specifies the number of minutes the master computer will wait for the next participant to register before starting the imaging process without reaching the number of computers specified by the clients option.

The session name must be a unique string to identify this multicast session. The session name string used must be identically entered on all workstations (both master and slave) that are going to participate in the session. This string is used to hash a multicast address, so a small chance exists that two different strings can result in the same multicast address. Multicast addresses are class D IP addresses. In order to ease wire sniffing, troubleshooting, and LAN traffic analysis, the imaging engine always uses 231 as the first octet in its address.

Start this process by using the `img session <name>` command. Each workstation waits until the user determines which station will act as the master. The master workstation should be the *source* workstation; all slave workstations are *destination* workstations.

To designate the master workstation, go to the workstation that contains the source drive. The workstation should be running the session command and should be waiting just like all of the other workstations. Press the m key on the master workstation. This designates that workstation as the master. At this point, all of the other workstations attempt to register with the master and receive a unique session identifier. If, for some reason, a slave station is rebooted before the session starts, it always receives the same identifier.

When the desired number of stations has registered with the master, the master displays a running count of the number of registered slaves, and then starts the session by pressing **g** on the master workstation. Any station attempting to join the session after the session has started is denied access. Contents of the master are now transferred to all of the slave workstations.

Once the session is over, the master workstation displays a list of the stations that did not successfully complete the image.

NOTE The multicast operations are dependent on the multicast features configured in your network equipment. Possible problems might include the routing of multicast packets not being allowed, stations outside of the defined scope of multicast on switches not receiving the packets, and so on.

Script Commands

The following commands perform some type of operation that would normally be activated only when the imaging engine is initially booted in manual mode. These are simple shell scripts that have been created for your convenience by the imaging system. Other script files exist, but these are the most useful to you.

- ▶ /bin/cdrom.s—Mounts the CD-ROM drive to /mnt/cdrom.
- ▶ /bin/config.s—Enables you to configure the SETTINGS.TXT file for the Linux partition.
- ▶ /bin/imaging.s—Runs the imaging engine in auto mode, just like the img a command.
- ▶ /bin/install.s—Creates the Linux partition and installs it onto the hard disk. It removes all partitions *unless* the Linux partition already exists; then it just updates the files.
- ▶ /bin/lilo.s—Installs the ZENworks Imaging boot manager system, making sure that this system is booted first on the drive.

## CHAPTER 15

Maintaining a Workstation

Once the ZENworks for Desktops 4 system has been deployed across the network, the workstations have the ZENworks for Desktops agent, and the workstation is registered, you can maintain and manage the workstation from any location in the network. This provides obvious benefits, because support technicians rarely have to visit the individual workstation. This is a significant cost improvement over previous methods.

To maintain any particular workstation, you need to right-click the workstation object in ConsoleOne and select Properties, and then on the tabs you can get to a list of maintenance actions that can be performed on that workstation. The following sections discuss the actions you can perform.

Reviewing Workstation Inventory

An extremely useful action you can perform on workstations you are managing is checking the inventory for the particular workstation you are working on. The inventory provides you with useful information about the hardware and software installed on the workstation.

Accessing the workstation's inventory enables you to determine whether there are any obvious hardware or software problems or incompatibilities in the system. For instance, you could determine that the workstation is running an outdated version of software that needed to be upgraded. You could then upgrade the application using ZENworks application distribution.

The following list details the specific information you can get from the Inventory list:

- *General*—General information gives you the basic information about the workstation such as the name, user, serial number, and so on. It also gives you login information.

- *Software*—Software information includes everything about the software installed on the workstation from the operating system to the specific drivers being used. The software option includes:

    - *Software Vendors*—Lists the vendors of the software installed on the workstation. By clicking on a vendor, you can see a list of applications by that vendor and determine which version of the application is installed.

    - *Device Drivers*—Lists drivers installed for each device on the system.

    - *Operating Systems*—Lists the operating system or systems installed on the workstation.

    - *NetWare Client*—Shows the version of the NetWare Client.

    - *Inventory Scanner Information*—Displays the version and mode of the inventory scanner that's running on the workstation.

- *Hardware*—Lists all the hardware installed on the workstation. This includes everything from hard drives to port information. By clicking a listed hardware component, you can get detailed information about that component, thus allowing you to assess the hardware needs of the workstation.

- *Network*—Gives you the DNS name of the workstation.

- *System*—Includes general information about the basic system components such as the motherboard and CPU.

Remote Controlling a Workstation

On some occasions, it is necessary to remote control a workstation from any other workstation in the tree. You can remote control a workstation via the IP or IPX protocol and from any workstation in the network; however, you must have Novell Directory Services rights to control the workstation. Before you can remote control a workstation, you must complete the following:

1. The proper remote control agents must be present on the workstation. This can be accomplished by installing the ZENworks for Desktops 4 agent that ships with the product.

   Additionally, you can deliver the agents to the workstation via the ZENworks for Desktops 4 Application Launcher. When ZENworks for Desktops 4 is installed into the tree, several application objects are created for the remote control agents for the Windows NT/2000/XP and Windows 98. If you have the Application Launcher launched from the login scripts of your user, you can force-run the deployment of these agents to ensure that all workstations have the proper agent.

2. The workstation must have registered with Novell Directory Services and have a workstation object imported and associated with the Workstation Policy Package if you want to use eDirectory rights to control who can remote control a workstation or a user. Alternatively, with ZENworks for Desktops 4 you can remote control this process using a password and IP address. This is launched from the Tools menu of ConsoleOne. The password you enter must be the same password that the user entered into the remote control agent.

   A good way to test that you have got a good association is to modify some of the policies associated with the workstation and determine whether the changes take effect. One thing to do is to change the remote control policy so that the icon shows on the taskbar or the desktop and then determine whether this takes effect on the workstation. By doing this, you know that the workstation is associated with the object and that the system is communicating properly with Novell Directory Services.

3. You must have rights to perform the remote control. When the remote control session starts, the session manager (program that runs from ConsoleOne) determines whether you have rights to remote control the workstation. Additionally, the agent also verifies that you have rights to control the workstation.

   The rights to remote control a workstation can be given in several ways. One way is through the ZENworks Manage Remote Operators wizard launched from the Tools, Management Remote Operator in ConsoleOne. This wizard walks the tree starting at the specified container and makes sure that the users specified gain rights to remote control the workstations. Additionally, you can go to the workstation object itself and add users to the Remote Operators page. When they are added to this page, they are given rights to remote control this workstation.

Once the system is set up with the workstation, you can remote control any registered workstation that you have rights to remote control. To remote control a workstation, you need to do the following:

1. Start ConsoleOne.

2. Browse in the tree to the particular workstation object for the workstation that you want to remote control. Highlight the workstation object. You can start remote controlling the workstation by right-clicking and selecting Actions, Remote Control on the workstation object menu, or you can view the details of the workstation and launch remote control from the Remote Management page, Remote Operations button.

3. The remote control session manager verifies that you have rights and then attempts to connect to the remote control agents on the workstation associated with the object. The agent then responds and begins the remote controlling of the workstation, and you are presented with a window on your machine that represents the desktop of the remote machine. You now have control of the remote workstation until you exit the remote control session.

You can configure the remote control from the remote control policy of the Workstation Policy Package discussed in Chapter 9, "Setting Up a Workstation Policy Package."

Using Remote View

The remote view enables you to monitor a workstation the same way that remote control enables you to remote control a workstation. By using the remote view option, you can observe everything that is being done on a specific workstation. You cannot affect the workstation like you can with the remote control option. This view helps you determine user errors that might be causing problems. The remote view uses fewer system resources than remote control on both the managed workstation and the management console.

You can configure the remote view from the remote control policy of the Workstation Policy Package discussed in Chapter 9.

File Transfer

The file transfer option enables you to copy, delete, or move files to and from any particular workstation. This can be useful when you need to get a new driver to a user or free up space by deleting extraneous files from a workstation. The file transfer window, shown in Figure 15.1, displays the local file system on the management console workstation in one pane and the remote file system on the managed workstation in another.

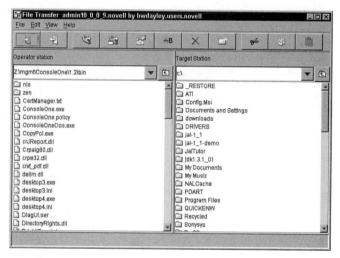

FIGURE 15.1
File Transfer window in ConsoleOne.

Remote Execute

Remote execute enables you to run an application or perform a command on a workstation. Selecting this option pops up a window that prompts you to specify a command to be executed. For instance, if two users have conflicting IP addresses, bound on their workstations, you can execute the following command on one of the workstations to resolve the conflict:

```
IPCONFIG /release
```

You can configure the remote view from the remote control policy of the Workstation Policy Package discussed in Chapter 9.

Workstation Diagnostics

There are occasions when it is beneficial to perform some immediate diagnostics on a particular workstation. From the ConsoleOne utility, you can perform immediate diagnostics on the workstation. These diagnostics perform an immediate connection to the agent on the workstation and then deliver to the administrator information about the workstation. Figure 15.2 shows the output screen from the diagnostics.

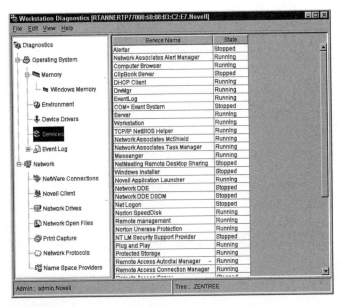

FIGURE 15.2
Workstation Diagnostics of a Windows NT workstation.

The diagnostics information includes the amount of memory available and used, the environment information, device drivers, services information, and the event logs. In addition it displays the network connections, drives, and open files. Also it shows client information, printers, network protocols, and name space providers.

This tool provides you with some real-time information about the workstation as you debug the system and repair your user's problems.

Remote Wakeup

Remote wakeup enables you to remotely boot up a system that is powered down. In order to do so, the system must have a network card that supports Wake-on-LAN. The Wake-on-LAN agent must be installed on the managed workstation. The Remote Wakeup feature enables you to manage workstations during off hours, thus minimizing the user downtime during working hours.

NOTE The Wake-on-LAN agent is installed on the managed workstation during the Remote Management Agent installation.

Remote Management Audit

The Remote Management Audit option enables you to store information about the remote management sessions running on the managed workstations as log files. This feature runs automatically when any remote management session is initiated with a workstation. These audit files are stored in the AUDITLOG.TXT file, which is created and updated when there are no remote management sessions in progress. The information that can be found in these files includes the following:

- ► *Start Time*—Start time of the event occurrence.
- ► *Duration*—Duration of the remote management session.
- ► *Console DN*—Name of the management workstation.
- ► *Console User DN*—Name of the remote operator.
- ► *Operation Code*—The various operations that a management console user can perform on the managed workstation. These codes are as follows:

```
Remote Control = 1
Remote View = 2
File Transfer = 3
Remote Execute = 5
Remote Diagnostics = 6
```

- ► *Operation Status*—The status of the event indicates whether the particular event was a success or failure. 1 indicates that the remote management operation was successful and 0 indicates that the remote management operation was unsuccessful.

An example of an audit record is as follows:

```
1005572546000 1000 workstation1 admin.novell 1 0
```

The AUDITLOG.TXT file will store up to 100 of these records in the system directory. You can store more records than this in a centralized database by installing the workstation inventory agent on every managed workstation. The inventory scanner will then collect the records and store them as scanned data files in the scan directory on the inventory server. You can then configure the number of audit records that can be stored for each workstation on the RM Audit tab of the Inventory Database Object.

Generating a Remote Management Report

Another extremely useful tool when managing workstations is the capability to generate a remote management report. This report shows you the number of times a particular workstation was remotely managed as well as errors managing remote workstations. This can help you troubleshoot management issues.

You can run a configured remote management report from the inventory database. Use the following steps to generate the remote management report:

1. Click on a Server object in ConsoleOne.

2. Click Tools, ZENworks Reports.

3. From the Available Reports list, double-click RM Audit Reports. Click Remote Management Report.

4. Specify the selection criteria for: Date of Operation, Console DN, Console User DN, Target Workstation DN, Operation, and Operation Status.

NOTE In the Reporting dialog box, you can use wildcard characters (*). The wildcard character is applicable to character data only. For example, PRV-WS* would retrieve PRV-WS001, PRV-WS002, and so on.

---

5. Click Run Selected Report. A status box appears displaying the progress of the report generation. When the report is generated, it appears in the viewer. Use the buttons on the toolbar to page through, print, or export the report.

Registering and Un-Registering a Workstation

There might be occasions when you need to unregister and re-register a workstation with eDirectory. When the ZENworks Management Agents were installed on the workstation, the executable file ZWSREG.EXE was installed in the following directory:

```
C:\program files\novell\zenworks directory
```

This executable can take an **-unreg** option to unregister the workstation. No options will cause the program to register the workstation. You can specify the Import server and the Import policy that you want to use.

## CHAPTER 16

Using Software Metering with ZENworks for Desktops 4

A major advantage included in ZENWorks for Desktops is software metering. ZENWorks for Desktops software metering gives organizations the capability to manage software licenses and track software usage through ZENWorks for Desktops application management and Novell's Licensing Services (NLS). Currently NLS cannot be administered in ConsoleOne, requiring that you administer the licensing in NWAdmin while managing ZENworks for Desktops 4 in ConsoleOne.

Once software metering is configured for an Application Launcher application, a license is used each time a user launches the application. In other words, every time a user runs the application, one of the licenses is also in use.

NOTE Applications must be delivered to the user through Application Launcher in order to take advantage of software metering. Application objects must also be associated with license containers.

To set up and use ZENWorks for Desktops software metering, you need to become familiar with the following procedures.

Using NWAdmin to Install and Administer Licenses

The first piece of software metering you should be familiar with using is NWAdmin to install and administer licenses. You should use the NWAdmin utility to create metered certificates as well as to add new ones to existing license containers. You can also use the NWAdmin utility to generate reports and view information about software metering.

To access the licensing features from NWAdmin, select the Novell Licensing Services option from the Tools menu, as shown in Figure 16.1.

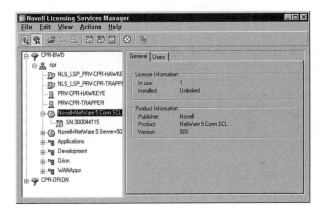

FIGURE 16.1
The licensing options in NWAdmin.

Installing a License Certificate Using NWAdmin

You first need to install a license certificate. When you install a certificate for an NLS-aware application, the system adds a License container object to the NDS database as well as a License Certificate object inside that container object.

To install a license certificate in NWAdmin, use the following steps from the tree browse view:

1. First select the container you want to install the license certificate into.

2. Then select Tools, Novell Licensing Services, Add Licenses (see Figure 16.1).

3. From the pop-up window, select License File and click OK. A window pops up enabling you to specify the license file you want to install.

4. From this window, navigate to the location of the license file you want to install and select it. Click OK and a window similar to the one in Figure 16.2 appears.

5. From this window, browse to the NDS context where the Certificate object should be installed. (The default is the currently selected container.)

6. Once both fields are completed, click the View button to view specific information about the license, or click the Add button to install the license certificate.

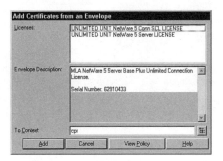

FIGURE 16.2
The Add Certificates from an Envelope window in NWAdmin.

Creating a Metered Certificate Using NWAdmin

The next procedure you should be familiar with is creating a metered certificate. Metered certificates enable you to track application usage. Using metered certificates enables you to track and manage the licenses for user applications even if they are not NLS (Novell License Services)-aware.

To create a metered certificate using NWAdmin, follow these steps from a tree browse window:

1. First select Tools, Novell Licensing Services, Add Licenses.

2. From the pop-up window, select License Metering and click OK. A screen similar to the one in Figure 16.3 appears.

3. From that screen, enter the name of the software publisher.

4. Enter the product name.

5. Enter the version.

6. Set the NDS context for the license certificate.

7. Set the number of licenses for the certificate.

8. Enter or select the number of grace licenses you will allow.

9. Set whether users will use a single license when launching an application multiple times from one workstation.

10. Click OK to finish.

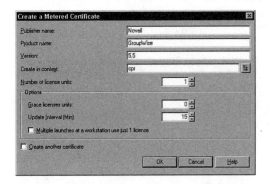

FIGURE 16.3
The Create a Metered Certificate window.

NOTE The grace licenses option enables additional users to run. If you do not enter a number of grace licenses, users cannot open additional applications beyond the number specified.

Assigning Licenses to Users Through NWAdmin

Once you know how to install license certificates and create metering certificates you need to know how to assign licenses to users through NWAdmin.

The NDS user who installs the license certificate is the owner. An owner can assign the following objects access to the licenses:

▶ User   ▶ Organizational Unit

▶ Group   ▶ Server

▶ Organization

For example, if an owner assigns a container object to use a certificate, all users in and below that container can use the certificate. Once license assignments are made, only those objects that have been assigned to the license certificates can use the license.

To assign and delete access to licenses using NWAdmin, use the following steps from a tree browse window:

1. Select the license certificate that you want users to access.
2. Right-click the license certificate and select details.
3. Select the Assignments property page.
4. Click Add to add objects.
5. Locate and select the object that enables the correct users to access the certificate's licenses.

Here are the steps for deleting assignments on a license certificate in NWAdmin:

1. Navigate to the Assignments property page of the License Certificate object you want to delete assignments on.
2. Select the user objects and click Remove.

Assigning a New Owner to a License Certificate Using NWAdmin

The next procedure you should be familiar with is assigning a new owner to a license certificate. Because the user who installs a certificate automatically becomes the owner of that certificate, you might want to reassign ownership at a later date.

NWAdmin enables you to assign a new owner to a license certificate by using the following steps:

1. Select the License Certificate object from a tree browse window in the NWAdmin utility.
2. Right-click the object and select details.
3. Select the Installer property page.
4. From the Installer property page, locate and select the object you want to assign as owner of this certificate.

NOTE Only a certificate's owner can reassign ownership of the certificate.

Working with Reports in NWAdmin

The final procedure you should be aware of is the capability to create reports about licensed and metered products in the NWAdmin utility. Because NWAdmin tracks data about licenses and metered products, you can create reports that help you assess and monitor usage and compliance concerning these products for the past 15 months.

These reports can range in information about a single license certificate to information about all license certificates currently being used for a given product.

Creating a Report

To create a report for license certificates, use the following steps from within NWAdmin:

1. Select Tools, Novell Licensing Services, Generate License Reports.

2. From this screen, shown in Figure 16.4, you can select to scan either the tree or a pre-defined catalog to generate the report.

3. Select a license container you want to begin the scan at and specify any specific publisher, product, or version filters you want to use for the scan. Click the OK button.

4. Once the scan is complete, a list of license certificates and containers appears. To create a report, simply select the license certificate you want to report usage on and select Actions, Create License Usage Report. A screen similar to the one in Figure 16.5 appears.

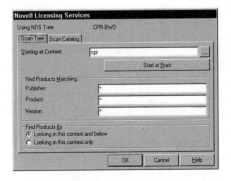

FIGURE 16.4
The Scan Tree tab on the Novell Licensing Services window in NWAdmin.

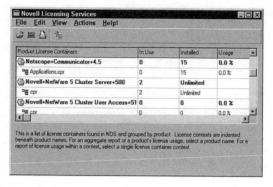

FIGURE 16.5
A metered license certificate report in NWAdmin.

Viewing a Report

Once you have created a report using NWAdmin, you can toggle between a graphical view of the report and that report's text.

To use the graphical view, click Graph, as shown in Figure 16.6, and a graphical representation of the data in the report is displayed on the screen. This view displays the number of license units installed and the number used. The dates along the bottom of the graph show the start and end dates that the report covers. You can change these dates to make the data more informational.

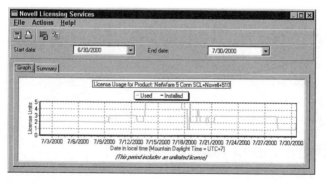

FIGURE 16.6
A metered license certificate usage report graph in NWAdmin.

To use the textual view, click Summary and a textual representation of the data in the report is displayed on the screen, as shown in Figure 16.7.

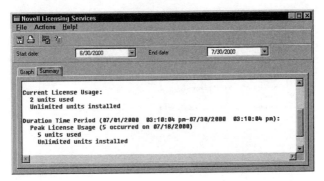

FIGURE 16.7
A metered license certificate usage report summary in NWAdmin.

The textual view provides the following information:

- ▶ The date and time you created the report
- ▶ The product
- ▶ The location or NDS context of the object
- ▶ Current number of licenses being used and installed
- ▶ The range of dates being reported
- ▶ Peak usage of licenses, including date the peak occurred
- ▶ The number of units used and installed during peak usage
- ▶ A list of possible dates out of compliance

Setting Up Software Metering

Now that you are familiar with using the NWAdmin utility, you need to understand how to set up software metering. Setting up software metering involves using the following procedures to verify the metering requirements and setting up metering certificates.

Verifying Setup Requirements

The first step in setting up software metering is to make certain that you have the correct system requirements met. The following are the current requirements for setting up software metering:

- ▶ You should have Supervisor rights to the [ROOT] of the eDirectory tree in which you install the Application Management portion of ZENworks for Desktops.

▶ Users must have Read and File Scan rights to the directory in which you install NAL.

▶ Users must have sufficient rights to the directories in which you install the applications they can access.

Installing Locally or on the Network?

Once the system requirements are met, you must make certain that the application is delivered to the user through the Application Launcher via the Application Launcher window or via the Application Explorer. Although software metering does not care where an application's executable file is located, it must be delivered to the user through the Application Launcher.

Ensuring Users Have Access to NLS

The next step in setting up software metering is to ensure users have access to NLS. Users must always be attached to a NetWare server that provides licensing services.

TIP By loading NLS on more than one server in your tree, and ensuring users have a connection to one or more servers with NLS loaded, you can ensure users have access to NLS. If a server running NLS goes down, NLS still works as long as it is running on another server and users have a connection to that server.

Assigning Users to a License Certificate Object

Once you have verified that the system and setup requirements for software metering have been met, you need to assign users to a license.

If no object is specifically assigned to a License Certificate object, anyone can use it. However, after assigning at least one user to a License Certificate Object, only the users, groups, or containers who are assigned to that license can use it. This limits access to the licenses.

To assign users to a License Certificate object, use NLS Manager or the following steps in the NWAdmin utility:

1. Double-click a Product License container.

2. Select a License Certificate object.

3. Right-click it and select Details to add users.

Creating a License Container and Metered Certificate Object

To set up software metering, you now need to create a license container and a Metered Certificate object. These objects enable ZENWorks for Desktops to track and control access to license objects.

The license container is a special container object in NDS to store Metered Certificate objects.

The Metered Certificate object contains the information you enter. License Containers can contain multiple Metered Certificate objects.

To create a Metered Certificate object and a license container, use the following steps in the NWAdmin utility:

1. Highlight the container where you want to create a Metered Certificate.

2. Select Tools, Novell License Metering, Add Licenses then License File; a screen similar to the one in Figure 16.8 appears.

3. From that screen, enter information about the application that you want to meter, such as software publisher name, software product name, and version or revision.

4. Click OK.

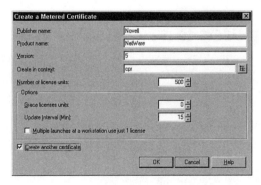

FIGURE 16.8
The Create a Metered Certificate window in NWAdmin.

Adding Licenses (Metered Certificates)

The last procedure you need to be aware of when setting up software metering is adding additional licenses; for example, if you originally installed a 50-user license of an application and want to extend this to a 75-user license. To extend the license of the application, you need to create another Metered Certificate object.

The license container is a container class object in eDirectory and cannot be renamed. The metered certificate is a leaf object of the license container. The metered certificate basically represents the individual license count. To get a total license count, the license container adds all leaf metered certificates beneath it.

To add licenses, you need to add Metered Certificates using the following steps in the NWAdmin utility:

1. Highlight the container where you want to add a license.

2. Select Tools, Novell License Metering, Add Licenses then License Metering.

3. From that screen, enter the same name as the original license container to which you want to add licenses.

If you enter the same software publisher name, software product name, and same version number, a new Metered Certificate is created below the license container. This metered certificate is added to those already located in the license container to form a new license total.

## CHAPTER 17

Integrating ZENworks for Desktops with ZENworks for Servers

A major advantage included in ZENworks for Desktops is its capability to integrate into the Tiered Electronic Distribution (TED) system that is included with Novell's ZENworks for Servers product. This integration enables you to leverage the powerful TED engine for application distribution. You can distribute desktop applications throughout your entire network, across tree boundaries, from a single source location.

The following sections describe what TED does and how to integrate a ZENworks for Desktops Application object into the TED distribution system to more effectively distribute applications to users on large networks.

How to Use TED with ZENworks for Desktops

The TED engine in ZENworks for Servers is comprised of Distributor, Subscriber, and Proxy agents hosted on NetWare, Linux, Solaris, and Windows servers throughout your tree. When you install ZENworks for Servers, the installation program creates Distributor and Subscriber objects for the TED agents that you install on each server.

Once you have installed TED, you can configure and manage the TED objects from ConsoleOne. This makes it easier to distribute files by grouping them into data packages (distributions) and hosting them in distribution channels made up of Distributor and Subscriber objects. You can add Application objects to the TED system as data packages by using the Desktop Application Distribution wizard to create a Desktop Application Distribution object.

TED then transfers the Desktop Application Distribution object from single or multiple sources to the subscriber server nodes in the distribution channel. This enables you to schedule distributions to take advantage of off-peak hours. It also sends notification of distribution statuses by sending e-mail messages, displaying real-time messages, logging events, database reporting, or sending SNMP traps.

About the Desktop Application Agent

The ZENworks for Servers 3 Desktop Application agent is the TED agent that allows you to distribute ZENworks for Desktops Application objects through the TED channel. The Desktop Application agent is responsible for keeping track of the Application object-specific information as the package is distributed through the channel so that it can be maintained when it reaches the destination subscriber.

Once you have set up the Application object through the wizard, the ZENworks for Servers distributor will read the objects' properties in eDirectory and determine the location of the source files. Next, it will determine the associations with other Application objects, application folder objects, chained applications, and containers. It will package the associations data into an .XML file and package it with the Application objects source files, including the source files of any associated Application objects, into a .CPK file to be distributed though the TED channel.

When the package is distributed through the ZENworks for Servers channel, subscriber servers extract the package including the source files and XML data and replicate the Application object in their tree locations. The subscriber can be in a different location and even in an entirely different tree.

NOTE You must install ZENworks for Servers policy-enabled Distribution Services to have access to the Desktop Application agent.

Using the Desktop Application Distribution Wizard to Create a Desktop Application Distribution

Now that you understand how the Desktop Application agent works to distribute a Desktop Application Distribution through a TED channel, you need to know how to create the Desktop Application Distribution object. ZENworks for Servers 3 includes a Desktop Application Distribution wizard to ease the creation of Desktop Application Distributions. The wizard allows you to specify an Application object that you want to distribute and then enables you to set properties that will determine how it is delivered. The following sections discuss creating a Distribution object, running the Desktop Application Distribution wizard to add an Application object to it, and setting the properties to distribute the application.

Create a Distribution Object

The first step in creating a Desktop Application Distribution is to create a TED Distribution object. Use the following steps to create a TED Distribution object from within ConsoleOne:

1. Select the container you want to create the TED Distribution object in.

2. Click File, New, TED Distribution.

3. Enter the name of the Distribution object in the object creation window shown in Figure 17.1.

4. Use the browse button to select the Distributor object that you want to distribute the application. The source files for Application objects that will be part of the distribution must exist on the local file system of the Distributor you select.

5. Click OK.

NOTE The source files for the Application objects you add to the distribution must reside on the Distributors' local file system. The subscriber must have Novell's eDirectory installed on it to extract the Application object and apply it.

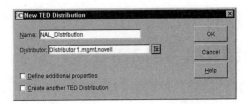

FIGURE 17.1
Distribution object creation window in ConsoleOne.

Configure the Distribution Type Using the Desktop Application Distribution Wizard

Once you have created the TED Distribution object, you need to define the distribution type as a Desktop Application. That way, you can use the Desktop Application Distribution wizard to define the Desktop Application properties and make the TED distribution a Desktop Application Distribution.

Use the following steps to define the Distribution type and start the Application wizard:

1. Right-click on the TED Distribution object you just created and select Properties from the pop-up menu.

2. Choose the Type tab, shown in Figure 17.2.

3. Select Desktop Application from the drop-down Type list to set the distribution type as a Desktop Application Distribution.

4. Then click the Setup button to open the Desktop Application Distribution wizard shown in Figure 17.3.

WARNING Do not edit Desktop Application Distribution objects manually from their ConsoleOne properties windows. Always go through the wizard to make changes to these objects.

The following sections describe how to navigate through the Desktop Application Distribution wizard to define the settings used when distributing the Desktop Application through the TED channel.

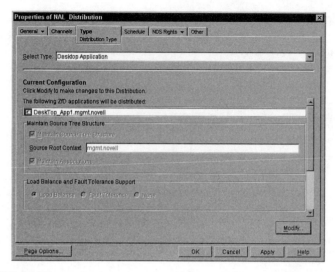

FIGURE 17.2
Type tab for the TED Distribution object in ConsoleOne.

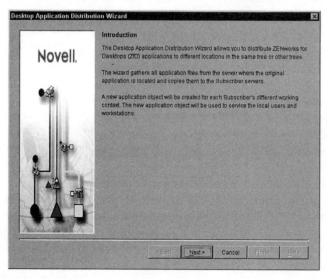

FIGURE 17.3
Desktop Application Distribution Wizard for the Desktop Application agent
in ConsoleOne.

Configure the Application Source Options

Once you click Next from the initial window in the Desktop Application Distribution wizard, you will see a screen similar to the one shown in Figure 17.4. From this screen you can configure settings that control what properties of the source Application object you want to maintain when it is distributed through the TED channel. You also define whether load balancing and fault tolerance are used.

The following is a list of the properties that you need to define in the application source options screen of the wizard:

▶ *Maintain Source Tree Structure*—Selecting this option duplicates the source tree's directory structure at the destination's location, which is the target subscribers' working context. This tree structure is then used to create the ZENworks for Desktops Application objects. You must enable this option if you want to use chained applications.

▶ *Maintain Associations*—Selecting this option will maintain the group and container associations of the Application object in its source tree, by replicating the associated groups or containers at the target location if they do not exist. User and workstation associations in the source location are not replicated.

▶ *Source Root Context*—This field specifies a container object to be used as the root container for the ZENworks for Desktops Application objects. The distributor will record directory data only from that container and its subordinate containers; therefore, when the subscriber extracts the package it will apply the Application object to its working directory as if the container had actually been the root. You can select Application objects from this root container and its subordinate containers.

▶ *Load Balancing and Fault Tolerance*—This setting allows you to specify whether to use automated load balancing, fault tolerance, or neither. If you use load balancing, ZENworks will automatically spread the Desktop Application Distributions of the servers being used. Fault tolerance is effectively accomplished through load balancing because multiple servers are involved. If you specify fault tolerance, ZENworks will allow a server currently being used for Desktop Application Distributions to assume the distribution role of another server that's down, however. If you select None, you can manually configure each Application object for load balancing or fault tolerance.

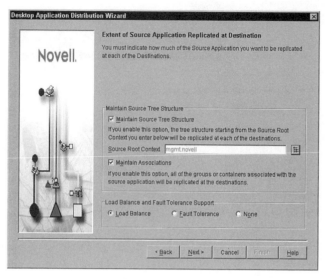

FIGURE 17.4
Application Source options screen of the Desktop Application Distribution wizard in ConsoleOne.

Configure the Application Source Objects

Once you have configured the options for maintaining information about the source Application object and clicked the Next button, you will see a screen similar to the one in Figure 17.5. This screen allows you to configure which Application objects you want to be part of the Desktop Application Distribution.

You must first specify at least one valid ZENworks for Desktops Application object. ZENworks for Servers 3 TED supports Application objects that are chained together. When you add an Application object that is chained, all associated objects will be shown on the Type panel of the Distribution object once you have completed the Desktop Application Distribution wizard.

From the Application Source objects screen, shown in Figure 17.5, click the Add button and select Application objects to be added to the Desktop Application Distribution.

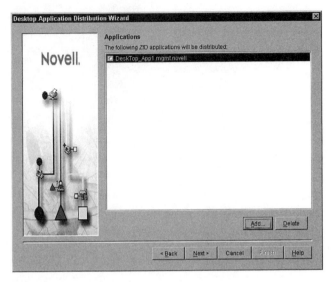

FIGURE 17.5
Application Source objects screen of the Desktop Application Distribution wizard in ConsoleOne.

Configure the Application Destination Options

Once you have selected the Application objects and clicked the Next button, you will see a screen similar to the one in Figure 17.6. From this screen, you can configure settings that control where the Application object's source files are extracted when it has been distributed through the TED channel to a subscriber. It is important to verify that the destination nodes have enough disk space to receive the Application objects.

The following is a list of the properties that you need to define within the application destination options screen of the wizard:

- ▶ *Destination Volume or Shared Folder*—This option allows you to specify a NetWare volume or shared folder that will store the source files of the Application object at the destination subscriber node. This volume must exist on the destination node. The default is **%DEST_VOLUME%**, which is a macro that indicates the use of the same volume name as where the source files are stored on the distributor.

- ▶ *Destination Directory Path*—You also have the option to use the default directory for the Application object to store the Application object source files, or you can enter a user-defined directory. If you select user-defined, the path is added to the destination path between the destination volume and the parent directory of the Application object's default path. For example, if the Application object's default path is \APPS\APP1\ and you enter VOL1 as the destination volume and \CTREE\ as a user-defined path, the effective path is VOL1:\CTREE\APPS\APP1\.

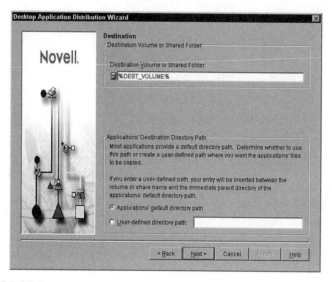

FIGURE 17.6
Application Destination options screen of the Desktop Application Distribution wizard in ConsoleOne.

View the Application Distribution Summary

Once you have configured the application destination options and clicked the Next button, a Desktop Application Distribution summary window similar to the one in Figure 17.7 is displayed.

Review the information on this screen carefully. If any problems exist, you can click the Back button and make changes. Otherwise, click the Finish button. The Desktop Application Distribution object is created and you can see the settings in the Type tab shown in Figure 17.2. If you need to modify these settings, you can run the Desktop Application Distribution wizard again by clicking the Modify button.

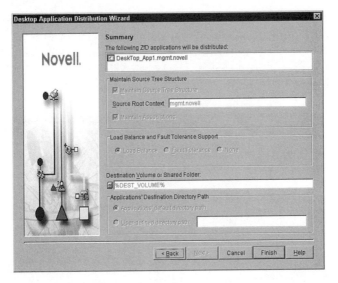

FIGURE 17.7
Site Distribution summary in ConsoleOne.

Configure the Desktop Application Distribution Object

Once you have set up and configured the TED Distribution object to be a Desktop Application Distribution, you need to finish setting up the Distribution object and schedule it to be distributed through the TED channel. The following sections discuss configuring the Distribution object's settings, channel, and schedule.

Configure Settings for a Desktop Application Distribution Object

You can configure the Desktop Application Distribution object's settings from the General, Settings tab shown in Figure 17.8. From this screen, you can specify the following settings, which the Distribution object has as it is distributed through the TED channel:

▶ *Active*—Activates or deactivates the distribution. If a distribution is inactive, the distribution is not sent to subscribers even if it is in a channel.

▶ *Use Digest*—Activates the TED system to use a digest on the distribution file.

▶ *Encrypt*—Activates distribution encryption, thus providing security for the distribution during transit between the distributor and subscriber. Typically, you would only encrypt a distribution that is sent through a firewall. You have the option to select strong or weak encryption.

▶ *Maximum Revisions*—Enables you to specify the number of revisions of the distribution that you will keep. Each time that a distribution is collected and a distribution file is created, this constitutes a revision. When the maximum number of revisions has been created, the oldest revision is discarded from disk (unless it is currently being sent to a subscriber, in which case it is discarded on the next distribution cycle). Each subscriber that receives this distribution will keep this number of revisions. This includes subscribers that act as parent subscribers but do not actually subscribe to the channel. You can also delete previous revisions prior to accepting the next. This is extremely useful in the case of large distributions because the subscriber frees space for the new version before receiving it.

▶ *Priority*—Specifies the priority of this distribution. The priority determines how it will be sent in relation to other distributions. A high priority means it will be sent before all medium- and low-priority distributions.

▶ *Distributor*—A display-only field that identifies the distributor that collects and transmits this distribution. This distributor is specified when the Distribution object is created. This distributor is the owner of this distribution. The owner of a distribution cannot be changed.

▶ *Description*—Enables you to have a free-flowing text description of the distribution. This is helpful in understanding the files and the purpose for the distribution package.

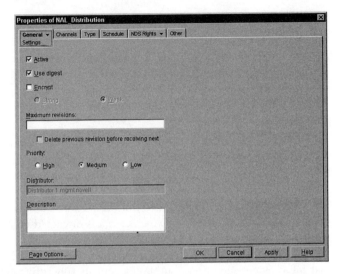

FIGURE 17.8
General Settings tab for the TED Distribution object in ConsoleOne.

Configure Channel for a Desktop Application Distribution Object

Once you have configured the general settings for the Desktop Application Distribution object, you need to configure the channel you want it to be distributed through from the Channels tab, shown in Figure 17.9. From the Channels tab, you can select the channels that contain this distribution. This distribution can be placed in any number of channels. All of the subscribers associated with each channel are sent this distribution by the distributor associated with this Distribution object.

To add this distribution to a channel, press the Add button and browse through eDirectory to select the channel. Once you have selected the channel, it is placed in the list displayed in the Channels box. To delete the channel from the list (thus removing the distribution from being distributed), select the channel and press the Delete button. To go to the property pages of the channel object, select the object and press the Details button.

Any distributions that are associated with channels also appear in the channel object under the Distributions property page.

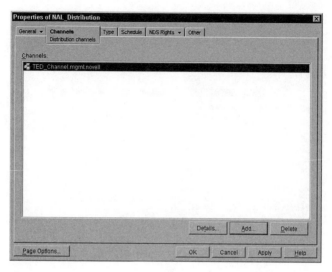

FIGURE 17.9
Channels Settings tab for the TED Distribution object in ConsoleOne.

Configure Schedule for a Desktop Application Distribution Object

Once you have configured the channels to distribute the Desktop
Application Distribution object through, you need to configure the
schedule from the Schedule tab shown in Figure 17.10. The Schedule tab
enables you to specify how often and when this distribution should be
gathered. Each time the server clock hits the specified scheduled time,
the agents are activated and the distribution gathered and compared with
the previous version to determine whether any changes have been made.
If there have been changes, a new version of the distribution file is created. The actual distribution of the file occurs based on schedules of the
channels.

The following choices are available to you for the scheduling of the
distribution: Never, Daily, Monthly, Yearly, Interval, Time, or Run
Immediately.

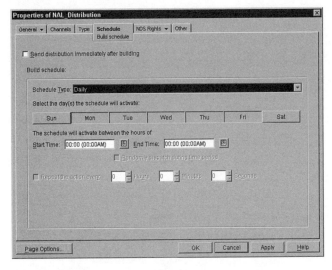

FIGURE 17.10
Schedule tab for the TED Distribution object in ConsoleOne.

Deploying Novell ZENworks for Desktops 4 in a Pure Microsoft Windows Environment

ZENworks for Desktops 4 runs on a Windows network without a NetWare server. ZENworks for Desktops 4 operates on Windows workstations regardless of the server environment in your network. ZENworks for Desktops 4 will function in any IP network running eDirectory, including Windows 2000/NT, NetWare 6 or NetWare 5.1 server based networks, and mixed environments.

ZENworks for Desktops has traditionally been deployed in NetWare networking or mixed NetWare and Windows environments. The initial versions of ZENworks for Desktops were dependent on many of the features and capabilities that existed only in a NetWare-based LAN. However, as the product has matured, features have evolved, allowing ZENworks for Desktops to provide significant functionality in a non-mixed, pure Windows environment. Everything that you require to run in a pure Windows environment, with the exception of eDirectory, is supplied in the ZENworks for Desktops 4 product.

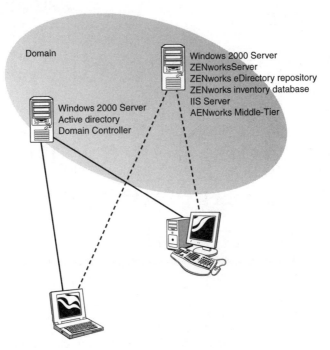

FIGURE 18.1
ZENworks for Desktops operating in a pure Windows environment.

ZENworks can be deployed, as depicted in Figure 18.1, into an Active Directory Domain and provide all the services in the product through Windows 2000 servers and IIS. All administration of user accounts can continue through the domain, whereas administration of applications, desktops, and the like is done using eDirectory as the repository independent of Active Directory, for example. ZENworks ships with other Novell products so you can automatically synchronize your users and passwords between Active Directory (or NT Domains) and the eDirectory ZENworks repository. ZENworks is agent-based and requires no Novell client on the workstations or laptops. It will quietly authenticate in the background to eDirectory and retrieve applications and policies, delivering them to your desktop through a browser, Start menu, window, or desktop icons.

This chapter discusses how ZENworks for Desktops can be deployed in a pure Windows environment and walks through the installation steps to set up a trial configuration.

ZENworks for Desktops Networking Setup and Requirements

Using Novell's eDirectory and DirXML products enables you to install ZENworks for Desktops into a pure Windows network with minimal requirements on the network side. In fact, the only requirements are that you have a Windows 2000 Server with IIS and SP2 installed in the domain.

In addition to having a Windows 2000 Server with IIS and SP2 installed in the domain, you need to set up the following:

- ▶ An Active Directory domain.

- ▶ ZENworks for Desktops 4 Server installed on a Windows 2000 Server with eDirectory and DirXML 1.1a and Password Synchronization installed; not the DC. This server must be in the same domain as the Active Directory DC.

- ▶ ZENworks for Desktops 4 Middle Tier installed on a Windows 2000 Server where Microsoft IIS is installed. This server must also be in the same domain as the Active Directory DC. This can also be the same server as the eDirectory and ZfD4 server; however, you should consider keeping the IIS server independent to minimize performance issues.

ZENworks for Desktops 4 Configuration Options

ZENworks for Desktops 4 can run in three modes on the workstation: Application Browser View Agent mode, Full Agent mode, and NetWare client mode. It is assumed that in a pure Windows environment the NetWare client will not be used; therefore, you need to determine which features you need in your network.

Application Browser View Agent Mode

In this mode, a single Application Browser View agent is delivered
when the user connects to IIS and opens an application page, provided
by ZENworks for Desktops 4. The Web agent is automatically installed
on the workstation, provided the user has rights to install local applications.

The Application Browser View agent will only deliver applications to the
workstation when the users connect to their personalized application
Web page. Dynamic local user account creation, hardware and software
inventory, automated imaging services, and remote management capabilities are not included in this agent.

Full Agent Mode

In this mode, the ZENworks for Desktop 4 agent is installed on the
workstation. The installation can be done by an administrator, part of an
image, or by the user. By installing the ZENworks for Desktop 4 agent,
you provide your users with all the capabilities inherent in the product.

Should you need Dynamic Local User account creation on the workstation, you must configure ZENworks for Desktops 4 agent to prompt
the user to log into eDirectory prior to the local windows login. When
configured, the users are prompted for their eDirectory usernames and
passwords (which should be the same as their Active Directory account
because they are being synchronized by DirXML). ZENworks will then
create a local account on the workstation if one is not present, and
then log the user into Windows with the same username and password.

If you do not require Dynamic Local User account creation, ZENworks
will silently retrieve the username and password from Windows when the
user logs into his workstation. The agents will then connect to eDirectory
using the given username and password in order to provide the applications administered to the user.

With the full agents installed on the workstation, you can still choose to
only deliver applications through the browser view.

DirXML Engine and Drivers

The DirXML engine is an eDirectory module that enables you to synchronization eDirectory data with any outside data service. The DirXML engine is designed such that it can have several drivers running that describe how output and input is sent between data sources.

The DirXML Driver for Active Directory (included with ZENworks for Desktops 4) is specifically designed to synchronize data between Novell eDirectory and the Microsoft Active Directory directory service. The synchronization is bi-directional; you determine whether information should flow to and from both directories, or whether information should flow only from one directory to the other.

There are many other DirXML Drivers available for other data sources, including PeopleSoft, JDBC, any LDAP directory, Lotus Notes, SAP HR, and WebSphere MQ. Check out `http://www.novell.com/dirxml` for new drivers.

DirXML's architecture uses a publisher/subscriber model whereby the publisher's responsibility is to place information into eDirectory, whereas the subscriber's job is to reflect changes in eDirectory back into the external, synchronized data source. The behavior of the publisher and subscriber and the attribute mapping is determined by a set of rules that are housed in eDirectory as part of the DirXML driver. DirXML drivers can be customized through XML rules to deliver just about any data configuration desired. See `http://www.novell.com/documentation` for more details on how DirXML can be configured. Check out the DirXML Novell site (`http://www.novell.com/dirxml`) to determine how you can customize your installation.

Installing ZENworks for Desktops 4 in a Pure Windows Environment

The following sections walk you through a standard installation of ZENworks for Desktops 4 in a pure Windows environment with Active Directory.

Configuration

For the purposes of developing your own test environment, the configuration used in this chapter is relatively small. Your systems can include, in fact, many servers for such needs as application execution, terminal services, and so on. This chapter uses the following network layout:

▶ Windows 2000 server, which is the Active Directory DC

▶ Windows 2000 server, which is the ZENworks server and is where you'll install eDirectory and the ZENworks Middle Tier server

▶ Windows XP Professional Workstation with the full ZENworks agents configured

▶ Windows XP Professional Workstation with the Application Browser View agent

In a more traditional system, you might want to put your ZENworks Middle Tier server onto another Windows 2000 server to provide maximum performance. This is not done here to minimize hardware requirements. Should you decide to put the Middle Tier server on another server, the only requirements for this server is a Windows 2000 Server running IIS with all of the appropriate support packs.

Installing ZENworks for Desktops 4

Now that you understand the network configuration required to install ZENworks for Desktops 4, you can begin the install process. The following sections discuss the pre-installation requirements to check before you begin the ZENworks for Desktops 4 install and how to install ZENworks for Desktops 4 into your pure Windows environment.

Pre-Installation Requirements

Prior to installing ZENworks for Desktops 4, you need to make certain that the required network components are installed and running. The following is a list of components that must already have been installed and functioning:

▶ DA-01—Windows 2000 Server with Active Directory (DA domain) and SP2 installed.

▶ DA-02—Windows 2000 Server with Support Pack 2 or greater, IIS, and a member of the DA domain.

▶ WKS-01—Windows XP Professional Workstation.

▶ WKS-02—Windows XP Professional Workstation.

Once you have verified the network components are installed and running, it's a good idea to download the following updates and documentation and save them for use during the installation process:

▶ DirXML 1.1a for Windows NT/2000 from the `http://download.novell.com` Web site. Choose DirXML product.

▶ DirXML Password Synchronization for Windows from the `http://download.novell.com` Web site. Choose DirXML Password Synchronization for Windows product. This will download version 1.0.

▶ DirXML Password Synchronization update (PWDSNC1.EXE) from the `http://support.novell.com/filefinder` Web site. Enter `pwdsnc1.exe` in the search field.

▶ Print TID# 2962702 from `http://support.novell.com` to learn how to apply the password synchronization update.

▶ eDirectory 8.7 or higher for Windows NT/2000 from the `http://download.novell.com` Web site. Choose the eDirectory product.

▶ The update DirXML Active Directory driver and utilities found in TID#2964748 from the `http://support.novell.com` Web site (through the knowledge base).

ZENworks for Desktops 4 Installation
Perform the following steps to install the ZENworks for Desktops 4 system into the identified environment.

Step One: Getting eDirectory
Download eDirectory and get a license from Novell for it. This is done by performing the following:

1. Go to `http://download.novell.com` and download eDirectory for the Windows 2000 platform.

2. Choose eDirectory 8.7 on Windows NT/2000 and download.

3. Go to `http://www.novell.com/products/edirectory/ customer_license.html`.

4. Press the I Accept button on the license agreement.

5. Select the appropriate eDirectory version from the list of licenses available.

6. Fill in the contact information. Make sure you put in your correct e-mail address, as your licenses will be sent to that address. Press the Submit button.

7. A license will be sent to your e-mail address. When received, open the e-mail and save the two files to a floppy disk.

Step Two: Getting Updated DirXML Drivers

Take the new AD drivers and support tools you downloaded from TID#2964748 and put them on the server in some directory you create (not in ConsoleOne) or onto a floppy. These files should include AD-DRIVER.XML, AD-DRIVER_EN.XLF, AD-DRIVER-SCHEMA.LDI, and READDOMAINGUID.EXE.

Step Three: Installing eDirectory

Install eDirectory onto DA-02 by following these steps:

1. Log onto the DA-02 Windows 2000 server as the administrator and launch the eDirectory execution program, which is downloaded in the pre-installation procedures.

2. Choose to install both eDirectory and ConsoleOne onto the server. Press Install.

3. The first step that eDirectory installation performs is the installation of the Novell client. Perform the following steps to install the client:

   A. Choose Yes on the license agreement.

   B. Choose custom installation and press Next.

   C. Verify that only the client is chosen on the modules list. Press Next.

   D. Choose IP only and Remove IPX if present. Press Next.

   E. Choose NDS to instruct the client to default to using NDS connections. Press Next.

   F. Choose Finish.

4. The eDirectory License Installation will begin automatically. Press Next.

5. Read the license agreement and press I Accept.

6. Insert the license disk you made in the previous step.

7. Select Install License Diskette, A:License and press Next.

8. Press Close on the licensing installation success dialog box.

The system will now install NICI cryptography system. Once that is installed, the system will prompt you to reboot.

9. Remove the floppy disk and press OK on the dialog box requesting to reboot. Once the system is rebooted, eDirectory will complete its installation.

10. When the system next comes up, you see the client login dialog box. Press Ctrl+Alt+Delete.

11. Choose workstation only and log into the system as the administrator. Press OK.

The installation of eDirectory will automatically continue.

12. On the welcome screen for the installation, press Next.

13. View the license and press I Accept.

14. Select the desired languages and press Next.

15. Accept the default installation path and press Next.

16. Press Yes on the dialog box to create the new directory that does not exist.

17. Choose to create a new eDirectory tree. Press Next.

18. Choose a tree name, context for the DA-02 server, and admin user object along with the passwords. At the very minimum you want the server and admin under a container, so append a *<dot>containername* (where *<dot>* is a period) after the server name. This chapter uses the **da** container name. So, for example, the tree name would be **DA-TREE**. The server object would be **DA-02-NDS.servers.da**, the admin name would be **admin**, and the context would be **da**. Press Next.

19. Accept the HTTP Stack Ports as default, because there will be no conflicting Web ports on this server. Press Next.

20. Accept the defaults on the Certificate Server Objects wizard page and press Next.

21. Proceed and create a certificate authority for the tree, pressing OK on the warning dialog box.

22. Because eDirectory will need to not interfere with the Active
Directory that is using the default 389/636 ports, you need to
change them. Change the clear text port to 388 and the SSL port to
635, as shown in Figure 18.2. Uncheck the Require TLS for Simple
Bind with Password option. This is necessary in order to allow
password synchronization to function. Press Next.

23. Accept the default NMAS Login Methods by pressing Next.

24. Complete the eDirectory installation by pressing Finish.

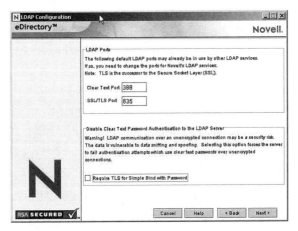

FIGURE 18.2
LDAP ports setting for eDirectory installation.

eDirectory will now perform its installation on the DA-02 server. When
completed, press Close on the success dialog box.

Step Four: Creating DirXML Administrator Account in Active Directory

In order to isolate changes that occur with other administrator accounts,
Novell recommends that you create a separate account for DirXML with
Administrator privileges in Active Directory. To create this account:

1. Log onto the DA-01 server as administrator of the domain.

2. Launch the Active Directory Users and Computers MMC by
launching Start, Programs, Administrative Tools, Active Directory
Users and Computers.

3. From Active Directory Users and Computers, select the container
where you want to add the DirXML administrator user, and then
click Create a New User.

4. Enter the names for the user. For example, enter `Novell` as the first name, `Dirxml` as the last name, and `Novell Dirxml` as the full name. The user login name should be `novelldirxml@da.com`.

5. Click Next, and then set the password for the new user. Mark Password Never Expires so that a password won't disable the driver unexpectedly.

6. Click Next, review the summary, and then click Finish.

7. In the Tree view, select Builtin, Administrator's properties, Members, Add.

8. Select the full name of the user you created (`Novell Dirxml`). Click Add, click OK, and then click OK again.

9. Close the Active Directory Users and Computers window.

10. In the Administrative Tools window, select Domain Controller Security Policy.

11. In the tree view, expand Security Settings, Local Policies, User Rights Assignment.

12. Set Log On As a Service, Security, Add, Browse.

13. Select the user you created (`Novell Dirxml`). Click Add, OK, OK, and then OK again.

14. Close the Domain Controller Security Policy.

15. Reboot the system.

Step Five: Installing ConsoleOne

The installation of ConsoleOne will now automatically start. Proceed through the wizard to install ConsoleOne onto the DA-02 server:

1. Press Next on the welcome screen.

2. Read the licensing agreement and press I Accept.

3. Select any additional languages you want to install. Press Next.

4. Accept the default installation path and press Next.

5. Accept the default set of components to install and press Next.

6. Accept the JInfoNet licensing agreement and press Next.

7. Press Finish on the summary page. ConsoleOne will now install on the server.

8. Press Close on the successful installation dialog box.

Step Six: Verifying That eDirectory Is Functioning

When ConsoleOne is completed, you need to verify that the tree is up and looks appropriate by performing the following steps:

1. Right-click the red N in the taskbar and select login.

2. Enter **user admin**, your password for eDirectory. Press Advanced and fill in the tree name, context of admin, and server, as shown in Figure 18.3.

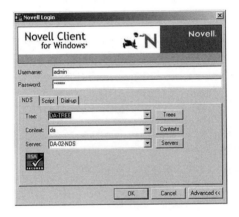

FIGURE 18.3
Advanced options for the Novell client login window.

3. Press OK. This should log you into eDirectory.

4. Verify that you are logged into the tree as **admin** by right-clicking the red N in the taskbar and selecting connections. Verify that you have a resource for the tree and the server and the username of **CN=Admin**. The authentication state on the server should be Directory Services and the tree should be **DA-TREE**. Close the dialog box.

5. Now launch ConsoleOne and see whether the tree is visible and the **admin** along with server objects are present, as shown in Figure 18.4.

6. Create a shortcut on your server for **c:\novell\nds\ndscons.exe**. NDSConsole enables you to view the state of the eDirectory tree and the services running.

7. Launch **ndscons** and verify that at least **ds.dlm** and **nldap.dlm** are running. You now have an eDirectory tree running on your Windows 2000 server.

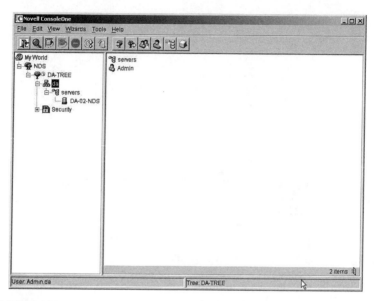

FIGURE 18.4
Tree view with admin user in ConsoleOne.

Step Seven: Installing DirXML

Now that eDirectory is running, you need to install DirXML so that users can be synchronized between your Active Directory Domain and eDirectory. Install DirXML by performing the following steps:

1. Log onto the DA-02 Windows 2000 server as the administrator and into eDirectory as the admin.

2. Launch the DirXML 1.1a installation program, downloaded in the pre-installation procedures (`nt\install.exe` after extraction).

3. Press Next on the DirXML welcome screen.

4. Read the licensing agreement and press I Accept.

5. Choose to install DirXML Engine and Drivers and DirXML Management Utilities on the component installation page, shown in Figure 18.5. Press Next.

6. On the following component page, choose DirXML Engine and the appropriate core driver (DirXML Driver 2.0a for Active Directory). Proceed with the installation by pressing Next.

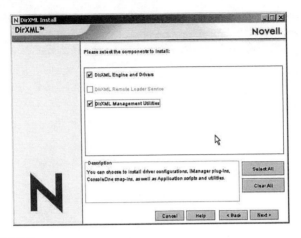

FIGURE 18.5
Component options of the DirXML installation.

7. Verify that the tree is appropriate and enter, or browse to, the admin user and password. Your admin username is CN=admin.O=da. Press Next.

8. Choose ConsoleOne Snapins for DirXML, and DirXML Preconfigured Drivers for additional installation. Press Next.

9. Deselect all of the preconfigured drivers except the appropriate Active Directory driver. Press Next.

10. Press Finish on the summary dialog box.

    The installation of DirXML will continue. First it will shut down eDirectory and then the installation will proceed.

11. Press OK on the dialog box warning about the possible conflict with eDirectory and the LDAP system. (You fixed that when you installed eDirectory.)

    When it is completed eDirectory will be brought back up.

12. On the final dialog box, uncheck Launch ConsoleOne DirXML Configuration Wizards and press Close. You'll be launching the configuration wizards at a different time.

You have now installed DirXML. The drivers need to be configured before synchronization will occur, so that's the next step.

Step Eight: Configuring DirXML Drivers

Now that eDirectory and DirXML have been installed on your DA-02 server, you need to configure your DirXML drivers and begin synchronization between your Active Directory Domain and eDirectory. Configure your DirXML drivers by doing the following:

1. Log in to the DA-02 server as the administrator and eDirectory as the admin.

2. Open a DOS box and execute the `readDomainGUID.exe` program. Make sure you run the tool from the `c:\novell\nds directory`. Cut and paste the GUID returned by the tool into a text file for later use.

3. Launch ConsoleOne.

4. You need to extend the eDirectory schema to accommodate the new Active Directory driver. This is accomplished by doing the following:

   A. Launch the schema import tool by selecting Wizards, NDS Import/Export from ConsoleOne.

   B. Select Import LDIF file; press Next.

   C. Browse to and select the AD-Driver-Schema.ldif file on your ZENworks floppy. Press Next.

   D. Enter `127.0.0.1` into the Server DNS Name/IP Address field and `388` into the Port field.

   E. Select Authenticated Login and enter your admin user object and password in the fields. Remember to enter the LDAP version of the admin username including the container (`cn=admin,o=da`). Press Next.

   F. Press Finish on the summary screen.

   G. You should get a scrolled output of the import. Verify that the total entries processed are three and that there were no errors.

   H. Press Close.

5. Create an Organizational Unit (OU) container in the directory under your **da** organizational container. Call this new OU DirXML. You'll create all of the objects related to DirXML under this container.

6. If desired, create a user Organizational Unit container under **da**.

7. Select the parent container (**da**) of the new DirXML organizational unit, and then choose Wizards, Create a New Application Driver.

8. On the creation wizard, select In a New Driver Set. Press Next.

9. Enter a driver set name, such as **ADDriverSet**. Browse to and select the DirXML container for the context and the DA-02 server for the server field, as shown in Figure 18.6. Press Next.

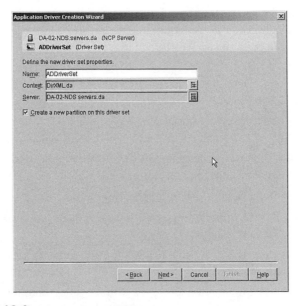

FIGURE 18.6
Application driver creation wizard for DirXML configuration.

10. The wizard will now create the objects for the driver set.

11. Select Import Preconfigured Driver and browse to and select AD-DRIVER.XML on your ZENworks floppy. Press Next.

WARNING The installation of DirXML places an **ADDRIVER.XML** file in the system. This will also come up on the list. Make sure you choose the new **AD-DRIVER.XML** file.

12. Now you must configure the driver parameters. They are all on the presented wizard page and are visible by using the scroll bar. See Table 18.1 for a list of fields and their description.

13. Press OK.

14. Press Yes to set the security equivalences of the driver.

15. Press the Add button. Browse to the `admin.da user` and add it to the list. Press OK.

16. Press Yes on the Novell Recommends You Identify All Objects that Represent Administrative Roles dialog box.

17. Press the Add button and browse to and select all users who are administrators of eDirectory. This will prevent them from being created in the Active Directory domain and synchronized. Press OK.

18. Press Finish on the summary page to complete the wizard.

TABLE 18.1 Application Driver Parameters for Configuring DirXML

FIELD	DESCRIPTION
Field 1	Driver name. Leave the name of the driver as the default.
Field 2	Active Directory Account. Enter the domain administrator account you created (`novelldirxml@da.com`) and the passwords.
Field 3	Authentication Password. Enter the password for the domain administrator account.
Field 4	Retype the Password. Re-enter the domain administrator account password.
Field 5	DNS name of Domain Controller. Enter `LDAP://<DNS name of DA-01>` into the address of Active Directory Domain controller field. Do not enter an IP address. This would be `LDAP://da-01.da.com`.
Field 6	Domain GUID. Enter the GUID for the domain. You can cut and paste the GUID that you saved in a text file into this field.
Field 7	Data Flow. Leave this to the default Bi-Directional.
Field 8	Active Directory Base Container. Enter the base container in Active Directory. This is the container where you want users to be synchronized with eDirectory (for example, CN=Users,DC=da,DC=com).
Field 9	eDirectory Base Container. Enter the container where you want your users to be created and synchronized with Active Directory (for example, `users.da`). You can browse for this container by pressing the browse button. If you are going to mirror the Active Directory containers, then this would be the top container in eDirectory.

TABLE 18.1 Continued

FIELD	DESCRIPTION
Field 10	Publisher Placement. Choose if you want flat or mirror. If you choose flat, all user objects coming from Active Directory are placed in the same container. If you choose mirror, the user objects and the containers are re-created in eDirectory.
Field 11	Subscriber Placement. See field 10 to choose your placement.
Field 12	Driver Polling Interval. Enter the polling interval you desire. In the lab it should probably be around 1 minute whereas in production you probably will want it around 15 minutes.
Field 13	Use Secure Authentication. Leave this the default Yes.
Field 14	Enable PasswordSync. Leave this the default Yes.
Field 15	Install Driver as Remote/Local. Set this to Local.
Field 16	Remote Host Name and Port. Ignore and leave as the default.
Field 17	Driver Password. Ignore and leave blank.
Field 18	Retype the password. Ignore and leave blank.
Field 19	Remote Password. Ignore and leave blank.
Field 20	Retype the password. Ignore and leave blank.

Before you can get the DirXML driver running, you need to install the
Password Synchronization software as described in the next step.

Step Nine: Installing Password Synchronization

Once you have installed eDirectory and DirXML, you need to install
Password Synchronization. This enables the User objects that you create
in Active Directory, which are automatically created in DirXML, to have
the same password as their corresponding user in Active Directory. This
is necessary to allow for single-login to both Active Directory and
eDirectory when your users log in to their workstations.

You should be aware that password synchronization requires that the
platform-specific password policies not be in conflict with each other.
Password policies that are in conflict will prevent successful password
synchronization. For example, if eDirectory passwords are required to be
at least eight characters, whereas Windows passwords have no length
requirements, users could create shorter Windows passwords that

wouldn't be accepted by eDirectory. In this case, the passwords will not be synchronized. Password synchronization does not override platform policies.

DirXML allows you to generate an initial password for an account based on the account's attributes or other information available through Java services. For instance, you can generate a password based on a user's surname plus a four-digit number. Generating an initial password requires driver customization, but is a great way to manage passwords when provisioning an account through your existing HR toolset.

ConsoleOne lets you set an initial password when creating a user account by marking the Assign NDS Password check box and then selecting the Prompt During Creation radio button. In this case, ConsoleOne sets the password before an account is associated in NT or Active Directory accounts, thus preventing the initial password from being synchronized. Passwords are synchronized only after the first password changes.

To avoid this delay, you can use one of the following methods:

▶ Unmark Assign NDS Password during user creation and assign the password later. A brief delay will allow account associations to be completed.

▶ Select Prompt User on First Login so that password setting is delayed until the account is actually used.

Microsoft Management Console lets you set an initial password on a user account simply by typing the password at account creation. The password is set before password synchronization can associate an eDirectory account with the Active Directory account, so the password synchronization service cannot update the eDirectory account immediately. However, the service will retry the password update and the account will be properly updated within several minutes.

Install password synchronization on your servers by performing the following steps:

1. Log in to DA-02 as the administrator and in to eDirectory as the admin. Ensure that ConsoleOne is closed.

2. Launch the installation of password sync that you downloaded from the Novell Web site.

3. Press Next on the welcome screen.

4. Read the license and press Yes to accept.

5. Select both the Password Synchronization Service and PasswordSync Snap-in for ConsoleOne on the component menu. Press Next.

6. Press Next on the review settings page. The installation will now copy the files to your DA-02 server.

7. On the Setup dialog box, select the DA domain and browse to the ADDriver object (`ADDriver.ADDriverSet.DirXML.da`) in eDirectory. Press OK.

8. Leave the object name as the default. For the Context, verify that it is the DirXML container that you have created. Press OK.

9. When asked to give the password sync object rights, select the container where your user objects, synchronized from Active Directory, are expected to reside. Make sure you give these rights for every container of users that you are synchronizing. Press OK.

10. When prompted to put filters on each Domain Controller, press Yes.

11. You will be given a list of Domain Controllers. Select DA-01 and press Add (as shown in Figure 18.7).

FIGURE 18.7
Password Synchronization Add Filters dialog box.

WARNING Adding the DA-01 domain controller will cause DA-01 to be rebooted.

12. Wait until DA-01 has rebooted and the dialog box shows DA-01 status of `Running`.

13. Press Close.

14. Press Finish.

15. Follow the instructions on TID# 2962702 that you downloaded. This will apply the update of password synchronization that you downloaded. Don't forget to reboot both DA-01 and DA-02 after applying the update.

Step Ten: Finalizing Configuration for DirXML Drivers

Now that you have installed and configured both the DirXML drivers and the PasswordSync driver, you need to finalize the configuration to make these drivers start automatically and function properly. This can be achieved by following these steps:

1. Log in to DA-02 as the administrator and to eDirectory as the admin.

2. Launch ConsoleOne.

3. Select the `ADDriverSet` object under the DirXML container in ConsoleOne and right-click to select Properties.

4. Select the DirXML, Drivers tab.

5. Select the ADDriver in the list and press the Start button. Verify that the driver has started by watching the status field change to `Running`.

6. Press the Properties button.

7. Select the Startup Option tab and change the startup to automatic.

8. Press Apply.

9. Press Close.

10. Open NDSCONS.EXE and verify that the `dirxml.dlm` is running.

Step Eleven: Verifying eDirectory, DirXML, and Password Synchronization

You now need to verify that your eDirectory, DirXML, and password synchronization are working properly in your environment. One way to do this is to create a few users in Active Directory and see whether they are automatically created in eDirectory with the proper passwords.

1. Log in to DA-01 as the administrator of the AD Domain.

2. Launch the Active Directory administration tool and create a test user in Active Directory (for example, `TestUser1@da.com`).

3. Log in to DA-02 as the administrator of the domain and as admin
   in eDirectory.

4. Open ConsoleOne and verify that `TestUser1` has been created in
   the administered container. Remember that you might have to wait
   for a synchronization cycle to complete before the user will appear
   in eDirectory.

5. Log in to eDirectory as that user and verify that the password is the
   same as was given in Active Directory and that you successfully
   authenticated to eDirectory. Remember that it might take another
   synchronization cycle before the password is updated.

6. For completeness, you can now create a user in eDirectory, using
   ConsoleOne as admin, and verify that the user is now in the domain.
   Log in to the domain as that user with the password you specified in
   eDirectory. Don't forget to log in to the directory as admin.

NOTE The default synchronization rules will not create an Active Directory user until
the full name attribute field is populated in eDirectory. This can be done under the properties of the user object, in the General tab.

Now that eDirectory, DirXML, and password synchronization are working
and users are being synchronized, you can proceed to activate your
DirXML licenses and then install ZENworks.

Step Twelve: Getting a License for DirXML Drivers

Now that you have DirXML and password synchronization working, you
need to receive an activator license to properly license DirXML and the
drivers. This can be done with the following:

1. Log in to DA-02 as the administrator of the domain and as admin
   in eDirectory.

2. Launch ConsoleOne. Browse to and select the DirXML container.

3. Select Wizards, Create a DirXML Activation Request.

4. On the welcome screen, browse to and select the DirXML driver set
   (`ADDriverSet.DirXML.da`).

5. Press Next.

6. Enter your Novell customer ID. Press Next.

7. Insert your ZENworks floppy and store the activator request onto
   the floppy.

8. Press Next.

9. Press Finish to exit the activator wizard.

10. On a machine that has Internet access, launch your browser and go to the Novell activator Web site (`http://www.novell.com/activator`).

11. Log in to the Web site with your Novell profile username and password.

12. Press the Browse button on the Web page and browse to and select the REQUEST.REQ file on the ZENworks floppy.

13. Press Submit at the bottom of the page.

14. On the Novell Product Activator page, select DirXML Password Synchronization and press Submit. This will generate an activator license for your DirXML 1.1a engine, the Active Directory driver, and the PASSWORD SYNCHRONIZATION driver.

15. You will receive an e-mail with an attached Activation Credential file (`<bunch of numbers>.act`). Save this file onto your ZENworks floppy.

16. Go back to DA-02 and log in as administrator of the domain and as admin in eDirectory.

17. Launch ConsoleOne. Browse to and select the DirXML container.

18. Select Wizards, Install a DirXML_Activation.

19. On the welcome screen, browse to and select the DirXML driver set (`ADDriverSet.DirXML.da`).

20. Press Next.

21. Insert the ZENworks floppy into DA-02.

22. In the Specify a File ... field, browse to and select the .ACT file that you saved on your ZENworks floppy. Press Open.

23. Press Next.

24. On the conclusion page, press View to see whether the activation file installed is considered valid.

25. Press Cancel.

26. Press Finish.

You have now completed the installation and activation of eDirectory, DirXML, and password synchronization on your server. Now it is time to install ZENworks into the system.

Step Thirteen: Installing ZENworks for Desktops Server

You are now prepared to install ZENworks for Desktops into your Pure-Windows environment. This section describes how to install all components of ZENworks for Desktops, although only a small portion is needed based on your desires. ZENworks for Desktops can be broken into five main categories: Policy Management, Application Management, Imaging, Inventory, and Remote Control.

You can also choose for your environment to have workstation objects in your eDirectory tree. This can impact whether certain features are available. See ZENworks for Desktop documentation for more information regarding these features (`http://www.novell.com/documentation`).

Now, you will install the ZENworks for Desktops server onto DA-02, where eDirectory is located. Follow these steps:

1. Log in to DA-02 as administrator of the domain and admin for eDirectory.

2. Insert the ZENworks for Desktops program CD.

3. Choose English.

4. Choose New Installation.

5. Choose Install ZfD Server. The installation wizard starts.

6. Read the welcome page. Press Next.

7. Read the license agreement. Choose Accept and then press Next.

8. Press Next on the information page.

9. Browse and select your eDirectory tree you installed on DA-02 (`DA-TREE`). Make sure the Extend Schema option is checked. Press Next.

10. Select all of the components of ZENworks for Desktops that you desire. Press Next.

11. Press Add Server and add `DA-02-NDS` to the server list. Select all of the appropriate components to install on this server, as shown in Figure 18.8.

12. Press Next.

13. Press Next on the Database file installation path to accept the defaults.

14. Select Configure Standalone for Inventory. The container should be the same as where your server is located (`servers.da`). Press Next.

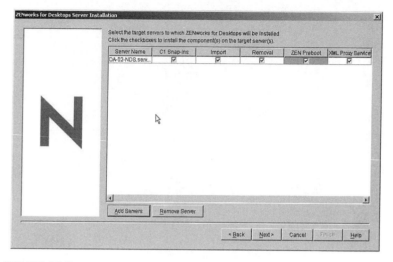

FIGURE 18.8
ZENworks for Server component installation options.

15. Press Next on the XML Proxy Configuration page to accept the defaults.

16. Press Next on the Remote Management File installation paths to accept the defaults.

17. Press Finish in the summary dialog box.

18. The schema will now be extended in eDirectory. Press OK on the Schema Extended Successfully dialog box.

19. A dialog box, similar to the one in Figure 18.9, pops up. It warns you about certain ZfD processes and services that cannot be running. Because this is the first time you have installed ZfD, none should be running. Make sure that you have closed ConsoleOne. Press OK.

20. The ZENworks for Desktop software and services will now begin to install on DA-02.

21. Press OK on the Please Reboot dialog box.

22. Press No on the View Log Files dialog box.

23. Reboot server DA-02 to complete the installation. When DA-02 comes back up, additional installation processes will be activated and completed.

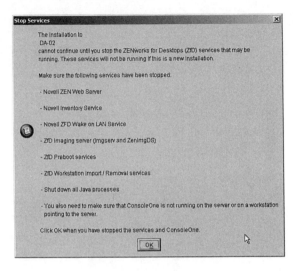

FIGURE 18.9
The Stop Services warning dialog box lists the services that must be shut
down prior to completing the installation.

Step Fourteen: Installing ZENworks for Desktops Middle Tier

Now you need to install the ZENworks for Desktop Middle Tier, if you
delivered your ZENworks for Desktop features through the browser and
over the Internet. You will install ZENworks for Desktops middle-tier
server on DA-01, where IIS is present. You need to be aware that the
installation of the Middle Tier requires the Novell client already be
installed on the server that runs the installation; therefore you will install
the Middle Tier onto DA-01 from DA-02 where the client is already running with eDirectory.

Install the ZENworks Middle Tier by performing the following:

1. Log in to DA-02 as admin of eDirectory and administrator of the
   domain.

2. Insert the ZENworks for Desktop Program CD.

3. Choose English.

4. Choose New Installation.

5. Choose Install ZfD Middle-Tier Server. The installation wizard
   launches.

6. On the welcome screen, press Next.

7. Read the licenses, and then choose to accept them. Press Next.

8. On the information screen, press Next.

9. On the Select Middle Tier Server screen, choose Add Server.

10. On the Add Server dialog box, choose DA-02. Then press OK.

11. Back on the Select Middle Tier Server screen, shown in Figure 18.10, enter the following into the sections devoted to ZfD Middle Tier Server on Windows 2000:

   A. Administrator login name (`administrator@da.com`) in the Domain Username field.

   B. The administrator password in the Password and Confirm Password fields.

12. In the section on Primary eDirectory Tree Information, shown in Figure 18.10, enter the following:

   A. DNS/IP—Enter the address or DNS name of DA-02.

   B. Users context—Enter the context of the eDirectory tree that contains the user objects that will use this Middle Tier.

   C. Admin username—Enter the administrators user object (for example, `admin.da`) and password.

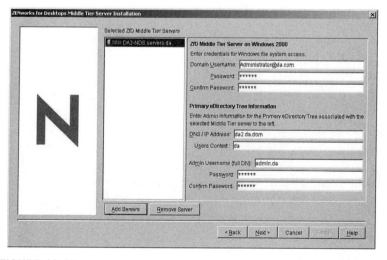

FIGURE 18.10
Entering the primary eDirectory tree information during the Middle Tier Server Installation process.

13. Press Next.

14. Press Finish on the summary screen.

15. The ZENworks Middle Tier system will now install.

16. Press OK on the Please Reboot dialog box.

17. Press No to not view the log files of the installation.

18. Reboot DA-02 to complete the installation.

Step Fifteen: Installing ODBC Drivers

Now if you installed inventory onto the ZENworks for Desktops server, you need to be able to run reports and queries against this database. To do this, you must install the ODBC driver for the Sybase database. This can be accomplished by doing the following:

1. Log in to DA-02 as admin of eDirectory and administrator of the domain.

2. Insert the ZENworks for Desktop Companion CD.

3. Open the ODBC container on the CD.

Follow the instructions in the README.TXT file on the CD to set up the address of the Sybase and verify that you can make a connection.

Step Sixteen: Installing the ZENworks Management Agents

Now you have a ZENworks for Desktops system running in a Windows-only environment. The next step is to install the ZENworks management agents onto your workstations and begin to use the ZENworks features to manage those devices.

The full agents may be installed on a workstation by running the SETUP.EXE found in `\\DA-02\novell\public\zenworks`. The Application Viewer agent is automatically installed when the user first goes to the MYAPPS.HTML page on the ZENworks server (`http://DA-02.da.com/myapps.html`).

If you want to have the Web page install the full agents (approximately 8.5MB), copy the SETUP.EXE file to the `\\da-02\inetpub\wwwroot` directory and replace the following line in the MYAPPS.HTML:

```
document.write("codebase=\"http://da-02.da.com:80/
ZfdWebSw.exe\"");
```

with the following line:

```
document.write("codebase=\"http://da-02.da.com:80/
setup.exe\"");
```

Conclusion

Now that you have completed the installation of ZENworks for Desktops in a pure Windows environment, you can configure and use the features of ZENworks for Desktops in your system. You can also install other ZENworks family products onto this same ZENworks server and have them work in your Windows-only environment.

Review the administrator guide found at `http://www.novell.com/documentation/lg/zdpr/index.html`.

You can refer to the following Web sites for updates and additional information:

`http://www.novell.com/zenworks`

`http://www.novell.com/coolsolutions/zenworks`

`http://www.novell.com/dirxml`

`http://www.novell.com/documentation`

## CHAPTER 19

Troubleshooting ZENworks

ZENworks for Desktops is an extremely powerful tool. It saves network administrators much needed time. However, because of the complexity of network environments, problems can occur that prevent ZENworks for Desktops from doing its job. This chapter covers how to troubleshoot and diagnose those problems in the following areas:

- ▶ Troubleshooting desktop management
- ▶ Troubleshooting distributed applications
- ▶ Troubleshooting policies packages
- ▶ Troubleshooting NetWare errors

Troubleshooting Desktop Management

Desktop management is difficult to troubleshoot because several network components are involved; this includes the server, clients, eDirectory, and the LAN.

The following sections discuss the most common areas to review when you are troubleshooting desktop management issues.

Reduce LAN Traffic

If you find that LAN traffic is unacceptable after you create and associate policy packages with objects, you might need to reduce the LAN traffic. One effective way you can reduce LAN traffic is by limiting how the system searches the tree for associations between policy packages and objects discussed in earlier chapters. Limiting the searches should reduce LAN traffic.

To reduce LAN traffic in this way, use the following steps in ConsoleOne:

1. Create a Container Policy Package. Right-click it and select Properties from the drop-down menu.

2. Enable the Search Policy on the Policies tab.

3. Highlight the Search Policy and click the Properties button.

4. On the Search Level tab, set the Search For Policies Up To field to Partition, and then choose OK to close the Search Policy properties window. This limits how many directory levels are searched for associations between policy packages and objects.

5. Select the Associations tab, and associate this Container Policy Package to the container where you want to make the Search Policy effective. Remember that the Search Policy affects all containers below the associated container, because the workstation manager looks for the container package.

Troubleshooting Workstation Import Issues

If an attempt to import a workstation was unsuccessful, you might need to troubleshoot import by using the suggestions covered in the following sections.

NOTE A workstation does not synchronize with eDirectory until after it has been imported and the Workstation Registration program runs again.

Verify Workstation Setup

The first step in troubleshooting workstation import issues is to verify that the correct client is installed on the workstation. This client can be installed from the ZENworks for Desktops CD, or can be downloaded from Novell's Web site.

Validate the Workstation Import Policy

The next step in troubleshooting workstation import issues is to validate the Workstation Import Policy. First verify that the Workstation Import Policy is enabled for the server in to which the user is logging. Do so following these steps:

1. From ConsoleOne, right-click the server that the user, not registering their workstation, is logging into and select Properties.

2. Click the ZENworks, Effective Policies tab.

3. Select the correct platform for the server that the user is logging into and then click Effective Policies.

4. There should be a policy package listed for the Workstation Import Policy. If not, you need to create-enable the Workstation Import Policy in a Server Policy Package and associate it to the server.

Check Registry Keys for Workstation Manager

Next check the Registry keys for Workstation Manager to ensure that the workstation is not already imported. Follow these steps:

1. Launch REGEDIT.EXE (or REGEDT32.EXE for NT/2000/XP).

2. Browse to the following Registry key:

   ```
   HKEY_LOCAL_MACHINE\SOFTWARE\Novell\Workstation
   Manager\Identification
   ```

3. Workstation registration might be in three states (No WS Import Policy, Registration, or Imported).

   If the workstation is in the No WS Import Policy state, the Registered In, Registration Object, and Workstation Object values will be either NULL or will not exist.

   If the workstation is in the Registration state, the Registered In and Registration Object values will be populated, but the Workstation Object value will not exist.

   If the workstation is in the Imported state, the Registered In, Registration Object, and Workstation Object values will be populated.

NOTE A good general troubleshooting step for registration is to delete the Registered In, Registration Object, and Workstation Object values. They will be recreated at the next boot up login attempt.

Verify the Trusted Tree for Workstation Manager

Once you have verified the Registry keys, ensure that the Workstation Manager Trusted Tree is set to the correct tree name by using the following steps:

1. Launch REGEDIT.EXE (or REGEDT32.EXE for NT).

2. Browse to the following Registry key:

   `HKEY_LOCAL_MACHINE\SOFTWARE\Novell\Workstation Manager\ Identification`

3. The tree value must *exactly* match the tree name the user is logging into. ZENworks is enabled for one tree at a time, and this tree name is listed here. If the tree you are logging into does not match this Registry value, all of ZENworks is disabled (including the Workstation Import Policy).

Ensure That the Automatic Workstation Import Is Running

Verify that the Automatic Workstation Import service is running on your server and that an import policy is associated with that server.

Also check to make sure that the workstation is pointing to the import service by having the string `"ImportServer=<DNS of the import service server>"` or `"ImportServer=<IP address of the import service server >"` in the following Registry key :

`HKEY_LOCAL_MACHINE\Software\Novell\ZENworks\zenwsreg`

View the Error Log

When troubleshooting workstation import issues, you can also view the WSREG32.LOG log file at the root of the C: drive. Look for errors and then continue troubleshooting from there.

Re-Register the Workstation

As a final option, you can re-register the workstation by running the register utility from the following location:

`C:\Program Files\Novell\ZENworks\zwsreg.exe`

Use the `-unreg` option to unregister and no parameters to register. Use `/?` or `-?` for additional options.

Troubleshooting Distributed Applications

The next area of troubleshooting ZENworks for Desktops is *distributed applications*. If users encounter problems using distributed applications, you can use the following procedures to help diagnose and debug the issues.

Troubleshoot Application Launcher and Explorer

The first place to start when troubleshooting distributed applications is Application Explorer. You can obtain information about Application Explorer to help you troubleshoot problems that your users encounter.

Open the Application Launcher Debug Window

You can see the applications and their states within a debug window to allow you to see, from the workstation's perspective, what applications are available and why or why not. This can be opened by launching the Application Windows or Explorer. Choose the About box from the menu. Then press and hold the F2 key and click on the More button. This will bring up the debug window and provide all the information about the application.

Review Information About the State of Currently Running Applications

The first issue to consider when troubleshooting the Application Launcher is getting information about the state of currently running applications. This helps you determine whether any resource conflicts or incompatibilities exist between different applications.

To get information about the state of applications currently running on a workstation, select Start, ZENworks for Desktops 4, Application Window and check the status of any running applications.

Re-create the Workstation Cache

You can remove the `c:\nalcache directory` from the workstation. This will remove all distributed information about the applications from the workstation. The cache will be re-created and repopulated the next time that you boot or run the Application Launcher.

Review eDirectory Tree Specific Information

Once you have information about files and running applications, you should look at Directory tree specific information about the tree the workstation is logged into. Select Help@, About Application Explorer and click the More button to view the login information and verify that the workstation is logged into the appropriate location to receive the application.

View and Edit User or Container's Application Launcher Configurations

Once you have looked at Application Explorer, you should view and edit user or container Application Launcher configurations. This helps you troubleshoot issues that are caused by problems with the setup of distributed applications in the user and/or container objects. To review the Application Launcher configuration for user or container objects, use the following procedures.

Use the Launcher Configuration Property Page

Verify the Application Launcher configuration tab on the properties page for user or container objects in ConsoleOne. You should review the following information:

▶ The effective Application Launcher configurations for a User, Organizational Unit, Organization, or Country object

▶ The Application Launcher configuration inheritance tree (where the current object gets configurations from objects higher in the tree)

▶ Set up custom Application Launcher configurations for the currently selected container object

Review User or Container's Effective Application Launcher Configurations

Once you have reviewed the previous information from the main Application Launcher page in ConsoleOne, you should check the effective Application Launcher configurations. Effective settings include custom configurations applied to the current object as well as configurations inherited from parent container(s). You can control how a Container object inherits Application Launcher configurations by using the Use as Top of Inheritance Tree option.

To view the custom Application Launcher configurations from within ConsoleOne, follow these steps:

1. Right-click a User, Organizational Unit, Organization, or Country object and click Properties.

2. Click the Application Launcher tab.

3. Choose View Object's Effective Settings from the Mode drop-down list.

Review Application Launcher Configuration Inheritance Tree

Once you have reviewed the custom Application Launcher configurations, you should review the Application Launcher configuration inheritance tree for the user or container object by following these steps:

1. Right-click a User, Organizational Unit, Organization, or Country object and click Properties.

2. Click the Application Launcher tab.

3. Choose View Configuration Inheritance Tree from the Mode drop-down list.

Review and Edit User or Container's Custom Application Launcher Configurations

Once you have reviewed the Application Launcher configuration inheritance tree, you should review the container's custom Application Launcher configurations for the Container object by following these steps:

1. Right-click a User, Organizational Unit, Organization, or Country object and click Properties.

2. Click the Application Launcher tab.

3. Choose View/Edit Object's Custom Configuration from the Mode drop-down list. If no settings appear in the list, no custom settings have been defined for this User or Container object.

4. Click the Edit button to customize the settings for this object.

Review User Object's Inheritance Applications

The next step in troubleshooting distributed application launcher problems is to look at the applications inherited by User objects. You might find that the user inherits two applications that are incompatible or that take up too much of the client's resources, and so on.

Use the Show Inherited Applications option on the Tools, Application Launcher Tools menu to see the Application objects that have been associated with the User object, including all applications either associated with or inherited by the User object. The applications are listed by mode of delivery, such as force run, App Launcher, Desktop, Start menu, and system tray. These categories come from the Applications property panel, which is available for User, Group, Organization, and Organizational Unit objects.

Use the following steps to list the applications that the user has rights to use:

1. Highlight a User object.

2. Choose Tools, Application Launcher Tools, Show Inherited Applications.

3. Expand the User object to view all associated applications.

Set Timed Refresh Frequency

A useful setting when troubleshooting distributed applications is the Set Refresh Frequency option, which lets you specify the refresh frequency in seconds. For example, if you set the refresh to 300 seconds, Application Launcher or Application Explorer updates applications from the network automatically every five minutes and might even run some applications depending on how you have set them up.

Although a short timed refresh interval is very useful in situations where you want changes to refresh quickly, it usually causes higher network traffic.

TIP If you are having problems with network traffic when distributing applications you should always increase the timed refresh frequency for Application Launcher and Explorer. You might need to play with the frequency value to match your specific environment.

Change Workstation Files in Use

Another useful step in troubleshooting distributed applications is to make certain that the workstation was properly rebooted with the appropriate files. Occasionally the workstation will not reboot or a file will be in use when the application was distributed, preventing it from being distributed properly.

When Application Launcher distributes applications, it might change workstation configuration files (for example, CONFIG.SYS, AUTOEXEC.BAT, or WIN.INI) depending on the settings in the Application object. The changes to these files do not take effect until after the workstation is rebooted. Application Launcher detects whether such changes are made, and prompts the user with a message stating that the workstation must be rebooted before the changes can take place.

Similarly, when application files are copied, the files they are replacing might be in use, and cannot be deleted or replaced. Application Launcher usually handles this situation. Generally, the new files are copied to a temporary area and then copied to their correct locations when Windows is restarted. However, if a problem exists with the temporary area or the workstation was not rebooted then the correct files will not be properly installed.

Clean Up Network Resources

The next step in troubleshooting distributed applications in ZENworks for Desktops is to make certain that network resources are being properly cleaned up.

The process of "cleaning up" means that the license for a particular network connection is removed. This prevents users from using a network connection when they don't need it. When the clean up Network Resources option is selected, drive mappings and printer ports associated with Application Launcher-delivered applications are removed.

NOTE If the resource (a connection, map, or capture) is already in use when Application Launcher or Application Explorer is started, Application Launcher or Application Explorer uses it and does not clean it up. Otherwise, the resource is created and cleaned up when all other Application Launcher or Application Explorer applications are finished using it. The connection to the server containing the resource is removed as well. If the applications that Application Launcher or Application Explorer launched are still running when Application Launcher or Application Explorer is terminated, the allocated resources remain intact.

When an application is launched, Application Launcher or Application Explorer monitors the executable of the application. When the executable terminates, the process of cleaning up network resources begins. However, it's possible that the executable filename is actually a wrapper that sets up environments, runs other executables, and then terminates. If Application Launcher or Application Explorer monitors the wrapper executable, it might prematurely start cleaning up network resources before the application has terminated.

To prevent Application Launcher and Explorer from prematurely cleaning up an application's resources, consult your application documentation about whether the application uses a wrapper executable. If it does use a wrapper executable, find out the name of the module that remains running, and then type this name, excluding the extension, in the text box provided.

Write Application Administrator Notes

As a network administrator, you should keep records for later use. When troubleshooting issues with distributed applications you should use the Administrator Notes property page to create a section of notes that only you, as the administrator, can view and edit.

For example, you might want to remind yourself about some special settings for a particular application. This is true especially when several administrators manage your system. You could use the Administrator Notes property page to provide a history of application upgrades and file changes so that work is not duplicated.

To write administrator notes for an Application Object, follow these steps:

1. Right-click the Application object and click Properties.

2. Click the Administrator Notes option from the Identification tab.

3. In the space provided, type the note, and then click OK.

Review Roll-Back Application Distribution

When troubleshooting application distribution you should be aware that if ZENworks for Desktops encounters an error during distribution, it rolls back or reverses all the changes made before the error and resets the workstation to the state it was in before the distribution began.

When you roll out or distribute a complex application using Application Launcher, changes are made to the targeted workstation. These changes might include text files (such as CONFIG.SYS and AUTOEXEC.BAT), Windows Registry entries, and .INI files. In addition, application files can be copied or deleted at the target workstation.

The method Application Launcher uses to roll back changes is simple. First, it creates temporary files and directories to store files and other rollback information on the workstation. If the distribution is successful, those files and directories are deleted. If the distribution encounters an error, Application Launcher uses the rollback information to restore the workstation to its original state. Once that is completed, the rollback information is deleted.

Problems rolling back can occur if a file is in use, the application is set to overwrite an existing application, and so on when the roll back occurs. Application Launcher is unable to roll back a file that is in use or does not exist.

Use Search and Replace Entire Application Object

A very useful tool in troubleshooting application objects is the Search and Replace Entire Application Objects option in ConsoleOne. You can use the Search and Replace dialog box to search the entire Application object for text strings.

For example, if a directory name is changed and the application object no longer functions, you could use this feature to correct the directory name every place it occurs in the application object.

To search and replace text strings in all property pages of application object, follow these steps:

1. Highlight the Application object that you want to search.

2. Choose Tools, Application Launcher Tools, Search and Replace.

3. Choose Options, and then choose the type of Application object settings you want to search.

4. Choose Match Case to make the search case sensitive.

5. Type the text you want to search for in the Search For text box, and then click Find Next.

6. If you want to replace that text with other text, type it in the Replace With text box and then click Find Next. Click Replace or Replace All.

Use Search Specific Application Object Property Page

A very useful tool in troubleshooting application objects is the Search Specific Application Object property page in ConsoleOne. You can use the Find dialog box to search the current Registry settings, .INI settings, or Application files property page.

For example, if a specific Registry setting was causing the application distribution to experience problems, you could use this feature to find the Registry setting in the application object.

To find specific application object settings, use the following steps:

1. Right-click the Application object and click Properties.

2. Click the Registry Settings, INI Settings, or Application Files option panels from the distribution tab.

3. Choose the Find option (in most cases this might appear on the File button).

4. Type the text that you want to find, and then choose Find.

Review Application Termination

When troubleshooting application distribution, make certain that the application was terminated properly. You can use the Termination property panel in ConsoleOne to view and modify how Application Launcher handles the termination of an application. If termination is improperly set up, users can experience problems when the application runs.

Use the following steps to view and modify termination of the application:

1. Right-click the Application object and click Properties.

2. Click the Termination option panel from the Availability tab.

3. Select and modify the appropriate termination behaviors from the drop-down list.

Send Message to Close Application

If users should close the application, use the Send Message to Close Application option. For example, if you set an interval of 20 minutes, Application Launcher sends a message (if one is active) to the user every 20 minutes until the application is closed.

Send Message to Close Then Prompt to Save Data

You can use this option when the application must be terminated; however, user data loss might occur. This option prompts users, for a specified period of time, to close the application on their own (this action is optional). When that period of time expires, the Application Launcher attempts to close the application. If users have not saved data, they are prompted to save it.

Send Message to Close, Prompt to Save, Then Force Close

Use this option when the application must be terminated, regardless of user data loss. This option prompts users, for a specified period of time, to close the application on their own. When that period of time expires, you can close the application prompting users, at specified intervals, to save their work. If users have still not closed within a specified period of time, the application is forced to close.

Send Message to Close Then Force Close with Explanation

Use this option when the application must absolutely be terminated and user data loss is not a concern. This option prompts users, for a specified period of time, to close the application on their own. When that period of time expires, the application is forced to close.

Troubleshooting Policy Packages

Another troubleshooting area that you should be familiar with is the policy packages. No formal method exists for troubleshooting the Workstation Policy Package; however, the following are some steps you can take to identify problems and find resolutions.

Review eDirectory Workstation Object

In the case of a Workstation Policy Package, make certain a valid eDirectory Workstation object has been created and is linked to workstations that use the policy package. This can be checked by viewing the values listed in Table 19.1 in the workstation's Registry.

TABLE 19.1 Identification Key in Workstation's Registry

KEY	VALUES
HKEY_LOCAL_MACHINE\ SOFTWARE\Novell\ Workstation Manager\ Identification	Registered In:REG_SZ:.OU=ZEN.OU=Site.O= Company Registration Object: REG_SZ: UserName, IPX_Network_Address, IP_ Network_Address, Station_Name, and so on. Workstation Object:REG_SZ:CN= StationName123456789012.OU=ZEN.OU= Site.O=Company

You are specifically looking for the Workstation object value. It identifies which eDirectory Workstation object the workstation is using when it is logged in. All Workstation Policy Packages need to be associated with this eDirectory Workstation object or to a Workstation Group that has this eDirectory Workstation object as one of its members.

If a Workstation Policy Package is not associated to the eDirectory Workstation object listed in the Workstation object Registry value or a group it belongs to, no Workstation Policy Packages are downloaded and applied. You can also check for effective policies on the effective policies panel of a container object's properties page.

Review Policy Package Type

Make certain that the appropriate type of policy package has been created. For example, if the workstation is running Windows NT/2000, make sure you have created a WINNT Workstation Policy Package.

Review Workstation Object Associations

In the case of a Workstation Policy Package, make certain that eDirectory Workstation objects have an association to the policy package. This can be verified by looking at the details of the policy package within ConsoleOne by clicking on the Associations tab.

Make certain that all the workstations that use the eDirectory Workstation object are listed there, are members of a Workstation group listed, or exist in a container listed.

TIP Make certain to look for potential problems with a Container Policy Package if you are only using the container to associate the eDirectory Workstation Object. If you are not sure, it is a good idea to associate the eDirectory Workstation object directly (as a troubleshooting step, not as an implementation design).

Enable Policies

Make certain that at least one policy is enabled to download. If no policies are enabled, the user cannot detect any change to the user/workstation environment and might question if it is working properly.

Review Trusted Trees

Make certain that workstations have the active tree listed as a trusted tree. The Workstation Manager component of ZENworks uses the concept of trusted trees, and Windows 95/98 or NT/2000 Workstations attempt to search for a ZENworks policy package only if the tree is listed as a trusted tree. This feature gives greater administrative flexibility as to which workstations are controlled by ZENworks.

You can set the trusted tree by selecting the custom installation of the Novell client for NT/2000 or 95/98. If Typical Installation is selected, it automatically sets the tree that you first log in to as the trusted tree.

To view the trusted tree property on a Windows workstation, view the Registry key directly at the following location:

```
HKEY_LOCAL_MACHINE\SOFTWARE\NOVELL\Workstation Manger\
Identification
```

Troubleshooting NetWare Errors

When troubleshooting ZENworks for Desktops you should always be aware of any NetWare error messages that are occurring. ZENworks for Desktops is heavily tied into the NetWare operating system, eDirectory, and file system. Therefore, any error occurring in NetWare could possibly affect ZENworks for Desktops as well.

NetWare Server File System Errors

When ZENworks for Desktops is having problems distributing applications, you should always look for errors in the NetWare file system. These errors often help you narrow down the problem to a specific cause and resolution.

For example, if the ZENworks for Desktops client gives the user the following error, you might suspect a connection problem with the server and could focus troubleshooting on finding the cause and fixing that problem.

```
918: This utility was unable to get connection information.
Error code: 89FF.
```

Table 19.2 contains common file system errors.

TABLE 19.2   Common File System Errors

CODE	TEXT	DESCRIPTION
0x8901	INSUFFICIENT SPACE	The station does not have sufficient disk space. Make certain that the minimum free disk space requirements are set up for the application object being used.
0x8980	FILE IN USE	An attempt was made to open or create a file that is already open. Set the shareable attribute if you want multiple users to access the file at the same time.

TABLE 19.2 Continued

CODE	TEXT	DESCRIPTION
0x8983	DISK IO ERROR	A hard disk i/o error occurred on a NetWare volume. Typically a bad sector has been encountered and cannot be migrated to the hotfix area. Replace the drive.
0x8999	DIR FULL	An attempt was made to write to a volume without available directory space. Make certain that you are not exceeding the maximum number of directory entries for the volume.
0x899C	INSUFFICIENT RIGHTS INVALID PATH	An attempt was made to access a path with invalid rights to the path or with an invalid path name. Make certain that the user has appropriate rights to the path and that the path name is correct.
0x89A8	ACCESS DENIED	Access has been denied. Make certain that the user has appropriate rights to the file.
0x89BF	NAME SPACE INVALID	An invalid name space was used. Make sure the correct namespaces are loaded on the volume being used.

eDirectory Errors

Another area you should always review when troubleshooting ZENworks for Desktops is the eDirectory error messages. ZENworks for Desktops uses eDirectory heavily, not only for normal authentication and access, but also as a service for controlling ZENworks for Desktops objects.

eDirectory errors can be categorized as follows.

eDirectory Operating System Error Codes

Some eDirectory background processes require the functionality provided by the NetWare operating system. These processes, such as communication and transaction servers, can return operating system specific error codes to eDirectory. These error codes are then passed to the eDirectory background process that initiated a request. In NetWare 4.*x*, versions of eDirectory (NDS) can also generate operating system error codes.

Usually operating system error codes that are generated by eDirectory have a negative numerical representation, whereas normal operating system error codes have a positive numerical representation. The numerical range for operating system error codes generated by eDirectory is -1 through -256; inversely the numerical range for operating system error codes is 1 through 255.

NOTE eDirectory returns the positive numerical error code rather than the negative error code normally used by eDirectory to the application to prevent any incompatibility. Therefore, any occurrence of an error code within the range of 1 to 255 or -1 to -255 should be treated as the same error.

eDirectory Client Error Codes

The next class of eDirectory error codes is the client error codes. Some eDirectory background processes require the functionality provided by other eDirectory servers. Use of these functions, such as bindery services, requires that an eDirectory server act as an eDirectory client to the server providing the functionality. Therefore, these functions often result in client-specific error codes being returned to the eDirectory background processes and operations.

eDirectory client error codes are generated by the eDirectory client that is built into eDirectory. The eDirectory client error codes fall in the range of codes numbered -301 through -399.

eDirectory Agent Error Codes

Another class of eDirectory error codes is the eDirectory agent error codes. eDirectory agent error codes represent errors that originated in the eDirectory Agent software in the server that are returned through eDirectory. These codes are numbered -601 through -799 (or FDA7 through F9FE).

NOTE Temporary errors are normal, because the eDirectory database is designed as a loosely consistent database. You should not be alarmed if eDirectory error conditions exist temporarily. However, some errors might persist until the error condition is resolved.

Other eDirectory Error Codes

Some eDirectory background processes require the functionality provided by other NLM programs, such as `timesync.nlm` or `unicode.nlm`. If any of these modules encounter an error, it can be passed on to the `ds.nlm`. `Unicode.nlm` and other errors in this category range from -400 to -599.

Tools for Troubleshooting eDirectory Errors

To effectively troubleshoot eDirectory errors that affect ZENworks for Desktops, you should be familiar with the tools available to troubleshoot eDirectory problems. The following tools are provided to monitor and repair error conditions with eDirectory.

The eDirectory Manager Utility

The eDirectory manager utility provides partitioning and replication services for the eDirectory database on a NetWare server. It also provides repair capabilities for repairing the database from a client workstation, which alleviates the network administrator's total dependence on working from the server console.

The DSREPAIR Utility

The DSREPAIR utility enables you to work from the server console to monitor and repair problems with the eDirectory database on a single-server basis. It does not correct problems on other servers from a single, centralized location. It must be run on each server on which you want to correct eDirectory database errors.

The DSTRACE Utility

The DSTRACE utility enables you to work from the server console to diagnose eDirectory errors. These errors might appear when you are manipulating eDirectory objects with the administration utilities. eDirectory errors also show up on the DSTRACE screen.

Table 19.3 contains common eDirectory errors.

TABLE 19.3 Common eDirectory Errors

CODE	TEXT	DESCRIPTION
-601 FDA7	NO SUCH ENTRY	The specified eDirectory object cannot be found on the eDirectory server that is responding to a request.
-603 FDA5	NO SUCH ATTRIBUTE	The requested attribute cannot be found. In eDirectory, if an attribute does not contain a value, the attribute does not exist for the specific object.
-625 FD8F	TRANSPORT FAILURE	The source server is unable to communicate with the target server. This error is almost always LAN-related.

TABLE 19.3 Continued

CODE	TEXT	DESCRIPTION
-626 FD8E	ALL REFERRALS FAILED	The object could not be found; however, it is still possible that the object does exist. It is likely that the server cannot communicate with another server that is holding a copy of the object.
-634 FD86	NO REFERRALS	The source server has no objects that match the request and has no referrals on which to search for the object. This is not a serious error, just a response. This error usually resolves itself.

Understanding eDirectory Changes

When ZENworks for Desktops 4 is installed on your network, it will make several extensions to your current eDirectory tree. These extensions enable new ZENworks for Desktops objects to be created and data linked to existing objects.

This appendix identifies the new objects that have been introduced to your tree and changes to existing base objects when ZENworks for Desktops 4 was installed.

New Objects for ZENworks for Desktops 4

Table A.1 contains the significant objects that are introduced into eDirectory for ZENworks for Desktops 4. This table describes all objects and not just objects that have been introduced since ZENworks for Desktops 2 (that is, ZENworks).

TABLE A.1   New Objects Added to the Tree for ZENworks for Desktops 4

OBJECT	DESCRIPTION
Application	This object represents a Windows application that you want to deliver to workstations and to users. This object contains links to the files to run or install as well as the administrative restrictions and configurations on how to present this application to the users.
	The administrator creates this object and associates it with users, groups, workstations, workstation groups, and containers. See Chapter 6, "Creating and Using Application Objects," for more details.
Application Folders	This object allows the administrator to specify a foldering view that can be presented to the users as they are given application objects. These folder objects enable you to specify the menu design used on the start menu to access the application.
	This object is created by the administrator and is associated with Application Objects. See Chapter 6, "Creating and Using Application Objects," for more details.
Computer Extensible Policies	This policy allows you to add .ADM policy files to the workstations in your system. In this policy, you can import and administer these .ADM files and then associate them to the registered workstations, applying when the workstation logs into the tree. Unlike most policies, this policy is cumulative, meaning that the system walks the tree (according to the search policy) and combines all of these associated policies. Most agents stop on the first policy they find.
	The Computer Extensible Policies feature is administered as part of the Workstation Policy Package (see Chapter 9, "Setting Up a Workstation Policy Package," for more details).
Dynamic Local User Policy	This policy holds the configuration parameters, used by the Workstation Manager agent on the workstation, for the creation of local user accounts at login. These accounts are created on the fly in the local Windows user database and represent users in the tree who log into the workstation.
	This policy is administered in the User Policy Package and therefore is associated with users in the directory. See Chapter 8, "Setting Up User Policies," for more details.

TABLE A.1 Continued

OBJECT	DESCRIPTION
Imaging Server Policy	The ZENworks Imaging agent that runs on the server uses this policy. This policy holds configuration information that tells the agent the configuration and addresses to assign to workstations. This policy also holds rules that allow the agent to determine which image to place on any unregistered workstation that contacts the agent.
	This policy is part of the Server Policy package and is associated with the servers on which the ZENworks for Desktops Imaging agent is located. See Chapter 14, "Imaging a Workstation," and Chapter 12, "Creating a Server Policy Package," for more information.
Novell iPrint Policy	This policy enables you to configure the Novell iPrint policy to install the iPrint client and to manage printers using ZENworks for Desktops 4. This policy can be configured from both the user policy package and the workstation policy package.
Remote Control Policy	This policy dictates the features that are activated in the remote control system. The remote control system includes remote control, file transfer, chat, remote diagnostics, and remote execute. This is a general policy and can be associated with either a registered workstation (any Windows version) or a user. If this policy is associated with both the workstation and the user of a desktop, the most restrictive permissions of the two policies are used.
	This policy is administered in both the User Policy package (see Chapter 8, "Setting Up User Policies," for more details) and the Workstation Policy package (see Chapter 9, "Setting Up a Workstation Policy Package," for more details).
RollUp Policy	This policy allows you to administer the next level of the ZENworks Inventory Service where the local server agent should send their information. This links ZENworks Inventory Service agents to other ZENworks Inventory Service agents in a hierarchical manner.
	This policy is part of the Server Policy Package and is associated with servers in the tree. See Chapter 12, "Creating a Server Policy Package," for more information.

TABLE A.1   Continued

OBJECT	DESCRIPTION
Scheduled Action Policy	This policy sets up schedules for specific actions to perform on objects associated with the policy package. This is a plural policy that can be added many times to a policy package. It can be configured from the Server Package, the User Package, or from the Workstation Package.
Search Policy	This policy tells the workstation agents the order in which to process any policies found in the tree. The default order is object, group, and then container, and then search to the root of the tree. Using this policy, you can change the order and stop searching up the tree to a container or partition level.
	This policy is part of the Container Policy Package and is associated with containers that impact any user and workstations in that container or sub-container. See Chapter 10, "Creating a Container Policy Package," for more details.
Server Group	In order to facilitate the association of policies to a set of servers, ZENworks for Desktops introduces the Server Group object. It allows you to create a list of servers. This server group is administered much like user groups and can be associated with Server Policy Packages.
SMTP Host Policy	This policy allows you to specify the IP addresses of the SMTP e-mail agent. There are several workstation and server ZENworks for Desktops agents that can be administered to send e-mail to an individual when particular events occur.
	This policy is part of the Service Location Policy package that identifies the resources in the network available for agents. See Chapter 11 "Creating a Service Location Policy Package" for more details.
SNMP Trap Target Policy	This policy allows you to specify the IP addresses of the SNMP monitors that will receive messages from the SNMP agents in the workstations. Unlike more policies, this policy is cumulative, meaning that the system walks the tree (according to the search policy), collects all SNMP policies, and combines them. Most agents stop on the first policy they find.
	This policy is part of the Service Location Policy package that identifies the resources in the network available for agents. See Chapter 11, "Creating a Service Location Policy Package," for more details.

TABLE A.1   Continued

OBJECT	DESCRIPTION
User Extensible Policies	This policy allows you to add .ADM policy files to your users. These .ADM files are used by Microsoft within the policy editor tool. In this policy, you can import and administer these .ADM files and then associate them to the users. The User Extensible Policies feature is administered as part of the User Policy Package (see Chapter 8, "Setting Up User Policies," for more details).
Windows Group Policy	This policy brings all of the attributes of Microsoft's Group Policy into ZENworks for Desktops. This policy, in ZENworks for Desktops, can be assigned to any group, user, or container. In Active Directory, it can be assigned only to a container. This policy is available only for those on Windows 2000/XP. This policy is administered in both the User Policy package (see Chapter 8 for more details) and the Workstation Policy package (see Chapter 9 for more details).
Windows Desktop Preferences Policy	This policy enables you to control the workstation desktop items such as desktop background, mouse, console, and sounds. This policy is associated with a user and will adjust any desktop that the user uses. This policy is administered as part of the User Policy package. See Chapter 8 for more information.
Windows Terminal Server Policy	This policy allows you to specify settings to manage your Windows Terminal Server NT/2000 system, user accounts. This policy is associated with users and is administered as part of the User Policy package. See Chapter 8 for more information.
Workstation	This object represents a registered workstation in the tree. A workstation registers with the tree through the ZENworks for Desktops Import agent that resides on a server. When the workstation registers with the agent, it creates a workstation object in an identified location and with a specified name (see Workstation Import Policy). The workstation then saves its workstation object name in the secure portion of the registry, and the Workstation Manager agent, on the workstation, logs into the tree as that workstation to gather policies and perform work for the administrator.

TABLE A.1   Continued

OBJECT	DESCRIPTION
Workstation	This object holds such information as a history of the users who have logged into this workstation, the critical hardware inventory information, any remote control restrictions, associated application objects, and the IP and/or IPX address of the workstation.
Workstation Group	In order to facilitate the association of policies to a set of workstations, ZENworks for Desktops introduces the Workstation Group object. It allows you to create a list of workstations. This workstation group is administered much like user groups and can be associated with Workstation Policy Packages.
Workstation Image	This object represents a ZENworks for Desktop image that has been taken on a workstation. This object refers to an image file (.ZMG) that is stored on an imaging server. The object is used as a reference to that file in other objects and policies. An administrator must manually create this object.
Workstation Image Policy	This policy contains the configuration and rules for applying images for registered workstations. When the ZENworks for Desktops Imaging agent on the server is contacted, it determines whether the workstation is registered and whether any imaging configuration has been set in the workstation object. If there is no configuration in the workstation object, this imaging policy is applied for the workstation. This policy is administered in the Workstation Policy package; see Chapter 9 for more information.
Workstation Import Policy	This policy holds administered parameters for the naming of workstations, the container where workstation objects should be created, and the number of imports that should occur in a given timeframe (in order to not overload your server). The ZENworks for Desktops import agent that runs on the server uses this policy to determine how and when to create the workstation object. This agent logs in as this policy to do its work, so the policy is given rights in the containers where the workstation is to be created. This policy is administered in the Server Policy Package and is associated with the servers that run your ZENworks for Desktops import agent. See Chapter 12 for more details.

TABLE A.1 Continued

OBJECT	DESCRIPTION
Workstation Inventory Policy	The Workstation Inventory policy allows you to administer the inventory system for ZENworks for Desktops. In this policy, you specify whether hardware and software inventory should be taken on the associated workstations. You also specify the Inventory Service object, which represents the inventory agent that is running on a server.
	This policy is part of the Workstation Policy package and is associated with workstations in the tree. See Chapter 9 for more information.
Workstation Removal Policy	This policy describes when the ZENworks for Desktops workstation removal agent should examine the administered containers to discover workstations that have not connected to the tree in a specified timeframe. These workstations are automatically deleted from the tree. If these workstations later reconnect to the tree, the import agent will create a new workstation object.
	This policy is administered in the Server Policy Package and is associated with the servers that run your ZENworks for Desktops import agent. See Chapter 12 for more details.
ZENworks Database	This object represents the ZENworks database that is stored on the server. This database is used to store logging information from various agents as well as the hardware and software inventory of the workstations in your tree. This policy holds such information as the passwords into the database, the drivers, and the IP address of the server.
	This object is created during the install process, but can be created by the administrator as well.
ZENworks Database Location Policy	This policy allows you to specify the ZENworks Database object that those associated with the Service Location Policy should use for storage. There are several workstation and server ZENworks for Desktops agents that use this database to store inventory and logging information.
	This policy is part of the Service Location Policy package that identifies the resources in the network available for agents. See Chapter 11 for more details.
ZENworks for Desktops Agent Policy	This policy lets you configure the workstation to use in ZENworks for Desktops 4 without using the Novell Client. It can be configured from the workstation package.

Modified Objects for ZENworks for Desktops 4

Table A.2 contains the significant objects that are modified to contain additional attributes following the installation of ZENworks for Desktops 4. It is assumed by ZENworks for Desktops 4 that these objects already exist in the eDirectory system. If not, an error will result at install time.

TABLE A.2   Modified Objects in the Tree for ZENworks for Desktops 4

OBJECT	MODIFICATION
Country	Modified to allow a ZENworks for Desktop policy package and an application object to be associated with the object.
Group	Modified to allow a ZENworks for Desktop policy package and an application object to be associated with the object.
Locality	Modified to allow a ZENworks for Desktop policy package and an application object to be associated with the object.
Organization	Modified to allow a ZENworks for Desktop policy package and an application object to be associated with the object.
Organizational Unit	Modified to allow a ZENworks for Desktop policy package and an application object to be associated with the object.
Queue	Modified to provide an attribute to attach a printer driver and printer information. In this manner, when users want to work with the queue, they will automatically get the proper drivers for the printer.
Server	Modified to allow a ZENworks for Desktop policy package and an application object to be associated with the object.
User	Modified to allow ZENworks for Desktop policy packages and application objects to be associated with the user. Also provides remote control administration capabilities and restrictions on the administrator for this user. Additionally, the object is modified to link users to the current workstation object representing the desktop they are using.

Using snAppShot to Create an Application Object Package

In this appendix, you review an example of using the snAppShot utility to create an application object package for distribution to other workstations. This appendix is split into the following two sections:

- Using snAppShot to package GroupWise
- Review of the created object template

Using snAppShot to Package GroupWise

This example uses the custom mode in snAppShot to set specific options for snAppShot. It then uses snAppShot to capture the changes made in an application object template package when installing GroupWise on a client workstation. This way, you can use the created template later to distribute GroupWise to several other clients.

You will use the custom mode of snAppShot to perform the operations described in the following sections in order to create the application object template for GroupWise.

Launch snAppShot

The first step to create an application object template for GroupWise is to launch the snAppShot utility by double-clicking the Snapshot icon located in the SYS:\PUBLIC\SNAPSHOT directory, as shown in Figure B.1.

FIGURE B.1
Folder displaying the snAppShot utility icon.

Choose Custom Mode from Main Menu

The next step is to select which mode you will use to create the application object template for GroupWise. This example uses the custom mode so that you can use some specific preference settings as shown in Figure B.2.

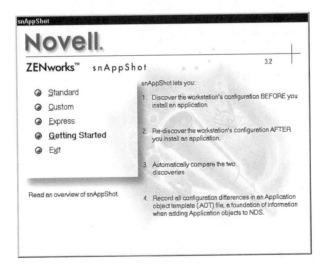

FIGURE B.2
Window in the snAppShot utility that allows users to specify which mode of discovery to use during application object template creation.

Choose the snAppShot Preferences File

The first window that comes up after you select the custom mode in snAppShot allows you to choose a snAppShot previously saved preference file, or use the snAppShot default settings.

Because you have not previously created and saved a preferences file in a previous custom mode, use the default settings here.

Name the Application Object and Icon Title

Once you have selected to use the default preference settings in snAppShot, you input the name that the application object will have in the DS tree (GroupWise 5.5) and a title for the icon that represents the application object (GroupWise).

Network Location of the Application Source (.FIL) Files

Once you set the name for the application object and title for its icon, you set the network location to store the application source files (.FIL) for the GroupWise object template to the following directory:

T:\Snapshot\GroupWise 5.5

Network Location of the Application Template (.AOT and .AXT) Files

Once you have specified a network location for the .FIL files, you set the network location to store the application template (.AOT and .AXT files) for the GroupWise object template to the following directory:

T:\Snapshot\GroupWise 5.5\GroupWise.AOT

NOTE By specifying a network location for these files, you can more easily access them when it comes time to create the Application object and distribute it to users. It's best to set the network location for both the source files and the application template files to the same directory. This makes for easier handling of the application object package.

Including or Excluding Parts of the Workstation

Once you have selected the network location to store the application object support files, you use the snAppShot screen in Figure B.3 to select the parts of the workstation covered in the following sections.

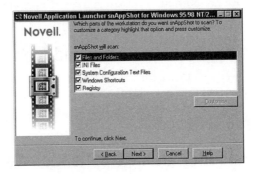

FIGURE B.3
Window in the snAppShot utility that allows users to specify which parts of the workstation to include or exclude.

Files and Folders

From the workstation scan customization menu in snAppShot, you can modify which files and folders you want to include or exclude. However, you do not need to ignore any specific files or folders in this example, so leave the setting at the default shown in Figure B.4.

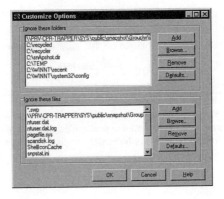

FIGURE B.4
Window in the snAppShot utility that allows users to specify how and which files and folders will be created in the application object template.

INI Files

From the workstation scan customization menu in snAppShot, you can modify which INI files to exclude. However, you do not need to ignore any specific INI files in this example, so leave the setting at the default.

System Configuration Text Files

From the workstation scan customization menu in snAppShot, you can modify which system configuration text files you want to include in the scan. You do have the NETWORK.BAT file that is executed when all workstations are booted, thus setting specific preferences. This file is specific to each workstation and even though the GroupWise install shouldn't affect it; you can add it to the list to be safe.

Windows Shortcuts

From the workstation scan customization menu in snAppShot, you can modify which Windows shortcuts to exclude. However, you do not need to ignore any specific Windows shortcut files in this example, so leave the setting at the default.

Registry

From the workstation scan customization menu in snAppShot, you can modify which registry hives you want to include or exclude. Leave the setting at the default for this example.

Specify the Drives That Will Be Discovered

Once you have specified which parts of the workstation to include or exclude, you select which disk drive to scan on the workstation to determine changes. In this case, because you are installing GroupWise to the C: drive, you only need to select the C: drive for scanning.

Read the Pre-Discovery Summary

Now that you have set all the preferences for the first discovery, a summary of the preferences appears in the next snAppShot window. The information displayed includes:

- ▶ Application Object Name
- ▶ Application Icon Title
- ▶ Template Filename
- ▶ Application Files Directory
- ▶ Snapshots Working Drive

- ▶ Scan Options
- ▶ Disks to Scan
- ▶ Directories to Exclude
- ▶ Files to Exclude
- ▶ System Text Files to Scan

> **NOTE** Notice that the file you selected as a system configuration text file to ignore is listed in the summary: C:\NETWORK.BAT. This is a good example of points to check before proceeding with the first discovery.

You can click Save Settings to save the snAppShot preferences you have defined thus far to a file. Later, if you use snAppShot to create a template for a GroupWise upgrade, you can use that preference file in the express mode.

Run the First snAppShot Discovery

The first snAppShot discovery runs when you click next from the Preference Summary window. The screen shown in Figure B.5 shows the status of the discovery and a count of the following items that have been discovered:

- ▶ Folders and files
- ▶ Windows shortcuts
- ▶ INI files
- ▶ System configuration files
- ▶ Registry entries

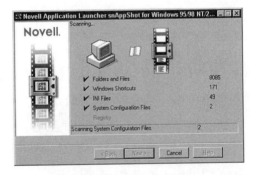

FIGURE B.5
Window in the snAppShot utility that shows the users the current status and statistics about the currently running discovery scan.

Run the Application's Installation or Upgrade

Once the first snAppShot discovery is completed, a Run Application Install button is available.

When you select the Run Application Install button, a file pop-up menu will appear and you will be able to navigate to the application install executable and execute.

Specify How to Handle the Creation of Files, Folders, .INI File Entries, and Registry Settings

Once the GroupWise installation is complete, snAppShot allows you to specify how to handle the creation of entries for the application object. From the screen shown in Figure B.6, you can set the addition criteria for the entries described in the following sections.

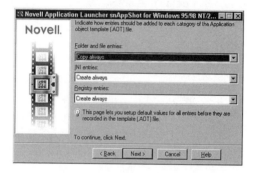

FIGURE B.6
Window in the snAppShot utility that allows users to specify how snAppShot will handle the creation of file, folder, INI file, and registry entries in the application object template.

Folder and File Entries

From the application object entry addition window in snAppShot, you can configure whether files and folders will be added to the application object by clicking the down arrow under the Files and Folders option and selecting the addition criteria shown in Figure B.7.

NOTE You use Copy if Newer Version because you do not want to overwrite any files that might have been added by the user in a local workstation specific installation.

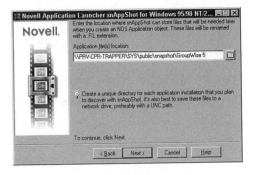

FIGURE B.7
Window in the snAppShot utility that allows users to specify how snAppShot will handle the creation of file and folder entries in the application object template.

INI Files

From the application object entry addition window in snAppShot, you configure whether INI files will be added to the application object by clicking the down arrow under the INI files option and selecting the addition criteria.

> **NOTE** You use Create if Does Not Exist because you do not want to overwrite any existing INI files that might have been added by the user in a local workstation specific application installation.

Registry Entries

From the application object entry addition window in snAppShot, you configure whether Registry entries will be added to the application object by clicking the down arrow under the Registry entries option and selecting the addition criteria.

> **NOTE** You use Create Always because you want to overwrite any registry entries that might be pointing to invalid file or directory locations that do not match the current application installation.

Enter the Path to the Application's Executable File

Once you have defined the addition criteria for entries into the application object, you specify a path to the application's executable on this workstation. To do so, enter the location of the GroupWise application installation files on this workstation in the text field as shown in Figure B.8.

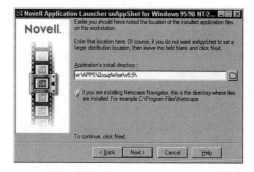

FIGURE B.8
Window in the snAppShot utility that allows users to set the path for the application's executable file.

Define Macros for Distribution Automation

Once you are finished with setting the path to the applications executable and you click the Next button, use the screen shown in Figure B.9 to define macros to control the distribution of application objects.

FIGURE B.9
Window in the snAppShot utility that allows users to add, edit, and remove macros to be used in the application object template.

Click the Add button in the macro definition window. You then need to specify a variable name and a string for the template data.

Run the Second snAppShot Discovery

Once you are finished with defining macros to automate application object distribution, you click Next. snAppShot runs the second discovery, as shown in Figure B.10. Once again, you can monitor the status of the discovery by noting the count of the following items:

▶ Folders and files   ▶ System configuration files

▶ Windows shortcuts   ▶ Registry entries

▶ INI files

Once the discovery is finished, snAppShot will begin generating an object template. This is where the actual differences between the two discoveries are discerned and the template files are created.

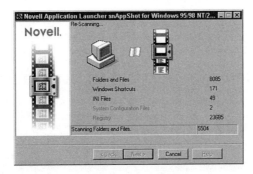

FIGURE B.10
Window in the snAppShot utility that shows the current status and statistics about the second discovery scan while it is running.

Read the Completion Summary

Once the second snAppShot discovery is completed and the template files are generated, a completion summary describing what took place is displayed. The completion summary contains information about the application template creation, including:

▶ The location of the new application object template (.AOT)

▶ The location of the new .FIL files

▶ The location of the textual version of the application object template (.AOT)

▶ The steps necessary to create the application object

▶ Statistical totals from the second discovery

▶ Statistical totals from entries added to the application object template (.AOT)

Review of the Created Object Template

Once you have reviewed the summary from running snAppShot and clicked Next, the process is complete and the application object template package has been created. You can now go to the network location where the application object template was created and review the items described in the following sections.

Directory Listing

Figure B.11 shows a directory listing of the files in the application object template directory. These files represent the packaged object ready for distribution. You can see the following files:

- .AXT file
- .AOT file
- FILEDEF.TXT file
- Various .FIL files

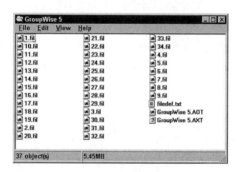

FIGURE B.11
Directory listing of the files located in the GroupWise application object template directory.

FILEDEF.TXT File

Looking at the FILEDEF.TXT file in Figure B.12, you can see the mappings of .FIL files to the actual GroupWise application files.

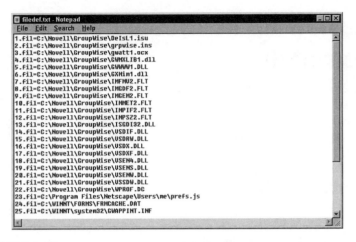

FIGURE B.12
FILEDEF.TXT file for the GroupWise application object package.

Application Object Template File (Text Version .AXT)

Looking at the text version of the GroupWise object template, shown in Figure B.13, you can see all the changes that snAppShot recorded from the GroupWise installation. These changes can be applied to other workstations when the application object is distributed.

Looking at the FILEDEF.TXT file in Figure B.13, you can see the mappings of .FIL files to the actual GroupWise application files.

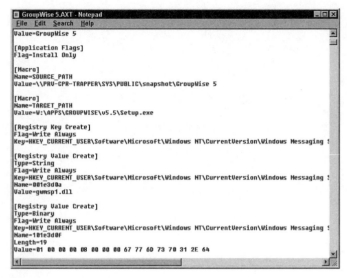

FIGURE B.13

Textual version of the application object template file for the GroupWise application object.

Other ZENworks for Desktops Resources

Many other resources are available concerning ZENworks for Desktops. This appendix describes a few resources that are available to assist you in your discovery and implementation of ZENworks for Desktops.

Novell Support and Online Documentation

Novell has set up a ZENworks Web site at www.novell.com/products/zenworks. On this Web site, you can find Novell's online documentation and announcements of updates to the product.

Additionally, from this page you can follow the links to support.novell.com/products, where you can find patches and fixes that have been released. ZENworks products are found under the NetWare and the Management Products categories.

ZENworks Cool Solutions

Many more uses of ZENworks for Desktops exist than can be described in a single book. Many customers use ZENworks for Desktops every day and get very creative in their use of the system.

Novell created a location on the Internet where customers can ask their questions to the actual ZENworks for Desktop engineers and can learn from solutions that other customers have created.

The Web site for ZENworks Cool Solutions is `http://www.novell.com/coolsolutions/zenworks`.

This site changes often and features articles from real customers and insiders on how to make ZENworks for Desktops hum in your network. The site also includes a list of frequently asked questions and answers as well as articles from other deployment specialists. You can often find a whitepaper at the Cool Solutions site that will have the information you need for your issues.

From time to time, this site also posts software that is not supported by Novell, but provided by some internal Novell engineers, Novell consultants, or customers. These tools can help you deploy and manage ZENworks for Desktops.

The ZENworks Cool Solutions site sometimes includes live discussions with experts whereby customers can get real-time answers to their issues. You might even see some job postings for companies that are looking for ZEN Masters to implement ZENworks in their environments.

Novell Consulting Services

Novell Consulting Services has many good engineers who are familiar with ZENworks for Desktops and who understand how it can help Novell customers. They can assist you, beyond support, in getting ZENworks for Desktops to do exactly what you want. Novell Consulting Services can help you with field consulting and help you tailor ZENworks for Desktops to your organization's needs.

Novell Technical Support Services

Novell has one of the best-trained and most responsive technical support services departments in the industry. Novell's technical support engineers help customers resolve installation, configuration, incompatibility, and software issues. They track those issues and create technical information documents (TIDs) that break down the symptoms. Those TIDs are available to you from the Novell Technical Support Knowledgebase at the following address:

`http://solutionet.novell.com/`

You can also access the Novell Support forums to view and post messages about questions you have. Novell's support engineers and other users can respond to these messages. The Novell Support forums are available from the following Web address:

`http://support.novell.com/forums/`

ZENworks Inventory Database Schema

ZENworks for Desktops comes with several views to retrieve information from the inventory database. However, those views might not always give you the information you need exactly how you want it. If you are familiar with the Common Information Model (CIM), Desktop Management Interface (DMI), and have a solid understanding of Relational Database Based Managed Systems (RDBMS), you can access the ZENworks inventory database directly by creating your own queries and views.

Accessing the inventory database can be a powerful tool for creating metrics to measure company growth, user and workstation status, product usage, and so on. The tables in this appendix define the schema and associations in the ZENworks inventory database. Also included in this appendix are sample queries that give you a jump start at accessing the database.

Database Class Associations and Attributes

The first concept you must understand when accessing the ZENworks inventory database is what is available and how it is available. The following tables help you understand the schema structure for inventory classes, class associations, association attributes, and class attributes for the following types of inventory objects:

- ▶ Miscellaneous Computer System objects
- ▶ ZENworks Site objects
- ▶ Client Software objects
- ▶ Network objects
- ▶ Disk objects

TABLE D.1 Computer System Objects in ZENworks Inventory: Associations and Attributions

LOOKUPCLASS	TARGET CLASS	ASSOC. CLASS	ASSOC. ATTRIBUTE 1	ASSOC. ATTRIBUTE 2	CLASS ATTRIBUTES
ZENworks.Bus	CIM.Unitary ComputerSystem	SystemDevice	PartComponent	GroupComponent	BusType, Version, Name, Description, Protocol supported
ZENworks.BIOS	CIM.Unitary ComputerSystem	SystemBIOS	PartComponent	GroupComponent	Manufacturer, InstallDate, BIOSBytes, Caption, SerialNumber, Version, PrimaryBIOS, Size
ZENworks_ OperatingSystem	CIM.Unitary ComputerSystem	InstalledOS	PartComponent	GroupComponent	OSType, Caption, CodePage, Role, Version, InstallDate, TotalVirtualMemory Size, TotalVisibleMemory Size, SizeStoredInPaging Files

TABLE D.1 Continued

LOOKUPCLASS	TARGET CLASS	ASSOC. CLASS	ASSOC. ATTRIBUTE 1	ASSOC. ATTRIBUTE 2	CLASS ATTRIBUTES
ZENworks_NetWare OperatingSystem	CIM.Unitary ComputerSystem	InstalledOS	PartComponent	GroupComponent	Accounting Version, InternetBridge Support, MaxNumberOf Connections, PeakConnectionsUsed, PrintServerVersion, QueuingVersion, RevisionLevel, SecurityRestriction Level, SFTLevel, TTSLevel, VAPVersion, VirtualConsole Version, InteranalNetwork Information
ZENworks. Motherboard	CIM.Unitary ComputerSystem	ComputerSystem Package	Dependent	Antecedent	HostingBoard, Manufacturer, NumberOfSlots, Description, Version

TABLE D.1 Continued

LOOKUPCLASS	TARGET CLASS	ASSOC. CLASS	ASSOC. ATTRIBUTE 1	ASSOC. ATTRIBUTE 2	CLASS ATTRIBUTES
ZENworks. ZENKeyboard	CIM.Unitary ComputerSystem	SystemDevice	PartComponent	GroupComponent	Delay, TypematicRate, Layout, NumberOfFunction Keys, Description, subtype
ZENworks. ParallelPort	CIM.Unitary ComputerSystem	SystemDevice	PartComponent	GroupComponent	Name, DMASupport, Address
ZENworks. SerialPort	CIM.Unitary ComputerSystem	SystemDevice	PartComponent	GroupComponent	Name, Address
CIM.PointingDevice	CIM.Unitary ComputerSystem	SystemDevice	PartComponent	GroupComponent	PointingType, Name, NumberOfButtons
ZENworks.Pointing DeviceDriver	CIM. PointingDevice	DeviceSoftware	Dependent	Antecedent	Name, Version
CIM.DMA	CIM.Unitary ComputerSystem	Computer SystemDMA	PartComponent	GroupComponent	DMAChannel, Availability, Description, BurstMode

TABLE D.1 Continued

LOOKUPCLASS	TARGET CLASS	ASSOC. CLASS	ASSOC. ATTRIBUTE 1	ASSOC. ATTRIBUTE 2	CLASS ATTRIBUTES
CIM.IRQ	CIM.Unitary ComputerSystem	Computer SystemIRQ	PartComponent	GroupComponent	IRQNumber, Availability, TriggerType, Shareable
CIM.PowerSupply	CIM.Unitary ComputerSystem	SystemDevice	PartComponent	GroupComponent	Description, TotalOutputPower
CIM.Battery	CIM.Unitary ComputerSystem	SystemDevice	PartComponent	GroupComponent	Name, Chemistry, DesignCapacity, DesignVoltage, SmartBatteryVersion
CIM.Card	CIM.Unitary ComputerSystem	Computer SystemPackage	Dependent	Antecedent	Description
CIM.Slot	CIM.Card	CardInSlot	Dependent	Antecedent	MaxDataWidth, ThermalRating
CIM.CacheMemory	CIM.Unitary ComputerSystem	SystemDevice	PartComponent	GroupComponent	Level, WritePolicy, ErrorMethodology, CacheType, LineSize, ReplacementPolicy, ReadPolicy, Associativity

TABLE D.1 Continued

LOOKUPCLASS	TARGET CLASS	ASSOC. CLASS	ASSOC. ATTRIBUTE 1	ASSOC. ATTRIBUTE 2	CLASS ATTRIBUTES
CIM.PhysicalMemory	CIM.CacheMemory	RealizesExtent	Dependent	Antecedent	Speed, Capacity
ZENworks_VideoAdapter	CIM.Unitary ComputerSystem	System Device	Dependent	Antecedent	Description, NumberOfColorPlanes, CurrentHorizontal Resolution, CurrentVertical Resolution, VideoArchitecture, VideoMemoryType, MaxMemorySupported, CurrentBitsPerPixel, MaxRefreshRate, MinRefreshRate, DACType, ChipSet, ProviderName
ZENworks.SoundCard	CIM.Unitary ComputerSystem	Computer SystemPackage	Dependent	Antecedent	Name, Description, Manufacturer
CIM.POTSModem	CIM.Unitary ComputerSystem	SystemDevice	PartComponent	GroupComponent	Name, Description, Caption
ManageWise.User	CIM.Unitary ComputerSystem	ManageWise. ObjectContact	Owner	Client	LastLoginName, CurrentLoginName

TABLE D.2 Site Objects in ZENworks Inventory: Associations and Attributions

LOOKUPCLASS	TARGET CLASS	ASSOCIATION CLASS	ASSOCIATION ATTRIBUTE 1	ASSOCIATION ATTRIBUTE 2	CLASS ATTRIBUTES
ZENworks.Site	CIM.Unitary ComputerSystem	SystemSite	SystemSite	ComputerSystem	SiteID, SiteName
ManageWise.NDSName	CIM.Unitary ComputerSystem	Designates	Designation	Host	Label, Tree
ZENworks.SystemInfo	CIM.Unitary ComputerSystem	Computer SystemPackage	Dependent	Antecedent	Tag, Model, Serial Number, Manufacturer, Description

TABLE D.3 ZENworks Client Software Objects in ZENworks Inventory: Associations and Attributions

LOOKUPCLASS	TARGET CLASS	ASSOCIATION CLASS	ASSOCIATION ATTRIBUTE 1	ASSOCIATION ATTRIBUTE 2	CLASS ATTRIBUTES
ZENworks. NetWareClient	CIM.Unitary ComputerSystem	Installed SoftwareElement	Software	System	Version
ZENworks. InventoryScanner	CIM.Unitary ComputerSystem	Installed SoftwareElement	Software	System	Version, LastScanDate, InventoryServer, ModificationTime
CIM.Product	CIM.Unitary ComputerSystem	InstalledProduct	Product	ComputerSystem	Name, Version, Vendor

TABLE D.4 Network Objects in the ZENworks Inventory: Associations and Attributions

LOOKUPCLASS	TARGET CLASS	ASSOCIATION CLASS	ASSOCIATION ATTRIBUTE 1	ASSOCIATION ATTRIBUTE 2	CLASS ATTRIBUTES
ZENworks. ZENNetworkAdaptor	CIM.Unitary ComputerSystem	SystemDevice	PartComponent	GroupComponent	AdapterType, ProviderName
CIM.NetworkAdapter	CIM.Unitary ComputerSystem	SystemDevice	Dependent	Antecedent	Name, Caption, Description, InstallDate, MaxSpeed, PermanentAddress, AutoSense
ZENworks. NetworkAdaptor Driver	CIM.Unitary ComputerSystem	Installed SoftwareElement	Dependent	Antecedent	Name, Version, Description
CIM. IPProtocolEndPoint	CIM.Unitary ComputerSystem	HostedAccess Point	Dependent	Antecedent	Address, SubnetMask
CIM. IPXProtocolEndPoint	CIM.Unitary ComputerSystem	HostedAccess Point	Dependent	Antecedent	Address
CIM.LANEndPoint	CIM.Unitary ComputerSystem	HostedAccess Point	Dependent	Antecedent	MACAddress
ManageWise. MSDomainName	CIM.Unitary ComputerSystem	Designates	Designation	Host	Label
ManageWise.DNSName	CIM.Unitary ComputerSystem	Designates	Designation	Host	Label

TABLE D.5 Disk Objects in the ZENworks Inventory: Associations and Attributions

LOOKUPCLASS	TARGET CLASS	ASSOCIATION CLASS	ASSOCIATION ATTRIBUTE 1	ASSOCIATION ATTRIBUTE 2	CLASS ATTRIBUTES
ZENworks.DiskDrive	CIM.Unitary ComputerSystem	SystemDevice	PartComponent	GroupComponent	Removable
ZENworks. PhysicalDiskDrive	CIM.DiskDrive	Realizes	Dependent	Antecedent	
ZENworks. LogicalDiskDrive	CIM.Unitary ComputerSystem	SystemDevice	PartComponent	GroupComponent	DeviceID, TotalSize, VolumeSerialNumber, Caption
ZENworks. Storage PhysicalMedia	ZENworks. PhysicalDiskDrive, ZENworks. Physicaldiskette, ZENworks. PhysicalCDROM				Description, PhysicalCylinders, SectorsPerTrack, PhysicalHeads, Capacity, Manufacturer, Tracks
CIM.DiskettDrive	CIM.Unitary ComputerSystem	SystemDevice	PartComponent	GroupComponent	
ZENworks. Physicaldiskette	CIM.DiskettDrive	Realizes	Dependent	Antecedent	
ZENworks LogicalDiskette	CIM.DiskettDrive	MediaPresent	Dependent	Antecedent	DeviceID
CIM.CDROMDrive	CIM.Unitary ComputerSystem	SystemDevice	PartComponent	GroupComponent	

TABLE D.5 Continued

LOOKUPCLASS	TARGET CLASS	ASSOCIATION CLASS	ASSOCIATION ATTRIBUTE 1	ASSOCIATION ATTRIBUTE 2	CLASS ATTRIBUTES
ZENworks. PhysicalCDROM	CIM.CDROMDrive	Realizes	Dependent	Antecedent	Manufacturer, Description, Caption
ZENworks. LogicalCDROM	CIM.CDROMDrive	MediaPresent	Dependent	Antecedent	DeviceID
ZENworks. LogicalDiskDrive	ZENworks. LocalFileSystem	ResidentOnExtent	Dependent	Antecedent	DeviceID, VolumeSerialNumber, Caption
ZENworks. LocalFileSystem	CIM.Unitary ComputerSystem	CIM. HostedFileSystem	PartComponent	GroupComponent	Name, FileSystemSize, Description, FileSystemType

Sample Inventory Database Queries

The tables in the previous section give you a glimpse at the schema of the ZENworks inventory database. The following sections list some sample queries based on those tables to help you better understand how to use them to perform queries and create your own reports. These sample queries retrieve the inventory information from the ZENworks for Desktops Inventory database.

Query 1

Retrieve the name and ID of all workstations from the database and also to the tree to which these workstations are registered. The query is as follows:

```
SELECT u.id$,m.label,m.tree FROM managewise.NDSName
m,cim.UnitaryComputerSystem u,
➡managewise.Designates s where s.Designation=m.id$ and
s.HOST=u.id$
```

Query 2

Retrieve the asset tag, manufacturer, and serial number of all the workstations in the database. The query is as follows:

```
SELECT m.Tag,m.Manufacturer,m.SerialNumber FROM
cim.UnitaryComputerSystem u,
➡zenworks.SystemInfo m,cim.ComputerSystemPackage s
➡WHERE s.Antecedent=m.id$ and s.Dependent=u.id$
```

Query 3

Retrieve all the software applications with their versions that are installed on the workstation 'SJOHN164_99_139_79.WS' registered under the 'NOVELL_AUS' tree. The query is as follows:

```
SELECT m.name,m.version FROM cim.Product
m,cim.UnitaryComputerSystem u,
➡zenworks.InstalledProduct s,managewise.NDSName m1,manage-
wise.Designates
➡s1 WHERE (s.Product=m.id$ and s.ComputerSystem=u.id$) AND
```

```
➥(s1.Designation=m1.id$ and s1.Host=u.id$) AND
m1.label='SJOHN164_99_139_79.WS'
➥and m1.tree='Novell_AUS'
```

Query 4

Retrieve the processor information for the workstation
`'SJOHN164_99_139_79.WS'`.

```
SELECT
m.DeviceID,m.Family,m.Stepping,m.OtherFamilyDescription,
➥m.MaxClockSpeed,m.Role,m.UpgradeMethod FROM cim.Processor
➥m,cim.UnitaryComputerSystem u,cim.ComputerSystemProcessor s
➥managewise.NDSName m1,managewise.Designates s1 WHERE
➥ (s.PartComponent=m.id$ and s.GroupComponent=u.id$) AND
➥m1.label='SJOHN164_99_139_79.WS'
```

Query 5

Retrieve the ID of the `UnitaryComputerSystem` used for the workstation
`'SJOHN164_99_139_79.WS'`.

```
SELECT s.host FROM managewise.NDSName m,managewise.Designates
s WHERE m.label='SJOHN164_99_139_79.WS' and
m.id$=s.Designation
```

Query 6

Having known the ID of the `UnitaryComputerSystem` for a particular
workstation from the query as shown in Query 5, Query 4 can be modified as follows:

```
SELECT
m.DeviceID,m.Family,m.Stepping,m.OtherFamilyDescription,
➥m.MaxClockSpeed,m.Role,m.UpgradeMethod FROM
➥cim.Processor m,cim.UnitaryComputerSystem u,
cim.ComputerSystemProcessor s
➥u.id$=? And s.PartComponent=m.id$ and
s.GroupComponent=u.id$
```

Substitute the ID of the specified workstation in place of the **?** value for
`u.id` in the query.

Query 7

List the IP addresses, IPX addresses, and MAC addresses of all workstations in the database:

```
SELECT ip.Address, ipx.Address, mac.MACAddress FROM
cim.IPProtocolEndpoint ip,
➥cim.IPXProtocolEndpoint ipx, cim.LANEndpoint mac,
cim.UnitaryComputerSystem u,
➥cim.HostedAccessPoint s WHERE (s.Dependent=ip.id$ and
s.Antecedent=u.id$) AND
➥ (s.Dependent=ipx.id$ and s.Antecedent=u.id$) AND
(s.Dependent=mac.id$
➥and s.Antecedent=u.id$)
```

Modify the same query to get the information for a specified workstation as follows:

```
SELECT ip.Address, ipx.Address, mac.MACAddress FROM
cim.IPProtocolEndpoint ip,
➥cim.IPXProtocolEndpoint ipx, cim.LANEndpoint mac,
cim.UnitaryComputerSystem u,
➥cim.HostedAccessPoint s WHERE (s.Dependent=ip.id$ and
s.Antecedent=u.id$) AND
➥ (s.Dependent=ipx.id$ and s.Antecedent=u.id$) AND
(s.Dependent=mac.id$ and
➥s.Antecedent=u.id$)AND u.id$=?
```

Use the query as shown in Query 5 to retrieve the ID of the specified workstation and substitute the ID in place of the ? value for u.id in the query.

Query 8

Retrieve the name and other properties of the drives on the hard disk of the specified workstation.

```
SELECT m.DEVICEID, m.TotalSize, m.VolumeSerialNumber,
m.Caption
➥FROM zenworks.LogicalDiskDrive m, cim.UnitaryComputerSystem
u,
➥cim.SystemDevice s WHERE s.PartComponent=m.id$ AND
➥s.GroupComponent=u.id$ and u.id$=?
```

Use the query shown in Query 5 to retrieve the ID of the specified workstation and substitute the ID in place of the ? for u.id$ in the query.

INDEX

A

B - C

Policies Property page (Server Policy Package), 310

Q - R

U - V